T0367406

Who we really are

Gadi Fishman

AuthorHouse™
1663 Liberty Drive
Bloomington, IN 47403
www.authorhouse.com
Phone: 1-800-839-8640

Published by AuthorHouse 10/25/12

ISBN: 978-1-4772-7624-2 (sc)
ISBN: 978-1-4772-7630-3 (hc)
ISBN: 978-1-4772-7623-5 (e)

Library of Congress Control Number: 2012918388

Relishing the blue sky from a hammock on the balcony of my current apartment, I cannot stop thinking about my past. So many years have gone by; where did they go? How did they manage to fly by so quickly, was I asleep? Half of my life went by in a flash, and yet it all seems as yesterday.

I am disappointed, realizing that I wasted significant years of my life, because, through all those years, I created nothing worthy. Therefore, when my time comes, there will be nothing to show that I walked this planet, and that I was here. I wonder what misled me, and when it happened. What did I do to deserve such tremendous feeling of guilt, and remorse?

In my youth, I thought that all my loved ones, and all of my affairs were everlasting; that nothing would ever change. As it turned out, I was living in denial; I took life, with everything in it, for granted, naïve to recognize the fact that very beginning always concludes at the end. Neglecting my free will, I let my destiny ride like a roll of dice, and in conclusion, my life path had designated for me, and not by me.

Now I grieve for those people I will no longer see; I will never hear their voices, it seems as if just yesterday we were full of passion and joy. Many years went by in a glint, today they are gone, and I am not the man I used to be.

I have come back to square one, and again, I am starting my life over. Only now, I have a quest to distinguish myself from today, and the way I used to be. Who am I? Why, back then, did I act so selfishly? Why did I obtain so many losses? How could I consume fluids that my body resented? Is it true that we all pay for our sins at one time or another? Did I pay for mine? On the other hand, am I still condemned? How much and how long does the punishment goes on? Will it ever end?

Sometimes, I think my life span is not enough to pay of my debts and start from a new page. Regardless, today I am certain that the mental punishment is greater than any material or physical loss.

I was born in Russia. At the age of ten, I immigrated with my parents to Israel. I enjoyed my youth in the beautiful state of Haifa. At the present, I live in New York, happy as I can be. Most of my acquaintances, including my shrink, have stated, "You are forty-two years old, and life with everything in it is ahead of you."

I never understood that statement, and it came as a surprise to me how they could know what is waiting for me, or where I will be tomorrow. Will tomorrow arrive for me? Where shall I place my past? How will I manage my future? What have I accomplished? What am I supposed to achieve?

I have so many questions, and often, those questions circle in my head, revealing exhausting thoughts that dissolve my wisdom, then I see myself on a crossroad to nowhere, standing there, I do not know where to turn.

How did I become so confused? It is odd that, with age, I recognize how much I do not understand. Because of my past, all those who loved me are long gone, leaving me with regrets and only shadows of good times. Now, I spend most of my time looking back, and hope to find the path, which rotated my life upside down. If I am lucky, I might also find a way to correct what is still correctable.

However, sometimes I wander, is hope the only engine that drove me through life, and onto the ultimate quest for tranquility and happiness? What is happiness? When I ask someone if they could define happiness, most say it is love. Well, we are all seeking love, but how often do we actually know what we are really looking for?

When I was younger, I was never satisfied with my credentials nor pleased with my lifestyle and was always seeking more. Everything my mother had taught me, and the way she brought me up apparently worked against me. Not recognizing nor cherishing the warmth that surrounded me, I comprehended compassionate feelings only upon their loss. I lived my life by one principle, one rule: "Trust no one, and no one will lie to you."

That rule grew in me and became my shield. It sheltered and preserved me from betrayal. Unfortunately, that same rule pushed away all my beloved people, until ultimately; I was on my own. Sad but true, back then, not for a moment would I recognize or realize my standing. In fact, I turned out to be doubtful and suspicious toward everyone I encountered. I always kept my distance, just to be on a safe side.

That behavior clinically labeled paranoia, and maybe defined as being overly suspicious. My ex-shrink stated that my only cure was trust, which I needed to learn and learn badly.

How could I have faith in others? How far did I need to extend that belief, and how deeply should it go? What must a person do for me to earn that trust and what should I grant him?

Not knowing the answers, I let suspicions overcome the pleasure of intimate feelings, so I decided to stay on the safe side and play a selfish role in life. As I matured, that role became a big part of my life, and soon, without warning, my ignorance turned me onto the road of selfishness. Egoism played a big part in my behavior. Though surrounded by people, I always kept my distance. With time, that neglectful space wearied me, and I felt obstructed and could not blend in.

It was not long before alcohol came to my rescue, and was my only comfort in my life. With time, it converted into my companion, my trustworthy pal that provided me with warmth and peace. I considered alcohol a friend, since it comforted me, and did not drill holes in my head as some people I have known.

In my youth, when I encountered alcohol for the first time, I did not like the flavor or its scent; moreover, I hated that feeling of dizziness in my head. Subsequently, all that changed, and alcohol showed me a newly colored world. Periodically, I lived in a dream world.

If life is all about choices, then the choices we make define who we are. There was a time I had to confront myself with difficult choices: what is acceptable, and what is secure to me? Should I explore people for what they are, by exposing myself to right and wrong, or should I stay in my new world with the friend that I know, and see where that dream world will take me?

I did not like or enjoy the atmosphere in my life. Therefore, I chose my new friend. The kind of friend I could purchase when I felt lonely or sad, "fueling" myself with that friend to the point of self-fulfillment and joy. Ultimately, without realizing it, my life turned upside down. All that I was and all I had known slowly began to perish from my soul. In my mind, alcohol created a world of my own, where I was the king, a ruler with tremendous abilities, apprehending anything and anyone in my way. I came to believe in my self-esteem. Whom do I trust? Me! Whom do I believe in? Me. Before I knew it, a selfish user and abuser is what I became.

When I was younger, twenty-five years younger, I thought I was the expert of all things. The world and everything in it was like a 24/7 store that was always open for me. All I had to do was reach out and grab whatever I liked. That feeling arose in me, and with time, it outgrew me.

It all began when I arrived in New York; I was eighteen years old, naive, righteous, and full of pure hope. Then without my consent, and reluctantly, my mother decided to send me to the United States because she was against the idea of me joining the Israeli army. She thought that, by sending me away, she was saving me from wicked and hideous tragedies that soldiers encounter in the army, especially during the war. And boy was she wrong!

She entrusting me to my biological father, whom I hardly remembered, and brought me the good news. "Al, I have great news for you! I spoke to your father, and you will be leaving to New York next week!"

"You must be kidding me! Right?"

"No, here are your tickets."

"Ma I was recruited! So how will I attend the lineup on Thursday if I depart on Monday? And why would you call him my father? You know who my pap is! I am not going!"

"Oh yes you are! And you will call him that for as long as needed! Besides, it's only for few years."

"What do you mean, a few years? My return ticket is in one week!"

"How naive could you be? That ticket is a masquerade for your sergeant; you will bring him those tickets along with this file and request to postpone your pledge."

"What is in this file, Mom?"

"Nothing important, your birth certificate proofs that he is your father and Tom's medical records states that he is very sick, and has less than one week to live.

"Is he really dying?"

"Okay Al; that's enough. Just go there tomorrow and I will handle the rest."

Back then, my mother was everything to me, and more! I was Mama's boy, so when she said, "Jump" my reply always was "How high?"

All I knew about Tom was that he was my biological father, whom I had not seen since I was three years old. He was now living in New York and I needed to go live with him.

While growing up in Israel, I had many great friends, and most of them dreamed to visit America. I also thought about the life in the USA, but never imagined that one day I would be actually visiting. I thought of America as a place were all dreams come true, and if I ever were to go there, wealth and happiness would be waiting for me upon arrival.

Mom's plan worked out fine, and just like in a dream, I arrived at the New York Airport. It was a great feeling touring JFK Airport and inhaling the scent of that new, affluent life; or at least that was my first impression.

Recalling all I had seen on TV, I thought, *Wow; here it is, all of it.* As I passed through Customs, somehow my eyes locked onto a man who turned out to be my long-gone father. I came to that conclusion by watching him waving and shouting out my name. When I approached him, we looked at each other as two strangers, and he said, "Come on, let's go to my car." That is all he could say.

A Lincoln Town Car. Wow. I had seen them only in movies. While we were driving, I could not stop thinking about this car, and what a luxury it was.

He probably has a big house, with a pool and tennis court. There are probably more cars there. I will select a sports car, and I will drive it everywhere. What a life! Mom was so right, and I am so glad I listened to her again!

My imagination took over me, and I let myself float through the rest of our trip; it was a new, great feeling. Until the moment when Tom shouted with joy, "We are here!"

As he was parking, I noticed a small, dilapidated, five-story building, so I thought that maybe he had to pick something up. Then I heard him say very scary words. "We are home, let's go!"

At that moment, I felt my heart dropping to my knees, thinking it could not be, but as he was pulling my suitcases out, unfortunately for me, that was my new home.

As we were climbing up the stairs, I thought, *oh well, how much worse could it get?* We arrived on the fifth floor, and it got much worse.

He turned left at the hall, and pushed the first door open, which appeared to be hanging there by some kind of miracle. "Come on in," he said.

I slowly walked in to a tiny hallway; there was a small kitchen up ahead. By the aroma, I could only tell that too many people were living there. Unwillingly, I turned my head to the right and saw a room filled with strangers, apparently waiting for my arrival, all seated by a long skinny table, mashed one to another like sardines.

Right there and then, all my dreams vanished and a huge dim cloud rolled over my eyes.

Meeting all those people, I came to realize I had a half brother; at the time, he was nine years old. There were cousins that I knew of from Mom's stories.

So there I was, settling in and living in Brooklyn. I learned later that my new neighborhood called Borough Park, and I missed my previous life very badly. Walking on the streets of Brooklyn, I found myself in a hibernating state, walking and thinking about my life transformation and not knowing of my next step.

Boredom tortured me, so after a few days of torture, I decided to approach my so-called father and ask him for a favor. "Can you help me find me a job?" I asked.

"Okay. What would you like to do?"

"Anything; I don't care, I have ninety dollars in my pocket, so any job will do."

"Let me make some phone calls; try to stay close. I don't want you to get lost."

A few days later, he found me a job, and I began working at the gas station on Tenth Avenue and 27th Street in Manhattan. Night shift was the only opening at that time, but I did not care. There I was, living in a dreamland as a gas attendant, pumping gas at night.

Tom and his family spent the nights at home, so he let me use his car. However, shortly after that, he also needed it, so I was left with a problem and needed my own car. I had no money, and had to confront Tom, but did not know where to begin. I needed to approach him for help again. In reality, I had no idea who he really was. My only option was to fabricate a story and hope he would buy it.

So come Saturday, I decided this was the day, and I approached him. I said, "You know I have no knowledge of the city, and most of all, I have poor English vocabulary. When I use the subway, I often get lost. I can't drive your car, so having my own car will make life easier for me. So I need your advice; how can I obtain a car?"

"Al, you see the way we live. We are not rich; in fact, I consider us to be slightly below middle class, but this is temporary. Anyway, what I am trying to say is, unfortunately, I don't have any money to give you. I wish I had."

"I see, so you can't help me. Maybe you know somebody that can give me a loan?"

"What loan? Nobody would give you a loan! You have nothing to show! However, I can get you a car loan; of course, you would have to pay it off! Can you?"

"Of course I can! I'm working now! Where do we have to go?"

"Let's go now; never postpone for tomorrow what you can accomplish today!"

Wow! All this time, that was the wisest thing he had said. That phrase impressed me.

He took me to a Dodge dealer. I did not know anything about Dodge, but did not care much either. There were so many great cars there my eyes began to jiggle. While looking at so many varieties, I became confused. At the end, I chose the most expensive one, but he quickly turned me toward a vehicle I could afford.

It was the cheapest car there, but it was new and supposedly, all mine.

I watched Tom, as he sat with the sales clerk in that glass booth for hours; then finally, they pulled my new car out and parked it on the opposite side of the store. Strangely, in a good way, from a distance, it looked different, maybe because there were no upscale vehicles nearby, or maybe because it was far away.

Nevertheless, I was happy. Considering where I came from, owning a car seemed as a fairytale to me. In Israel, most people could not afford that luxury, especially eighteen-year-old kids. When I drove away from the dealer with my new Dodge, that fairytale turned in to reality.

Successfully arriving and parking by the dilapidated building, I was a bit tense, bearing in mind that this was my first time driving in the area. As I sat there playing with all the buttons and being acquainted with my new toy, suddenly, out of nowhere, he appeared.

"How do you like it?" Tom asked.

"I like it a lot! Thanks!"

"Come on; we have to rejoice this occasion! Let's celebrate!"

"What do you mean?"

"Well, come on, and you'll see! You have a lot to learn."

As we entered the crummy apartment right off the bath, he pulled a bottle of scotch and poured two shots.

I looked at him, then at the glasses, and said, "You know I don't drink. Didn't my mother tell you?"

"We spoke only of your immigration issues, and nothing else."

"Well, anyway, I don't drink; never tried and don't wanted to, either!"

"Listen, don't be embarrassed. I was shy also at first, but I was younger than you and still overcame that fear, so be a man, and see what it feels like!"

Sipping my first shot ever, it felt as if a ball of fire glided down my throat, and when it arrived below, my stomach exploded. Suppressing that burning feeling, I thought of this celebration as a taste of hell, and tried to retreat from his enjoyment, but he would not let me go.

"Hey, where do you think you are going? The party has just begun!"

"No, thanks I can't drink anymore. Besides, there is no food here."

"Food is for chumps," he commented, and poured me another and another. After a few more drinks, I passed out on the living room couch.

When I woke up, I went to the kitchen and there he was, still by the table, clutching an empty bottle of scotch in his arms, and out cold.

Now I knew what rejoicing really meant in his vocabulary, and my version of rejoicing was still pounding in my head. I rejoiced nausea with tremendous vomiting, and complete body wreckage. I sat in the bathroom for an hour, and I could not stop thinking about how cruel destiny can be.

In some strange way, and somewhere very deep in my soul, I really felt sorry for Tom. After all, he was my father and his lifestyle was so pitiful. I wonder what he did to roll down so low, and become who he is today. Maybe that is why he drank in the evenings; so the alcohol would blind him and he would not see what surrounded him.

With all those years behind us, I never understood why he never tried to reach out to me. Eighteen years had passed, and my mother had made our connection possible, but she did not do it for him. She probably knew that Tom with his family had no need of me. Regardless, she convinced them to accept me.

He always talked about his hardware store, and that, because of it, everything would change very soon, and they would become kings of the city. However, not once did he include me in those fairytales.

Alcohol helped Tom to cope with his existence, because after consuming a few shots, he became a happy man, and sometimes, a wealthy man. Observing him under the influence, he seemed as if he were living large. It was odd, to see how alcohol changed Tom's mood and his way of thinking; what illusions it created. Worst of it all, he believed in what he saw, and was happy for those few hours of living in illusion.

Then, he reminded me of my stepfather, because he lived the same lifestyle, and my mother always fought with him about drinking. The only difference between them was that Pap was not a dreamer sober or drunk. He was never concerned with wealth or a better way of living. Everything always suited him, and the only engine that constantly attempted to push him forward was my mother.

Unfortunately, most of the time, Pap was drinking. Regardless, I always loved him. Jimmy was his real son, and meant more to me than a brother could; he never complained, but maybe sometimes envied me because I receive more attention than he did.

Pap had great knowledge of machinery skills; he worked as maintenance director at the largest hospital of Haifa, so most of his time he dedicated to work. As a result, my mother and two of my sisters received no attention from him. Periodically, my mother complained that she never felt as a woman should feel next to him.

Thinking about Tom, it hit me, maybe he lived with regret because nothing worked out with my mother, and maybe by having me next to him, he was trying to turn things around.

While mulling over the state of affairs of my family, I began to feel better. Though it was a bit early for me to go work, I decided to live, anyway. There was nothing else for me to do; moreover, I did not what to stay in that place, especially with Tom.

The best part of going to work was driving there. I had a great feeling of freedom, control, and self-confidence because I could go anywhere at anytime I desired.

Suddenly I noticed a change at my work site. The area began to fill with half-naked women. Judging by their clothes and the way they waved at every passing car, I realized that they were probably prostitutes. They occupied every corner. I had never experienced this kind of scenery before, only read about it in magazines, and seen it in moves.

I was stunned while observing those women. It was a cold night and they walked around with practically nothing on, except a mini skirt and tiny top, freezing and simultaneously smiling. Watching them walk toward cars brought me excitement. I was also shocked when I realized that most of their clients were Hasidic Jews. I would never have believed it if I had not witnessed it with my own eyes.

I always thought religious people stood as role models, however, that day proved me wrong, that would explain why they pray twice a day. I got skeptical and wanted to take closer look, so I got out from my booth for a smoke.

While I enjoyed my cigarette, one of the women approached me.

"Do you have a light?" she asked

"Yes; of course."

As I extended my arm with the lighter, she looked at me, lit her cigarette, and said, "How do you like this weather?"

"What's to like? It's cold."

"Tell me about it; I'm freezing my ass off."

"Of course you are! I mean, look at you; you are practically naked."

She laughed and said, "Baby, that's the only way to get with the right client! I have to show my goods. More visual honey equals possible extra money!"

"Forgive me for prying, but what do you mean the right client? Aren't they all the same?"

"Oh, honey! What are you doing here, sleeping? Did you see to whom the girls are running?"

"No, not exactly"

"Okay, let me enlighten you! Orthodox Jews of course, who else? They are the best clients ever! Although they smell like a horse shit, and never tip, but they are very quick and quiet. Also steady customers, unlike the drunks I get on occasion. Those assholes can't ever get it up, and afterward, they blame me for it and ask for a refund."

"Do you have a refund policy?" I asked her, smiling, but she was not insulted.

"Who are you kidding? I mean, come on . . . look at my lips."

"What's wrong with your lips? They look fine to me."

"Oh, honey, please. I got these fruit lips from blowjobs. Do you know what a blowjob is?"

"Frankly, no."

Suddenly she began laughing hysterically, and I wondered why.

"I thought so. Listen, kiddo, and some day you will find this lecture useful and quite enjoyable, I might add. Let's see . . . A blowjob is when a woman, or even a man, attempts to turn . . . let us call it a hanging pickle, what you men carry between your legs . . . you know! So, how am I doing so far?"

"Go on; you were referring to our penis?"

"Yes! Okay, so, by sucking on it and mostly using our lips, we arouse you. Then a scrawny pickle turns into a giant cucumber, only in my dreams of course. On most cases, I end up with a tiny banana. Anyway, men find it very pleasant, so it's very practical during sex. Are you following me so far?"

"Yes. I am, I think! But why fruit lips? I don't get it."

"Oh, dummy. Sometimes, no matter how hard I try, it will not rise. That happens mostly with drunks, my lips work overtime and get swollen; get it?"

"So why do you do it?"

"A satisfied customer is a must for good business!"

"Are you married? Do you have a boyfriend?"

"Why, you interested?"

"I'm just curious."

"Don't sweat it, kiddo. Do you like animals?"

"Yes, of course. Dogs mostly; why?"

"Because, I like animals; I have a few foxes in my closet, on rare occasions a tiger in my bed and a Jaguar parked by my window. So you see, for me there is no need for a relationship. I possess precious creatures, and lack the most important one. That is why I do what I do."

"So tell me, which one?"

"A donkey that can pay for it all! Oh, I have to go! That is my baby coming around. It was nice talking to you, kiddo. Take care."

"You too! Maybe I'll see you again!"

I went back to the booth, thinking that, in some ways, she was very creative. However, why did she use that terminology of, banana and pickle, talking to me as to a child, and why did she call me kiddo? Did this mean that I looked like a kid?

After a few nights, I was sitting in the booth as usual, watching the pumps through the window, and then at sunset, a gorgeous creature slowly approached my booth, her appearance stunned me. She floated above the snow on long, toned, stunning legs that extended from a perfectly shaped body. The darkest long hair surrounded her face. Her dazzling green eyes were on a smooth, ravishing face. Her unforgettable smile could light up the city and melt all her surroundings.

I was galvanized when she gently opened the door, and looked in.

"Hey! What's up?" Her soft voice pleasingly rolled into my ears.

"Nothing" Speechless as I was, I answered.

"Would you like to have some fun?"

"What kind of fun?"

She placed herself on my lap. Damn, she was cold, ice cold, and my sweating knees began to shiver. I did not know what to do next, and was completely helpless.

I though I knew what she wanted, but I did not feel comfortable asking her. Actually, I froze at that point. Bear in mind that I had never experienced intimate feelings before.

While she was on my knees, I noticed a glowing red light blinking on the desk phone. I remembered what the owner had told me. "When the red light on the phone is blinking, it means that someone is using the exterior public phone. They are connected to each other."

She gently turned my head, and said, "I guess you are busy, so I'll go!" She kissed me on the cheek and quietly vanished.

I decided to pick up the phone and listen in, and I heard two people talking about me. The last thing one of them said was, "Let him pick up more cash; then you move in."

At that point, I became confused. They were talking about me, my actions. It could only mean that someone was out there watching me. I looked at the building across the street, then at all the parked cars, but I did not see anyone, and had no idea what to do next. The phone line was busy, so I could not call the cops, or find any other solution. The only rational move was to go out and confront them, and then see where it would lead.

I grabbed a can of motor oil, placed it in my coat inner pocket, and sat, waiting for them to come around, waiting for the unknown. Strangely, I was not afraid. Actually, I had no feelings at all. Maybe it was tension.

Suddenly a group of people approached the station. There were six of them, and some had hoods on. I came out and moved toward them. I marched with confidence, as if a squad of solders where backing me up.

When I came closer, one of the members looked at my coat, then into my eyes, and said, "How much is the gas?"

I thought to myself, *Wow, what a stupid question.* "Don't you see? Look at the sign!" I said, pointed my finger toward the price tag.

Of course, he did not look. Instead, he turned around and commenced walking away. Suddenly and unexpectedly, a huge blast went through my head. It sounded like thousand bells where ringing simultaneously, then everything turned black.

When I opened my eyes, a group of people surrounded me; some appeared to be cops Somehow I had ended up back in the booth with something soft over my head, and a huge headache.

"Are you okay?" someone asked.

I looked up and saw an ambulance medic. "Yes, I'm fine; thank you."

"You need to go to the hospital."

"No thanks. I'm fine."

I stood up, and there she was, that same beautiful woman who was sitting on my lap a few moments ago. Now, for some reason, she was talking to the cops.

One of the police officers approached me and said, "Please sit. Tell me what happened."

"I don't know. I don't remember."

"Well, let me tell you what we know. Do you see that women talking with my partner?"

"Yes."

"She saw the whole thing and called for help. You should be grateful; it could have been much worse if not for her. One of the guys hit you in the back of your head with a metal pipe, while the other, distracted you. Luckily, we were close by, and when they heard our siren, they decided to split."

All the time he was talking, I was looking at her. I watched her walk away again, thinking, I *do not even know her name.*

"Did they take anything? Are you missing anything?" cop asked.

"No, I don't think so."

"Do you carry a weapon?"

"What do you mean?"

"Do you have a gun on the premises?"

"No, I don't have a gun, or any kind of weapon."

"Can you describe that individual you spoke to?"

"No, they all looked alike to me."

"Okay, tell me about yourself, and where you live."

I told him what he wanted to know.

Then he stated, "You know, you can't stay here unarmed. Please lock up, and go home. Give this case number to your boss, and tell him to call for a police report."

After they all left, I closed the station down and drove home.

While staying home and relaxing on the bed with all my clothing on, all I could think about was that woman and why she came into my booth.

Maybe she did save me; I only wish I knew her name. Why did I not ask for her name?

From that day, I stopped judging people. I came to believe in a phrase, "Don't be judgmental, and you shall never be judged." How we earn our living or what we do through our life path does not necessarily relate to who we are.

As I was trying to recall what happened, a thought crossed my mind. *I always kept the money in my sock; is it there now?* I reached into my sock and pulled out a bundle. Yep, it was all there, eight hundred and seventy dollars, lucky me! Damn, I would have to give it all to the owner.

Next day, when I returned to work, the owner was already there, and I thought he was waiting for me.

"Oh, you're here," he said.

"Yes, I came to work; you seem surprised."

"Why did you leave the station last night?"

"I was robbed! Here is the number for the police report. They said for you to call them."

"Is that what happened?"

"Yes."

"I don't care, because you didn't call me! So it's not my problem, and I will not pay you for that shift!"

"I was battered; didn't call anyone. I could hardly drive myself home! Besides, the cop told me to lock up and leave!"

"Is that a fact? Then ask the cop to pay you! Now, where is the money from that night?"

"I have it. Take it; it's all here."

"Okay, we'll see about that! If all the figures check out, Anthony your manager will call you, and you will return for tomorrow's shift but for now, go home." I turned around and left.

While driving back home, I could not believe what just happen to me. Why would he treat me this way? I did not do anything wrong. I could have kept all the money and state to the cops that they took it. Why was I so stupid? This was not right. Unfortunately, honesty brings nothing but pain, and righteousness is not valued.

What a cheap creep my boss turned out to be. There had to be a way to make him pay for this misconduct, and I was desperate to find it.

The following day, I was preparing myself for work as usual; suddenly an idea came to mind, and with that, I recalled a phrase, where there is a will, there must be a way!

So on the way to work, I purchased a small electrical water pump and some hoses, then when my shift commenced, I served customers as usual until ten p.m. Afterward, cabbies and limousines began to arrive, that's when I decided to slightly alter my service and provide a privilege; only to the most familiar customers, of course.

When the first taxicab approached, I did not hesitate, and asked, "How would you like a full tank of gas for only half price?"

"Are you kidding?" he answered.

"No, just park in the back by the yellow circle on the ground! It is very important; no one must ever know my terms with you! Do we understand each other? "

"Most definitely, you can count on me!"

That yellow circle was the cover of the main gas tank supply. I removed that cover, lowered one end of the pump hose into the tank, and with the output, fueled up the cabby. A few minutes later, the cabby was full, and I was ten bucks richer. From that moment on, I provided those terms on every shift, with practically all the taxicabs and limousines.

That mutual understanding and need grew between us, and, they kept it quiet. No one ever found out about my privileges. Three hours per shift, six shifts a week, for one month plus. Yes, I generated serious money until one day, at the shift exchange, my replacement coworker approached me, and stated.

"Al, watch your self! The owner is in a panic!"

"Why? What happen?" I asked.

"Apparently this gas station has begun to lose revenue, and I mean big time loss!"

"But I observed him while he was comparing pumps readings with sales, all the numbers were apple for apple."

"Yes, all the numbers match! However, he is buying more gas than usual, and receiving less revenue."

"Wow, that is odd" I replied, and my heart overflowed with joy.

Then, out of nowhere, that greedy asshole appeared in front of me, he had a strange look on his face, as if his brains were constipated. "Do you know? I'm purchasing more gas than you guys are selling!"

"What do you mean?"

"I mean that gas sales have dropped and use has increased! Clearly, somehow my gas is vanishing."

"Maybe it's evaporating?"

"No, dummy; probably the tanks are leaking!"

"So what do you want us to do? Should we stop pumping and wait until you resolve this issue?"

"No, I will lose all the customers! You both continue as if nothing happened, and I will get professionals in here as soon as possible."

He hired a company, and they began to run pressure tests on each tank. I called that day a judgment day. On that day, they found some pressure loss, which led to one conclusion: the tanks were leaking, so now, without a doubt, repairing or replacing was now necessary. In either case, the situation was major.

Luckily, he did not have enough funds for the needed procedures; so instead, they offered him a minor interior repair. They added some liquid to the tanks, hoping that it would clog any cracks.

Due to the low-cost repair, he was very happy with that process, and I was even happier, because, I began to live the New Yorker's life. Unfortunately, I was also stealing while working, but because of my boss, I felt good about it. That was my first step away from ordinary people's life routine.

Because I had no friends or acquaintances, most of my free time, I was alone. I felt the need to quit my job while I was ahead, but how could I? Instead, I cut my shifts by half. With so much free time, I applied myself toward cruising around the city, and further. On a few occasions, I visited Tom's hardware store.

It turned out to be very small, and had no customers in it. I felt sorry for him, and when he was not looking, I dropped some cash in his register, until one day he caught me.

"What are you doing?" he asked

"It's not what it looks like; I'm just putting some money in."

"Yes, I know you are, because there was nothing there in the first place! But I want to know why."

"Well, like you said; there was nothing there, so I filled it up a little."

"Listen, I don't need your donations! How could you possibly get so much cash? And so fast! Don't tell me! I don't want to know, but I'm sure it's dirty! So take that shit back, and go away."

"Okay, fine! And for your information, it's not dirty. I work hard nights for it; it is as simple as that."

"Hard, huh? As you can see, we all work hard, but my pockets are empty!"

"That is because your store is always empty! Every time I come here, there is no one but you! I could change that; I think I can help you. Let me try and you'll see!"

"So now you want to tell me how to run by business! Is that it?"

"No, I just have some ideas that will pay off."

"I run this place, and no ideas are needed, especially from a crook!"

"I am not a crook, and you don't run this business, YOU JUST SLEEP IN IT!"

"Get the hell out of here NOW!"

I left, and that was my last visit to his department of sleeping goods.

Often, I thought about my family and the people I had been close to who I had left behind; maybe that is why I called my mother every chance I had. On the phone, my mother and I would discuss that lost time between us, and she would tell me about the deeds of my two sisters, my pap, and my brother Jim. Hearing her voice and her stories made me realize how much I really missed them.

Once, I wrote her a poem, telling her how hard it was for me here, living on my own and without family, how I missed my friends and my previous life doings. I wrote about my disappointments with everything that had happened in New York from day one, well, almost everything. That poem was very depressing. I spilled all my pain and sorrow into it, and I knew it was a bad idea to let her know how awful I felt, but I had to get it all out.

Sometimes, my mother would call me at work, but one phone call was quite unusual, and most definitely unexpected. That night she sounded very upset, and I could only assume that my poem had played a big role. "I have received your letter," she said.

"I'm sorry for distressing you, Ma. I didn't mean to go so deep."

"I could not stop crying. Leave everything behind, and come back home."

"No way Ma, I will not run! I did that once, when you made me run from the army, remember. And so far, nothing good came out of it. Anyway, why you are so upset? What happened?"

"We bought a knitting store."

"That's great news. Congratulations!"

"Thanks, but there is a problem. We took a loan for this business, but there is not enough revenue, and now we cannot pay it back."

"So what are you going to do?"

"Well, I wanted to ask you for a favor, can you send us a thousand dollars?" That question had really shocked me.

"What? Mom, I thought you were upset because of my letter. Now it seems that it means nothing to you. Did you understand my situation? It's all there, in black on white!"

"Yes I did. I just thought, you living in America and all, it has to be easier to get that amount. After all, what is one thousand dollars in the USA?"

"It's a lot! Especially when considering my situation. You know, I will have to borrow that money from a stranger, and at this point, this stranger does not exist in my life. So bear with me until I find him."

"I understand, but don't worry; we will pay you back."

"Sorry, Mom, have to go back to work. Bye." I hung up on her for the first time ever.

So there I was, thousands of miles away, lonely and confused, looking for some support from the closest person in the world, but instead, I get a cry for help. Actually, I had the money they needed, and more, but no one was supposed to know about it. The fewer questions asked the simpler affairs.

So I began asking around, and as bad news travels fast, one night a limousine driver approached me. "I heard that you are looking for a loan," the man said.

"As a matter of fact, yes; I am."

"Here, take this and call those people up; they may help you."

"Who are they?"

"Think of what you need and not who they are."

Without thinking, I grabbed the phone, and when he left, I dialed the number. Only then did I realize it was almost midnight. I was about to hang up, but a male voice answered.

"Yes," the rugged voice said.

"Hello, a friend of my give me this number and . . ."

"I know. How much do you need and when do you need it by?"

"A thousand dollars as soon as possible; I have to send it to my mother"

"Give me the address and we will send it to her."

"Really? She is in Israel!"

"Just give me her name and address," he said.

Can he do that? I thought to myself. Oh well, I have nothing to lose, and so I gave him the needed information.

A few days later, I was in deep sleep, and the phone began to go crazy. Unwillingly, I picked up the phone.

"Hello son! Sorry to wake you."

"Hello, Mom. What happened now?"

"I couldn't wait to tell you! I have great news for you!"

"What is it?"

"Your brother Jimmy has decided to join you."

"What? Are you sure?"

"Yes, aren't you glad?"

"Most definitely, when he his coming?"

"In two weeks. Write down the information; you will have to meet him at the airport."

"Of course I will."

"And thanks for the money."

"Did you receive the money already?"

"Yes; some man dropped by and give me the cash, then he said that it's from you."

I could not believe that. I was lost in excitement. Jim was coming! He was one year younger than I was. Although we were not blood related and he was not even my half-brother, we always considered each other as blood brothers and more, much more.

I looked at the calendar with anticipation. Those two weeks were exhausting, and every day seemed like an eternity. I never had any patience, but waiting was the only thing I could do.

I have never experienced the feeling of a perfect moment in time; some say it happens in a moment when time seems to stop, and you can almost live in that moment. On Saturday at eleven a.m. in January 1985, I was at JFK terminal, looking for Jimmy. When I saw him walking toward the exit, at that particular moment, I felt as if everything around me had frozen. Jim commenced to walk in slow motion; suns bright light was bursting through the windows shining everything around him. Then the crowd disappeared; there was no one else but him, and for the first time in my life, I experienced that moment.

It had been two years, and he had not changed a bit. He still looked just like I remembered. There we were, hugging as if we had not seen each other for centuries.

"Jim! Long time no see."

"Too long, Al. How are you doing?"

"I am fine, and now I could not be any better!"

While driving back to my beloved neighborhood of Brooklyn, he told me all about our family, friends, and his ordinary life ordeals. As we entered my temporary residence, I glanced at Jimmy's reaction and, for a moment, he looked like he had lost his breath.

Then we entered the apartment.

"Hi, nice to meet you," he said to all the house members.

"Hello! How was your flight?" my so-called father Tom asked.

"Fine, thanks"

I showed him the way to the bedroom, as Tom stated, that it would be our room for now. It was the only separate room in the apartment.

Tom, with his wife and their son, were sleeping in the five by eight foot space of the living room, on a foldaway bed, sharing that space with some furniture and mice; the situation was stressful but we did not care.

The next morning, I had to go to work. When I got there, a strange feeling came to me. I felt the need to move on. I could do more with my life, and it was time for a change, time to put things into normal perspective. I also knew that my luck would run out and, eventually, everybody would know, so I decided to quit.

I told one of the workers to relate my message of leaving, and that was it. Just like that, my nightlife was over.

On my way back home, I had plenty of time to kill, so I decided to drive around, and acquaint myself with the area. Passing a few blocks, I pulled onto a parking lot, and went to a coffee shop across the street.

When I walked in, a man's voice shouted my name. "Al! How are you doing?"

"Fine thanks. Do I know you?"

"What! You don't remember me. It's me, Mike!"

Of course, I remembered; he was one of a few customers who spoke Russian.

"Hi, Mike. Sorry I didn't recognize you."

"What brings you here?" Mike asked.

"I just quit my job, so I came in to celebrate over a cup of coffee,"

"Talk about being in the right place at the right time. How would you like to park cars?"

"Okay. What is the pay?"

"Two fifty per week."

"Great! Thanks; when can I start?"

"You can start in two weeks, at six in the morning!" Mike said that with a smile on his face.

"Thanks; I'll be there. By the way, where is your place?"

"The parking lot is across the street from here. Look for it; you can't miss it!"

In less than one hour, my life has turned around. It is strange how things sometimes work out. That quick turn showed me that, every segment of time is another chance to start over, and all I needed to do was to go with the flow without hesitation.

I guess that is one of many gifts which life has to offer. When I came home, I gave my news to Jim. After hearing me out, he became a little upset. "What is the matter?" I asked.

"I can't stay home anymore; why didn't you offer your boss a replacement? I could take your place."

"I don't think it's a good idea for you to work the night shift, especially in that area, with all the prostitutes and who knows what else!"

"Hey, bro; you know me! I can handle that. Just talk to him."

"Okay, I will call him."

"Can you please call him now? I can't stay in this place anymore!"

It was not clear to me why he would be so ambitious, wanting to work so badly, when only a few days had passed since his arrival. Maybe something was wrong. I thought he would need time to adjust, but then again, two years ago, I was the same way.

When I called, I did not get much pleasure from talking with the gas station owner. He kept asking questions, and I kept on sincerely lying. At the end, he agreed to accept Jimmy; however, the location was different.

"Jimmy, guess what! There is another gas station on Lexington and 76th Street in Manhattan in need of a gas attendant. It's also a night shift, but the good news the location is great and you can start tomorrow."

"Sure I will; that's great. Thank you, Al!"

"However, the owner would like to see you today, so let's go. I will take you there."

After his interview, on the way back, Jim was excited.

"Are you ready to make some big bucks?" I asked.

"Are you kidding me? I can't wait."

As I was driving, my car had made several loud and unpleasant noises, which shortly proved to be mechanical issues.

The following weekend, Jim was watching a movie and I decided to take this matter to my Uncle Abe, as I called him.

"You need to dispose of it," he said.

"Really? And how am I supposed to do that?"

"I will see you tonight, around nine p.m. Wait for me."

He came in with a smirk on his face and said, "Give me your car keys and don't worry about anything! Go home and wait for me there. I'll be back soon."

I watched TV for two hours and still there was no sign of Abe. Another hour went by, and not a phone call. I began to worry.

Jim looked at me and said. "Don't worry, Al. He is probably driving around looking for fun!"

"Thanks, Jim! As always, you are a great comfort."

Suddenly, I heard a knock on the door. I jumped and pulled the door in, and there was Abe, his clothing half burned, and smelling like gasoline and smoke. Most of his hair and eyebrows had burned; he appeared as he just expelled from hell.

He walked in slowly, leaving a huge mess of smoke and ashes in his path. He sat himself down and proceeded to stare at me as if we were strangers. "You wouldn't believe what happened to me!" he stated.

"Judging by your appearance, I would believe anything! However, I don't know if I want to hear it! Anyway, tell me; did you rescue someone from a fire? Oh, where is my car?"

"I told you I would get rid off it, and I did! I think."

"You think? What is that supposed to mean? Also, you never told me how you planned to accomplish that task! So Abe, what did you do?"

"Okay, I poured some gas on the rear seats, and some on the floors, then I lighted a match, and fire commenced, but I was unable to get out! The car alarm locked all the doors automatically; why didn't you tell me about this alarm before?" he shouted, and then became furious.

"I didn't known you were planning to burn it, so it didn't seem important. Anyway, how did you get out?"

"I placed the key back into ignition, the doors unlocked, and I jumped out. I realized my clothes were burning, so I rolled around the sidewalk. Afterward, I went back to the car, shut the door, and helplessly waited for this monster to burn. Unfortunately, the flames began to recede, probably because the windows were closed, so the fire died out. That's how I got these burns."

"Give me back my keys; where did you park? Jim, let's go!"

"I don't have the keys! I left them in the ignition."

"Damn you, Abe! Just take us there!"

No matter how hard Jimmy tried to hide his feelings, laughter burst out of him and he could not stop laughing. Then he said, "Abe, don't look so twisted. Better luck next time!"

I approached Tom and asked, "Will you drive us to pick my car?"

"Why, what happened to your car?"

"Nothing; I loaned the car to Abe, and he forgot the keys in the ignition."

"Fine; let's go."

Approaching the location, Abe slowly pointed his finger toward my car, and there she was, nicely parked and looking as good as new.

As we got out, I asked Tom, "Can you please follow us?"

"Where we are going?"

"Abe said there were some mechanical problems with it, so I would like to take it to the repair shop where I work."

"You don't need a repair shop; this vehicle is new, remember? Go to a dealer in the morning, and use the warranty."

"Yes, I remember. I just want for our mechanic to check it out first."

"Fine; let's go."

When we arrived at my ex-station, I went to talk to the gas attendant. "Hey, I need a few five gallon canisters."

"How many you said?"

"Two canisters, five gallons each, and fill them up and then my car, while you're at it."

"Why would you need two full canisters?"

"My friend got stuck with no gas. I'm on a mission to help him."

"So, you need two cans for that?"

"Yes, he has a big car. Hey, aren't you supposed to pump gas? I used to work here, and I am acquainted with your boss. Wait until I will tell him of your curiosity; all talk and no work! We shall see what he will say about that!"

"Sorry, I meant no disrespect."

"No problem; just get on with it."

It actually felt good putting that kid in his place. In some strange way, my performance had inspired me to proceed with the plan.

While driving, surrounded with the aroma of gasoline and Abe's burned remains, I was scanning for an isolated place, and had no idea of where I was going; meanwhile, Tom was following us all the way.

We entered uptown and passed 180th Street. After a few miles, I saw a construction site, then it became obvious to me; I had finally found that deserted area.

As I was about to slow down, I heard Jimmy yell out, "Wait; stop!"

"Why, what's the matter?"

"This is it! It's perfect! Look to your right. A construction site and there's no one there."

He was right; it was the perfect spot for my purpose. We pulled over and Tom stopped behind, with good intentions and no idea of what he was about to witness.

He said, "Do you know where we are? You took a wrong turn back on the west side highway. I was flashing you with high beams; why did you kept on going?"

"Sorry, we got lost; please wait here!"

"Where are you going?"

"Just wait here, on this side of the road; we'll be right back."

We drove toward the site and down the slope onto the construction field.

"Stop here. Let's do it here," Jimmy said.

Without any further discussion, we both knew our agenda, and the next action each of us shall commence. Jimmy pulled out the portable gas tanks from the trunk, ripped the sleeve off his shirt and gave it to me I poured some gas on the sleeve, slid one end into gas tank extending the other away. It did not extend that much; it hung only a few inches from the gas tank.

Meanwhile, Jimmy had emptied the two containers into the car interior.

"Jim! What are you waiting for? Light it up."

"My hands are all wet from gasoline, so you'll have to do the honors."

"Okay; first, climb back up toward Tom's car, and I will do the rest."

"Don't forget to run!" Jimmy screamed while running up the driveway.

Without much thought as to how far away I actually needed to be, I lighted the sleeve and began to move away. Looking back, it dawned on me that I was still too close. With all my effort, I struggled to retreat further, but unfortunately, I did not get far.

Suddenly, a tremendous explosion occurred; the blast wave threw me into the air and I landed on my back. I saw my car lift up and light up the sky like a huge ball of fire, glowing like the sun. It flipped around several times before falling back to the ground of the construction site, crushing everything it hit, and dismantling into pieces.

I never anticipated such an enormous outcome, nor have I ever witnessed anything like that sight.

We climbed back up and onto the road, and then jumped into Tom's car. Tom was sitting in his car like a statue. He grasped the steering wheel as if his life depended on it.

I shook him and said, "Let's go!"

"What was that? What happened?"

"Nothing much, please go. Now!"

"What do you mean nothing much? I heard an explosion, and then I saw a ball of fire going up in the air. What did you two do?"

"Oh; yes, okay. We had a small accident; I lost control while driving down there, and then suddenly the car began to burn, so we had to jump out, and then it exploded. Luckily, we got out in time. Now please drive us out of here before the cops show up. They may get the wrong idea about all this!"

He pulled out in a hurry; and asked, "Are you okay?"

"Yes, thanks for asking."

"You know, you and your brother are something else. Never have I imagined that you are capable of something like this. If you really think I am buying that Israeli bullshit story, you are dumber than you look!"

"Do I look stupid? Hey, Jim, do I?"

"No, Al; he is just upset."

"I am not upset. I'm very angry with Al. I have never broken the law and he placed me at risk. Now tell me! What have I done to you to deserve that exclusive treatment?"

"It's what you haven't done that counts the most; besides, since you are an accomplice, I strongly recommend that you forget what happened!"

"You think that you have an answer for everything, don't you? That's because you are still young, but life will catch up with your doings and then one day you will stand speechless."

"We'll see about that."

I need a drink," Jimmy said.

"When did you start drinking?" I asked.

"Right about now. Tom, can you drop us by a bar?"

"Jim, aren't you seventeen? Never mind; I'm going home. And you two, are on your own. There is a bar a few blocks away from us; enjoy!"

"Fine thanks. We will walk."

We were seated at the bar, relaxing, then Jim said, "You know, when you got all those gas containers, I speculated that you were about to burn that car. Nevertheless, I never anticipated that crazy, uncalculated approach of yours! Tom was right. What you were thinking? Did you see how close you were? You almost got blown up also."

"Well, almost doesn't count. Besides, I didn't have time to calculate. When I saw Abe and the way he was, my brain overheated."

"Yeah, that cousin of yours is a gift from another planet. Let me ask you; why did you lie to Tom? He is you father, after all, and he is trying to become your friend. You just don't see it."

"There was no other way for me. He is a stranger to me, and I don't trust him."

"In that case, you better learn how to lie, because that story sucked. Any kid would laugh at it. You are really a terrible liar."

"What would you know about lying?"

"Are you kidding me? I grew up in orphanage remember! Nobody tells the truth there. Honesty is the last place in line, as simple as that."

As we talked, we forgot what happened, and strangely, I noticed that Jim knew how to handle his alcohol; those beers were rolling in like popcorn.

His behavior reminded me of my mother's story, when she told me about his life at the orphanage, and that most of the kids there abused alcohol and drugs whenever they could. That was the first time I had actually seen Jim a little drunk. I guess some stories are true. However, alcohol was never my favorite interest, and so I struggled with one beer. I could not keep up with Jim even if I tried.

The next morning, I rushed to the kitchen, and, boy was I thirsty, I assumed it was due to a hangover from last night's one beer. As I was sitting by the kitchen table enjoying my drink, the phone rang, and it kept on ringing until I realized that I was home alone.

When I answered, it was my uncle Abe. I had not spoken to Abe for a while, not after what happen to him on his adventure with my late car. He said, that he was acquainted with a girl through his relatives. Apparently, they went out once and did not click, so he thought, she would be perfect for me.

"So, Al, are you up for it?" Abe asked.

"Yes why not!"

"Let me ask you, when was the last time you went out with a girl, or had sex, for that matter?"

"Let me be completely frank with you; none of your business!"

"I'm just asking. Maybe you need some pointers. I would help, just say the word."

"No. thanks. I'm still shaking from your last help attempt!"

"Okay, whatever. Here, take her number."

He gave me her number and I called her the same day. We did not talk long on the phone. The way Abe described her; I wanted to meet her as soon as possible. She did have a pleasing and soft voice, and I hoped the voice would fit the image.

When we met, it did. Man, I was astounded when I saw her coming out of the building. She was wearing glossy black leather pants with a short leather jacket. She had a perfectly shaped body, big blue magnetizing eyes, and an unforgettable smile. She reminded me of a Barbie doll, and I felt just like that cartoon wolf in the scene when his eyeballs pop out and his tongue rolls down.

When she approached the car, I did not know what to do. She waited for a minute and opened the door. Boy, did I feel stupid. I thought I was supposed to get out and open the door for her, but that moment was long gone.

"Hello. I am Victoria; how nice to meet you!"

"Hi; nice to meet you to" I struggled to get those few words out, but was grateful for that achievement. Thank god, she was talkative, and not only beautiful, also very clever as well. What a package!

As she talked, I made her believe that I understand and agreed with all she was saying, but the truth of the matter was, I could not speak even if I wanted to. I was hopelessly hooked on her and there was nothing I could do about it; not that I wanted to. If men we'r created from steel, she was a magnet toward all men kind.

We went out a few times, and then she introduced me to her parents. Her father seemed nice, however, her mother, for some reason, was always in a bitch mood.

As it turned out, Vicky was the only child, and daddy was very committed to spoiling her. Also, it was difficult for me to meet with Vicky. She lived in Queens and I was in Brooklyn. On every occasion, I had to approach Tom and ask for his car. One Friday night, we were all watching TV.

Jim was at work and Tom had to offer his opinion about me using his car. "Al, you are working now. Don't you think it's time for you to buy your own car?"

"I don't make as much as you might think. Why would you bring this up? Am I interfering with your plans?"

"No, however, I never know when or what might happen, and for a family, it's always good to have a vehicle on standby."

And that was it! I had him trapped. I had wanted to approach him and ask for his assistance in purchasing a car, but after what had happened, I was hesitating. Now, he brought my needs into the open!

And I said, "The insurance paid in full for that Dodge, yes?"

"Yeah. So what?"

"You are correct; I am in need of a vehicle, but I can't buy one. However, I saved enough for down payment; would you sign a loan for me again?"

"What did you say? After what you did last time, you must be out of your mind!"

"It won't happen again! I promise; that Dodge was a junk, and this time I know exactly what I want! Besides, no one took a loss!"

"Oh yeah? So what is it this time?"

"Pontiac Trans-Am. I saw an ad; that car is awesome!"

"Okay, Al. Go into the kitchen. Let me speak with my wife about that."

On my way to the kitchen, somehow I knew that this car would be mine. I could see myself driving it, and it was only because he was discussing that matter with Silvia.

Silvia had a great heart and a soul of an angel. When I met with her for the first time, I judged her by the way she appeared; she was overweight and had a manly, deep voice, so my opinion was very low. However, with time, I realized that, on the inside, she was completely the opposite. Tom was diabetic, and had an alcohol problem, among other issues. Regardless of all that, she was always by his side, and anyone else for that matter; she never needed a reason or explanation to help or assist someone in need. For that, I respected her.

"Hey, Al; come in."

"Yes."

"I will sign a loan if you will provide me with a stable payment plan, only because I cannot afford to get stuck with that car."

"Of course, I understand, and I have a plan. It's quite simple actually. Jim and I will pay it off. Our income is more than enough to cover our needs and the loan combined!"

"Have you spoken to Jim about it?"

"No, but I will tell him tomorrow morning, at the dealer!"

"So you already decided to go tomorrow. I see you got this all figured out. And what makes you so sure that Jim will agree?"

"Because, he is my brother! Besides, I can't pull this off without all of you!"

"Okay, Al. We will get your car tomorrow! I just hope this time you will be wiser!"

I could not wait until the next sunrise. At six a.m., I was all dressed up and ready to go. I sat in the kitchen and waited for Jim to walk in, and shortly after, he did.

"Hey Al, you look like those hookers, all dressed up, and no one to blow! What are you doing sitting here like this, and so early?"

"Good morning to you to! I am happy to see you in a good mood, and I'm waiting for you, actually. We are going to buy a new car!"

"No way! And how we are going to do that?"

Then Tom walked in. "Hey, guys; you are both here! Good, I wanted to talk to you both. Jim did your brother tell you about the deal we are about to make today?"

"No, what deal?"

"Bro, listen. Tom is willing to get us a loan for a new car. I have the down payment"

"You said for *us*, Al. How do you see us using one car at the same time?"

"Bro, that's simple. We work different shifts. I will use it during the days, you will use it at nights, and on weekends we will take turns."

Jimmy stood there for a moment, and said, "Okay; let me go change."

As Jim left, Tom had to put his five cents in. "You know, Al, I never thought you were a manipulating individual. I cannot believe he agreed to your bullshit plan. How do you do it?"

"I did not do anything! I told you before; he is my brother and I would do the same for him and more! So I was not manipulating anyone."

"Oh, yeah? I don't buy it," he said that, and walked away laughing.

I was really speaking form my heart, and did not see anything wrong with my plan, Tom's statement confused me; however, that did not matter, because afterward, we all went to the Pontiac dealer.

When we got there, three was only one Trans-Am left in the showroom, and right there and then; I knew it would be mine. Tom sat with the sales clerk for over an hour again, and I began to speculate that he might have a thing for sales clerks.

Finally, he walked out, and said, "Okay, Al; it's all done. I cannot believe those sales clerks. He tried to rip you off for an additional five hundred dollars, but we got it all straightened up. The down payment is a thousand dollars; do you have it?"

"Yes, here it is."

"Not now; you will give it to me at home. I paid with a check."

"So, it was only one thousand? I thought it would be more!"

"Apparently my credit history had improved, so the down payment was at a minimum. However, your monthly payment will be $640. Can you handle that?"

"Yes, we can. Where are my papers?"

"They will come by mail, and they are not yours; they are mine. The loan is in my name, remember?"

"Oh, yes, of course; thank you!"

Jimmy and I were standing outside when they pulled our new car out. Man! What a beauty she was. We were both speechless, we stood there with a huge smile on our faces, looking at that vehicle, and then at each other.

"Al, look at that white eagle on the hood! Wow; you know this car looks better in black!"

"Yeah, it's exactly like the one I saw in the advertisement. Jim, will you do the honor and drive us back home"

"I don't think so, Al. Why don't you be the first one to feel her?"

"Hey, man; you refer to this car like she was a woman! I like it. Get in. Let's see what she's got!"

That car had great power; as we took off, the rear wheels lost traction, spinning and burning tires leaving black marks on the concrete behind us.

"Al, take it easy. Treat this baby with respect!"

"I had no idea how powerful this car is I guess I'll have to be gentle with the gas peddle from now on."

When we arrived, Jim was tired and went home to rest, and I drove to see Vicky. I could not wait to show her my new toy. I parked by her window and honked for few times, but she didn't look out, so I went upstairs.

"Hi, Al. What brings you here without notice?"

"Sorry to show up like this, but I have great news, and wanted to show it to you. Can you come down?"

"Sure, let me get dressed. If you don't mind, wait for me downstairs."

I waited for a while until my patience ran out, and I decided to go back and remind her. As I reached the front entrance, she almost walked into me.

"Al, what happened? Why are you rushing back in?"

"I could not wait any longer; look at that!"

"Wow, is that yours?"

"She will be in a few years. You like?"

"Yes I do, very much so!"

"Get in; where would you like to go?"

"Funny you ask. I have a job interview not too far from here. Why don't you take me there?"

"Sure, show me the way!"

I looked at her, and I noticed something odd through her window. "Vicky, what are those white strings hanging on the tree?"

"What string are you referring to?"

"Right there; white thick strings on that tree, below your window."

"Oh, you mean those things. Probably balloons."

"They don't look like balloons to me. I have never seen balloons like those before, and who would throw them out like that?"

"I don't know, and why would it matter? Let's go!"

"Okay. You look great. I never had a chance to ask you before; how did you know my Uncle Abe?"

"Make a right here and go straight. I met him at my friend's party."

"Did you find him attractive? I hear that most women do! However, I don't know what they see in him; he is a klutz."

"Yes, he is. Turn left at the next block and stop. You know, he is not my type. However, I felt sorry for him. He looks like he is lost in his own world, but some women like that."

"No kidding; I wonder why?"

"Okay, we are here and right on time."

"Can I come with?"

"Of course; let's go!"

"Please be gentle with the door. It practically closes itself."

"Al, I am gentle by nature, and stop worrying about this car, It's just metal on wheels; remember that!"

We walked into a real estate store. She showed me to a chair by the door, and walked in. I could see her talking to an older man, and I could hear them laughing, as well.

What she said about my car had really bothered me, and then, she called to me.

"Al, come in."

I thought she was about to introduce me, but as I was walking in, she was on her way out.

"Come on, Al, let's go! And Gerry, remember I would do anything for you!"

"You just called for me, why are we leaving?"

"He had a call, said it was important, so let's go!"

"I didn't hear any phones ring, and what did you mean when you said 'I would do anything'? What was that?"

"Oh, boy; you are a jealous type, aren't you? I came here to get a job; work wise, it is just a figure of speech. It means nothing."

"I never heard that figure of speech before!"

As we walked back to the car, she jumped in and slammed the door so hard I saw the rearview mirror shake. "I thought you were gentle by nature! What happen? Is this your definition of being gentle? Have to say, I don't want to see you rough."

"Can you please drive? Take me back home."

"Look, I did not mean to upset you; however, evidently you show no respect for other people's property."

"Oh, I have no respect, and how would you know that? You don't know me that well. Actually, you don't know me at all, so please let's keep it quiet and drive, thank you!"

"You know, you are very sexy when angry. I guess to me, you will always look sexy!"

"Al, are you trying to be funny? Do you have any music here?"

"Yes, and yes, but I don't feel like listening to music now. At least I made you smile; was it a bad thing?"

"Of course not. Okay, we're here!"

"Let me walk you, and . . ."

"I know, be gentle with the door!"

As we walked to her building and passed that decorated tree, I noticed some balloons on the ground. "Look, Vicky. I think one of the balloons landed. And it does not look like a balloon to me. What would you say it is?"

"Where do you see it?"

"Right there on the grass, to your right."

She did not look at it; instead, she turned and asked me, "So, what do you suppose that is?"

"I don't suppose; I know it's a condom. The question is whose is it?"

"A couple lives in the apartment above me. I guess they throw away what they use"

"You think?"

"Look, Al, thank you for coming. I wish I could say I had a great time, but I haven't, so maybe next time we'll enjoy each other's company. Have a great day; goodbye."

As I watched her leave, she showed her great body, and that stayed with me the whole way back home. When I arrived, the apartment was empty and Jim was still asleep, so I had to wake him up. "Jim wake up, I have to tell you something!"

"What time is it, Al?"

"Three in the afternoon, come on, wake up"

"Man, I have some time to myself and you had to ruin it. What's up?"

"Abe has introduced me to this girl, and I have to say, she is amazing!"

"I am happy for you, Al! Congratulations! Now let me go back to sleep!"

"No, Jim. Please get up. You see, I met with her this morning, and we got off on the wrong foot, so I need to go back to her and repair the damages. So get up; get dressed. I'll drive you to work, and then I will go see her again!"

"Al, what about our arrangement?, let me drive you, and I will take the car to work."

"No way, I will get stuck there. The arrangement is in effect. Please just once make an exception."

In spite of everything, he was the closest person on earth to me. How could he say no? Evidently, my plan worked, and after driving Jim to work, I unexpectedly turned up at Victoria's place.

"Al, what are you doing at my doorstep again? Don't you know of the phone?"

"I could not stay away, especially after this morning. I wanted to apologize in person, so here I am, and I'm very sorry."

"Sorry for what?"

"Well, you know, for my behavior."

"Ok, stop blushing. Come on in and say hello to my parents. Mom, Dad, you remember Al!"

Her father looked at me from my toe to my head and backward, then said, "Al, where do you buy your clothes? Or someone has donated them to you?"

"Hello, sir, Bob . . . I bought them; why?"

"I was just wondering; good looking guy like yourself, and no taste whatsoever."

"Well Bob, I am dating your daughter!"

"Dating? She said that you are a friend!"

"Yes I am, and I hope to be very close friend."

"Keep on hoping; my daughter is very smart. I have seen many guys ended with nothing but hope!"

"Thank you, sir. I'll keep that in mind! Come on, Vicky, let's go!"

"You are welcome, and keep everything in your pants, if you know what I mean!"

"Where are we going?" she asked.

"I'm hungry; let's go to a restaurant."

I was not that hungry; I just wanted to get out of there. Her parents had gotten under my skin, and I felt like an alien from another planet.

Afterward, most of our encounters were at her place, when nobody else was there. From that point, any free time I had, I spent it with Vicky, and by the end of each workday, I would rush to her, forgetting anything and everything else in need for my attention.

I always missed her, even when she was present. She was extremely sexy and full of passion; she turned to be my first and only priority. While we were snuggling, I wanted to go further, but she would not let me. Our passion never went beyond kissing and touching. Feeling her soft and tender body turned me into a wild and fanatical person, and I was going out of my mind.

Those encounters continued for three months; for three months, she drove me crazy, but I did not believe in self-satisfaction, that was never an option for me. Instead, for three months, I was lifting car bumpers, and it helped to get some pressure out of my system, until one weekend when I visited her in the morning.

Her parents were gone and it finally happened. At last, we had sex. At least, I thought we did. With all the excitement, I was done before she got started. She was my first love, and when I finally penetrated her, it was over for me in less than a minute. I could not understand what was happening to me, and thought that maybe that was the way it was supposed to be.

Man, I was confused. I recalled watching porno movies, where they were getting it on for half an hour, tumbling around, groaning and moaning with extreme pleasure and passion. For some reason, my experience was quite different, and I expected much more, so it made me think that maybe something was wrong with me, or maybe it was because I was tremendously aroused by her, and because of that, it took only a minute for me to explode.

Suddenly, she hugged me and asked, "Al, were you a virgin? Was this your first time?"

"No, I had a girlfriend before. Why do you ask?"

"Well, it's just that I've seen this before. Guys are very quick their first time. Or, did this happen to you in the past?"

"Can you be more specific? I don't get it."

"Okay, we didn't make love; we did not have sex; and actually you left me in anguish. So, tell me, were you a virgin or are you just fast?"

"Anguish, I left you in anguish? Let's talk about anguish! What about those months when you aroused me, then told me to go home, sending me out with my penis ripping through my pants. How do you think I felt when every time I left you with a hard on, I didn't know what to do with myself? You think that was pleasant or what?"

"Oh, I had no idea, poor baby! Okay, forget it. I just hope you are, or should I say were, a virgin!" She then smiled and went to the shower.

Of course, I lied to her. Actually, there was a girlfriend in my life, but I had never had sex before. Considering that she was my first and I had no knowledge of intimate relationships, what I experienced, in some strange way, was satisfactory to me.

She was older than I was by two years; therefore, she probably knew more about sex than I ever anticipated. At that time, she was the best thing that ever happened to me, so, complicating things was not my intention. I decided not to take those issues any further, and didn't think of them ever again.

"Hey, Vicky, how was the shower?"

"Great. I was expecting you to join. Why didn't you?"

"I was deep in thought!"

"What about? Look, if our intimate relations made you uncomfortable, don't be. With time it will get better, I promise!"

"It's not that. Well, it is. However, my main concern was that I lied to you about being with another woman. I'm sorry. I will never lie to you ever again!"

"Oh, I knew that all along, but, I appreciate your honesty. Thanks!"

"So, you were saying something about intimacy correction. Hey, did you hear that siren?"

"Yes, why?"

"Strange but it sounded just like the siren in my car! You know; the sales rep told me that they are very unusual, and easy to recognize."

"Honey, where did you park your car?"

"Babe its nine a.m. Who would try to mess with it in bright daylight? Shit!"

As I looked out from the window, I saw my car zooming past the red light, and into the unknown. "Vicky, please call the cops. I just saw my car leaving me for good."

I waited until the cops showed up, then called Jim, and told him the bad news. To my surprise, he took it easy.

However, Tom was not as understanding. "Hello Al, how is your ride?"

"Hi, funny you ask! Actually, I just saw my ride driving away from me pretty fast!"

"What? What do you mean you saw it drive? And where were you? What happened?"

"You won't believe this, but my car was stolen right before my eyes!"

"You're damn right I don't believe it! What did you do this time; drive it off a cliff? You know, I thought this car would last you for a while, but you got bored with it sooner than I anticipated! So, what now Al? Which ad you'll be referring to this time? Ha! Where shall we go now? Don't tell me, I know! We will go to a Mercedes dealer! Would a 500 SLS do for you? No! Okay, then let me pick. Let's go for a Bentley; that way I would get lucked up for the rest of my life!"

"Oh, please stop with that. I'm telling you the truth! Besides, your credit line is not that good!"

"Yeah, thank God it's not! Be a man and tell me what happened. Where did you crash?"

"I don't have to listen to this," I said, and I hung up on him.

"Vicky, my father thinks I had something to do with this."

"Why he would think that?"

"That's a long story, you know. It's like this; once caught stealing, always will be called a tiff". I have to go, and will call you later."

I took a cab back to what we called home, thinking about the positive and negative things mixing on a daily basis, without my consent. At that juncture, it was clear that fate never asks for permission.

When I got home, I knew hard explaining was awaiting me, but I did not anticipate what was about to happen next. On the way into the kitchen, I saw Tom sitting there, browsing through the newspaper, and gazing at me with a doubtful look.

"Can you sit for a minute?" he said.

"Sure; honest to God, I was telling you the truth."

"Never mind that car. It brought you so much happiness; I knew it would not last."

"Why?"

"Because nothing good ever lasted with me, and you are my son. Whether you like it or not, our paths will be similar. An apple does not fall too far from its tree, and if it does, people call it a miracle. Are you a miracle, Al? Look, there is some other issue you need to attend to."

"Okay. It's been a long morning; tell me already."

"You and your brother will have to move out."

"What! Why? What happened?"

"Well, mostly it's because of you."

"What did I do? Is this because of what happened?"

"Don't play with me, Al. I see the way you look at my wife."

"What way? What do you mean?"

"What do I mean? You looked at her as if she was a sex object. I understand that you are alone, but I won't tolerate that behavior in my house."

While I was listening to his preposterous accusations and the fragments floating in his alcoholic head, I thought maybe he was drunk again, but he looked sober to me. So probably because of alcohol abuse, his brains were fried, and he was lacking thinking equipment.

I looked at her; so what. I like her because she is a nice and good-hearted person, but he said sexually. Damn. That thought alone terrified me. If we where the only two people on this planet, I would gladly cut off my balls, before even considering her as a sex object.

It was interesting to me how he conceived that fantasy. I tried to imagine her sexually appealing and attractive appearance . . .

She was five feet tall, a square shaped person weighting at least three hundred pounds, maybe more. What could be sensual and arousing about her? Maybe watching her as she rolled from one room to another, cracking the floors, and simultaneously shaking the walls with her gently erotic bass voice.

Presumably, he thought at that special moment my hormones would rise, and that intimate thoughts were circling in my head. Right; what a psychopath, and he said I look stupid.

However, they say that all creatures have a taste for their own. That is probably what a dog is thinking while licking his own balls, so Tom, in his own way, found Sylvia attractive, then assumed that my feelings for her was mutual. I never marked heavy rounded women, and some men find them very attractive. However, I have always admired the opposite visual effect.

He is most definitely attracted to her, so he thinks that everyone else is. How else could I explain his resentful behavior? I could only interpret his conduct in one way; he wanted me out, and that was a good excuse. Selfish, but practical.

Presumably, he has shaded his eyes, which explain why he is drinking every evening, listening to him babbling, I actually felt sorry for him.

Poor man, how did he fall so low, living this lifestyle with no enthusiasm or ambition? He became a living corpse, and called himself a family man. I guess he deserved that life. Nothing in life happens without a reason. We all pay for our wrongdoings, even when we manage to bypass the law, thinking now it's behind us. However, it's just a matter of time before a higher power steps in, and hits with a force, where it hurts the most.

My mother told me about Tom; she told me of how they met, and what he was like when I was born. "He was a handsome devil," she said, worked as a tour guide and always arriving home late with the aroma of women's perfume on him.

And if that was not enough, he reported to my mother with whom and how he had spent his time. That was the main reason why, she left him.

Once, I confronted him with that story, and his reply was, "What can I tell you? Yes, I was young and stupid."

Well, I thought, nothing had changed except, he became old. Look at him now, sitting there like a skeleton, with one scrawny hair on his head, which he ran around on his scalp in circles, in attempt to hide his baldness. If that hair stretched out straight, it would be a mile long.

My mother called Tom a gigolo! I saw him as a fiasco with pride! Unfortunately, for unknown reason, I found him repulsive, and nothing I could do about that.

"Hey, are you listening to me?" the gigolo said, babbling.

"Yes. Clearly!"

"Well, did you understand me?"

"Yes I did. Please give us some time; finding a place on my own is all new to me."

"Okay, but I expect you to start looking immediately!"

Jimmy and I began browsing through newspapers and it did not take long before we found something!

"Hey, look! One bedroom apartment completely furnished, and ready for rent," Jim said.

"That was fast; call them, although the rent is a little high for our blood."

"Can we afford it?" Jimmy asked.

"I don't see why not; we are both working."

The arrangement was easy. One month rent with a security deposit, and we were in. We packed our stuff quickly and moved out.

Walking away from Tom and his miserable lifestyle was the greatest feeling ever. We liberated from that hellhole with moles, and freedom ignited our lives.

Finally, we have a place of our own, peace and quiet at last! What a life. This apartment was enormous and we were two young guys, eighteen and nineteen years old, with no supervision and unconditional freedom. All we were lacking was money, and I needed lots of it!

As I was comfortably floating on someone else's couch, suddenly out of nowhere it hit me. "I don't have a car." I still had some money left, so it seemed to be a good idea to start looking for one. Then, I remembered one hot ride for sale at the parking lot.

"Jim. Let's go to Manhattan; we need wheels. I saw hot wheels for sale at the parking lot."

"What kind?"

"79 Pontiac Trans Am. Believe me when I tell you, you have never seen anything like that car before."

That car was still there when we got to the lot, glowing under the sun in black shiny color, with chrome custom rims. Man, that thing was hot!

"Hey, you are early. Twelve hours early, what happened?"

"Hi, Mike. This is my brother, Jimmy. I'm interested in that Pontiac. Do you know who owns it?"

"Sure," Mike said

"Can I talk to him?"

"You are talking to him! Do you like this car?"

"Oh yes; how much is it?"

"Only three thousand dollars."

"Damn, that's a lot!"

"I'll tell you what. When you start working here, I will arrange a pay off plan for you. When you pay it off, it will be all yours!"

"You see, I had a small accident with my vehicle, so now I need wheels badly. I brought some money with me, and the rest I'll pay off, like you said, but I must have it today."

"No problem. Temporary plates are at my office. You can have it today. I will take care of the paperwork tomorrow."

"Thanks Mike! I owe you one!"

"Not a problem; just don't let me down," Mike said with a smile.

Some people point their down noses while walking; Jim and I looked up at the sky as we walked toward our car, and that day turned to be a good day for both of us.

While driving back home, we discussed our schedule. I would pick up Jim from work at five thirty a.m., afterwards, he would drop me to work, and go home. Same day, at five thirty p.m., Jim would pick me up, drive himself to work, and I would take the car for the rest of the day, or wherever my urges would require. It was perfect.

As we talked about it, that arrangement excited us both. At the same time, I noticed unfamiliar scenery flashing by my side window. Then we passed some road signs I had never seen before.

Jim said, "Al, I think you are lost."

"How do you know, and what do you mean, *you*? We are both here; remember?"

"How do I know? I don't recognize this road, that's how," he shouted

"Calm down; what is the big deal? Let's ask somebody."

"Oh, yeah and who are you going to ask? We are on the highway, going eighty miles an hour! By the way, it would be a good idea for you to slow down, or maybe you want to crash into someone and ask them for directions?"

"Okay, we'll just keep on going. I read somewhere about New York roads. Apparently they are all connected, so you see, eventually we will get back where we came from!"

"What? How they are connected? What is the matter with you? Going straight, we will reach Canada! Then how would you get us back to New York? Oh, you did not read about that, did you?"

"Well, they said that all the roads cross each other, so we need to keep on going until a sign appears with a familiar road name and we'll follow it."

"Do you know any road names?" Jimmy asked.

"Yes! 10th Avenue and 26th Street, or 11th Avenue and . . ."

"Pull over, and stop," Jimmy shouted, and continued to scream. "That is the only road sign you know? Highway signboards are different! Are there any highway names you know?"

"Well yes; I know BQE and . . ."

"And what else?"

"And that's it," I said

"Oh, shit. We are SCREWED!" Jimmy shouted.

We didn't know our whereabouts for four hours, and we were still zooming along highway I–95. While passing through the unknown, I began to ponder. I pondered of our faith; I pondered at how fast this thing could go; and I pondered about the gas gauge. Then, I stopped pondering and focused on the gas gauge, because for some reason it pointed toward empty.

While flying by a sign that confirmed our way to New England, I began to ponder some more. Should we stop in the middle of nowhere, or keep on going into the unknown?

The lack of gas was causing me to behave erratically; I decided to get off the highway and find a gas station. It was the only rational thing to do.

"Jim. We need to get off this highway."

"Yes, get off at the first exit."

"Oh, by the way; we are out of gas."

"What? No gas?"

As Jim said that, the engine stalled and the steering wheel stiffened, then the brake pedal felt like a rock and would hardly move. Without looking on my right side, I veered the steering wheel to the right, and we began to slide off the highway. We then unexpectedly rammed into a vehicle that was driving along our side.

I heard someone scream, and then both our cars glided from the freeway, and onto the side road, where we finally came to a stop.

"Are you okay?" Jim asked.

"Yes, I'm fine! What shall we do now?"

"Well, now you can ask for directions! And there is your chance coming toward you!" Jimmy said.

We both looked at the man getting out of the other car.

As he approached us, he shouted, "What the hell is wrong with you? Are you blind?"

"I'm okay, thank you; and how are you?"

He came closer, then looked at me, nodded his head, and went back in to his vehicle.

It was eight o'clock in the evening and we were stuck on the highway, with nothing to do but turn our ears to the radio.

Shortly after, a cruiser pulled over. One of cops approached my window, showing one hand on the holster, and, with the other, pointed a flashlight into my eyes. "Your license, registration, and insurance," he said.

When I gave him my license, I immediately detected an abnormal look on his face.

While waving my license around, he asked "What is this book?"

"That's an international license. It's valid in six countries."

"What language is it written in?" the cop asked.

"Hebrew; it's Israeli."

"All international driving licenses are written in English! What in the world is this?"

"No, please keep on flipping the pages; there is some English content there, I know. I've seen them before."

He kept flipping the pages while walking back to his vehicle. After a while, he returned and said, "What happened here?"

"I was trying to change lanes, and that man ran into me, hitting me on the side."

"He stated that you hit him suddenly; is that true?"

"No!"

He reviewed my documents and said, "Here is your report number. I dispatched a tow truck, and you must stay in the vehicle at all times."

The first tow truck arrived in less than an hour. He picked up our neighbor's car, and then drove away.

At dawn, the second tow truck showed up. Fifty bucks for five gallons of gas, that was the rate for the people stuck on the highway, but at least he gave us directions. Then finally, we were on our route back home.

It took us over two hours to get home; on our way, we explored some of the Bronx Boroughs, and got a little lost again, but we finally arrived.

Home, sweet home, I do not know why, but on the way, I stopped by the liquor store and purchased a bottle of vodka. Jim went to a Chinese restaurant. A funny feeling came over me. Just by holding that bottle, suddenly most of my problems went away. Go figure.

At last, we entered our new apartment. Jim carried the Chinese food and I held one bottle of what Jim had described as complete relaxation in a promise land.

"Jim, go set the table." I rushed for glasses. Man was I hyper. We dropped a couple of shots down our stomachs. It seems very odd, but it actually felt good, because all the thoughts in my mind went away.

I found myself somewhere extremely quiet and comfortable; without talking or eating much, we emptied that bottle of pleasure and from that point, I didn't know where I was. But in a way, it certainly felt great.

The world I created had everything for my needs, and more. I felt overly comfortable, at first, it was scary, but then some questions arose. Why would I stay in reality when my dream world was better than I could ever imagine. I knew that the real world would always be there upon my return, so any doubts vanished without trace.

The next day, I felt actually good; no hangovers, no head aches, except for a small problem that occurred upon my arrival to work.

I arrived before six a.m. Punctuality was always my ambition.

"Good morning, Mike!"

"Hey Al, you're early. Are you trying to impress me?"

"Actually no; that's how I am."

"Good for you. I like it! Hey, wait a minute, what happened here?"

"What do you mean?"

"That dent along the side of my car. How the hell did you manage to do that?"

"That's my car, remember! Anyway, I had a small accident; no big deal."

"Listen to me closely; this is not a minor issue. The entire side is dented, so until you pay me in full, that car is mine! Do you get it?"

"Yes, I do; sorry"

"Don't be sorry. Pay me the balance or we fix it here and the cost will be on you!"

"Ok, fix it then! But I need a loaner!"

"Al, I will give you a temp car! But if anything happens to it, you would wish . . ."

"I get the picture, and will be extremely careful!"

"Okay, God help me! Now, each week, I will deduct one hundred dollars from your pay. In a few months, you'll pay off the repair. Now, let me show you around; your task is to stand here by the entrance. When a car pulls in, just ask how long they intend to stay. Short timers are on the left and long term to the right; all else will come to you as you go!"

This job turned to be easier than I expected, because most of the clients already knew the parking process by heart, as if Mike trained them personally, and some of them guided me to their preferred parking space.

My work was very simple, and very boring; nevertheless, I needed to find a way to keep myself occupied, and make more money so I could pay off my debts.

One ordinary day, I was standing by the gates as usual. Suddenly, a person appeared in front of me; he looked very casual, except for the large black suitcase that he lugged.

"Hey, man! I have some systems here; real cheap!" he whispered.

"Like what?"

"Look here! I have car stereos, VCRS, I have . . ."

"How much is the VCR?"

"Which one? Panasonic, or . . ."

"That one! JVC, how much?"

"Oh, this one! Hmm, sixty bucks."

"That is way too much for me!"

"Hey! You picked the most expensive unit; let me see what I can do for you! Forty dollars and that's it."

"I'll give you thirty!"

"No man, I can't. It's brand new! Besides, this one has a remote! The remote alone is twenty dollars, and you want to buy the system for only ten bucks? Get out of here!"

"Okay, let me see it again."

"Here you go! But don't break the seal; you can't open it!"

Why not?."

"You have to buy it first, that's why. Can't you see that this thing is new?"

"Yes! I see; okay here is your forty bucks, Thanks."

When he handed me that VCR, I was thrilled. At first I wanted to open that box, but feeling its weight, and observing all the labels, I decided to wait for Jim. That way we would open our first purchase together.

So by the end of my work day, Jim arrived. As I got into the car holding our new toy, he asked, "Wow, where did you get that?

"I bought it this morning, right here!"

"Don't tell me Crazy Eddy came to visit you!"

"Who the hell is Crazy Eddy? What is the matter with you?"

"Don't you watch TV anymore? That is the biggest retailer of electronics; they advertise all the time!"

"No, I guess I missed him. Anyway, there was this guy with a bunch of stuff, and I bought this from him for only forty bucks! Can you believe that, or what?"

"Actually I don't believe that. Have you checked the system? Does it work? It might be stolen, you know!"

"I bet it is, but who cares! And no, I did not check it yet. I thought we would do that together."

"Okay, let's go, and while I'm working, you better pray to God that this box will work!"

After dropping Jim at work, I arrived home, changed my clothing, and then periodically looked at that box. I wanted to open it with Jim, but what he had told me really bothered me, so instead of praying to God, I broke the seal and ripped the box open.

At first, there was some newspaper, then another heavy layer, and more newspapers, and more, and then nothing else. That was an emotional shock, as I never experienced before. What a fraud. Now, for the first time, I was in the shoes of a schmuck.

When I called Jim and described my purchase to him, he commenced to laugh and did not let me finish talking. I listened to his laughter for a moment or so, and then tried to join with him, but I couldn't, so I hung up.

A few days later, I forgot about my stupidity, and Jim stopped riding me with his wiseass comments. I was at work, thinking the usual thoughts. Suddenly I heard someone screaming his guts out in Michael's office. When Mike came out, I recognized the man at his side; he was the Mercedes owner who parked here all the time.

Mike approached me and asked, "Have you seen any strangers entering the parking lot during your working hours?"

"No, no one went in; not even the customers. In addition, during lunchtime, or when I visit the bathroom, you always replace me. Why, what happened?"

"That man you saw bursting out of my office claimed his radio was stolen here.

"He has a pull-out radio. Maybe he forgot it somewhere else, and besides, I didn't notice any radio while parking his junk! However, that would explain his tone."

"Okay, just keep your eyes open from now on!"

I always kept my eyes on the fashionable cars, especially on the radios they had, and if it was removable, then I removed it of course.

The next day, same man drove in, and I made the courtesy of asking him, "Hi, I heard your radio was missing."

"Stolen, not missing, it's a Bose System. Eight hundred dollars and sold only at the dealers. If I catch that guy, I will . . ."

"Look, I know somebody who can get you the same radio for only two hundred. However, he carries only used; let me know if you are interested."

"It's probably hot, isn't it? Who is this guy you are recommending?"

"I know what you're thinking. It could not be him. He lives in the Bronx, and besides, he never shows up in this area. I would have to pick it up for you, and that will cost you another fifty."

The next day that man drove in, got out of his car, handed me two hundred and fifty dollars, and said, "Go get it! When will I have it?"

"Well, I will go after work, and will bring it tomorrow for you."

The next day, I brought his radio with me. The exterior box had minor damages, and I added some tiny stains with a red marker, so it would not look familiar to him, then waited for him to show up.

"So, did you get it?" he asked.

"Yes, here it is. He told me it works like new."

"I can't use this; the box is broken."

"If you like, I can buy a new box for you and replace it; they sell for forty bucks plus labor."

"Well . . . Okay, do it."

And so I did. As bad news travel fast, before I thought about it, people were coming up to me and requesting the same removable box. I was doing two, sometimes three cars per day, and that turned out to be my small but very profitable operation.

A few days later, at the end of the day, Jim stopped by. He found me in a Jag, at the completion stage. Looking in through the window, he asked, "What are you doing?"

"I'm almost done; this is my new self kickback."

"I see; so you are installing radios now, and preparing them yourself for future easy stealing?"

"Hush! I call it alteration work. I'm placing them into a Benzie box. That way, people can carry the radio with them at all times. It's a new thing, and quite profitable!"

"Really, how profitable?"

"Well, I get eighty bucks per unit, and this is my third car today!"

"Wow, that's not bad. Does Mike know about it?"

"Yes and no. He doesn't have to know all the details."

"So, when will your car be completed? I'm tired of the subway routine."

"Funny you should ask. It's done; we can take it out today! And give back that piece of shit Mike loaned me!"

"You know, I don't feel like working today, so I called in sick. Since you getting rich, let's do something else!"

"Okay; do you have any ideas?"

"Well, let's go to a bar; maybe I'll get lucky!"

"Okay, my shift is almost over. Wait for me in the coffee shop. I'll come and get you later."

At the end of the day, we went to that bar. While getting smashed, we both forgot the main cause of our being there. Instead, we were deeply discussing the management of our future profits up to the moment when Jim came up with the question of the day.

"Al, tell me; do you love your mother?"

"Of course I do. What kind of question is that? And why did you bring this up? If my future plans don't interest you, or you have a better idea, then, be my guest, but don't change the subject."

"I did not mean to interrupt you like that; its just you are earning more money now, and I have never seen you sending anything back home, so I wondered why."

"Be more specific. What exactly do you mean?"

"Okay. Why won't you help your family? You know they need it. Is that specific enough for you?"

"I did help them, and I did that when I was in the most need ever. By the way, I still owe because of my family. Besides, who would help me? Answer that, why don't you?"

"Hey Al, calm down. I was just curious, that's all."

"I don't think so. You are not the type. You don't ask questions out of curiosity. So tell me, bro, what's eating you?"

"Okay, I am sending my mother a few hundred every month. I just wanted to know if we were alike in this matter."

"I don't know what to say to that! Placing myself in your shoes, I would never help your mother."

"Why not?"

"Because she gave you away when you were little, and I recall what Pap told me. In Israel, he asked for your custody, and wanted you to live with us, but she refused, and decided it would be best for you to stay at the orphanage! So what kind of mother would do that?"

"She is my mother!"

"Okay, but why would you think she deserves your help?"

"Because, she is my mother! Forget it; you wouldn't understand. Is it true what father told me, how your mother smashed tomatoes in your face? Was that noble treatment from your mom?"

"She had a good reason!"

"Really! Tell me more."

"I was only seven then. She asked me to visit the market and pick up tomatoes. This was close to the end of summer. You must remember how it was in Russia during that period; markets were half-empty. Anyway, I took a bus there, and when I got off the bus, luckily for me, the first rows were full of tomatoes. So I got what I came for, and then jumped on the next bus home."

"I don't see any harm in that."

"That's because I've haven't got to that part yet. Hey, bro, get another round, will you? Okay, back to my story. On my way back, at every stop, people were coming in, and the bus filled up. Shortly after, I was jammed in the crowd like a sardine in a can. When the bus pulled to my stop, I had to squeeze myself out of there, and finally, I got out in one piece. However, tomatoes in the bag had turned to ketchup, but I still felt good about my task. Unfortunately for me, my mother did not share my enthusiasm, and when she opened the door, her first words were, 'Where are the tomatoes?'"

I was holding the bag behind my back. I slowly handed the bag to her. She looked in, and then shoved her hand in the bag, and, while pulling out tomatoes chunks, she said, "What do you suppose that is?"

"Tomatoes, Mom!"

"Tomatoes, you say! Is this what you call tomatoes?"

Then she slammed her palm full of tomato into my face and began to rub them in. I just stood there, frozen like a statue. She continued rubbing that souse into my face, and yelling, "This is your breakfast, lunch, and dinner."

I tried to explain, and said, "Mom, please listen. The bus was crammed full; people were squeezing me the entire way. It's not my fault, besides, most of the tomatoes look okay!"

"Really you say! Not your fault, you say. They look okay, you say! Go to your room!"

"Have to say Al, it took a lot of courage for you to show up the way you did. I would thrown them away"

"Good idea, but I was one honest kid!"

"Yes, and now you are a grown up crook! Just kidding; it must be the alcohol talking."

"Don't sweat it. Maybe I am; I don't know who I am anymore!"

"Well, in some ways you are little tricky, but maybe it's all thanks to your mom and the way she treated you. I understand her point, trying to make a man out of you, and all. But, come on! Her methods were a bit frightening, don't you agree?"

"Maybe, she used to tell me, when her father died and I was born, she saw him in me, so she always expected more from me."

"That would explain who you are!"

"Oh, and according to you, who am I?"

"Your ordeals! And your approach toward them."

"Bro, now you lost me."

"Okay, what I mean is, it's always easy for you to find a way out. You seem to have a solution before problems occur. Do you remember when we were kids, going to school together?"

"Yes, so?"

"You may not remember this, but I surely do. It was the day our teacher give all the kids in school a task. We were given school stamps, and the task was to collect funds for our school from people in our neighborhood."

"Yes, so what is your point?"

"So my group and I walked from building to building collecting donations, and for the money we received, we gave back an equal amount of stamps. Do you remember what you did at that same time?"

"Yes I do! Why bring this up now?"

"Because, you were the only one in school who returned all the stamps, and not a dime of the donations. Imagine that! Thousands of students and only you came in empty! And what was even more surprising is that everyone believed you; moreover, they felt sorry for you!"

"So what? Were you jealous?"

"Judging by the smile on your face, I can tell that you have reconciled with your memory, so maybe now you can tell me. How did you do it?"

"Jim, I don't think I follow you!"

"Al, stop it. You're pissing me off. I mean, come on! So many years have gone by, and we are in a different country, for crying out-loud. Stop playing!"

"Okay, I'll tell you, Detective Must-Know-It-All! Actually, it was quite simple, and as in every scam, the simpler it is, the harder it is to reveal. That day was most memorable, because I did make tons of money! And so what? There were so many of you out there collecting, more than the school needed, don't you think?"

"Well, maybe, but that's not what I asked you!"

"Yes, I know. Let's have another round and I'll get to the details."

"Fine, can't wait; bottoms up! By the way, Al, I never saw you drink before! What happened, and when did you start?"

"Tom taught me! Boy, that one had a hard time rolling down my stomach! As I was saying, it was simple! I was walking around with a notebook, and upon every so called "donation," I wrote people's names and addresses, stating that the school would be mailing them a receipt shortly afterward!"

"That's it?"

"Yes, that was it."

"Unbelievable! A take like that never crossed my mind. No wonder no one doubted you, and back then, I thought you were stealing, and people actually gave it to you. WOW! Wait a minute; you mean to tell me that no one asked you about those stamps? It cannot be. I have encountered a few people who knew and were expected a stamp in return, so how is it . . ."

"Hold your horses. Of course, there were a few. Actually, if memory serves me right, there were more than a few snoopers. Anyway, I said to all of them that I ran out, but to keep collecting and be in the lead, I needed their name and address, and they would get the stamps in the mail from the school; get it?"

"Yeah, I get it. You see, that's what I meant before; you always find a way."

"Jim, there are many ways, and they are always there for everyone, including you! Maybe you are not looking, or not concentrating while looking. I believe that if there is a need, there must be a way. Try to live by it! It works!"

"Easier said than done, Instead; let's try to get out of these chairs and go home."

"Good idea, I'll drive."

"Al, can you drive?"

"Of course I can! Why do you ask?"

"Because, you walking the wrong way. We parked on the other side of this street. Besides, look around you. What do you see?"

"Okay, I see. There she is; my beauty!"

"No, Al, there is snow everywhere. It's winter now, remember? Roads tend to be slippery. Take it easy with your beauty tonight."

"Okay, I will drive slow and carefully."

"Thank you; although for some reason I doubt that very much!"

"Hey, look; we're approaching Brooklyn Battery tunnel."

"Fine, take the tunnel; just stop at the red light."

"Of course I am not blind. You see that fine curved road leading to it?"

"Yes, I've seen it hundreds of times; so what?"

"I bet you this baby can make that turn at eighty miles per hour."

"Al, there is no vehicle that can take this turn at that speed!"

"This one can! I'll show you, as soon as the lights turn green."

"NO, Al. You are drunk; don't do it."

"HERE WE GO! HOLD ON!"

"Al, slow down . . . AL . . ."

That was the last thing I heard Jim say. Afterward, everything went blank.

"Al, wake up! Wake up, Al!"

"Oh, man! Where am I? What happened?"

"We had an accident; stay in the car, Al. I'll go get help."

"Al, let's go; get up."

"Where are we going? Damn, what's my baby doing in that wall?"

"You killed your baby, Al; now get in there."

"Hey! Whose car is that?"

"No, no . . . Al. Get in the back, and lay low, I mean on the floor, Al."

"Hello!"

"Bro, who is that woman?"

"She is a friend; besides, she is nice enough to stop and get us away from this mess. Now keep it quiet."

"Listen, I think your friend is drunk! You said he was hurt; he looks fine to me! So I think you both better get out."

"Bro, I though you said she was nice. What a bitch she is!"

"Okay! That's it; get out now!"

"No, please drive. I'll pay you. Here is a hundred dollars. If it's not enough, I will give you more at our place! Just get us out off here, please!"

"I don't need your money. Fine, just keep you junky friend quiet."

"Junky? Whom do you call junky? You mucky..."

"Al, shut up! Please drive, if we stay, we'll be arrested. He made a mistake; it can happen to anyone. Besides, he will pay for it. Look at his car!"

"Okay, you seem nice. What are you doing hanging out with someone like that?"

"He is my brother, and as people go, he is okay, I think."

"You think? You mean to tell me you don't know your own brother?"

"Act normal, we are passing the toll now!"

"So what! There, we passed. Happy? I assume he is an asshole anyway!"

"You meet a lot of assholes in your life?"

"No. Yes! From time to time, I do."

"How is it, a beautiful lady like you meet that kind of people?"

"Well, my work, I guess."

"Really, what do you do?"

"Listen, bitch! If you think I'm asleep, you have another think coming to you!"

"Well, well, the asshole speaks again. I though he told you to shut up! What possibly can be coming to me from someone like you?"

"Whatever it is, you won't be able to handle it! Cheap whore; picks up anyone on her way! Be careful, Jim, she might rob you!"

"Who do you think you are, calling me names, in my own car? No good deed is unpunished! I made a big mistake picking you up!"

"Al, you will walk home; go back to sleep. Please don't pay any attention to him; just drive. By the way, I don't know your name. I'm Jim."

"Hi, Jim, my name is Betsy."

"Nice too meet you Betsy."

Then I fell into a deep sleep.

"Al, wake up!"

"Jim, is that you?"

"Yes. How do you feel?"

"I have a terrible headache. We have to stop drinking. What a nightmare I had. You would not believe the dream I had!"

"Oh really? Tell me."

"There was an accident. You were also there, and my car. For some reason I don't remember the details."

"Let me see if I can help you with that! We were sitting in the bar, talking, recalling our childhood, and then you smashed into the Brooklyn Tunnel wall! Was that your dream?"

"Yes! Now I remember! How did you know that?"

"Because I was there! Your dream was my reality, Al. Your car is ruined Sorry."

"Oh my god! Now I remember. Where is the car now?"

"After we brought you home, I went back to my station, borrowed the tow truck, and towed you car to your parking lot. It's there now, or what is left of it. I told you not to race into that turn, but you were so persistent. Needless to say, it was a bad outcome."

"You said *we*. Who else was there?"

"Some nice girl that give us a ride home, the one you called bitch all the time! Don't you remember?"

"Yes, now I do; sorry"

"Al, what are you doing?"

"Exploring our new apartment"

"No, you are not. You are snooping around for alcohol! And it is not our apartment, remember?"

"Okay, fine! Whatever. Damn, there is nothing in here. What are those people, cheap shits?"

"Al, those people don't drink. You just said we have to stop drinking."

"Considering the circumstances, I will commence that phase tomorrow. Now I need a drink; help me find something"

"Stop it. I'll go to the store"

When Jim returned, I was sitting in the kitchen supporting my head with my arms. Suddenly I heard a bang, so I looked up and saw Jim slamming two bottles of vodka on the table. I looked at him and said, "That was fast! Where did you get those?"

"You know, I have noticed, recently no matter where I live or work, for some reason, there is always a liquor store around the corner. Why do you suppose that is?"

"There is a reason for everything. Don't ask questions. Be grateful for what you have. Besides, would it be better for you to walk a mile or two instead?"

"Of course not! That is not the point."

"Yeah, well, let's celebrate! My car is fixed, we are making more money, and you are my tag along tail."

"What are you saying? Your car was destroyed, where do you see a celebration in that?"

"Listen, like I said, there is a reason for everything. You brought two bottles; the second bottle will be dedicated toward her funeral."

While drinking, neither of us noticed how a bottle of alcohol was joining us on every other evening. Sometimes at dinner, sometimes for no reason at all, and on occasion, we would look for a reason. However, that night was the most memorable of all.

As we were calmly sleeping, suddenly I heard someone knocking at the door and screaming. At first, it seemed like a dream, but then I began choking and had great difficulty breathing, and that was for real.

I woke up and found myself on the living room couch surrounded by smoke. The smoke gathered in the room rapidly and it became hard to see the light in the hall.

As I raised my head, with one bang the entrance door dismantled and flew into the living room. As it landed next to me, firefighters rushed in.

Lying on the couch, I froze as I watched the firefighters perform rescue activities. They broke all the windows and began throwing our things out, including some of the furniture that was on fire.

I did not understand what was going on. One of the firefighters approached me, grabbed me by my hand, and said, "Come on, let's go!"

"Why, what's going on?"

"You have to get out; there is a fire here."

He pulled me away from the couch and into the corridor. "Wait, my brother is in there!"

I broke loose and ran back in. As I ran into the bedroom, Jimmy was sleeping on the bed, surrounded by a cloud of smoke. His mattress was burning and yet he slept like a baby.

"Jimmy, get up."

Luckily, he woke up. "What?"

"Come on! We have to get out of here!"

Then firefighters entered the bedroom. "What are you still doing here? Get the hell out of here!"

We ran out of the apartment and toward the building exit. As we got out of the building, many people were standing there, they gathered around and enjoying the show. We joined the crowd, and watched our stuff flying through broken windows, accompanied by rented furniture.

"How this could happen? All I recall is that we were drinking and feeling good about it, and then I went to sleep. Jimmy, did you start a fire?"

"Me? No way"

"Oh yeah, then tell me, why was your mattress smoking? Tell me that!"

"I don't know"

"My guess is that you went to bed with a lighted cigarette, and then fell into deep sleep, and Walla! Now everything is gone, including our apartment."

"Are you the tenants of the burning apartment?" the firefighters asked.

"Yes we are," I answered.

"Who was in the bedroom?"

"I was," Jimmy said.

"So you are the responsible one?"

"Responsible for what?"

"The fire started in the bedroom; you probably fallen a sleep with a lighted cigarette. Apparently, you dropped the cigarette on the mattress and that is how this mess started. You should be grateful for standing here. We have seen this before, and in most cases people suffocate from so much smoke."

Jimmy stood there, looking like a zombie, and had nothing to say. I could tell he was upset, guilt chewed him up, and nothing I could do about that.

Shortly after the firefighters left, we went back in. The entire place was a disaster zone. We looked at each other and knew the main reason for what happened; however, neither of us raised the question of alcohol.

The firefighters chopped into pieces most of the furniture, including our TV. Pieces of furniture had gone out the window, and placed on the sidewalk; the only good item was the couch I slept on in the living room. Walls were stained everywhere with black smudges, and our new place smelled of smoke and stink from overcooked clothing.

As we circled the rooms, I went into the kitchen, then into Jimmy's bedroom. The firefighters had really done their duty. They demolished all that was in their way, including some of the floor.

I just do not understand the need to destroy it all, or the purpose of it all. I guess I will never know.

"Jim, where is your stuff?"

"I saw some of my shit outside on the sidewalk. All I have left is that suitcase in the closet and what you see on me now."

"I can relate to that, except there was a laundry bag in that closet as well. Go check it out. There may be some clothing we can share."

Keeping all the money in the car had turned to be a good idea.

I tried to make him feel better and take his mind off the incident, however I was taller than Jim by a few inches, and my clothing would not fit him.

My attempt to surround Jim with comfort was brief, because he set down, looked at me, and said, "Who ever told you that we were the same size?"

"I just thought that maybe you would compromise."

"Compromise what? Are you kidding me, no way? I have some money. I am going to get some new clothes in the morning. You are welcome to tag along!"

"Oh, I forgot. You are going to work tomorrow."

"Yes, I have to be there at six p.m."

"Okay. Go do your shopping. I guess from there you will go directly to work."

We went back to sleep as if nothing had happen. Next morning, Jim woke me up with a strange question. "Okay. What are you going to do?"

"I'll call Mike, and ask him if my car is repairable. Also, I will tell him that I need a day off, and then I will try to clean this place."

"Okay, good luck!"

When he left, I was standing in the middle of a nightmare with many things to do, and no knowledge of how. I told him I would clean the place up, but looking at it, I considered that unrealistic. Actually, I felt depressed. One thing after another; it is true what they say. "When it rains, it pours." It felt as if my life was flooding with bad luck and I was sinking in it.

Picking up a few saved chairs and placing them next to the three-legged table, I decided that was enough cleaning. Therefore, I took myself out for some food. Luckily, there was a pizza place around the corner, and surprisingly, a liquor store right next to it. Without my consent, my brain instructed my legs to stagger into the liquor store, and I walked out holding a gallon of vodka. Afterward, I took myself to the pizza place for a pie with extra cheese and pepperoni.

Holding the pie in one hand and vodka in the other, I was hiking home with tremendous speed. I had no idea I could walk so fast. If this were a marathon, I would probably take first place. Strange but true; somehow, the thought of alcohol consumption granted me extra speed.

Somewhere I heard that best cure for morning hangovers is the addition of more alcohol. According to my subconscious, I was badly in need of that liquid; my brain began sending signals of ASAP to my body.

Finally, there I was, sitting by the three-legged table, holding a slice of pizza and a glass of pleasure. After a few slices and one third of the bottle gone, all my thoughts began to change.

Suddenly a war zone had turned into the Garden of Eden, where everything was comfortably nice. All my worries were left somewhere behind me; all I could think about was that I needed to share that pleasure with someone. But Jim was gone, and I was alone, so I kept pouring myself shot after shot.

Until I heard a voice "Now hear," the voice said. "You have to walk away."

"Why?" I asked.

"Follow me, and I will show you the way."

"I like it here! I do not wish to walk anywhere."

"Walk with me. I will show you the way."

"No . . ." But my feet began to walk anyway.

"Keep your eyes on the ground, and observe the footprints behind you. Keep your eyes on those footprints at all times, and walk."

I did not wish to walk nor look at some stupid print, but I did it anyway.

Then there was a terrible, loud ringing sound. I woke up and realized that apparently I had been sleeping. It never occurred to me that a dream could be so real that it was frightening.

The loud noise came from the phone, so I answered. "Hello."

"Are you Al?"

"Yes, I am."

"I'm Sergeant Belatsky from the 69th precinct. Your brother Jimmy was arrested for theft, and you will have to come down to the station."

"Certainly; I'll be there shortly."

As he kept talking, I looked at the clock. It was midnight, and I could not believe that I had slept for so long. My head was pounding like a dozen tractors, and I could not think straight.

With no further questions, I hurried to the police precinct. When I walked in, Jimmy was sitting on the bench, handcuffed and downhearted.

Luckily, for him, they have given me some forms to sign and released him under my supervision and personal guaranty. Actually, I had no idea what exactly I was signing, but as long as Jimmy would go free, I did not care.

When we walked out, I could not help it, and had to ask, "Tell me, why in the world you would steal?"

"I was short of money, and needed an extra pair of jeans!"

"Have you completely lost it? You know you are walking around with a temporary visa. They could deport you for something like that. What were you thinking?"

"I don't know. I didn't think they would catch me, that's for sure. Hey, did you drink?"

"Why?"

"Because your breath smells of alcohol."

"Don't be trying to flip the record to another side; I'm still playing my music. Tell me, what's with the bag?"

"New clothes! Don't worry, I paid for those."

"Oh really! Then why did you get arrested?"

"I tried new pair of jeans in the dressing room, didn't pay attention, and left them on. When I got out, the alarm sounded, and that's how I ended up in here, still have the jeans though."

"What? Where are they?"

"On me; look!"

"I can't believe it. Tell me, where is my car?"

"What car? Old habits, die hard, huh? How did you get here?"

"Car service, damn! I forgot about the car, have to call Mike."

"Well then, the cab is our ticket home."

On our way back home, or to what was left of it, my mood slightly changed. As we recalled our incident, I have to say, in some way, we found it amusing.

Ultimately, I did not feel quite myself, considering, my accident, Jim's arrest, plus our place became a pile of junk, however, after all that had happened, at that particular moment, Jimmy's freedom comforted me.

I tried to understand his behavior. We all possess positive and negative thoughts; now and then, we make a choice. Unaware of the consequences, we act on that choice, and only afterward, we realize what we have done.

Sometimes, luck steps in, and at the end of the day, wrongdoing goes unpunished. However, most often, when committing to a choice and acknowledging a wrong action, thinking that this time I might get away with it, in most of those cases, and often sooner than anticipated, a wrong choice becomes obvious, then people get caught and no one likes to face the consequences. There are two sides to any incident, worthy and wicked. If I could learn to see the positive in every difficult situation, with time, similar incidents would be easier to admit.

Life is all about choices. From my youth, I intended to find that right choice; unfortunately, often with good intention, I would select the opposite. In spite of how hard I looked for that right angle, eventually, without warning, at the end of the day, somehow all my actions backfired on me, deeds that seem to be righteous, turned to be a mistake.

Nevertheless, I was determined to change things around, but due to my lack of knowledge, I did not know where to begin. Possibly that is why most of my accomplishments at some point or another had gone wrong.

Thinking about those issues, mulling them over, I came to realize that I could not recognize beforehand the right choice from the wrong one. Therefore, I would change my attitude, and my life would not be about choices; instead, it would only be about me.

I decided not to handle situations, nor deal with them either, instead, accept all that came my way, take the good for myself, and pass the leftovers to someone else.

The current situation was awful, so I would act accordingly. I would have to be vile; perhaps there were no other options or choice for me, so if that was the case, so be it.

That night, my intellectual spirit changed, my savoir-faire had vanished, and it became clear to me that, to live with coyotes, I needed to howl like one.

That night, I became a different man. Actually, it was that easy, and after that, the only important people were Jimmy and I; everything and everybody else became a drop in the ocean.

I turned to Jim and asked him, "You know, I think we have to set our priorities straight, and find a way of making more money!"

"And how do you suppose to accomplish that? Get another job and work 24/7? Is that it?"

"No, don't think so small. I actually thought of a way to make it happen, and it would only take a few hours a day."

"Sounds good; what is it?"

"There is a guy I borrowed money from a while ago; in fact, I still have not paid him."

"So now you want us to work overtime so you can pay him back? Is that the plan? By the way, how much you owe him, and when do you have to pay him back?"

"My debt to him is irrelevant. I am telling you about him for other reason. We also need to find another apartment and move out. Don't you see! That guy is our only chance to accomplish our needs."

"Well, I trust you, Al. Why don't you talk to him, see what he has to offer us?"

"Okay, let's go home, and I will call him."

So, I called him.

"Hey, welcome to the lost and found! Long time no speak!" the voice said.

"Yes, sorry. I was busy at my new job parking cars."

"Okay, enough about that. You have my money?"

"Well, I don't, actually. That is why I called you. I thought you might have some work for me. That way, I would pay it off faster."

"Did Mike say anything to you about me?"

"No, I had no idea you were acquainted."

"We are not. I'll stop by your work tomorrow, and will post you with details then. You had better be straight with me, or there will be a world of problems for you! "

"Of course I am. Thanks."

I hung up the phone and went to the bedroom, thinking to give Jim the news, but he was sleeping. The last few days had worn me out, so I decided to lie down as well.

The next morning, I attended my post at the parking lot as early as possible, walked around my car, examining the damage I'd done. It was my desire to repair the damage, but I knew that this time my baby would not stand a chance to get back on the road.

As I stood there looking at her with remorse, Mike appeared next to me, and said, "So, Al, this time you have overdone yourself. Ha!"

"What do you mean?"

"A car like this, destroyed like that. You have taken her where no man has gone before!" Then he began laughing.

"Oh, you think it's funny? We could have been killed."

"Sorry, I did not mean to laugh at your expense. So tell me, what happened?"

"I crashed into a Brooklyn Tunnel wall."

"Wow, I was right! You did take her to no-man's-land. What are you going to do now?"

"I don't know. Can this be fixed?"

"What! Are you kidding me? The damage is tremendous. I mean, that car is in need of major repair!"

"Okay, stop. I get the point. So what will I do for wheels?"

"Let's take a walk in the lot."

As we walked toward the end of the parking lot, Mike stopped, pointed toward some metal scrap, and said, "You see that! This is the car for you!"

"You got to be joking; it's junk on wheels. I won't be sitting in this jumble!"

"Never judge a book by its cover. This vehicle is reliable, and will always get you where you want to be! With this tank, you can crash into a wall and keep on going, and for only two hundred dollars, it's all yours. Is it a great deal or what? Get it before it's too late!"

"You know, I don't see myself crashing into walls some time in the near future, however, two hundred, you said? It is tempting; is it running? Or do I have to invest my savings into that before it'll start?"

"Go ahead. The keys are in the ignition. Let her rip!"

"Wait a minute. You keep the keys in it?"

"Yes. Who would want to steal this junk?"

"Oh, so I am the only smart one paying for it?"

"Look, stupid; all I am trying to do is to keep you safe, and that is it. Don't think for a moment that you have driving expertise. You have a long way to go, and this is your ticket there! Hey! Don't look so dull; drive it. Save some money. Then, who knows, you may have enough to repair the car that fits you!"

"Okay, Mike. I'll take it."

"Start it first. Listen to the engine!"

Mike was right. That monster started upon a half turn of the engine.

"How old is this car? What is it, anyway? I never saw one on the road before!"

"Of course not, and I don't believe you will see one, either. This car is one of a kind, an antique 1964 Chevy Malibu; very significant car."

"I'm sure she is. Damn, that thing is older then me. You have the title?"

"Yeah, wiser as well, I'm sure. I do have the title. My insurance broker will register for new plates this week; meanwhile, you can use our dealer plates."

"Thanks Mike. Let me park it up front, and go back to work."

Sometime around noon, that guy arrived. We spoke for a few moments, and from what I understood, it was a simple job. However, there was only one thing that puzzled me. Who would pay four hundred dollars to deliver one package? However, at that point, all I could think about was how many deliveries he would give me.

I could not wait to tell Jim about it, so I called him. "Hey Jim, I'm almost done here. I will head home soon, and I will be driving home, so get ready."

"No way! They repaired your car?"

"No man. I bought another."

"Already! Where did you get the money?"

"I practically got it for nothing. I'll tell you about it when I see you. I will sound the horn three times for you to come down."

"Okay, I will."

When I pulled up to our building, the horn did not work, so I came up. "Hey Jim; we are set for tomorrow."

"Set for what? I thought you would honk for me. What happen?"

"Nothing, the horn in this tank on wheels doesn't work. Anyway, listen to our next ordeal. All we have to do is deliver some envelopes to certain locations. The best part about it is they will pay us four hundred dollars per address."

"You've got to be shitting me; how many deliveries did he give you?"

"I don't know how many yet."

"Where is the pick up? Oh, and what's in the envelopes?"

"No pick up. He will come to my work, and I don't know nor do I want to know the contents of the envelopes. Hey, do you want to see my new wheels?"

"Of course; let's go!"

"Man, Al, where did you find this metal box? It is huge. Tell me, what is this bottle doing here? It looks like you had yourself a party. Were you drinking and driving?"

"No. No party. I was a little upset, so I bought that on the way here. Hey, let's toast our new idea, what do you say?"

"Considering the potential . . . sure, why not?"

"Jim, have your ever driven anything like this?"

"No, never."

"Well, go on. Take it around the block. See what it is like to drive a boat!"

"Okay, get out. I'll be right back."

I waited for him for a while. I could not understand what took him so long, and then finally, I saw him returning.

He got out in a hurry and said, "It was not my fault!"

"What do you mean? What happened?"

"I tried to stop at the stop sign, and the car slid into the stop sign. Did I damage anything?"

I looked around, then said, "Jim, don't worry. It's minor, besides, dents look good on this car. Let's go home."

When we returned home, the drinking commenced again, and that was the first time I saw Jim drunk. Maybe that's why he opened up and told me of his life. In the past, I thought I knew of his life and his struggles; apparently, I did not. There was a lot unknown to me. Actually, I was a bit surprised when he told me about his mother.

Evidently, she was epileptic, and in his youth, when he was seven, he walked around with a spoon in his pocket because he never knew when an attack might happen. She couldn't bear for him to continuously witness and experience her suffering, so when he was eight years old, she placed him in the juvenile facility and he was there 24/7. That place became his new home.

We recalled those times in Russia when he was visiting my family and me. He stayed over the weekend several times a year. One of those weekends, they left us home alone, so we decided to go out into the forest to look for mushroom and anything else that might appear on the way.

"Jim, look. Do you see that field with roses?"

"Yes, let's go check it out."

When we reached that plant, Jim began to tear them off, one by one.

"Hey, what are you doing?" I asked.

"Taking some home to your mother; she will be grateful, trust me."

"I don't think we are allowed to do that. Look, there is a man rushing to us; let's get going."

That man had a shotgun. While running toward us, he commenced firing into the air. We ran so fast that Jim had lost all the roses, and I lost my house keys. Sweaty and out of breath, we finally returned home. I sat down on the porch and waited for my mother.

A few hours went by and she appeared. "Hey guys, what are you doing sitting here?"

"Mom, we were in the woods, and I lost my keys."

"Those were my keys, and the only spare we had. I cannot wait until your father shows up. We need to get in."

"And how do you plan to do that?" I asked.

"I will not do anything. You lost the keys, so you will be the one responsible. Come with me."

She grabbed me by the arm and pulled me into the building and to the fifth floor.

"Mom, we live on the fourth floor; why are we at the fifth?"

"You'll see soon enough."

She knocked on the door, and a strange man appeared.

"Can I help you?" he asked.

"Yes, please. My son lost my keys. Can you let us onto your balcony?"

"What has balcony to do with that?"

"Well... You see, he is very athletic; I want him to slide down from your balcony to ours."

"Are you crazy? He is just a little kid. What if he slips and falls? I can't take that responsibility."

"Don't worry; I will not hold you liable. Please, there is no other way."

He stood there for a moment, mulling thoughts over, and then to my surprise, he decided to let us in.

"Mom, I can't do it. I'm scared."

"Yes, you can, and you will. Look, it's not that far away; besides, those that like fast rides should be ready for unexpected outcomes."

"What do you mean? I don't understand."

"You were irresponsible and careless; you neglected to protect what was important. Now you must face the consequences, so no more pleading."

I went; climbed over onto the exterior side of the railing, and began to lower myself down. I was only nine, and could not hold on very long. My grip was getting weak and I could not hold on any longer. I looked up and saw that man watching me. By the look on his face, I could tell he sensed I was losing control. At the same time that I lost my grip, he grabbed me by my arms and held me hanging.

"Don't worry, kid, I got you. I will swing you into your balcony, then I will let go. Try to land on your feet!"

"Okay, I will try. Please, tell me when you will let go."

He swung back and forward for a few times, then shouted, "Jump," and I did. Landing on that floor at the right time and in a perfect way came as surprise to me. I was sure he would miss, or I would land on my head. However, it turned out fine, as we had practiced that stage before.

From that day, I never took any keys with me, and always tried to avoid responsibility, especially at home and in school.

While recalling that incident, Jimmy was still talking about his ordeal with his mother, but I was not listening. After a few years, we all immigrated to Israel. Shortly after, Jim, with his mother, followed us. Unfortunately, she was a selfish woman, because she refused to give him up to his father and have him live with all of us.

Instead, she placed him in a juvenile facility again. During that time, I always thought he belonged to our family; regardless, we hardly ever saw each other.

I was seventeen when I began to work part time in the hospital of Haifa. Jim's father, my stepfather, held a director position of hospital maintenance; I worked there every summer as an electrician helper.

One day my stepfather brought Jim to our workplace. I remember that day very well. I was very surprised when, at the end of the day when we went home, Jim stayed behind. When I asked my stepfather of why, his reply was, "That's the way it has to be."

Shortly after, I learned that Jim was sleeping there, in one of the old hospital terminals. He had run away from the facility and had nowhere else to go.

Consequently, my part-time workplace became Jimmy's home, with free bed and free hospital meals. My mother would not accept him because of his bad habits, as she described them; they included smoking grass and drinking alcohol.

Her children, including myself, had no taste for those elements. I guess she was worried about us. As they say, "Bad habits are catching."

I disagreed with her policy, but what could I do. It was depressing hearing him telling all of what had happened to him and the lifestyle he had inherited. I did not know what to say, or how to react I just listen, and rationalize my mother's thoughts. However, no matter how hard I tried, I could not find any reasonable explanation for her behavior.

He was young and nobody would give him a chance to start over, or prove himself to others. Although my mother had said, "We have tried to take him from the institute!" However, they did not have any success. Jimmy's mother put up a fight. She would not allow us to adopt him. Then when he was old enough to decide, I was scared, because he became very different and was not a child anymore.

I related that story to Jimmy, and all that my mother had said about him. By the look on his face and his reaction, it was obvious I should not have told him that story. He sat there like a statue, with tears in his eyes. He tried to suck them in and not cry, but a few drops glided on his cheeks anyway. Maybe Jim had no sense of security, domestically and financially. I tried to retreat from our conversation, but I couldn't.

He became angry and disappointed. Finally, he said, "You know I got tired of doing what was expected of me, so, by coming to the US; I did something completely out of my character. I have to say, it really felt liberating!"

"Okay Jim. Let's go to sleep. I work tomorrow, remember?"

"No, wait; I see you are worried."

"Actually, this conversation is very unpleasant, and I am very upset!"

"Inhale and exhale; it will help you relax."

"Okay, are you trying to be funny? Talk about wrong timing!"

"No, please try it! Inhale, and exhale! Back in the orphanage, the psychologist told us this process helps to retreat from the world of problems."

"No kidding!"

"Yes, I recently began this method again, and it really helps me to shift into a relaxing state of mind."

I thought Jim was fabricating that story to get his mind off the main issue that hurt him the most. He also began laughing.

I interrupted him and said, "Right; pour me some more of that liquid, and I will show you how to relax the old fashioned way! And while you're at it, let me ask you, have you ever tried drugs? Did it take you to a place of great happiness? I'm asking because some users state that for a fact; is it true?"

"Everyone takes a different journey. Besides, I don't do that anymore!"

"Why not?"

"Because afterward, I wake up and the same shit still surrounds me, only the day is different!"

"How unfortunate for you. People say they trip quite often; it helps them with their ordeals on a daily basis." I was kidding. Jim, however, took it very seriously. "Jim, you need to give up the illusions; get a bite of reality and stop living in a dream world."

"Al, I'm getting tired of your counseling. Besides, you have no idea what you are talking about!"

"Really? And how would you know that?"

"Because, I turned my dreams to reality."

"Jim, you are not being ethical; that's the alcohol talking."

"Not true, you say? Some of my dreams came true."

"Oh yeah! Prove it. State one!"

"A while ago, I was In Israel, dreaming of America. Now I am here! Aren't I?"

"That's a good point!"

"Al, this is one of those days when nothing went well. We have to change our strategies before acting, and you . . . please don't make any assumptions or judgments. I'm going to sleep. Good night."

In the morning, I drove to work. On the way there, I thought of our last night's discussion, and Jim's suffering. No matter what, it became important for me to remember that sometimes I needed to kick myself backward, slow down, and look around me. This could be a very exciting time, and I needed to release myself from the past, focus on today, and carefully plan for tomorrow.

I had to be realistic about what I could and could not do. I would not let my stubborn and sometimes-unreasonable attitude draw me into an unnecessary aggravated situation or struggle.

While thinking about my options, and the choices I was able to make, self-confidence and reassurance where growing inside me. I felt powerful and willing to take on any agenda, and to chase after my goals, which meant to turn my plan into satisfaction.

I needed to be proactive on all sides; the objective was to stand my ground, so that day, I promised myself, no matter what happens, I shall never back down.

I was a little tense coming to work that morning. When I arrived, Mike was not at the entrance as usual. Turning my head left to right looking for Mike, I missed the entrance and brushed the side of the car against the post. I stopped, and looked around for a minute, then drove in. Thank God, no one had seen me!

I parked all the way in the back, trying to hide the damage. It was my car, so I did not feel like explaining myself to him again. Slowly, I began to walk toward the office.

Out of nowhere, Mike showed up, and reamed my mind with questions. "I saw the way you drove in! What's the matter with you?"

"I was reckless, got lost in my thoughts. Sorry."

"Sorry! Sorry won't cut it. Don't think for a minute that I let you use my insurance for that again."

"What do you mean again? I paid for the repair last time!"

"Oh, yeah, and who do you suppose paid for the other damages?"

"Oh, I didn't know about that. Okay, deduct the cost out of my salary."

"Really, deduct for the car, deduct for the post repair. Have you forgotten how much you make? For your information, with all the deductions, it's not enough! Since you have used and abused that vehicle in full, which obviously you have, it is most definitely yours; therefore, I need for you to pay the balance in full."

I had nothing to say to him. All that mumbling, for a few hundred dollars. What was the matter with him today! I went back to the parking lot. I sat down waiting for clients and thinking about Mike and what an asshole he turned out to be.

At first, I considered Mike a decent man. I had never seen him scream or raise his voice at any point in time. If someone should ever ask me about him, I would happily reply that Mike was okay!

However, with time, he showed me another side to his coin. He always looked at women with some urge, and I could tell by his expression what he desired. Within a short time, I noticed Mike flirting with women, all kinds of women; looks and age meant nothing to him. Upon arrival of a female, on every occasion, he would go out of his way to get under her skirt, and with every denial, he would proceed with persistence the next time round. That man's main agenda was, getting laid. He tried to screw every female who was in his sight. He reminded me of the phrase; "He screws all that walks and crawls." However, in his case, and from what I had seen, he only screwed with his eyes, and finish with his nose!

Recently, his biggest purchase was a used Dodge Van, which he called with joy, "The Love Mobile." That van had dark tinted windows. The interior had two front seats and a full size bed in the rear, curtains on the windows, one red bulb, and a few posters of naked women.

He had found a unique space to park that pimp mobile. The rear faced the emergency parking lot exit, and the front was facing the entrance. That way, when he got into the van, I never saw who came in from the rear, and I did not care much either. Besides, in that neighborhood, no one but whores walked during closing time. That was when Mike sometimes visited his love mobile.

Mike had a son. Apparently, we were almost same age, so one day, he visited his father, and Mike introduced us.

"Hey, Al, come on into the office. I would like for you to meet my son!"

"Okay, Mike. I'll be there soon."

When I walked in, I saw a huge bald guy standing by the window.

"Paul, meet Al, my number one guy! Al, meet my son, Paul."

"Nice too meet you Paul!"

"And you Al!"

When we shook hands, I heard my bones crushing. "Hey, Paul, take it easy! What do you do for a living? Massage elephants?"

"Sorry; no, actually, I mostly work out. You can tag along next time around."

"Thanks, but will have to pass. The day is too short as it is."

"Al, Paul needs to get his things from his previous work place. Can you drive him?"

"Yes, Mike. I can, but my car is all the way at the end. I can't pull all those cars out."

"No need. Take the van."

"Is it drivable? I thought it was parked there forever!"

"Of course it's drivable. I've just had no use for it in awhile now."

"Okay. Come on, Paul. Let's go. By the way, where are we going?"

"Up town, to seventy-Fourth Street, and Lexington Avenue."

While driving there and talking, our friendship improved. As it turned out, Paul was a jeweler; also, he was a nice guy.

"Okay, Al, we are here. Wait for me here. I will be right back."

He returned after twenty minutes, with a small toolbox and a white bag.

"Paul, where have you been for so long?"

"Sorry, I got hungry, went for a snack. Do you like falafel? Here, I got you one, as well."

"Of course I do, but I can't eat and drive. By the way, which way should we take back? Can I make a right and drive down Second Avenue?"

"No, you need to avoid the traffic. Take West Side Highway, instead. Drive and I will show you."

So we drove, and I got onto the highway. Paul was persistent, and finally persuaded me to take a bite while driving. I have to admit, that falafel smelled so delicious I could not resist.

"You see, it's not that hard. You know, Al, at times like this, I thank God for giving us two hands!"

"Paul, how come you don't drive?"

"I do. My license got revoked recently, so in six months or so, I will be back on the road."

"Let me guess the reason. Was it because God give us two hands?"

"No, it's a long story. Maybe some day I will tell you. Hey Al, watch that bump!"

"Watch what? Oh, shit!"

"Al, turn left, turn left! What are you doing?"

"I am turning. LOOK! The wheel won't respond! Shit! Paul, hold on; there is nothing I can do!"

"AL! SLOW DOWN!"

That was it. The steering wheel was flipping around on its own. I was pumping the break pedal until it fell down and stayed there. From that moment; there was nothing I could do but sit tight and watch through the windshield as we shifted lanes, then crashed into a concrete column. Upon the crash, I felt the rear of the van lifting.

As we were helplessly sitting there, Paul shouted, "Al, are you okay?"

"I don't know! Paul, what is happening? Did we stop?"

"Jesus Christ, I think the van is flipping forward. Al, we need to move back!"

"Stay where you are, Paul. Don't unbuckle yourself!"

As I yelled those few words, the mattress slid to the front and slammed against our seats. I was face down holding the steering wheel, my body was hanging upward, bound to the seat by the seat belt.

At that moment, front of the vehicle was smashed against the road, and the rear wheels were up in the air. We stayed in that position maybe for a few seconds, and then Paul asked me, "Al, are you okay?"

When I thought this was the end of it all, there was a cracking sound and I yelled, "Paul! It's not over yet!"

The van tilted forward, and then flipped over the guardrail. We were freefalling onto the highway beneath, and then landed on a vehicle going in the other direction. Then, I fainted.

Upon revival, I found myself upside down. I looked around and Paul was gone, then the door opened and someone grabbed me by my waist, shouting, "Come on, and help me. Pull yourself out!"

Finally, someone pulled me away, and onto the side of the road. The scenery was woeful. Mike's love machine was all smashed, resting inverted on the top a large car. Behind it, cars piled up as far as the eye could see.

Shortly after, Paul appeared.

"Paul, where have you been?"

"I went to call for help. The cops are on their way. Are you okay?"

"I don't know. I feel weak."

"Maybe you are still in shock! The ambulance is coming, as well; why don't you go with them?"

"No way. I am fine. Give me a hand. I need to stand up."

"Man! Look at this mess! I can't believe we created this."

"What do you mean, we? I was driving."

"Al, before we crashed, the van was driving itself. I saw you turn the steering wheel right and the van drove left; don't you remember?"

"Well, it's coming back to me in pieces. Paul, did you call your father?"

"Are you kidding me? No way!"

"I see!"

Soon enough, somehow people managed to unwind the situation. Everyone got into their cars and slowly drove away. Only Paul, me, and the owner of the other car stayed in the center lane next to our vehicles. Then that person looked at Paul and said, "How did you manage to go over the rail guard?"

"We lost control, that's all I know, ma'am!"

"Here come the cops. You guys better be sober!" She said that, and walked toward the cruiser.

I turned to Paul and asked, "Now what?"

"We shall see; don't worry, Al. It was not your fault."

"Thank you for the support. I don't care about them. My main concern is your father!"

"Oh! Yeah, that will be a problem."

While the cops were taking my statement and doing a breath test, suddenly, I heard a big slam. A tow truck had dragged the van down from the car. That poor van had turned into a crushed can. I was stunned. We got into the tow truck and drove back to the parking lot, dragging behind what was left of Mike's love mobile.

When we arrived, I whispered to Paul, "Ask the driver to unload the van along the sidewalk, and I will go look for your father."

There was no one in the office. I walked around and could not find Mike anywhere. When I got out and walked toward the van, Mike was standing beside it talking to Paul, so I approached then slowly.

"Al, where have you been?"

"I was looking for you!"

"So Al! Tell me, did you like the way this van handled the road? I replaced the tires, and wanted to check how they would hold on the highway; but never got a chance. Look at those wide monsters now! By the way, west Side Highway was my idea, so you could refer to me if they paid off. But, at this point it's clear; no need to ask!"

"Mike, I don't know what happened! Honest!"

"Don't get excited. It was not your fault. The ball-joint popped out. That's why at first you lost steering, then when the wheel came off its arm, the brake line ripped. That is why you had no brakes!"

"How do you know this?"

"My mechanic inspected the left side wheel. You see the way it's hanging away from where it is supposed to be. What, you didn't see it?"

"Dad, he was in shock; he could hardly stand."

"I am surprised you are both alive, and no scratch on neither of you. It's amazing!"

"Mike, I would like to go home now."

"Yes, of course, go. Are you okay?"

"Yes, thank you."

I got into my car and left, and after a while, my body began to shiver. I could barely keep my eyes open. On its own, my mind replayed the most terrifying moments from the accident; some of those moments I did not recall. It was as if I was going through the same thing again.

Finally, I arrived home, and somehow got out of the car. I practically crawled up the stairs, and when I got in side the apartment, Jim was on his way out.

"Hey Al. What's the matter with you?"

"There was an accident. Be a pal; help me to bed."

"Is everything okay?"

"Yes it is! Yes it is. I just need to sleep it off. I will tell you what happened later."

I woke from a nightmare, sweaty and restless. The nightmare appeared to be real. Things were exactly like what took place yesterday, or maybe it was just a dream.

I was confused and did not know what to believe, so I took a quick shower and rushed to work. When I arrived, that love box was at rest parked by the curb. Unfortunately, my nightmare turned out to be yesterday's crisis.

I needed to get free of my problems. It was time to act on my earlier thoughts, to make more money and pay for the damages.

By ten o'clock in the morning, most of the vehicles had arrived; some self parked. I decided to proceed with my task, and made a phone call. I never knew his name, but as soon as I said hello, he recognized me.

"Are you ready for the task?" he asked.

"Yes, that is why I'm calling."

"So, you ready then?"

"Yes; very much so!"

"Okay then! Remember, there is only one rule. Never, and I mean not ever, open the packages!"

"I understand. Tell me, when I can start? Also, can my brother assist me?"

"Whatever. I will come to your work by the end of the day. We'll talk then."

When he hung up, I impatiently waited for the day to end.

Time passed and the parking lot emptied out. I had to be discrete, so I waited for Mike to leave as well.

As he was leaving, he said, "Look, don't worry about the van. My insurance will pay for all damages. I am grateful that you both are okay, and you should be too!"

"Thank you, Mike. I will clean my car and go!"

"Okay, make sure to lock up. See you tomorrow."

That was it; they were all gone. I waited for him for over an hour. Finally, he arrived, rolled down the window, and asked me to come forward.

When I came up to his car, he said, "Take this bag; there are three packages inside. Each has an address. Make sure they get there today. You have two hours!"

"But how will I . . ."

He interrupted me and said, "You will get paid the next day." He handed me a black bag and took off.

At first, I was a little confused, and then I thought to myself, *what is the big deal? Actually, there is nothing to it, piece of cake!*

I drove home, picked up Jim, and we were on our way.

On our delivery, we encountered with a few strange people. I observed each one; the way he grabbed the package, and clutched his arms around it, holding it tight. It was clear that the contents were very important to them.

I could not forget that person on our last delivery, because he was holding on to the package like it was the last gulp of air. Jim and I looked at each other and both knew there was something peculiar about those packages.

I did not feel comfortable about it. Jim tried to hide his emotions although I could see it in his eyes. What really bothered me about Jim's behavior was his silence.

"I wonder what was in those bags," I said.

Jimmy laughed and said, "Drugs! What else could it be? Did you see those people! Man, talk about people in need! By the way, do you know what will happen if we ever get caught?"

"I'm trying not to think about that. We need the money, remember?"

"All I'm saying is that we have to be extremely careful. When you see that guy again, talk to him about that!"

"And what do you suppose I should say? Or, how should I define *careful* to him?"

"I get the point. Just ask him; maybe he has a plan! Considering his line of work, he should have."

"Okay, I will. It's almost five p.m. Let me take you to work."

I dropped Jim at his station and went home. Lying on the couch, I began browsing through newspapers looking for apartments for rent. At last, I found a suitable one-bedroom apartment, in a co-op building. Wall-to-wall carpet, fully renovated, located in a nice neighborhood. That place seemed perfect for us, so I called. Luckily, the owner was there and willing to show me the place right away.

When I drove up to the building entrance, there was a woman standing at the lobby. She was half-naked, and looked just like those whores I had seen in the past, except she appeared to be old.

I approached the entrance, and saw her up close. She was wearing a tiny black nightgown covered with red and white roses. Her face was frightful, with enormous amount of makeup.

She waved her short arms at me, then walked toward the entrance and pulled the door open.

I walked in, and we were acquainted with a few minutes of conversation. I realized she was actually a very nice person. She reminded me of the old phrase, "Never judge a book by its cover." We went up to see the apartment; the rent was high, but now, affordable.

I looked around, thinking the place was superb.

"Do you like it?" she asked.

"Yes, I do. When can we move in?"

"Did you say *we*? I thought you needed it for yourself. "

"Sorry, I neglected to tell you; my brother will be staying with me, but this is temporary. He came to visit from Israel and will be going back soon!"

"Oh how nice. Well, I need one month security and one month rent, then you can move in what ever you feel like!"

"Okay, here is four hundred dollars deposit. I will bring you the rest by the end of week. Is that okay?"

"Yes, fine; welcome to our building!"

That evening, I had made a deal on a great place. I wondered what Jim would say; although I was sure, he would like it.

From that day, everything went very well. Nevertheless, I was short by one thousand dollars, which I expected to be the payoff from the day's deliveries. On the other hand, that man was unreliable and unknown, so there was a big possibility of getting nothing. However, I decided to wait for tomorrow and hope for the best.

The next morning, I picked up Jim from his work and we drove to my parking lot. On our way there, I told him all about the apartment, and he was overexcited. Therefore, we were about to move again.

"Would you like me to pack your things?" He said that while laughing hysterically. I assumed he was laughing because there was practically nothing to pack!

"Yes, please; pack everything. Don't forget the suits! Anyway, we need to move in today."

"I thought you said Friday?"

"Hopefully we will get paid, and money talks, so I think she will let us in sooner."

"Hey, slow down. That's your station. Look, there is a car already waiting for you there!"

"Where do you see it?"

"That car, along the side of the repair shop. Is that the guy?"

"Shit. Yes! That's the guy's car!"

"Don't forget to talk to him about some precaution plans."

"What precaution plan? Are you nuts? You really think he cares about our safety?"

"Just ask him! It won't hurt to try! You know what they say; 'Those that try it all live through it all'."

"Oh, really! They also said, 'Those that don't try it all, don't live at all.
"Okay. Go home, I'll call you later."

I did not approach him right away. First, I opened the parking lot gates, then, went for a cup of coffee. On my way back, I passed alongside his car. It had the darkest tinted windows I've ever seen; that car in it self gave me the creeps.

"Hey, good morning," he shouted while getting out of his vehicle.

"Good morning. I didn't expect to see you so early!"

"Had nothing else to do, so I thought I'd stop by on my way there. Get in; we need to talk."

"Is there a problem?"

"No, relax! Here, that's for you."

He handed me a small paper bag, folded in half. I took it, and it seemed that there was nothing in it. "What's in it?" I asked

"Your cut! Twelve hundred dollars, three addresses times four hundred dollars each. I always keep my end of the bargain. Good job, by the way, the clients were a little nervous, new faces and all. But at the end, they were happy, and that's what counts the most!"

"Was there someone else in my shoes? I mean, prior to me doing this. Did you have anyone delivering before me?"

"Well, yes. He was a good man but stupid, I might add, or maybe greedy!"

"Why did you said was? What happened?"

"You seem like a nice kid, so I'll remind you again; never open the packages!"

"Yes, I memorized that part well!"

"Apparently he had forgotten, and the rest . . . Well, use your imagination. Okay enough about that. I have another assignment for you. There are six locations in this bag: Upcoming Saturday, nine to eleven p.m. is your delivery period. I will deduct half of your share toward the loan I gave you; with time, locations and quantities per week will increase. Let us hope you can handle that! Now get out. I'm late; have to go."

Afterward, I went to the bathroom. I wanted to see what he had given me. In addition, I needed to think about the man who had delivered before me, because, when I thought about it, I did not like where it led me. Regardless of how hard I tried to imagine a normal situation, each story that I imagined came to a blind alley. There could be only one rational explanation. He opened the packages, probably liked what he saw, most possible cut something for himself, and at some point, he was caught. What happened next is unknown, and I did not want to find out.

Thinking about that man had made me forget about the bag in my pocket, so I checked it out. I did not trust him. Therefore, money was the last thing I expected to find in that bag. Then, when I discovered twelve hundred dollars in there, I was very surprised and it really made my day.

When I walked out, Mike was standing there, as a ghost always appearing at the wrong moment. "Was it that good?" he asked.

"What do you mean? Are you spying on me?"

"No, I just never saw anyone come out of the bathroom with a big smile on their face. What did you do in there? Was there anyone else with you? Is she still there?" He burst into the restroom with a question on his face, and then walked out, disappointed.

"What? It's empty. Whom did you expect to find there? Stop fantasizing. Can a person be in a good mood just because it's a nice day? You should try it some time; it's nourishing!"

"I do not think so; not in New York! I will see how long that mood of yours lasts; go back to work."

He went out of the office, and back to whatever he was doing.

I decided to call Jim, and tell him with the good news. At last, we could begin to rise to the top, and the way things were going for us, in a few months we would became financially stable. I just hoped for all of this to last.

Come Saturday, Jim and I were on our route again. Five of the locations were easy, because we had been there before and were acquainted with the usual routine. However, the sixth one was new and unfamiliar.

"Al, what's with this address? It says 55 Green Street! And that's it!"

"So, what is wrong with 55 Green Street?"

"How should I know? My point being, they did not specify a city!"

"That is probably because all our deliveries are in Brooklyn! We always get only numbers and street names! So what else do you need?"

"You dumb ass! That's because none of the other street names repeat themselves; this one does!"

"Okay and how do you know this?"

"Because, I toured the Green Street in Manhattan! It's lower downtown; some call it the Village and others SOHO. You know, quite a nice place! I saw some cool . . ."

"Stop with your fairy tales. We might have a problem here! Shit! This could be bad!"

"I know! You need to call that guy and ask for a correction."

"What correction? Do you think we deliver for UPS?"

"So now what?"

"I'll tell you what now; we go with the plan! Be rational; all our prior locations were in Brooklyn! Right?"

"Yes!"

"So why would this belong in Manhattan? It makes no sense! Am I right?"

"I believe so"

"So do I! Go to the Green Street in Brooklyn! Hey, what's the worst that could happen? We turn around and go to the city."

"Okay, Al. I hope you are right."

When we arrived, the place gave me the creeps, and by the look on Jim's face, he wasn't too thrilled about it, either. The street was dark and very quiet.

We sat in the car for a while, and then Jim said, "So, whose turn is it to knock on the door?"

"We never took turns! Why now?"

"One of us needs to stay in the car and cover the other."

"What cover? What are you talking about, and how do you plan to cover me? Or, with what?" Jim, I think you have been watching too many movies. We are just dropping a package, remember!"

"Okay, then. I'll go!"

As he said that, I opened the door and stepped out. I walked slowly toward our destination while observing the surroundings, and when I got to the door, I knocked a few times. There was no response, so I turned around and yelled, "Hey, Jim, it's the wrong address."

But Jim was not in the car.

I ran back to the car, looked in, and I felt a hard poke on my back. A voice said, "Get your head out of there slowly, and turn around."

I turned around, and saw four large men standing in front of me. They had hoods on, and one of them held Jim with his hands behind his back.

"What are you girls doing here?" He asked.

Jim replied, "It's a free country, isn't it?"

The other man turned around and punched Jim in his stomach, then said, "Yes it is, little lassie. Just remember, that this freedom of yours works both ways, and I can deal with you as I please!"

"Hey listen, let my brother go. We arrived here by mistake. Our parents asked us to deliver a letter, and we thought it's here. Apparently, it's in the city. Go look for yourself; the envelope is in the car!"

And so he did. As he walked back around the car, he stated, "55 Green Street, and no names! Why is that?"

"They are our relatives, Bunny and Joe!" I answered.

"Ron, let him go!" He continued talking, and at the same time slowly placed our envelope into his inner coat pocket. "So, you both were supposed to be in Manhattan, and instead, you ended up here! What a coincidence! However, I don't believe in coincidences! And neither do my men! Which means this envelope belongs to us. Don't worry; we'll make sure that your relatives get it! Now get the hell out of here before I'll change my mind!"

We both jumped into our car, and rushed away.

"Wow, Al. I don't believe what just happened! Did you see those guys! Talk about monsters!"

After driving a few blocks, Jim said, "Al, why are you stopping? And why are you turning! You must be nuts!"

"Look, Jim, without that envelope, our world as we know it will turn into a nightmare! Odd, I was talking about a situation like this with our employer. When I asked him what happened to his former deliveryman, he said; 'Use your imagination!' Do you get it?"

"Yes, I get it. However, I'd rather wait and see were it leads us, than die here and now instead! Have you any idea what they will do to us when they see us coming back?"

"They won't see us, but we need to follow them and think of a way to get our envelope back."

"Okay, Al. Stop here and don't get any closer. Look! They are still standing outside. What the hell they are up to?"

"I don't know, and don't intend to find out. I just want that envelope back."

"Al, we need to be smart about this. Look at them; those animals will rip us into pieces, so we cannot confront them. Not to mention, that we are bare-naked. I told you before; we need to carry guns, but no, better modest than sorry, you said! Well! Aren't you sorry now? I know I am!"

"Jim, having a gun, is like agreeing to kill, and I am not about that! Besides, look at them. We would not have enough bullets to put one of them down!"

"Yea, they are big alright, but not too bright!"

"What do you mean?"

"That talkative guy never opened the envelope, did he?"

"No, I don't believe he did. What a moron!"

"Okay, Al. They are getting in the car. Let's follow them, but keep a long leash; I mean very long!"

Those idiots cruised around that neighborhood for over an hour, and we had no choice but to tail behind for a long and tiring drag around.

"Al, I think we are going back to Green Street."

"Yes I believe we are!"

"Don't turn into the street; stop here at the corner! Look, there are lights in that house, and that van wasn't there before!"

"Jim, are those guns they pulling from the trunk?"

"They look like shotguns to me!"

"I think we need to call the cops!"

"Yes, good idea! And tell them what? Look, Al, they are taking their jackets of, get the crowbar! Damn, something bad is about to happen here; we need to be fast."

"Okay, they're walking into that house. Let's go!"

"No, Al. I'll go. When I flash the envelope, you drive in and get me. Give me the crowbar and wait here!"

When Jim went out, those men went into the house. By the time Jim reached their car, gunshots had transpired, and from overexcitement, I neglected to watch Jim, instead, I was observing that house.

When I looked at their car again, Jim was gone and there was no sign of him anywhere. I became paranoid and lost my concentration. I did not know what to do or what I could do.

Then the shooting stopped, and Jim emerged alongside of my passenger door and looked in.

"What are you doing? Get in!"

He jumped in and said, "We're good! Let's go!"

"No! They might see us! We stay for now!"

A moment later, gunshots transpired again, and then two of those men ran out from the house. As they got into their car and drove away, another two men ran out, and jumped into the van and pursued them rapidly.

Jim and I looked at each other, and then he said, "I think we can go now."

"Did you get it?"

"Of course! Let's go to Manhattan."

"Okay. Hey, where is the crowbar?"

"Shit, I left it in their car. It must have dropped when the shooting started. Maybe you'd like to catch up and get it back, as well."

"Very funny Jim; so, which of the windows did you break?"

"I did not have to; the doors were open. And why didn't you drive by like we agreed?"

"Because of the shoot-out; and I think it worked out well! However, only two of them came out. I wonder what happened to the other two."

"I don't. Just keep driving. Let's get it over with and go home!"

We arrived at the right location, and both of us walked to the door. As I was holding that envelope in my hand, I realized it became our key to our freedom.

After Jim rang the doorbell, a tall man in his pajamas opened the door, looked at us, then said, "Is that for me?" He then grabbed the envelope, and tried to pull it away from my hand.

"Al, let go! Let go, Al."

"Hey! Give it here! What's wrong with you?"

So, I let him have it.

Jim said, "Look, we had car problems. It has been a long night, but, we are here as promised!"

"You are four hours late! That is way off the promised time. I was about to call someone else. Lucky for you I didn't!"

"What is in that envelope anyway?"

"Jim, stop with the questions."

"Oh, you mean to tell me that you don't know? He did not tell you. Of course he didn't! It is my ticket to heaven; quite a few tickets actually! And thanks to you two bozos, I got time for only one trip."

"Come on, Jim; let's go."

When we finally came home, I fell on my bed with all the clothing on me, but could not fall a sleep, Jim's question circled my mind. I thought why he would be interested in the contents of that envelope. Before I fell asleep, one rational answer appeared. He must have taken something out. There was plenty of time to accomplish that on the way back to my car. Damn, why did they only use plan Scotch tape for a seal! That is so stupid.

The next morning, I woke up and yesterday's ordeals did not matter to me, or to anyone else.

Days went by, followed by weeks and months. I was making more money that I actually needed, and so was Jimmy. We completely furnished our apartment and life was great. I had no need for anything else; at least, that is what I thought at that time.

At that time, everything was going well for both of us, I was financially secure, had a girlfriend that I admired, and I became one happy dude.

Then again, Jim somehow was invisible to me, my eyes and thoughts were concentrated toward a new feeling. I felt something that I never felt before, and did not pay any attention to anything else. Unfortunately, I was unaware of that situation.

All I thought about was my Vicky, and a feeling that seemed to be love. Somehow, without recognition, it developed into a codependent emotion, and at the same time, by chance, I was neglecting Jimmy.

Apparently, he was not too happy about my situation. We hardly ever saw each other. Besides that, I had to cut him off from using my car.

One day, I dropped by our apartment. I needed a change of clothes and was running late. On my way to the bedroom, I glanced in the kitchen. Jim was sitting there looking at the empty walls. Observing his appearance, he looked depressed, so I stood there for a few seconds; I walked in, and sat across from him.

He raised his head, looked me in the eyes, and said, "Hey, welcome to the lost and found."

"Jim, how are you? What's wrong?"

"Nothing is wrong! I'm fine!"

"So why are you sitting here with a dull look on your face? Who died?"

"No one died. I'm exhausted from my daily routine. Work, home, home, work, there is nothing else for me. I'm sick of this lifestyle."

"Jim, don't mark your destiny. It could be worse. Stop complaining. What about your friend, that guy you went to concerts with?"

"Never mind him. Hey, how about a drink? I have a bottle of vodka here!"

"Is that what you have in your glass?"

"Yes it is. I also have good news. I purchased a car!"

"Congratulations! What kind?"

"Same as yours, only this one is white! And it's a stick shift. I have to say, what incredible power that car has. And it's all mine!"

"Good for you! I don't understand why you are upset. And why are you home? Don't you have to go to work?"

He emptied his glass down his throat, poured himself and me another. Then he said, "Enough with the questions. Anyway, I called in sick. So come on, bottoms up! Tell me, Al, how is Victoria? Do you get along? How long are you planning to date her?"

"Don't know; not long!"

"Well, that's a big addition to my great package of news. Let's toast to that! I hardly see you anymore."

"I think I will marry her!"

"What! You are kidding me. Why would you? You've only known her for a few months; you think it's enough?"

"Time is irrelevant. I want to be with her because I love her!"

"Let's drink to love! However, I don't know if I should be happy for you, or feel sorry for you."

"Jim, do we have any food in the fridge?"

"You and your food. Yes! Some Chinese leftovers; be my guest!"

"Thanks; by the way, I didn't know you'd get so upset."

Actually, he was somewhat angry. We kept on drinking and after a few shots, I could not resist. I had to ask him, "So tell me, what is eating you? Why would you feel sorry for me?"

"Man, are you blind? Don't you see; she is a butterfly! Besides, she is manipulating you, flipping your mind upside down. One day she will sculpt you into her own world, and then, at the end, you will be left heart broken!"

"How would you know? You saw her only once! You don't know her well enough to fabricate a story like that. You are insulting me and her, with no reason or proof!"

"Oh, aren't we defensive. Just wait and see; as always, time will show, and then you will get your proof. Too bad you are not smart enough too listen, and are constantly learning the hard way. You know, I like to watch your mistakes, because it prevents me from duplicating them; it helps me to avoid similar situations. You are a good example for a failure, and wrong ordeals. By the way, for your information, if some day you decide to change your perspective, let me give you a word of advice. In order to find out the truth of the mess you are in, step aside and look at the picture from the side view."

"Are you done? Tell me who died and made you the king. You are giving me advice. Learning from my mistakes, you said! Yeah, right! So what have you learned lately?"

"That's for me to know, and for you to discover!"

"Jim, just one hour ago you were grieving to me of how your life sucks. Why you are trying to turn me away from the best thing that ever happened to me, and for what? You want me to join your suck world so we could grieve there together. Is that it?

"Oh, please. I never asked you to join me!"

"Maybe you are jealous. Or is it the alcohol talking? What a sober man keeps in his mind, the dunk spills through his lips! Besides, if you are learning from me, then why are you sitting here moaning like an old fart? Go out there, make mistakes, live the life, and have fun like me. You know, by being to cautious, you will miss great opportunities, and sit all alone! Look at you now! "

"Fuck you! Who do you think you are, calling me an old fart?"

"Hey, I said you are behaving like one."

"I'm not, and I'm certainly not jealous, and most certainly not drunk. That is I talking to you, fool! She has you by the balls, and you call it fun. How convenient for her, you thinking with your dick. Sooner than later, it will backfire at you, and then we will see what kind of fun you will have."

"What if you are wrong? Have you considered that for a moment?"

"No, because I know that I'm right. Tell me, except fucking, what else do you do? Where did you go with her lately?"

"Well, we went to a movie, and went out a few times to some of her friends."

"That's it! That is all you did for the past months?"

"Yes! So what's wrong with that?"

"Don't you see? You are obsessed with her sexually, and I can understand that! After all, she is a very appetizing woman, but that's all she is. It's not love for her. I don't think she knows what it means. You should call it 'Mediterranean Sea of Splendor.' Enjoy it while it lasts."

"Okay, keep your comments to yourself. I remember your girlfriend, or so-called friend, as you putt it. She looked like a used sponge too me; but did I say anything, now, learn from that, why don't you!"

"What gives you the right to call her a sponge? Regardless, I never thought of marrying her. We had our fun, and then she was gone; end of story. Let's finish our drink. I'd like to go for a ride!"

"Ride! What ride? You're in no condition to drive. I will come with you."

"Sure, let's go!"

That was the first time Jim and I really argued. I did not understand his point. Maybe he was jealous, but what if he was right? Unwillingly I am sure; he had destroyed my emotional state.

When we approached his new car, I tried to persuade him not to drive, but he was stubborn, and took the wheel anyway. I was worried with him driving. We had drunk a little too much, and if that's not enough, Jim decided to take the freeway. He said he needed the speed to get rid of his anger. Fortunately, we were stuck in traffic.

We were hardly moving (thank God), but Jimmy became very furious. He looked like a balloon that was about to explode.

"Look at that asshole trying to cut in front of me," Jim said.

"Jim, let him pass; we have plenty of time!"

"Fuck him; he needs to stay in his lane."

"Maybe he is in a hurry; let him pass!"

"No! Fuck him! Nobody lets me in. I always have to wait, so fuck him."

As Jim said that, the asshole fellow impudently decided to cut in.

"Look at the nerve on this fucking guy." Suddenly, Jim released the clutch, crashing his new car into the left side of the assholes vehicle. Then, they both got out.

"What is wrong with you man?" the asshole screamed.

"Motherfucker!" Jimmy shouted back, while bursting toward the asshole. He went down on him like a ton of bricks.

Jim was steaming, that poor guy tried to protect himself from Jimmy's blows, but wasn't successful. As Jimmy was beating him, I ran over there, got between them, and broke them loose. Then I grabbed the asshole by his hands, and twisted them backwards.

"Why are you holding me? Hold your crazy friend!" Asshole shouted.

Jim was trying to get back in for more, screaming, "You're still breathing, motherfucker. Al, let him loose, come on! You fuck face, let's dance/"

"Jimmy. Go sit in the car! And you! Get the out of here while you still can!"

I pushed Jim toward the car, and made sure he got in; meanwhile, the asshole strolled into his busted vehicle, and just sat there.

I looked around, and saw cars had stopped. People were watching us and enjoying the show. Apparently, the highway was blocked.

"Jim, drive around him, and let's get out of here," I said.

We finally drove away from that scene.

"What came over you? Do you feel better now?"

"Not really, but it serves him right, cutting me off like that. He had it coming."

"Listen; learn to control your temper. What about the training you showed me? Inhale, exhale; or was it all bullshit? Your first priority is, do not get involved in unnecessary fundamental interactions. Moreover,

I would like to pass on to you some great advice. Don't ever fuck with anyone you don't know."

"Who gave you that advice?" Jim asked.

"It doesn't matter; the important thing for you is to follow it."

"Yes; Right! So according to your advice, I was supposed to ask for his credentials, and then kick his ass?"

"No, dumb ass; All I'm saying is you were supposed to avoid him!"

Jim lost his temper, and screamed, "Look who is talking, reminding me of those foolish rules. What is unnecessary for you; may be necessary for me. For your information, fights and sex, in my book are anxiety release, and you on the other hand are also hot-headed!"

"What makes you say that?" I asked.

"Because I never seen you calm in the same kind of situations."

"That's because you never saw me creating those kinds of situations, Jim. You are a clever person, but sometimes you behave like an idiot. Just think for a moment; what would happen if you let that person pass? Nothing, right? The worst thing about it, he would end up in front of you! Big deal! Then we would be on our way, happy dudes!"

"No, you would be happy. And maybe he would be, too, but not me. I'm not happy, and what's with the names? Why are you calling me an idiot?"

"I said you behave like one; there's a big difference."

"You know, I'm getting tired of your lectures. I need a drink."

"We finished that bottle, don't you remember?"

"Yes, I know. That is why I am going to get another."

And so, he did. I thought there was nothing wrong with that. He was distressed, and I just went with the flow.

That evening, I was supposed to call Vicky, but how could I? We were drinking that night like there was no tomorrow. The last thing I remembered was that plate of Chinese food, because it was so close to my face and yet so far. I wanted to taste it so badly, but for some reason I couldn't.

Then that voice! I heard it again! "Follow the footprints; follow them."

"Who is this?" I asked.

"Follow the footprints; follow them now! Before it's too late."

"Hey, wake up."

"Jim, is that you?"

"Yes, it's me. Who else would it be? Are you okay?"

"I'm fine, why?"

"Why, look at you, the way you are laying on the floor like a cripple, with Chinese food all over your face. And why were you saying 'footprints'?"

"What?"

"You repeatedly said foot, foot. Get up. Let's go to the living room; you can rest on the couch. And wipe that stuff of your face."

"I had a strange dream. I heard someone say 'follow footprints'."

"So that's why you were shouting 'foot, foot'?"

"I was? Don't remember that."

"Yes, you woke me up, you klutz."

"Damn, I have a terrible headache."

"Learn how to handle your liquor. Drink this; it will help you feel better."

"What is it? Smells awful."

"The same shit you drank last night. I didn't hear you complain about it then!"

He was right; I did feel better. That day, I swore to myself that I would not take another drop of that poison, and so the day had begun.

It was around ten o'clock in the morning when Vicky called. She was very upset, yelling, and yapping. "Where have you been?"

"Home. Why?"

"Why? What do you mean why? I was waiting for you, don't you remember."

"Sorry, honey; I forgot."

"This is unbearable; your behavior is abnormal. How do you plan to keep a relationship?"

Through the phone, she managed to drill holes in my head. The feeling of guilt made me listen; however, I did not understood what she was saying. All I could think about was how long can that woman go on yapping. To my surprise, it was a very long yap, so I forgot my whereabouts, and all that I needed to do.

At the end she said, "I need to see you."

I said fine, hung up the phone, took a short shower, and was on my way.

When I entered the elevator, unfamiliar men were standing there, apparently coming down from a higher floor. I got in, turned around, pressing the lobby key. I heard a large blow behind my head, and then darkness took over.

I opened my eyes in some noisy place, sitting in what looked like a bus chair, with a seatbelt around my waist.

Then a man approached me. He was holding a syringe in his hand. For some reason, my head was pounding, and I was very thirsty. I looked at him and said, "Where am I? Do you have any water?"

Then he stuck that needle in my arm, and I felt into a deep sleep.

I woke up in large white space. While sitting there, I thought I was dead. Trying to move I realized, they handcuffed me to a chair. That room was strange. Walls, ceiling, and floor were in pure white; there were only two chairs in that room and nothing else.

I sat there for an eternity, until finally a man walked in. He was wearing an Israeli military uniform. I should know, because not so long ago, they gave me a similar uniform, only without stripes.

He walked around me in circles, then, stopped, and said, "Are you Alan Cogan?"

"Yes. What am I doing here? Who are you?"

"Listen, kid, you will answer my questions, and mine alone."

"Okay, but please tell me, where am I? How did I get here? AND I WANT SOME WATER!"

He opened the door, and yelled, "Moshe, bring a glass of water!"

"Here is your water. Now, you are at an underground military facility of ZAHAL."

"Under what ground? And what is ZAHAL?" I asked.

"Under Ben-Gurion Airport, in Tel-Aviv, Israel. Don't play dumb with me, ZAHAL? Israeli Army? What, you don't remember? You use to be one of us. And now you are a DESERTER!"

Of course, I remembered. I just had no idea that something like that was possible, and after all this time. Go figure! I guess those people at the elevator got me, but how did they find me?

"Listen, I'm an American citizen. Take those cuffs off me."

"You are an Israeli citizen. We gave you a pass to go see your father. According to documents you provided, he was dying; you were supposed to return in one week. By the way, your father is fine and in perfect condition. Did you forget you were in the army?"

"You have kidnapped me; that is against the law."

"You signed yourself to us, and now you are an outlaw. Do you know what would happen to Israel if every soldier would run! You will serve time, then you will serve you country, and afterward, maybe we will see what we can do for you."

"I married someone; my country is America now. She is a citizen, and I want an attorney!"

"Are you trying to tell me you got married? When?"

"Yes, recently, but we dated for a long time. We love each other. You will lose your rank over this, I can promise you that!"

He then jumped out of the room and disappeared.

In a matter of minutes, a civilian walked in, took the handcuffs off me, then spoke to me in Hebrew. "Are you hungry?" he said.

"Place me on the first plane back!" I screamed.

"Lower your voice. I work in the kitchen. The sergeant is very nervous; what did you say to him?"

"Never mind what I said. Tell me, who took me?"

"What you didn't know? MOSAD, who else!"

"Those sons of bitches; Hey, listen, if you want to have a friend in New York, keep me in the loop!"

"Okay! I will try!"

When he left, I sat there forever, not knowing how my life would change or what they would do with me, and that made me very nervous. One thing I knew for sure; if I was sitting there for so long, they did not know what to do with me, and that was a good sign.

Afterward, another civilian walked in, a much older and intelligent man. From the way he looked into my eyes, I knew right then that he was not an ordinary man.

He stared at me with a very deep look. Then he stated, "Son, I represent MOSAD. We selected you back when you enlisted. I'm here to ask you to join us. All criminal charges against you will be dropped if you join now."

"Why did you pick me?"

"At basic training you showed skills. With such potential, why would you run from the army?"

"I did not run. I have fallen in love!"

"You are a fine shooter, among other things. Our academy needs you!"

"Have you also selected my friend?"

"I don't know to whom you are referring; however, a few of your mates died."

"I see. So you want me to follow them!"

"You should know better than that!"

"Look, sir, with all due respect for you and MOSAD, I don't think I will do that."

"Can you state why?"

"Well, first, I don't wish to become a killer. And most importantly, I have a family now. I did not plan for that to happen, but it happened. We love each other, and I am sure she is worried sick about me by now. The New York police, and whomever else she could find, are looking for me at this moment. So you see, I have to go back! They will find me anyway."

"Okay, legally we cannot hold you here against your will. When the next plane leaves, rest assured you will be on it."

Boy, was I relieved to hear that.

Then that sergeant walked in, and said, "Here! That is you flight pass; we apologize for any inconvenience."

"Can you bring me some food? And don't worry about that; no hard feelings."

"You know, you are the luckiest guy I have ever seen. You better cherish that love of yours."

"I'll keep that in mind!"

When he left, my new Israeli friend walked in, holding a big tray with salads and meat.

"Hey, listen, I have been through a lot lately. Get me some alcohol, will you? Your guys must have some bottles here, located under an airport and all, so, please do it."

"We don't have large selection."

"Anything will do; just go get it fast!"

In a matter of minutes, he rushed back in with a bottle of vodka under his jacket. What a day!

Then he asked, "Will this be okay?"

"Perfect! Thanks. What's your name?"

"Moshe"

"Here is my number in New York. Memorize it, and call any time."

"Oh! Thank you. Maybe I will; have a safe flight home!"

Finally, that was the end of it all. I ate, then went up to the terminal, walked around with that bottle under my jacket, and could not wait to get on the plane.

Then, finally, I was on the way back to New York. Thanks to that bottle, I was drunk in a matter of minutes, and fourteen hours passed for me in a glint. Finally, I was back at JFK. When we landed, I realized that all that I had on me was my driving license and eighty dollars in cash. How would I explain to Customs my arrival without a passport?

As anticipated, I was stopped, and then escorted to a room, this room was simple I felt right at home. It did not take long, and the interrogation has continued. "According to your driving license, you are Mr. Alan Cogan!"

"Yes."

"So, what is your story? How did you manage to get here?"

"You see, there are many problems in my life. I got drunk and after a long walk, I lost my way. Suddenly, I saw myself in the terminal. I did not know where to go. So I joined the crowd that walked by me, and here I am."

"You know, I thought that I had heard all possible fairytales; however, yours is the legend of all. Do you really expect me to believe that?"

"Yes sir!"

"Listen, wise ass, you were walking on international arrival path! There is no way you could have gotten there by chance. So, for the last time, where did you hide your passport?"

"Sir, I don't have a passport. The driving license you are holding is all I have."

"Okay, then. We shall see about that. You better pray that this plastic is real!"

He left, and I stayed there alone. After a while, I got up and walked toward the door. Looking through the glass, I saw a man in a uniform standing in the hallway. I looked back and thank God for the countertop attached to the wall. I decided to get some rest, and arranged myself comfortably on its surface. As I was about to relax, the door opened and a nurse walked in. She must have slammed the door behind her, because simultaneously, my temporary bed detached, and I landed on the concrete floor.

"Oh God! Are you all right?" she asked while running toward me.

"I really don't know what to say to that!"

"Please let me help you. Sit down. I need to take a blood sample from you."

"Why? What for?"

"I'm sorry, but I don't know"

"Okay, take my blood! Why don't you take my dignity while you are at it?"

"Sir Please!"

"Is that a yes?"

"Okay, I'm done. Have a nice day!"

When she left, I crawled back on the countertop and finally fell asleep. When I woke up, the clock on the wall showed around six. Morning or evening, and what day it was did not matter to me anymore. All I wanted to do was go home.

Then, around seven, that man returned. He came in holding a file, sat on the chair, and said, "What are you doing down there?"

"Napping"

"Please get up. I have some documents for you to sign, and then you may go."

"So, after all, you believed me!"

"No, I did not! Your driving license is authentic, but your name did not appear on any flights, and your blood is bursting with alcohol. Therefore, I have to accept your story, regardless of how absurd it is."

"Where do I sign?"

"Here, and there, also sign on that page. It states that we did not mistreat you in any way; however, by the look of you with that countertop, I take it you have done some damage to yourself."

"I am sorry about that. Thanks; can I go now?"

"Yes you can!"

As I opened the door and was ready to leave, he stated, "Before you go, off the record, can you tell me honestly how in the world you appeared in restricted area?"

"I really don't remember. Bye!"

I ran out of there like animals running from a fire. I got into the first available cab, and was on my way to see Vicky. On the way there, I knew there was a slim chance for her to believe me, but I had no choice. I decided to be honest. However, as I sat in the cab, I had all my fingers crossed.

When I arrived, she opened the door, and stood at the doorway looking like a dragon ready to burst with fire. Right then, I knew that was it.

Then she yelled. "Where have you been? You were gone for three days! We were all worried sick! Oh, and I called the cops!"

"Look, it's a long story, and I am very tired. Can I come in and catch my breath?"

"Yes, come in, and don't try to make one up. Just be straight with me!"

"Okay, I will. I was in Israel," I said, and ran to the bathroom.

"What Israel? Is that the best you can come up with?"

"Israeli Army, and MOSAD. They wanted me to join, and I said no. Because I love you!"

"Okay. Who is she?"

She said that very calmly. The zone appeared to be safe at that moment, so I decided to get out of the bathroom, and give her a hug. "Babe, who do you mean?"

"Don't touch me! The bitch you spent all this time with! I called your brother and your work; no one knew where you were. Oh, and your brother was covering for you, I could feel it. So who is that BITCH?" She said that yelling her lungs out.

"Listen babe, I told you I was in Tel Aviv, Israel, under ground!"

"You are an asshole. You don't have a passport. How would you get to Israel? I don't believe what I'm hearing; of all the lies in the world, you came up with something that only a smock would buy. Why are you doing this to me? Why!" Then she began to cry.

"Oh no, Honey don't cry. I am telling you the truth. They took me; actually, they kidnapped me, and then I was interrogated, and then . . ."

"Stop! That's enough. Get out!"

"But I'm telling you the truth. I was sitting down with a MOSAD officer. We talked and then they placed me on a flight back."

"Okay. You want to play this game, fine. Then tell me, why would the Israeli Army, MOSAD as you say, sit down with you? WHO THE FUCK, DO YOU THINK YOU ARE!"

"I know it's hard to believe. But it's true. They wanted to recruit me to MOSAD, and they kidnapped me and flew me in. I woke up in Israel."

"And how did you manage to get back, exactly?"

"I told you. You are not listening. They placed me back on a, EL/AL flight with a pass voucher!"

"Show me the voucher!"

"I can't. The flight attendant took it."

"They took it? How did you get through customs?"

"That was not so hard. I had my driving license!"

"Driving license!!! Did you say driving license? You are a son of a bitch. Get out now!"

Then she became hysterical. I had to leave. I stood by her door for over two hours. My patience ran out, and I became furious. The door was unlocked, so I went back in, and before she could say a word, I threw her on the couch in the living room, and the rest was history.

Apparently, rough sex finally calmed her down. Afterward, she laid there like a nourished baby; at the end, we both fell asleep.

However, she never bought my true story. Unfortunately, in her eyes, I turned into a liar for no reason at all, and when she came around, she looked at me calmly and said, "Please go home now."

Therefore, I had no choice, but to turn around and leave. When I arrived home, at first I called in sick, then I called Jim and told him that I was okay and everything was fine. Then I took the bottle from the fridge, got myself wasted, and went to sleep.

The next day, around lunchtime, I decided to go see Vicky again, thinking I would be more successful on my second attempt. When I parked by her building, I could not help but notice her talking to a person. The way she was smiling at him, and playing with her hair sparked a doubt in my mind, and I decided to observe her very closely. Watching her, I thought maybe Jim was right; that maybe she was a butterfly, which would indicate that she was a two-faced person. If that was the case, maybe I was blind.

I could not sit in my car any longer. I thought I would sneak in behind them and listen, but as soon as I got close, she turned around and, with a joyful voice, said, "Hey! I did not see you coming."

"Hi, baby; who is this?"

"Oh, that's my friend Ralf."

"I didn't know you had a friend called Ralf. Hello, Ralf."

"Hello!"

"Bye, Ralf! Come on, let's go home."

"Why you were so rude to him? Wait, let me say goodbye to him."

She went back to him, extended her head, and gave him a kiss to his cheek. They exchanged a few words, and then she floated back to me, just like a butterfly.

On the way to her place, I could not stop thinking. What was that? Jimmy was right. How could I be so foolish, believing her and thinking she was the only one for me? I could not believe that I wanted to marry that bitch.

Then she opened the door and said, "Come on in. What is wrong? You look pale."

"Nothing, I'm fine. Tell me, why did you kiss that guy?"

"I didn't kiss him! It was a goodbye gesture. You know, when people say hello they kiss, and then, upon goodbye, they also kiss! You know what I mean!"

"No, I don't know! And I don't kiss everyone I say hi to, and which people are you talking about? I don't see people kissing each other on the street everywhere. It's only you. I don't want you to kiss anyone anymore! No hellos and no goodbyes; no more kissing!"

"Al, calm down. It's harmless. I have known Ralf for quite a long time; don't be so jealous."

"I'm not jealous! I don't care how long you have known him! Actually, tell me, how long have you known him? Did you sleep with him?"

"Okay, that's enough. Let's change the subject."

"Fine! Only if you promise me no more kissing."

"Okay, it will not happen again. I promise!"

"Oh, baby, I missed you so much! Let's go to the bedroom."

"Wait, first I want to show you something. I wrote a letter to my boss. Tomorrow it's his birthday. Would you please read that? I'd like to know what you think."

I read it all right, through the bullshit and right to the end where she wrote, "Sincerely yours!" At that moment, I became furious. "Vicky, honey, can you come here, please!"

"Yes, sweetie, what is it?"

"Vicky baby! Tell me, please, are you planning to fuck your boss on his birthday?"

"WHAT? What did you say?"

"You heard me. What the fuck does "sincerely yours" mean? When exactly do you plan to become his?"

"That is a figure of speech, you idiot! That's how people express gratitude."

"Oh, a figure of speech, is it? Well, the way I see it, it's your figure wrapped around him. Some gratitude you are willing to express; what a fucking bitch you are! No wonder you kiss every dumpster that's on your way!"

"You are a sick, stupid, asshole! Sick because, of your illusions, and stupid, due to the lack of your English vocabulary! Why don't you go to school and get some knowledge, you stupid ass!"

"Don't change the subject. You will not get off that easy. What will you have? No wait, let me rephrase myself. When would you have your boss? Are you planning to screw him on his birthday? Also, why didn't you tell me that you are fucking him and half of your neighbors too, not excluding your friend Ralf, of course?"

"You know, that's enough! I do not want to talk to you anymore! I don't wish to see you. Get out of here, NOW!"

And there she was, hysterical again, crying and screaming at me without reason. It felt like a continuation of yesterday. "Why are you screaming at me? Is it because I revealed a fact? Well, sure it is! Truth is always painful, especially to those who lie."

"I said get out of my sight, and out of my life!"

She then began to throw things at me, so I ran out. At first, I felt good about it; placing everything in the open was the right thing to do. Of course, she did not like it; who would?

After all, she kissed that person right in front of me, and I took her for an intelligent woman, a woman with high standards. There was only one thing she was right about; I am an idiot for trusting her all this time.

Her parents seemed very intellectual and normal people, but I didn't know they way she was raised. However, she grew up to be a cheap slut, and me being with her knowing that fact hurt the most.

'A cute little piggy was born, and with time, it grew into a big stinky pig.' No one can predict the changes of nature. Now I am talking to myself; shit! I think I am losing my mind.

All the time I was driving, I kept seeing that miserable look on her face, especially when she was crying. That image evolved into a painful feeling inside; I tried to ignore it, but I could not, and the longer I fought with that feeling, the stronger it grew.

Where was I going? On which road was I driving? I had no idea where I was, so, after a while I decided to follow the road signs, and go home.

As I got home and opened my door, the phone began to ring. "That's probably her; she's calling to apologize."

I ran in to answer. "Hello; listen, Vicky!"

"No you listen to me, and who is Vicky? Never mind that; why did you skip work? And not tell me! Who do you think you are?"

"Mike, is that you?"

"You're damned right it's me! I was looking for you everywhere; what happen to you? No, forget it; I don't want to know." Suddenly, he shouted, "You are fired! Don't show your face around here anymore." He then hung up on me.

Well, that went just fine. I was sure I had called him yesterday, or maybe I miss-dialed his number. Shit what a day, and why didn't I go to the parking lot? What had come over me? Maybe it happened because of that bitch. Apparently, my memories had all mixed up.

She destroyed my day and my life; this morning I thought everything would get back to normal, and in only a few hours, my life had turned upside down. That is so weird it is scary.

I had to stop thinking about her; needed to find the liquid ecstasy. I remembered when Jim and I last partied, there was over half of the bottle left, but where was it? I looked everywhere in the apartment. Eventually, I got my hands on it, and was on my way to paradise. The thought alone calmed me down.

One gallon of vodka, and I had half of it all to myself. I decided to gulp to the end; I just did not know where the end was.

It felt better with every shot I swallowed right down to my guts. Suddenly it all became clear to me. She was a sex maniac. That was it!

That is why she was so upset when we had sex. One person was not enough. She needed more, and all that time she was playing a role of Mother Teresa.

After a few more shots of my medicine, I decided to call her. I needed to put my foot down, I promised to myself. It is about time I slam my hand on the table!

"Hello," she answered the phone, apparently very upset.

"Tell me; are you horny all the time? Is that why you want to fuck your boss, and kiss everybody on your path? Just tell me; don't be afraid!"

"Who is this?" she asked.

I could hardly speak and probably tripped over my tongue as well. However, I knew that there was a need for me to continue and say it all. Therefore, I did. "Listen, I know everything now! I know that you are a sex maniac, but that's okay, because this disease is curable. Don't worry. I will fix you up. I found a way. Listen! I will buy you a vibrator! That way you can screw yourself all the time, and everywhere. Then, soon enough, you will be over that issue. So, do you approve of my brilliant plan? Yes. No? Say something! "

"Who the hell are you? I am going to call the cops! You twisted pervert! How dare you talk to me this way?"

"Oh, I'm very sorry, miss; wrong number! Please don't call anyone. So sorry, bye!" Only then, I realized I had dialed a wrong number. How could I do that? Maybe it was for the best, and maybe it was a sign.

I needed a few more drinks, needed to think this over. After a while, when I could hardly see the phone, I reached out and dialed Vicky's number again, only that time I was very careful, pressing each digit slowly and confirming that was the right number.

"Hello, who is this? Al, is that you? Why won't you speak?"

"Oh, yes! Vicky, it is you. Thank god. Sorry, something was stuck in my throat. How are you?"

"Is that why you are calling? After insulting me, the way you did, now you want to know how I am doing. You are out of your mind. What gave you the right to say those things about me?"

"Yes, because I was right! And you are . . ." Then she hung up.

Why is everyone hanging up on me today? I wish people would express their feelings normally. Hey! What the hell; my only friend was right by my side. Yes, baby, although you are liquid and soon will end. Nevertheless, you do make me feel good when you are around; too bad you cannot talk. I am glad there is a lot of you still left in this bottle. I do not feel like going out for you today, so please help me, and try to reproduce yourself in that bottle.

Listen, the phone is ringing again, or maybe it is in my head? No, that is the phone for sure! I think its Michael calling. He has realized how much he needs me; he probably decided to apologize.

"Hey, Mike; you want me back? Okay, then, I want a raise! And make it a double!"

"It's me, you dumb ass! And, you are drunk."

"Vicky, is that you?"

"Yes; how much did you drink?"

"Did? Hey! I am still drinking. Have to tell you, that white, oh no, I meant clear liquid is a great refreshment. You have to try it; it would do wonders for you, I promise! So, would you like some?"

"I'm on the phone, you buffoon! Please listen to me and don't interrupt!"

"Okay, I am listening, baby. Just a second, let me move; there is something under my ass. Oh, it's your photo. Sorry, baby, I don't know how you got there!"

"Maybe it will be better if I call you tomorrow; you are a mess right now."

"No, no, I am listening, baby. Please continue, and speak softly. I can't bear when you scream!"

"I just called to say; actually I'm calling you because I want to explain to you the meaning of 'sincerely yours'. I think you need to know, no matter what happens between us; it is best if you knew."

"Okay, baby. We are here for you!"

"Stop referring to alcohol as a person! Anyway, when a person or in this case employee is referring in writing to his superior as 'sincerely yours', all that means is that they are willing to be truthful to him as a worker, and that's it! Like I said, it's a phrase; do you understand?"

"Yes, I think I understand. Can I call you right back. Please!"

"Okay, go ahead."

That was some theory she presented to me; she was a good storyteller. Yes, I guess she was the queen of fabricating stories. But, what if I was wrong? I had to stop and think on my own. I could not think straight, I needed a drink. What if she was truthful, what was I supposed to do then? I have to test her theory. But whom could I ask? Who would be honest with me, and whom could I trust? Jim of course, on the other hand, maybe not. Jimmy would not know that phrase. I know! Michael. Yes, he is the one; he has no reason to lie to me. So let us call him.

"Hi, Mike."

"Al, is that you?"

"Yes, don't get angry. I just need to ask you something. Is that okay?"

"Okay, ask!"

"Mike, I want you to know that I am, and always will be, sincerely yours!"

"What the fuck? Are you gay? What makes you think I need this? Get off my phone line." Then he hung up again.

I knew my theory was correct, so what could I do now? This was so very exhausting, I needed to sleep on it, and so I went to bed. I woke up at four o'clock in the morning with an awful feeling. Why did I drink that toxic waste last night? What a moron, I had become. I swore to myself before, and broke that promise, but whom could I complain too? So be it, what ever happened was all for the best. "Am I right?"

"I guess so; are you talking to yourself or referring to me?" Jim said.

"No, I'm just thinking out loud; why are you home so early?"

"My replacement came in a few hours earlier, so here I am. Happy?"

"Oh yeah, very much so!"

"Wait a minute, Al, what is that bottle?"

"Which bottle?"

"You know, the bottle lying next to you. What did you do with it?"

"Oh, that bottle. Look, it's in my bed. Strange, I don't remember!"

"Man, you finished all of it. Why would you do that? What happened?"

"Nothing happened, although you heard me saying, "Whatever happens, it's all for the best."

"I think you are still intoxicated; how do you feel?"

"Fine! Almost like brand new."

"Come on, get yourself together, and get in the shower. Water is all you need right now. Can you walk?"

"I don't think so. Somehow, I have lost my balance. Damn! Where is it?"

"Okay, let me help you. It will be better for you to take a bath, and stay in there for as long as you can. While you're in there, tell me what happened."

"Well, where shall I begin? Let's see; I broke up with Vicky because I called her a bitch, then I got drunk, and afterwards, I got fired. Oh, also I told Mike that I'm forever his! Apparently, he didn't like that idea. Hey, why are you laughing?"

"I must say! You are some gift to society. Why would you tell Mike something like that? Was it because you were drunk?"

"Not really; I needed to check out Victoria's statement in regard to a phrase. She said 'sincerely yours' doesn't mean anything, and I say it does. So, I tested my theory on Mike; evidently, he misunderstood me!"

"So you experimented on Michael? Were you satisfied with the results?"

"Yes I was! Mike proved me right!"

"No, you nut case, you are wrong! All it means is respect and truthfulness; it does not mean that you belong to someone."

"If you are so smart, then tell me why Mike reacted the way he did."

"Probably because of the way you said that to him. Besides, I never heard anyone use that expression verbally, so get ready."

"Get ready for what?"

"I see a lot of apologies in your future, and all done strictly by you! Have fun. I'm going to sleep."

Yes, I guess Jim was right! There will be a need for me to apologize, I have to think about this, actually, there is nothing to think about, I have to approach those people and ask for forgiveness, but how should I do that? I knew that no one would talk to me on the phone, so I decided that appearing in person was my best option.

First, I went to see Michael. He should be easy, and I had a justifiable cause and honest excuse. Vicky, on the other hand, was a different cake all together. She would probably suck the living soul out of me before she decided to forgive me.

There was no other way, so, Se la vie.. What ever will be will be.

Since I was the one creating the soup of the day, I was the one who would have to eat it!

Walking to the parking lot very slowly looking for Michael, in some way I was hoping he would not be there. But there he was. "Mike, can I talk to you? Please!"

"Didn't I tell you to stay away?"

"Sorry, I just want to apologize. You see, I had a fight with my girlfriend; we split up and I got drunk. I am very sorry for what I did and said. I also argued with Jimmy and we had a small accident; basically, I had tons of problems."

He was surprised hearing my story, and did not expect me to show up like that. He stood there, scratched his baldhead, looked at me, and said, "Okay, did you come back to work today or just to apologize?"

"Both, but I'd rather start working tomorrow. I don't feel very well."

"I wonder why? Fine, but remember, Al, if you disappear one more time, I will erase you from this station forever; do you understand?"

"Yes, I do, and thank you so much!"

Well, to my surprise, it went better than I thought it would After all, Michael is a cool person, and now I respected him even more than before.

The only thing left for me to do was to attend to the disaster zone, and face the consequences.

It was eight o'clock in the morning when I knocked on Victoria's door. At first, I thought there was nobody home. Then, the door slowly opened, she moved to the side, and with her small palm, showed me in. Boy was I ever nervous.

I said hello she then hung onto my shoulders and began to cry.

"Vicky, I'm so, so, very, sorry, I don't know what came over me. I know it's probably impossible to forgive me, but can you try?"

"I forgive you, and I'm not mad at you; just don't call me those names ever again, and I mean it."

"Never again; I promise, Vicky; I really love you, very much so. Would you marry me? Please?"

She gazed into my eyes with a strong, warm look. In those few moments standing there, I felt vulnerably naked, and then she said, "I love you too, Al, and yes, I will marry you!"

That was it; it was nothing close to what I expected. She must really love me, forgiving me like that, and she accepted my proposal.

Damn. I proposed to her, and she said yes, so now what? This is all new to me, and I think I am blushing.

"Honey, are you blushing? How sweet," she said.

"No, I'm not; it's hot in here. Do you want me to drive you to work?" I asked

"Not today; let me call the office."

I had never seen her so happy. It was strange the way things turn out. One minute I was single, and the next I was mar . . . mar . . . married. I could not even think the word. How could I say it aloud?

She insisted on making it official, and I did not understand the rush, but I never give it much thought. Soon, we went to the city hall. As we were entering, Ralf was strolling around; for some reason I became very annoyed with him, especially with his existence.

"Vicky, look! It's your friend Ralf. I wonder why he is here."

"I called him; we need as a witness."

I was amazed at how quickly people were getting married, and sooner than I anticipated, I became one of those who signed their life away.

We went back to her home. We got drunk and sequestered ourselves for several hours. Yes, we tried it all; she was doing things to me that I had never encountered before. I tried to pull some stunts of my own, but she would not let me.

I was shocked at what a woman could do to a man, that is, if she was in the right mood. Apparently, at that point, the mood was overly right for her. She used every inch of her body on me and around me, especially near my gifted area. She raised my spirit repeatedly, and inserted my emotional state into her great hall of pleasure, then took me to the point of no willing return. I wanted to stay there forever, but after a few hours, my genitals stated it was time to go.

She had worn me out, and then some! I had no knowledge of the things she could do; it made me speculate where she learned those acts and how she knew to perform them. The biggest question of all: Did she practice? and with whom?

Those thoughts became the leading problem. My mind turned into my main enemy. I had to ask! "Wow, baby; you are something else. Where did you learn to do all this?"

"Did you like it?"

"Oh, yes, did someone teach you to do that? Who was he?"

"Stop it; you know that I like to read."

"So, you read books about sex?"

"No, I read all kinds of books, including about sex. Al stop reviewing what happened yesterday, and start planning for tomorrow."

"What do you mean?"

"Enough digging in my past; learn to enjoy the present moment. Oh, my parents will be coming home soon; we will have to tell them."

"No, baby, you will have to tell them. I can't do this now. I will talk to them later."

I got my clothes on, gave her a passionate goodbye kiss, and left in a hurry. I do not know why I was rushing, but I was.

While driving, I could not stop thinking about what she has said. 'Start planning for tomorrow' What did she mean by that? I did not like to plan; never did, and never will.

It was six o'clock in the evening and there was nobody at home. I needed to talk to someone, so I went to see Michael. Who else could advise me?

When I arrived, Michael was closing the shop and the parking lot. This was a good thing, a great opportunity to acquire some of his knowledge.

"Hey, Al, what are you doing here?"

"I am just passing through"

"Passing from where?"

"From Victoria's place; actually I wanted to talk to you about her."

"Well, come on into my office. Tell me, what's eating you?"

"Listen, I don't know how to say it, so I will just say it; I got married."

"You did what? No way! Are you sure, it was not a dream? "

"You heard me; I am sure!"

"And when did it happen?

"Today; we went to the city hall, and got married."

"Well, congratulations. Is it a happy day? Or, I am missing something? And where is the bride?"

"She is home, giving the news to her parents. Do I look happy to you?"

"You can't stop surprising me. In less than two days, you managed to fight with everyone, and now you are married, and I am not saying anything about accidents. Tell me, what's next on your agenda?"

"That is why I came to talk. I don't have any agenda; I lost my agenda. What am I supposed to do now?"

"Oh, man, what makes you think I know?"

"I don't know; you being older, I just thought you might help."

"So, where are you going to live?"

"I don't know."

"Do you like her?"

"I love her."

"This is not what I asked. Do you like her? There is a big difference!"

"Okay, tell me the difference."

"You have to know the person to like the person. Love comes and goes, because it's mostly chemical, but when you like someone, it turns in to respect and stays with you forever."

"I think I like her, but I don't know her that well."

"I don't know what to tell you, my friend. Have you told the news to your brother?"

"No, not yet."

"Good luck! If I were you, I would go talk to him."

"Yes, you are right. Thanks for your time and advice; it was helpful."

"Take care, and remember: think before you act. We are rational, but reason has its limits."

Michael confused the hell out of me. Now I was puzzled and completely lost. What I was thinking asking him for advice? Maybe Jimmy would help, although somehow I doubted that.

When I arrived at Jim's workplace, I wondered why Jimmy was happy to see me. What could have happened?

"Hey, bro, you look good. Feel better?"

"Yes, I guess so."

"Why so glum?"

"I'm just tired."

"Why, what did you do now?"

"I was running around, made up with Michael, and Vicky has forgiven me."

"Good, so now you are back on track."

"Yes, I am. Oh, I also got married."

"You did what? Why? Why would you do that?"

"I don't know! It happened so fast, and I like her; yes, I do."

"Well, that's a good enough reason, I think. Anyway, I'm happy for you. Congradu-fucking-lations! I can't believe she got you!"

"What do you mean, she got me? I proposed to her!"

"Yes, like there is a difference. The main thing is, now she has what she wanted. Tell me, how did this happen? You just came to her, said hi, let's get married?"

"No, actually. I came to apologize, and she started to cry. Then we made up, and then I proposed. She said yes, and we got married!"

"So, it all happened in one day? Isn't this a little odd? What a way to apologize! No wonder you never apologized to me."

"Don't be sarcastic; it happened so fast. I am confused."

"I just hope it's for the best!"

"Thanks, Jimmy, me too. Let me go' I will see you later."

Boy, it was a long day, I came home, threw myself on the couch, and tried to relax a little, but then the phone rang.

"Hello, Al. Or should I call you dear?"

"Hi Vicky, how did it go with your parents?"

"Okay, I guess, although my mother said I need to take time to myself and think it over before we plan the wedding."

"Well, do you need to think it over?"

"No, of course not, but I do need some time, though, so I decided to go away for two weeks. Do you mind?"

"No, if that's what you want. Go ahead."

"It will be good for both of us, trust me!"

"Fine, so when are you planning to go? And where will you go?"

"Al, I will leave in two days to Israel; my parents will arrange it for me."

"Really? And I thought I was fast. Wait a minute; you can stay with my family. They live in Haifa, which is a beautiful city, by the way. You will love it there! And they will take care of you. Also, it would be a good thing for all of you to get acquainted."

"That's great! Let me go tell my mother. When will I see you?"

"I have some problems at work, so probably I will have to work late, but I will see you before you leave."

When we said goodbye, somehow it felt as if we would never see each other again, but I let that feeling slide. During those two days, I was busy with work, not to mention, we had more deliveries that I had to complete. I could not turn down those people, especially the mysterious guy; not that I wanted too. The days flew for me, and then that day came, "the departure day."

We had not spoken during the last two days because I did not call her and she did not call me. When she went to the airport, I stayed home. I have to admit it was not easy neglecting her like that, but it was not by choice. I was upset; the whole situation became very confusing to me.

Why would she leave so suddenly? Why would she go without me? And why now? I could not explain or rationalize her behavior; there was no logic in it and I did not think there would ever be a rational explanation.

However, I knew that I had to inform my mother of the news, including the arrival of her daughter in-law. I could imagine my mother's reaction, how her eyes would glow from all the excitement, and she would be pleased with my good news. However, in reality, I knew my mother would be disappointed. I was scared shitless.

The next day I dialed her number. We spoke for over an hour. I don't remember her being so upset; most of the time she was crying and asking me why.

"Why did you do that?" she said.

I didn't have any answers. When she finally calmed down, I asked, "Mom, did Vicky call?"

"No, she did not."

"Are you sure?"

"Al, what exactly didn't you understand? Would you like me to define the word NO for you?"

"Calm down, Mom. I got it."

"I'm a little worried. She arrived yesterday and was supposed to call you. As far as I know she has nowhere to go, so where the hell is she?"

"Well, she didn't call, and why didn't you tell me about it before? Why did you wait?"

"I don't know."

"Tell me, Al, what happened? Did you guys argue?"

"No, we did not."

"So, what happened then; why would she leave you?"

"She did not leave me, Mom. She just needed some time to herself."

"Oh, please; how naive can you be? Didn't I teach you anything? She left in such a hurry two days after you married, and went so far away. Why?

"I don't know."

"What do you know? How well do you know her? You better get your act together, you hear!"

"Yes, Mom, I do. Can you please find her?"

"Okay, give me her information and call her parents. I'm sure they know where she is."

"Thanks, Mom. Please call me as soon as you know anything; goodbye."

Right after I got off the phone, I called Victoria's parents. Her mother answered, and that is when I was very shocked. Apparently, she had no idea of our marriage. I understood that from our conversation, because she said nothing about our marriage, nor was she happy or sad.

And she was angry with me because it was four o'clock in the morning. But I did not care.

Vicky had safely landed in Israel, and was enjoying her time at the great hotel of Tel-Aviv. I did not ask anything else. I just wanted to get her number, which eventually she gave to me.

I dialed her number all night. On every occasion, the hotel reception stated that she was not in the room. Fortunately, for me, I spoke Hebrew and, playing a role of a nice person, I asked room service to check on that room. When they did, there was a 'Do not disturb' sign on the door, and my nightmare began.

Right away, I called my mother, and told her of the situation. I practically begged her to go check on Victoria. After a long talk, she finally said that she would.

I looked at the clock; it was five in the morning. I had been up all night. What a marriage.

How was I going to face Jimmy and Michael? She had made a fool out of me, and she said that she loved me. Is this love? Apparently, Jimmy was right. I could not get it out of my head. Why would she leave in such a hurry? Maybe it was her way of paying me back for all I had said.

Then why did she not call my mother, and why didn't her parents know of our marriage? So many whys, Fuck it; what did I do to deserve this?

I went to work, and on my way, I determined not to get myself aggravated, so I decided to keep it quiet. No one had to know of my problems; then again, I did not know if they were problems. Actually, I did not know what I had; I just knew that it was bad.

It was busy at work that day, which was a big plus for my self-esteem, because all the bad thoughts somehow vanished from my mind, and I felt good. That was a great day. I just hoped that frame of mind would last two weeks; that was when Victoria would come back. I really missed her. I missed her voice, her smile, and the way her aroma filled the room.

I came home looking for some peace and quiet, and thought I would surrender myself to a nice bath, but destiny had another plan for me.

I realized that when Jimmy approached me, and said, "Hey, bro; your mother called."

"What did she say?"

"She said for you to call her back. Glad you are home. I was about to leave you a note; have to run."

"Thanks; are you going to work?"

"Eventually, but first, I have two deliveries. It won't take long, so I'll see you tomorrow."

"Oh, man, I forgot about that. Sorry; do you need a hand?"

"No, I'll take care of this. Don't sweat it. Just call your mother. She sounded very agitated."

"Okay, have a good one."

When he left, I was a little concerned. Why would my mother be disturbed? I did not feel like calling her right away. Suddenly, the bad thoughts returned, and in some way, I was afraid to call her. I postponed the phone call because I knew she would only raise questions, questions that I wouldn't have answers to. Then again, maybe she would have some answers for me that I was longing for.

So, I called. "Hi mom, how is everything? Jimmy told me you called."

"Hello son; you called me at the right time!"

"In time for what?"

"It seems that my daughter in-law enjoyed a most common degree of popularity, for a woman, unintelligent, poor, and single."

"What do you mean? Can you be more specific?"

"I mean that your wife is a whore, Al."

"What? What did you say? Mom, how can you say something like that?"

"Al, please wait, and I will enlighten you! Al, I have discovered a lot about her. Still, if you find me wrong, please feel free to stop me at any time."

"Mom, what's going on? What are you talking about?"

"Apparently, your significant other was about to get married. According to her story, she came back to finalize her relationship with her fiancé. Meaning, to break up with him. Unfortunately for Vicky, as I looked for her, I asked my friends for assistance, and my friend confronted her in the park."

"How do you know it was her?"

"She responded to her name, and the rest she told me herself. Wait: Vicky, am I wrong?"

"No!"

I recognized Victoria's voice in the background; she sounded upset, and cried.

"Mom, why she is crying? Tell her not to worry. Ask her to come back. I will understand."

"She will come back, but not to you. Al, I don't know how to tell you this."

"Tell me what? What happened?"

"Victoria, I think you should have the honor. It seems she is wordless. Victoria, stop dropping those crocodile tears and wipe out that innocent look from your face. We both know who you are. Talk to Al and tell him why you came here!"

"Mom, don't hold me in suspense!"

"Did I raise you like that or you are naive by nature? Don't you get it? She was caught in the park with her fiancé when they were being intimate."

She left me speechless.

"Hello, son, are you there?"

I hung up.

I had never experienced such betrayal. At first confusion set in, then I wanted to go there and shoot her dead, and I think, if I could have, I would.

That evening, afterward, I took myself to a bar. I could not bear to contain the feeling of betrayal while sober.

Victoria's behavior was eating me alive. In my wildest imagination, I could not see this coming. However, others did. That meant I was blind when it came to relationships.

I recalled that phrase again, never judge a book by its cover, although her cover was exactly like her book, and I could not see it. I should have listened to others, what a bitch she turned out to be.

Some great philosophers said, "We all get what we deserve; nothing less, or more." It made me wonder what I had done in life to deserve such gift. I recalled her saying, "We both need this; trust me." That phrase turned my guts upside-down. Because of her, I would never trust another human being ever again, especially women.

It got to a point where I needed to get away from those thoughts, so I began to booze. I have to say, it worked. Sitting in the bar and thinking, I floated deep into my thoughts, then the bar attendant approached me and placed a drink next to mine.

"Thanks, but I still have one."

"This one is from that lady across there; you see her?"

"Yes, I do; thank you!"

I drank my shot of scotch, looked at her, then moved toward her. As I got closer, somehow she began to look different. Actually, she was not my type at all. I guess what attracted me, was her joyful smile, and the warm look she had.

I set myself next to her, and said, "Thanks for the drink."

"Hello; what drink?"

"Didn't you buy me one a minute ago?"

"No, sorry." She then began to giggle, and I was about to explode.

I looked around.

"Who are you looking for?" that giggling statue asked.

"My destiny," I replied.

"Good luck!" the statue said, and began to laugh aloud.

I wanted to slap her so bad, but instead, I got up, strolled around the bar, and began to return to my original seat. Someone gently pulled on my coat. "Hi there," a strange, lovely voice said.

I turned my head, and there was my landlady. That nightmare was all dressed up and ready to go. What a scary sight.

"Hi, Mrs. German."

"Call me Anna."

"Okay; hello, Anna."

"What's with you? Another one bites the dust?"

"Oh, you mean that woman? I mistook her for someone else."

"You mistook her for me."

"What makes you say that?"

"You thought she was interested in you because of the drink? Yes!"

"Yes; how did you know?

"Because, I bought you that drink. Aren't you surprised?"

"No. Yes, very, actually; are you looking?"

"Don't be foolish. I'm married; just want some company. Is that wrong?"

What a relief! "Of course not! Where is your husband?"

"He is home, sleeping as usual."

"How can he sleep with someone as beautiful as you?" With her, there was no need to wake up.

"Thank you, that was nice of you. Do you come here often?"

"Actually no, depends on my mood."

"Likewise, so what happened? A handsome guy like yourself, sitting in a place like this all alone?"

"Not much; I got married three days ago. Maybe, four days ago."

"Congratulations; why celebrating alone? Don't tell me, she is preparing for the wedding; am I right?"

"Almost! In fact, she is already prepared for divorce."

"What do you mean, divorce?"

"She has a fiancé."

"Well, that's a new one for me."

"Yes, I can relate to that. Her fiancé is in another country. She went there to break up with him, so while she was at it, she decided to fuck him. I guess there is no harm in a goodbye fuck, is there?"

"I guess not. I meant, poor baby, did you known about him before?"

"No, I just found out a few hours ago, so I'm here and he is probably still fucking her as we speak."

"Calm down; have another. You need to take your mind off it."

She then placed her hand on my lap and began to chafe it. Maybe she was coming on to me, I hoped not; that was all I needed, mixing myself with my property owner.

So, I said, "You know, I think it is time for me to go."

"Yes! me too. Would you mind if I came with?"

"Of course, not; we both live at the same building. Let's go!"

When we went into the building, I had no idea that she lived two stories above us. As I was about to get out from the elevator, she said, "How about a night cap?"

Should I reject her? No, that would not be polite. "Sure, why not?"

"Okay, you go on, and I'll be down in a minute."

I went in and my confusion had multiplied. What would I do if she decided to stay over? If I refused, she might get angry, and that might interfere with our monthly routine. After all, she was our landlady.

Maybe she was looking for friendly conversation. There was only one-way to find out.

"Sorry, I knocked but no one answered, so I let myself in. I hope you don't mind."

"That's alright. I did not hear you. Please come in and feel at home." It was her home, stupid.

"I like what you did with the place."

"Thanks. I had help from my brother."

"That's nice. By the way, where is he now?"

"He is working."

"I thought you said he was visiting."

"Yes, he was, but then he decided to stay; go figure!"

"Good for him. Let's drink to that, and to our families."

We boozed ourselves into blindness. The next thing I remember, I woke up in my bed, and it was morning. I didn't remember anything after that last toast.

She woke up next to me, then rolled herself on top of me, and afterward went into a deep sleep.

Dreadful vibes were growing in me as I felt her nude bony body on top of mine. It was a traumatized experience for me. I tried to squeeze out, but I could not. I tried to push her away, but then she clutched even harder, so I decided to tickle her. Then she began snoring.

As she snored, the aroma of rotten cabbage commenced to circle in the air. I could not stand it anymore, and my blood began to boil, so I pushed her away. Not recognizing her weight, I slightly overextended my force. As a result, she flew right into the wall, and then landed safely on the floor.

I had no idea how light she was until I pushed her. That scarecrow was a tiny leather bag with nothing but bones and wrinkled skin. I was very surprised to see, after a hard landing, that she kept on sleeping and kept on snoring.

I got up and looked at her expecting some movement, but there was none. A few minutes later, she stopped snoring. I became very nervous, and did not know what to do with her. Maybe she died. I panicked; that was all I needed, a dead naked nightmare in my bedroom. How would I explain it to anyone, and who would believe me?

I could not wait anymore, so I flipped her over, placed my ear to her flat bony chest, and listened. There it was; her heart was beating like tractor engine. Thank God, she was okay.

It was awful looking at her the way she was, so I decided to place her on the bed, and to dress her before she woke up. I still could not believe this was happening to me.

While putting her dress on, a strange feeling came on me. I felt as if someone was watching me, so, I turned around, and to my appalled surprise, there was Jimmy. The way he stared at us, then at her, then at me, I thought his eyeballs would pop out of his skull.

"Hey, Jim, how was your shift?"

"What the fuck are you doing? What did you do to that old geezer? Are you into antiquities now?"

"Stop with the comments and help me."

"Okay, so who is that old bag? Man! Did you sleep with her? How could you?"

"She is our landlady, and I did not!"

"What? Fuck it. I'm not helping you with that. Tell me, is this how you pay our rent?"

"Jim, I need your help. I can't do this alone; help me dress her, and stop laughing!"

"I am not touching that! You undressed her, so you dress her!"

He did place his hand here and there, and finally, we dressed her, repositioned her on the living room couch, then I placed an empty bottle of vodka in her hand, and left her there. Then we both went into the kitchen.

"Al, when will you stop testing your destiny? Do you realize how bad this situation is?"

"Yes, I do; however, I do not think she will stay."

"So, what she is doing here in the first place, and why she was naked in your bed?"

"I can only assume that I went to bed, and she followed me. And without my consent, she laid next to me."

"That is the fishiest story I ever heard. You know. That bullshit tale about Israel made more sense. Why would she follow you, Al?"

"We were both drunk, that's why. She must have thought she was going to her bed, and I was her husband."

"By the way, where is her husband? What if he is looking for her?"

"How would I know where he is? Besides, you saw her; who would be looking for something like that? He is home celebrating, I'm sure!"

"What seems like trash to you could be someone else's treasure. Get rid of her and do it now!"

"And how do you suppose I shall do that?"

"Hey, it's your mess."

"I know. Let's get her up to her place. We'll say that we found her like that in the lobby!"

"Great idea, good luck! I'm going to sleep."

"Wait, I need you assistance!"

"Al, she is a tiny creature. I'm sure you can handle it."

So, Jim went to sleep and I went to the living room, waiting for her to wake up. Suddenly it came to me. I had to go to work, so, I needed to wake that drag up. I began to shake her. After a few minutes of brutally shaking her, she woke up, thank God.

She looked around, then looked at herself, and said, "What am I doing here?"

"Good morning, Anna. Last night you fell asleep after you drank that bottle you're holding."

"Is that a fact? Well, maybe you can explain why my dress is inside out."

"Maybe you wore it like that and didn't notice!"

"Please, Al; stop with the tales and tell me what happened."

"You really don't remember?"

"Well, I remember us finishing this bottle, then you asked me to escort you to your bed, then, you took your clothes off and passed out."

"Is that all you remember?"

"Yes, what else was there? What did I leave out? Tell me."

"No, nothing. Believe me, if there was anything else, I would tell you. Now if you don't mind, I have to be at work."

"Oh sure. We'll talk about this later. Goodbye."

"Goodbye."

When she left, I began mulling over why it was that, everywhere I went, and whatever I did lately, I always ended up in bizarre situations. I went to Jimmy's room, and woke him up. "Jimmy, let me ask you; have you encountered any strange or problematic situations lately?"

"No, why do you ask?"

"That's great. From now on, I'm spending all my free time with you!"

"Okay! Go away Al; let me get some rest."

And so, I did.

Boy, I had a great time. We saw ten concerts in less than six months; most of the groups were heavy metal, and all new to me. What I experienced was awesome, and it will stay with me the rest of my life. We also went clubbing on almost every weekend, and especially on delivery days.

It was odd. They began to add up, and I was making sixteen hundred dollars a week. There was no reason for me to work at the parking lot, but I decided to stay there, only because that job was steady and I knew that deliveries might end as quickly as they had started.

One day on my way to work, I notice a huge sign posted on the building across the way. A nightclub had just opened in that building.

This was startling news for me. Because of its location, half of block away from the parking lot, I saw a remarkable opportunity of extra income. When they announced the grand opening that evening, I came back to the parking lot and posted an announcement of my own. "Now we are open after hours." I turned on the lights and waited to see what would happen next.

Well, what I predicted happen. In the first few hours, I received nine cars, which was not so bad considering five bucks per car, and no expenses.

Then, around eleven o'clock, the unpredictable happened. I could not believe my eyes; cars were accumulating at the driveway and along the street. I was running my ass off and barely had the time to gasp. The parking lot developed into a massive used car lot, and my pockets were swarming with cash.

Suddenly, a memory rose in my head; I recalled the time of the attempted robbery at the gas station. That recollection woke caution in me, so I hurried to my car, opened the trunk, and threw all the money in there. Man, was I relieved.

I thought I'd sit there until morning, but strangely, just after one a.m., people began to return, and before I knew it, in a matter of few hours, the lot was empty.

I could go home, but needed to share this event with Jimmy, so I went to see him. When I arrived, it was half past three in the morning; the gas station was empty, and so were the streets. I walked into the office, and saw him sleeping like a baby.

"Hey, give me all your money," I shouted.

He jumped up from the chair. "Al, couldn't you just say hello, quietly?"

"What's the fun in that? Come with me. I need to show you something." We went to my car; I opened the trunk and said, "So, how do you like them apples?"

"WOW, that's a lot of apples! Where did you get it? Hey, who did you rob?"

"No one, why would you ask me that?"

"Just kidding."

"Actually, I need to talk to you about them apples." I told him the whole story. Jimmy was excited about joining in my little business. In addition, considering that he was working seven days a week, it seemed the timing was perfect to take a little break from his station.

As a result, next evening, we were working together, parking cars while collecting the profits. It appeared that Sundays were busier than Saturdays. Jim was a big help; cars were no longer accumulating, and there was practically no waiting line like before.

The following weekend, we were operating like clockwork, and we really enjoyed ourselves doing that. I thought of our work as a missing ingredient toward our vision of fulfillment. We had always daydreamed about a business of our own, and this was our first ticket there. After a few months or so, that daydream could become a reality.

However, good things never last. It did not take long for our partnership to crack, and that happened on the night I saw Michael enter the parking lot. Right then, our dreamland collapsed, and I was a sitting duck waiting for the water to boil.

He got out of his car, looked around, and slowly walked toward me. "Al, I see you decided to work overtime. How enterprising of you. I will place you on the board at my office as employee of the month"

"Michael, I don't see anything wrong in what I am doing. The station was closed during this time anyway, so, what's the big deal?"

"Nothing, if you would inform the owner. But you didn't! Did you?" Then he began to shout.

"No; I did not think it would last."

"You are not supposed to think here! That is my job!"

"I think its greed shouting at me; you never yelled before."

"Did you call me greedy? This is my lot! Had you consider asking me before opening after hours? Moreover, if something bad would happen? Who do you suppose would be liable then? I tell you who, me! That's who. Where is your conscience? If you would have asked me, the situation might have bean different, but now, I want half."

"You want half, half of what?"

"Don't play stupid with me, half of all you guys make. I see your brother is here, as well. That's good."

"Will you trust me with the counts?"

"I won't have to! Today I will count on your dignity, but tomorrow I'll give you parking vouchers, and I will hold you accountable; see you!"

That cocksucker left, Damn him, and his vouchers.

"Jimmy, come here; we need to talk."

"Yes, what's up?"

"Did you see who just visited?"

"Yes, why do you think I walked away?"

“The asshole wanted half the profits.”

“How would he know our total? What an idiot.”

“Unfortunately, he isn’t that stupid. He will make us to use vouchers. That way we will be under his control, any suggestions?”

“Sure, tomorrow you’ll give me one voucher as a sample, and I will make duplicates. We will use some of his and most of ours.”

“Damn, Jim. What are you doing at the gas station? You should be in politics!”

“I know; maybe some day I will.”

Jim was right and it really worked. Michael was getting less than one third of the profits; and he was happy about that. Moreover, I was getting it all back and more, because when we obtained those vouchers, I decided to use them during the day as well, and I did that right in front of his nose. It was not about the money, for me. It was a matter of principle, so I took advantage of his greed, and used his self-indulgence to my satisfaction for as long as I worked there.

Another three months passed, and one evening, I was sitting home watching TV and feeling lonely, so I picked up the phone, and called Jim. We talk about our future and timing. I told him that it was about time for us to start something of our own. Like a gas station, or car repair shop, or both, but Jim did not like this idea. He said we should stay where we were, and for as long as possible. He made it obvious that no business would bring us as much money as those three trades combined. I tried to convince him otherwise, but at the end, I had no success. We spoken for hours, until I got tired, and then the subject glided away, as Jim continued talking.

Then I heard in the background someone say, “Get up, motherfucker, and put the phone down.” Then, the line disconnected.

Now who would say something like that? There could be only one option. I did not like the thought in my mind, but somehow I knew exactly what was happening there.

I ran out half-naked, got into my car, pressed the pedal to the metal, and took off like a fanatic. It was late, past midnight or so. Luckily, the freeway was only a few blocks away, and I was the only lunatic zooming on the freeway. I don’t know how fast I was going, and before I could get my mind straight, I was approaching the Brooklyn Battery tunnel.

Without hesitations, I busted right through the toll. I drove at incredible speed, and I flew out of the tunnel like a cork from a bottle of champagne. Then, right along the side of the concrete barrier, the car could not handle the turn.

I stayed there for less than a second, and took off again. This time, I heard sirens coming from the rear. I looked in the rearview mirror and saw a number of patrol cars on my tail.

The rational voice in my head said stop and accept the consequences, but the thought of Jimmy being in trouble erased that voice, and I was willing to accept any outcome as long as Jimmy was safe.

I flew through seventy-six blocks; luckily, most of the intersections were cars free, and presenting mostly red lights, but who cares. Police cars were massing together, chasing after me, and getting closer. They were in heavy pursuit, but I achieved my goal and finally I arrived.

I raced onto the station, then immediately was surrounded by cops. When I rushed out of the car, Jim was laying on the ground; a person was standing beside him holding a baseball bat in one hand and a gun in the other. Before I could budge, cops were all over me. They handcuffed me and pinned me down on the ground, then in a few moments, they took me in, and we drove away.

Later that night, they questioned me, and at the same time, I learned that Jim was in the hospital and he was doing okay.

Apparently, my hunch was correct; there was a robbery in progress, and I arrived there with cops before they could leave.

They interrogated me until morning, and afterward, they suspended my license, granted me a bunch of summonses, and then I was released. From the precinct, I went to the hospital. It turned out that Jimmy had a minor concussion. He received some medication and rested in bed awaiting discharge.

I went in quietly, thinking he might be asleep, but he was awake.

"Hey, Al, what are you doing here?"

"Didn't you know? I am everywhere!"

"Yes, I heard. Man! You are crazy!"

"What did you hear?"

"They told me what happened in the ambulance, and everyone in here is talking about that incident; you are a hero now!"

"Oh, please; that was no big deal!"

"You know, sometimes I worry about you. What were you thinking?"

"Well, the truth is I wasn't thinking at all."

"That's what worries me."

"You know, you look good in white."

"Thanks, if I didn't love you, I would say try it some time!"

"So, Jim; you want to talk about it?"

"No, thanks, I've done enough talking for one night."

"Please, tell me what happened. Be brief; I think I deserved a story from you."

"Well, while we were talking on the phone, I saw a guy walking around the pumps. There was nobody else there, so I became suspicious, but then he was gone. We kept on talking. Actually, I remember I did the talking. Anyway, I was not concerned with the pumps anymore. And then, that same guy burst into the office with a hand gun, and . . ."

"Yes, I know the rest."

"So you heard? You know, I always knew you were coming. Can't explain how or why, but I knew that you would appear. Didn't expect to see so many cops along with you. Nevertheless, what is unexpected from most, could be expected from you! That I already learned!"

"Should I take it as a compliment?"

"I believe so, however, only in this case!"

"Hey, rest. I have to go get my car."

"Why, what happened to your car? Have you smashed again?"

"Well, this time just a little. It's funny. I hit the same turn in the tunnel, only this time, on the outbound; can you believe that? What are the odds? Anyway, the cops have impounded my car, so, I need to get it back."

"Yes, it's very funny, actually. Go figure! Maybe you and that tunnel have magnetic attraction!"

"Maybe! From now on, I shall use only the bridge."

"Thanks for the heads up, then. I will use only the tunnel!"

"Okay, see you later. Stop laughing; get some rest."

I spent the rest of the day getting my car back, and the worst thing about that day was that I neglected to call Mike and inform him of my situation.

It was three o'clock in the afternoon and I was searching for any excuse not to call him, but there were none. Beside, when facing a blow, its better to be hit right away and get it over with. So, I called him. "Hello, Mike. Before you scream, please listen!"

"Scream? Why would you think that? I wiped you out! I have no reason to scream; there is no one on the other side of this phone." He then hung up.

I redialed, but the line was busy, so I decided to confront him, and I went there.

When I drove in, Mike was standing in front of the parking lot acting as barricade.

I got out and said, “You are behaving like a child. First listen, and then fire me, if you wish.”

“You won’t tell me what to do; didn’t I tell you to inform me of all outcomes?”

“Yes, you did, but I was locked up, and then interrogated. I could not call anyone.”

“Again with fairytales, Al, why won’t you become a writer instead? With your imagination, you would bring more satisfaction to yourself and society!”

“You really think this place will hold without me? Think again! You will never find a suitable replacement for me.”

“We will see about that; now go away!”

“Mike, if I will leave now, the outcome will be on you; remember that!”

“Oh really? What outcome are you referring too? What, you are going to burn this place down? Be my guest. I’m fully insured!”

“You and you’re fucking insurance; I am repulsed by how small you think. I will go all right, and get me a job on 22nd Street. Rest assured; all your clients would transfer there sooner than you can scratch your shiny skull. In addition, I will do everything possible and impossible to work there, and destroy your business. Remember that, why don’t you!”

I left furious. While backing away, I glanced at Mike’s face. It turned yellow. When I turned around and drove away, I looked in the rearview mirror, and he was still there, frozen in the same spot. I meant what I said, and this time, what I said would happen.

Finally, I got home. Jim was lying on the couch and it seemed that he was drinking. The music was playing so loud; he didn’t hear me come in. That was his favorite song, “I wish you were here,” by Pink Floyd.

It made me think that maybe he did not see me at the station, but then again, he was unconscious when I got there.

I stood there waited for the song to end, and watched him drink the liquid oblivion. I decided not to bother him, and quietly went to my room, fell on my bed, and surrendered to a deep sleep.

I woke up from that nightmare, the dream about a foot commenced to hunt me. What a strange state of mind. Most of the time, I had that dream only under the influence, but now it appeared regardless of my condition.

"Hey Al, I did not know you were here."

"I thought you were sleeping and decided not to bother you. Some night, huh?"

"Yes, what a night. So, did you get your car?"

"Yes I did! I also got fired, so now I am jobless!"

"Really, why?"

"No big deal. Tell me, what were you thinking about back then, in the living room? Is it about what happened to you? Are you in shock?"

"No, it's not that. I was just replaying the incident in my mind. I got hit on the head, and the next thing I saw was darkness, visions of gray and black, with complete serenity, I have to say, I really liked that feeling; very much so."

"What kind of feeling you are talking about? You couldn't have had any feelings; you were out!"

"Yes, but I did. It was amazing! Suddenly there was no pain, and only complete comfort, as if I had been born into a new world where there was peace and ecstasy. However, you would not understand, even if you tried."

"Is that the phone ringing?"

"Yes, stay there. I will get it. Al, it's for you!"

When I answered, Mike was on the line. "Hello, Al. Look! I was wrong. I guess you caught me at the wrong moment. Anyway, what I am trying to say is, forget about what happened, okay?"

"Yes, that's fine by me!"

"So, I will see you tomorrow?"

"Are you sure that you need me there?"

"Yes, of course I'm sure; why would you doubt that?"

"Well, because lately, you've changed your mind so often I'm not sure what to expect next! I need some reassurance, that's all."

"Okay, what do you want?"

"I want a raise. That way we both will be on the same page!"

"Fine, you got it. Is that all?"

"Yes, I want to receive that up front; let's say tomorrow!"

"Okay, I'll give it to you tomorrow. Are you satisfied now?"

"Yes, Mike. Thank you, and so you know, I don't remember any of what happened. See you tomorrow."

When I returned to the bedroom, my mood had slightly improved. "Jim, guess what?"

"What now?"

"That was Mike on the phone, and I got my job back!"

"And that's a good thing, I gather!"

"Yes it is, nevertheless, let's retrace our thoughts. Where were we? Oh, yes, you were saying about peace and ecstasy! Let me tell you version of what happened to you. What you experienced is called a black out, and nothing else!"

"I know what I felt, and it was real. No matter how I try to present it to you, you will never understand."

"Yes, you are right. I don't understand and don't want to, either. I'm just thankful that you are okay. That's all that matters."

Afterward, I couldn't go back to sleep, so I went out for a walk. On my way out of the building, the old mush walked in.

"Hello! Al; are you going out?"

"No, Anna, I'm coming in!"

"Really? So what are you doing on the inside of the building going out?"

"Well, as I was coming in, I thought maybe I should hang out a bit longer."

As I was saying that, Jim came out of the elevator. "Jim, where to?"

"Hello! And you must be Al's brother. What a pleasure."

"Yeah, same here! Al, your mother is on the phone, she asked me to get you, so come on, let's go. She is on the phone waiting."

"Bye, guys," Anna said.

We rushed into the elevator, and Anna stayed behind.

"Wait for me, youngsters" Anna shouted.

"Fuck her; let her wait!"

"Jim, have some respect! You keep forgetting she is our landlady, and an old lady."

"Old lady, you say? Respect, you say. I didn't hear you say that when she was naked in your bed!"

"Why do you dislike her so much? She was so nice to you."

"Would you feel better if I bang her? Anyway, you never told me what happened that night. How is it that that creature ended up in your bed, not to mention the way you were trying to dress her. Man, what a sight! Wait a minute; you were both naked. Did you and her . . ."

"What? Don't even go there! How desperate do you think I am? Damn, actually, I don't remember. What a nightmare. The thought alone makes me vomit. And why are you laughing?"

"Because, this is hilarious' wouldn't you say so?"

"No, I would not. There is nothing to laugh about, and it's embarrassing."

"Okay, we are here. Go; your mother is waiting."

I picked up the phone and there was nobody there. I figured she hung up intentionally to waive the call charges; besides, she knew I would call back, and so I did.

"Hi Mom, Is everything all right?"

"Yes, and then some! I have great news for you, but first tell me, how you are doing? Is that whore bothering you?"

"No, Mom, I'm fine. Tell me the news."

"Okay. Let me ask you, would you be happy to see us?"

"Are you kidding? Sure I would."

"Then, get ready, because we are coming!"

"That is great. How long will you be visiting? And who is coming?"

"We all coming, and we are coming to stay!"

I was stunned when she said, "coming to stay." That phrase pounded my ears like a thunderstorm, and showered me with tremendous joy, I became speechless.

"Son, are you there?"

"Yes, Mom, Give me few seconds. What exactly did you mean, we coming to stay? Are you willing to immigrate?"

"Yes we are. We lack just one document, and you need to provide a letter stating that you are accepting legal responsibility for us. That's all we need for our visas!"

"Okay. I understand; anything else?"

"We are selling all of our belongings. All we need is that letter, and we will be on our way."

"I'll get right on it. Where should I send it?"

"To our address of course, where else? However, please expedite it. Most of our stuff is gone, and I don't want to sit on the suitcases. Do you understand?"

"Yes, mom, I do. Still I can't believe it, though. I can't wait to tell Jimmy."

"No, don't tell him. Let it be a surprise."

"Mom, I have to tell him. I need to go. I will talk to you soon; bye"

I hung up the phone, and could not get up on my feet from the excitement. I was immobilized.

"Jim, get in here, quickly."

"What's up?"

"Man, you won't believe what I just heard."

"What's all the fuss about? Tell me!"

"They are all immigrating to the US. Our family is coming here! I still can't believe this!"

"Neither can I! What do you mean, immigrating here? You probably misunderstood her. Call her back; do it now!"

"There's no need. I'm sure they are coming. Aren't you happily surprised?"

"Shit, well, surprised, yes. Happy? Don't know. I thought they had a great life there. What will they do in this country?"

He sat himself down and stared into my eyes. I saw his face altering into a tightfisted figure. I knew he was hurting, but did not realize why. "What's the matter with you? Didn't you hear what I said? Our family is coming!"

"Come down, Al. I heard you. You mean your family. I don't have a family, and never had one, either."

"What are you talking about? Your dad and your sisters, aren't they your family? In addition, my mother . . . well, let's put her aside for now."

"I know he is my dad legally; however, I don't recall him as my dad. I never spend any time with him. He is more of a dad to you than he ever was to me! I also realize that I have two sisters, but I hardly ever saw them. I don't know them at all. I also have a mother; however, she was always away. As a result, I never had a family. Don't you see? There is a difference between your life and mine!"

"Please calm down. Give them a chance, and you will have a family sooner than you know!"

"No, Al. There was a time when I dreamed about family, but now I do not want it anymore. I would not know how to behave. Especially when my life is getting together, I have a job, I have a car, and I have my apartment. I am a normal person now, comparing to Israel, where I was nobody for so long! So, no thank you. I'm better like this, on my own!"

"It would not hurt to try; what is the big deal? What do you have to lose?"

"Everything! I can lose everything! Besides, I tried and it hurt. So it is a big deal for me, and why didn't your mother ask me? Maybe I don't want them to come. Where they will stay?"

"I think they will stay with us, but it will be for a short period, until they find a place of their own."

"There you go! You see! It's already beginning; they are coming to take our life away from us. No. Let me rephrase that correctly! They are coming to take my life away, and to be more specific, your mother will take it. Let's go to a bar, or I will explode!"

So, we went to the bar, and were quiet while driving there. Jim seemed upset, so I did not want to continue that subject, it was best to wait for the right time.

We sat in the bar, had a few drinks, and I waited. As I waited for the unknown, Jim was consuming his fourth drink.

"So, you feel better now?" I asked him.

"I feel calmer rather than better."

"Since you are calm now, let me ask you, what makes you think that somebody can take away your life?"

"I did not say somebody. I said your mother, and if they come, be forewarned, it will happen. Al, you must think I'm stupid. Tell me, where is Victoria?"

"What does she have to do with any of this?"

"I told you then about her, and you disregarded me, so after all this time, you learned that I was right. Don't get me wrong, not for a moment am I happy about it. However, the fact of the matter is, you are not with her anymore, and I knew that would happen from the time you began to hang out with her. I just did not want to dig in where you were bleeding, so I didn't talk about it."

"Yes, you are right. So what? That was a different case all together. I did not know her that well, but, I know our family, and they will not harm us."

"So what, you say! You are about to repeat your mistake. Your mother is not looking to harm anyone. She does it unwillingly, and most likely, only misfortune will find its way toward me."

"Jim, those people are not strangers. Please think it over."

"Al, don't let them come here. Stop them. If it was up to me, I would, but I can't. Only you can accomplish that. Let's call them, and you tell them to stay put, that you will go visit. I will pay for it."

"Jimmy I can't. I miss them too much. I can't."

"I anticipated that. What else did she say to you?"

"She said the only thing that's holding them up is a letter of guaranty. Besides that, they are ready to go. Also, they sold most of their stuff. So you see, now it's too late. I can't stop them."

"Yes, you can. They still have the money. Don't they? So ask them to buy everything back. Hell, I will buy it for them. Call your mother. Call her now, please!"

"Jim enough. They are coming and we will all be a family again, including you, and that's how it should be; whether you like it or not!"

"Why do I have to go through this again? Tell me Al, why? Why, why?"

"Everything will be fine. Get this into your head; nobody will distress you. I won't let them, I promise. And you know that, don't you? Besides, it will not come to that."

"That is where you are wrong, and the sad thing about it is that you don't even know it. She already got to me; as of now, I am distressed, and this is just the beginning, the beginning of my end."

Jim was a bit drunk, so I took him home. He went to sleep, and I stayed on my beloved couch, mulling over what Jim said, and the things my mother told me. I have to admit, doubts were forming. I considered Jim's intuition, and had some concerns. However, if the power of chance has decided, nothing can stand in its way, so there was no need to interfere. I strongly believed that what meant to be would be.

Me? Well, I could only go with the flow, and hope that Jim would come along.

A few days later, I fulfilled to my promise and mailed that letter to Mother. Afterward, I felt relieved, as if a weight had lifted from my shoulders. I couldn't explain it, but it certainly felt right.

Weekend came, and I stayed home all morning hoping that my mother would call me. Instead, around ten o'clock, someone knocked on the door. When I opened the door, I thought I was dreaming.

Vicky was standing there, right in front of me, with a smile on her face as nothing had happened. "Hello, Al, can I come in?"

"Hi, of course; what are you doing here? And when did you get back?"

"Thanks, a few months ago! How have you been?"

"Couldn't be better! Thanks. Why do you ask? And how did you find me?"

"Michael, your boss told me where you live. I met him at the restaurant. We talked, and I asked about you, so here I am! By the way, you have better watch him. He is dishonest toward you!"

"What makes you say that? Like you were any better!"

"Okay, I will not fight about that. However, he tried to get into my panties."

"Tried? Didn't you give him a tour? Also, tell me, do you know anyone who didn't get in your panties!"

"Stop insulting me. It's not appropriate for you to say something like that. Besides, your mother caught me with my fiancé, not with some stranger!"

"Oh, your fiancé? We were married! Doesn't it count for anything? And what about my friends? I presume they were not strangers to you as well, or were they?"

"What are you talking about? Which friends?"

"Those guys that live in my mother's building. You have forgotten that I grew up there! Alex and Max called me right after you left, and they both said you were coming on to them. Don't tell me. Let me guess. They were lying. Right?"

"Please; enough. Didn't you miss me? And what about them? Don't you want them anymore?" she said, while placing my hands on her breasts.

"I want them, but I don't want you! You may leave them, and go!"

Resting my palms on her breasts for a few seconds, I gave in, and could not resist the temptation. I ripped her cloths off, nearly tearing some into pieces, then stood her up, swiveled her around, and penetrated her with so much anger it hurt. There was no making love, and not even close to normal sex. It was pure dirty animal screwing, with no feelings whatsoever. All the anguish I had received from her went right back into her.

I thought in the beginning she was enjoying me, but then it sounded as if she was in pain. She started to scream, "Stop, you are hurting me."

Regardless, I continued, and yet harder. I thrashed her so hard that I started to hurt, and I could not stop. All my anger and all my suffering blasted out on her. I never knew the extent of the anguish I contained until that moment, or I should say, the entire hour? Because, that is how long it took me too relieve myself of her betrayal.

Eventually, I stopped and let her go. She fell, and I sat down exhausted and soaked in sweat.

We did not speak. She got up, dressed herself in a hurry, and left. It was pitiful watching her leave, all torn up and barely able walk.

At first I was not happy with what I had done; however when I considered it as payback, In a way, I felt good, considering my situation.

Soon after she left, the phone rang. It was my mother.

"Hello, Mom. I was actually expecting your call"

"Hi, Al. Well that's it; we have our visas and tickets, so we are ready to leave sooner than predicted. Thanks for the letter."

"That's great. So when will I see you?"

"We will be arriving in New York this coming Tuesday, at nine in the morning. I can't wait."

"Me, too, Mom. Give me the flight information and I will come to get you."

We spoke for a few minutes longer, and said goodbye. When I hung up the phone, confusion set in; I was both happy and sad. Happy because my family was coming and finally we would all be together. Sad because of Jimmy's intuition. What if he was right, what will I do then?

Four years had gone by. In that period, I had come to love my single life. Therefore, I hardly saw myself as living with my parents. I only hoped that they would not stay with us for long. In the worst case, it would be onerous if we did not get along. I would help them to stabilize, and then, they would leave.

It is strange how time seems to slowdown when waiting for someone with anticipation. For me, it was torture. It was as if time almost stopped and minutes developed into hours, hours turned out to be days, and days appeared as eternities.

With such excitement, I could not sleep on Monday night. I had no choice but to wait until Tuesday came, and eventually it did. It was a beautiful day when I got out of the house. The sun was glowing in the bluish sky, and the sky was clear and free of clouds.

That day was a wonderful experience of nature; I realized that life is truly a sensational gift, and I evolved a desire to cherish it.

I arrived at the JFK airport two hours early. I walked around the terminal and could not find myself a calm spot there. I guess my nervousness played some role in that. Unfortunately, Jimmy decided to skip that blissful reunion, and I did not try to convince him otherwise. Therefore, there I was waiting and waiting for the plane to land, I began to stroll around. I was a nervous wreck. I was strolling around the terminal and circling the waiting area at speed, until I became tired and set my ass down.

I observed as people stumbled upon each other with so much happiness and joy; it made me think of my encounter with my family. I remembered my mother, my stepfather, and my sisters, especially my baby sister.

Valerie was born on my fourteenth birthday. She was, and I thought that she would always be, my best gift ever. I loved her more than life itself from the first time I held her in my arms. I cared for her from day one. When I held her sweet tiny body, an enormous emotion of joy ignited within me. That was an unforgettable memory that I carried with me through all our years apart.

She became a part of me, just like one of my essential organs. Unfortunately, life's circumstances caused me to let her go. Back then, wherever I went, she always followed me. I recall one time when that little figure on her little legs ran after me it was hilarious, because, she could never keep up. I watched her following me, so I would intentionally accelerate and then hide. The best part about it was observing her approach my location. She would stop, stand there for a minute, confused look around, then with her adorable sweet voice call my name.

I had to leave my family when she was three years old. She stayed in my memory as a beautiful, clever little child.

My first year away was very tough. I could not tolerate the fact that we were apart from each other, and separated by thousands of miles. However, with time, accepting that fact somehow eased my sorrows.

Returning from my thoughts, I noticed people were coming from customs walking toward the exit. I stood up and looked around; hoping to see my beloved family, but did not make out any familiar faces, so I continued to wait.

One of the things I despised the most was waiting. I always hated waiting, but in this case, there was nothing else for me to do but wait. Time passed by, and everyone slowly vanished from the waiting area, accompanied by the awaited or beloved. Me? Well, I was still there, sitting all by myself and waiting.

Then it hit me. Maybe I was waiting at the wrong place. Damn. That would be disappointing to me, as well as to my family, so I began to look for assistance.

As soon as I turned around, I heard someone say, "Al, Hey son!"

I slowly turned my head and saw them; my family was approaching me, or was it them? As they came closer, I stood there stunned, traumatized by the sight, and could not move. Who are those people? That woman who came to me was shouting my name, and somehow looked like my mother, but to my recollection, she was not.

Then she hugged me and said, "Al, my son, finally! How happy I am to see you."

Apparently, she was my mother, although she seemed in some way different. I did not know what to do. Of course, I put my arms around her, but she did not feel at all like my mom.

She was aware that something is wrong, because soon afterwards she retreated and asked me,

"Where is my son?"

"Mom, it's me. Do you not recognize me?"

"I did. It's just that you look different and have matured. You turned into a man, and I remember you as a boy."

Then I approached my stepfather. I called him dad; he was always like a father to me, and more! Just goes to show, blood is not always the issue, and he appeared as before, except for the gray hair.

I looked down, searching for the little one, but she was not there. Instead, there were two grown-up girls standing by my side and staring at me. I was never close with Lora; she is my younger sister, as well, but somehow we had lived in different worlds.

What really knocked me off my feet was when I saw Valerie. That dazzling little baby was gone, and in her place stood some unfamiliar girl, observing me closely. She was completely a stranger to me, and judging by her gaze, I thought that feeling was mutual.

We were all quiet driving back to our home, except my mother. She was the only one talkative, but later I could not recall what she said.

The whole situation seemed peculiar. I could not understand how such a dramatic change had transpired so fast. Four year had passed, and in those years, my family grew to be strangers to me.

I parked by our building, and began taking suitcases from my car. I saw that scarecrow walking the ugly, tiny creature she called a puppy. I tried to avoid her but somehow she managed to pinpoint me, and of course, right then that witch was determined to come up and begin a conversation.

"Hello, Al; long time no see."

"What are you talking about? We met in the lobby just a few days ago, or have you forgotten that?"

"Oh, aren't we moody today? What happened? I don't remember ever seeing you this way."

"Really? Well, get used to it, because that is the way I am."

"Al, stop it. You are scaring me. Tell me, who are those people?"

"Mom, why don't you meet Mrs. German. She is our landlady."

"Hello, how nice to meet you. How was this tenant? Have you experienced any troubles from him?" my mom said.

Periodically and unwillingly, my mother could hit the bull's-eye with her questions. Although for her the question was meaningless, suddenly, the person began to shiver, and in this case, that was Mrs. German.

"Hello, nice to meet you as well," Mrs. German said, then grabbed me by the hand, and pulled me aside. "Al, have you told your mom about us?"

"Are you out of your mind? And what do you mean us? There is no us; we had a couple of drinks, and that's all it was."

"A couple of drinks? Really? So how will you explain us in bed, naked? And what did you do to me that night? I still can't get this out of my head."

"Don't flatter yourself. Nothing happened. How many times do I have to tell you that? We were drunk; especially you, and now I have to go. We'll pick this up again later."

"Okay, go. I take it that is your whole family there!"

"You take it right. So?"

"So, I did not rent you a motel. Make sure it's a short visit this time!"

"Bye, Mrs. German. Oh, and tell your husband that I need to talk to him as soon as possible!"

"Why, Al? Why would you need to talk to him?"

"It's personal! Goodbye, Mrs. German."

I gave my family a short tour of our apartment. They liked the place, but it was small for all of us. The suitcases alone occupied half of the living room.

When Jimmy arrived, the gladness around us grew beyond recognition, and huge warmth began to circle our atmosphere.

That evening, we all sat by the table, joking, and laughing like in the old days, except this time, the present of alcohol contributed to our joy, and especially mine. Those contributions continued on every other evening, I was not aware of how fast it twisted into a cycle, and before I knew it, we were drinking every day. Threes company, Pap, Jimmy, and me.

Eventually, those stimulations grew into complexity, then scandals emerged between our parents, and it was not delightful sight anymore.

Jimmy and I decided not to abuse alcohol in the house. In fact, from that period, I hardly drank in the house. Whenever I heard them argue, I would just go to the bar. Jimmy would join me, and that was the best resolution for both of us.

Nevertheless, for my mother it was not enough. Regardless of our evening absenteeism, Dad continued to drink and the arguments between our parents grew into mutual irritation.

Shortly, because of space shortage, the arguments evolved into a mental distress, and our living conditions became messy. Jimmy and I had slept on our beds in the bedroom; our parents were in difficult situation. They slept on the living room floor, and my sisters shared the couch.

From the day they arrived, I wanted to give them our bedroom, but they all refused; furthermore, they insisted on those terrible arrangements.

The mood in our place was gloomy. As soon as I got home, I felt the need to get out of there, so, most evenings I spent my time at same bar; shortly after, it became a second home to me.

One Friday, Jimmy decided to tag along, maybe because he was off the next day, or maybe he just missed my company, as I missed him. However, as soon as we got there, he said, "Everyone, hello. I'm buying! This round is on me!"

"Jim, tell me you are joking."

"No! I am buying!"

"Maybe you should reconsider. I mean, look; there are many people in here. Do your math! It will cost you a fortune!"

"I'm not blind, and I don't care."

"Well, it's your money."

"You're damn right it is, so drink up. By the way, tell me, was I right about them coming here? Just tell me that; I need to hear it."

"Okay, you were right. Happy?"

"No, somehow I anticipated a different reaction out of you, but, nevertheless my prediction was correct. Too bad no one listened."

"Maybe you are gifted, you know, like a fortuneteller."

"Maybe I am!"

"In that case, tell me what's next."

"For you or for me?"

"For all of us.

"I can speak only for the two of us! I also heard that Michael has bought a station."

"Yes, I know; with three bays in the repair shop, by the way. He was asking me if I wanted to lease it."

"Well, you see. Maybe that is what's next for you."

"Listen, Jimmy, I'm glad you brought this up, because I wanted to ask you about us leasing it together. We could do a lot with a place like that, and the rent is reasonable, so what do you say?"

"I say two words to you: no way!"

"Jimmy, pleas; you need to get out of that business. Those deliveries are not safe anymore. Besides, we will make good money there, you'll see."

"I am not going anywhere, and those deliveries were never safe, but I like it. I don't spend much time and I get what I want, so forget it. I wish you luck, though!"

"Jimmy, are you using? And please be honest; think before you answer." I asked him that only because there was no other reasonable explanation for his choices.

He took his time thinking, as well as gulping one drink after another, and then he said, "Yes, I am using. You look surprised, and all this time I thought you knew."

"Well, I did know, but was hoping to be wrong about it, as I was on all other matters."

"I guess this time you hit the jackpot. Listen, I am not into drugs. I'm just playing with it whenever I'm sad, or glad!"

"Yeah, that means all the time! I bet all the users say that. All I'm saying is you have to quit before it is too late, because if you don't, eventually this will take you to the boulevard of broken dreams, and Jimmy, there is no return from there. Do you know what I'm talking about?"

"Yes, better than you think, but it is my choice, so I will decide, not you or anyone else!"

"I'm not deciding. I'm just asking. Actually, I'm begging you; leave that business and your gas station. Let's start over together."

"Al, stop with that. You begin to sound like a broken record! I respect you. You know that. So, don't do anything to change that. Now, do me a favor."

"Okay, what?"

"Please go; I need to be alone."

"Okay, I hope you know what you're doing!"

I left, and from that night, our relationship changed. We hardly saw each other, and did not spend any time together. I could not say that I missed him; because of my new establishment, I was busy with my new business and myself.

On grand opening day, at first, it was slow. However, considering that this station was closed for over six months, I did not anticipating any business for first few weeks. Regardless, I assembled gas attendants and a few car mechanics, and we all waited. Yes, the worst thing in my life is waiting. In less than one month, I turned that place around, and began to get revenue. The feeling of getting it running on my own was beyond description.

Through that period, Jimmy reacquainted with his old girlfriend, and was barely at home. Our dad found a job and became a storefront mechanic, a profession that was completely outside of his training.

However, for some reason he was happy about it; our dad was a true perfectionist. Everything he touched would turn to mint shape. His hands and his dedication made him practically the best in every field. I had never seen anyone with such magnificent capabilities. In Israel, he was a machinery mechanic and welder; afterwards, they promoted him to division director. However, back here, when I visited his workplace, he was assembling aluminum storefronts and greenhouses. That was completely different knowledge from the work he had been doing. Nevertheless, I was stunned at the way he learned his new profession. It looked like he had been doing it all his life.

"Hello, Pap. Where did you learn to do that?" I asked.

"I learn as I go!"

"How is that possible? You had to know where those clips attach, and how to connect the vertical with the horizontal profiles. Someone must have showed you!"

"No, son, it is not that difficult. Anyone with minor tool skills can do this. Look and learn; all you really need is patience and willpower. Acquire those traits and you can build anything!"

He had mentioned the two traits I lacked the most. And I had no desire to get them any time soon. "Can you teach me?"

"Sure I can, but I won't have to. When you decide to pursue that line of work, I will guide you, and the rest will depend on you."

Pap was a hard worker. All his life he dedicated to his work. No matter where he worked, or what position he had, he always came up on top. He did that for one reason only, a need to provide for his family, and that was the only way he knew how to be. All his earnings found their way to my mother, and somehow she would always find a way to spend it all, on who knows what!

That was the main reason for our family to be short of money. No matter how much he would bring to her, it was never enough.

Soon, my two sisters went to school, and I thought they were doing okay, but my mother, on the other hand . . . well, my mother was not happy. Mainly because, as we all knew, the place was too small for all of us. One day, she decided it was time to move to a larger place, and who could blame her. When we talked about moving out, I did not think she meant all of us. Evidently, she did, and without much consideration, I agreed.

Then she had told me of her conversation with Jimmy, and I found out that Jimmy was fuming about this suggestion. He did not like the idea of us moving together, and I did not understand why.

One day, Jimmy and I crossed each other at the building entrance. I told him he could stay and have the apartment with all its contents to himself.

He then said, "I told you they would take my life from me. Well, it is happening."

"Where do you see that?"

"They are moving, and you are going along. I have no choice in this matter. There is nothing left for me to do. I can't afford that place on my own, and you know that."

"Look, we've been living together for a few months now, and I didn't see any difficulties except the lack of space, but we will change that and then we all will be fine, so why resist?"

"I am not resisting. We are just talking, fine. I will tag along, so we'll see where this will lead me."

I left with the thought of us moving together; all else we had talked about, I ignored.

So we did it; we finally moved to a nice house on Avenue J. That house was old but affordable, with three bedrooms, and more than enough space for all of us.

In addition, I thought we would all be happy there, but as usual, I was wrong. Somehow, I got used to the fact of always being wrong. I could not say it did not bother me, because it did. However, nothing I could do about it.

Concerning our apartment, there was one final act for me to complete. It was necessary to return the keys to our ex-proprietor. I hated meeting with her again, so going over there, I was praying to God for her husband to open the door. However, God was probably busy, and the scarecrow showed instead.

"Al; hello, handsome. Come on in."

"Thank you, but no thank you. I don't have the time."

"Come in; we can always make time. My husband is working. Did I tell you he is a limo driver? What a loser, don't you think?"

"Look Mrs. German, I came to return the keys and to tell you that we are leaving. Actually, we already left, so please take them."

"What? Are you out of your mind? Leaving like that without notifying me first"?

"I'm notifying you know; take the keys."

"No, you keep the keys and the apartment until I will find a new tenant.

So where is my rent?"

"You are nuts. I told you we left. Now, take the damned keys."

"I will sue you for all that you have. You disgust me. Give me the keys."

"Listen to me, scarecrow, if you consider proceeding with any action against me, your skeleton figure will be posted in the daily news in the lost and found section. By the way, are you permitted to sublease? I don't think so; therefore, shut the fuck up and cherish your existence while it lasts."

I left that building with a huge relief, and felt like a ton of bricks had lifted from me. That is how much weight that creature placed on me, and had no idea until now.

When I came to our new home all the family gathered by the table, according to tradition, and we had to toast the new home. This tradition continued for several days.

Then, for the men in the house, it became a routine. Every day one of us would bring a bottle of vodka for dinner, and every day, we would finish that bottle. It was a standard 750-gram bottle, and of course, for the three of us, it would be more than enough.

This lifestyle continued until one day I noticed that our parents didn't get along. I recognized that from fights they had. However, as the arguments between them grew, so did the alcohol use between the three of us.

I was never concerned about them arguing. I thought it was a marriage thing, until one day, and that day stayed with me forever.

As I came home from work, my mother was very upset, and she was crying.

"Mom, what happened? Why are you crying? Is it because of Dad? Tell me."

"No, it's not because of him. Actually, I hardly see him anymore."

"So why are you upset? Did something happen to the girls?"

No, they are fine. It's you brother."

"What happened to him? Where is he?"

"He is okay. Don't worry. He is probably at work now."

"So tell me, what happened?"

"Jimmy insulted me last night."

"What are you talking about?

"When you went to sleep, by accident you locked the door, and I tried to open it but I couldn't, so I started to yell. Then Jimmy began shouting at me with a terrible voice tone, using foul language."

"Mom, why did you yell?"

"I was worried about you. You probably don't remember, but last night you were completely drunk, so I wanted to check on you."

"Okay, I understand. Tell me what Jimmy said to you."

"It doesn't matter anymore."

"No, I want to know."

"Well, he was screaming at me, saying, 'Why are you knocking at our door? He is still sleeping. Leave him alone'."

"So I told him to mind his own business, this is my house, and I will do as I please. Then he began to shout, and said, 'It is not your house, and nothing in here belongs to you. What are you, stupid? You were supposed to find your own place, so find it, and get the fuck out of our place!'"

"Mom, are you sure he said that?"

"Of course I'm sure. I don't have a memory loss, nor am I stupid."

Her story has completely derailed my train. Deep inside, I was exploding, so being a mama's boy, and not thinking with my head, I picked up the phone and called Jimmy. When he answered, I said, "Jimmy listen to me, and listen carefully because I will say it only once."

"Al, wait. I accepted your call. Please hear my side first!"

"Oh, so you know why I'm calling. Don't you ever show your face here again, and consider this day your lucky day."

"Al, please wait. I want . . ."

"I don't want to hear you, and I don't want to see you ever again; remember that for as long as you live." And I hung up.

When I hung up, I felt as if half my soul had departed into that phone line. I felt emptiness inside my body, and I was standing by that phone completely numb when, my mother came up to me

She said, "What did you do? He has nowhere else to go. Why did you say that?"

"Mom, get away from me. I don't want to talk, and he will come home, you will see."

"No, Al, he won't. Jimmy loves you and respects you. He will not come here ever again!"

As she was saying that, conscious arose in my mind and I opened my eyes, and realized the consequence of my deed. What had I done? How could I have said that to him? What the fuck came over me? Somehow, I managed to calm myself down, and the thought of Jimmy insulting my mother actually helped me.

Nevertheless, in actuality, alcohol was the best medicine for my situation. That day, I drank myself useless, and the next morning, and the next evening, until I became sick. It was the first time in my life that I was alcohol poisoned. What a terrible stage. I vomited all morning and could not drink nor eat through the whole day.

This alcohol related fact came as a surprise to me. I had never encountered anyone who drank so much and I by no means had experienced that agony before. Until this, a hangover was my worst result. Eventually I got over it, and after a few days, my life was back to normal, although my behavior toward Jimmy literally consumed me.

Not a day went by without me thinking of him. Every evening when I drove home, I hoped he would be there. While driving, I would see him in my mind sitting on the couch and watching TV. I would speed up to get home quicker, but upon my arrival; there would be nobody there except the usual faces.

Nothing could cheer me, and no one could help, not that anyone tried. It appeared that in just a few moments, I had destroyed a lifetime connection, and for what? I could not bear the thought anymore. I needed to distract myself from the feeling, and I had plenty of time, so every evening; I would enter the home, look at the faces, turn around, and drive to the bars.

Meeting new people and getting loaded with alcohol somehow facilitated my emotions, but, when it was time return home, I was back to square one, this lifestyle seem endless. One most peculiar night was when I came home so drunk that I did not notice my mother and sister were not living with us anymore.

I woke up my dad. "Pap, where is Mom?"

"They left us a few days ago."

"Why didn't you tell me?"

"Because you are drunk all the time, and still are. What are you doing to yourself? When are you going to stop?"

"Ha, look who is talking. Did you ask yourself that question?"

"Go to sleep. Call your mother when you sober up. Her number is on the table. Good night."

That night pap was clear as a glass of water, and I wondered why. I pulled out a bottle from the fridge and continued boozing, then said to myself, "Why wait for tomorrow, if I can call her tonight? So I did.

"Hello, Mom, how are you? And where are you?"

"Al, is that you? Why are you calling me so late? Are you all right?"

"Yes, I'm fine. I was worried, and why did you leave?"

"I despise this behavior, and will not tolerate it anymore. Most of all, I felt sorry for the girls, seeing the two of you in that condition. What kind of example are both of you setting? That's why we left, and we are not coming back."

"Okay, Mom, as long as you all doing well, I'm happy for all of you!"

"Go get Jimmy. Now the three of you can drink until you drop. Good night, and next time be sure to call me only with a sober head."

"Good night, Mom."

The next morning, I skipped work and went to see Jimmy. Although it was a bad idea to keep the station closed, I figured that my state of affairs with Jimmy was crucial, and it was time for me to apologize. Surprisingly, it did not take long to find him, because when I came up to his station, he was there, working. Apparently, his shifts had changed around, so now he worked days.

"Al, what are you doing here? I was under the impression that you were disgusted with me, or maybe you came to beat me up. Is that it? Okay, go ahead then; help yourself."

"Actually, I came to apologize. I was wrong. I'm very sorry; please forgive me."

"Man, I wish I had a nickel for every time you were wrong. I wouldn't have to work as much."

"So, does that mean I'm forgiven?"

"What else am I going do with you? Do you remember what I told you? If you do, welcome to reality."

"I know, but still, I don't understand any of it. How could something like that happen?"

"There is nothing to understand. Your mother needed to toss me out. She has found a great excuse, and done it through you. Excellent choice, by the way."

"She left with the girls, so let's put this behind us. Tell me, when are you coming back home?"

"Tonight, thanks to you. I bought myself new clothing, so there is a little packing for me to do."

"Jimmy, I'm really sorry. I will work hard to make up for this!"

"Don't worry about it; you look like shit. Go home get some rest."

Not only did I look like shit, I felt like shit as well. Apologizing never becomes easier. Actually, it gets harder and harder, maybe because of the feelings, and mainly the feeling of guilt.

Jimmy came home that evening, as promised. I do not remember him ever breaking his word. That evening, we talked for several hours, but in some way, I felt distant from him, and I think the feeling was mutual. In that short period, we had grown apart, and never were tight again.

The three of us went back to a so-called normal routine. We were hardly drinking, and if so, only during weekends. During a few weeks, I practically did not see either of them; however, on a few occasions, I had the pleasure of encountering Jimmy, and it was weird.

Mostly because, of his appearance, for the previous week, he had walked around the house with an abnormal look on his face. When I tried to confront him, he would be brief in his answer, and then quickly slip away. One evening when I was driving back home, (it was Friday), I decided to ask him out. I thought a night out might fast track us back to how we used to be. When I walked in, Jim was watching TV. "Jim, do you remember that nightclub we used to park cars for!"

"Sure! Why do you ask?"

"It just hit me; we never checked that place out. We worked right there for months, and never went; don't you find it strange?"

"Actually, I don't! You're forgetting that we worked there all night, and when our work was over, so was the club's!"

"Yeah, but we could have chosen a different day!"

"I suppose we could have. What difference does it make? It was in the past; why bring this up now?"

"No reason. I was just wondering."

"Al please, wonder about something else, and keep it too yourself, I'm watching a game!"

"Okay, let's go to the club tonight! When the game is over?"

"Okay, let's talk then."

At ten o'clock, Jim approached me and said, "So, you really want to go out, huh?"

"Yes, I do."

"Do you mind if we will go to a different place?"

"No, what place are you talking about?"

"I've visited this place quite often lately; it's practically my home. I think you will like it."

"Okay, let's go."

"On one condition. I'm driving!"

On the way there, I was sitting in Jim's car and thinking aloud. The last time we did something together was so long ago that this seemed like dream to me. He acknowledged with a smile, and did not reply.

We arrived, and I had no idea where we were. That place was really booming; the music inside was so loud it was heard on the street. Some people were dancing on the sidewalk while waiting in line.

Jim took me by my arm, and said, "We don't have to wait in line; follow me!"

At the entrance, one of the guards stamped my hand with red ink and let us into the lobby. The lobby was dark, and filled with people.

"Jim, what are all those people doing here?"

"This is the busiest night of all, and it's probably overcrowded. There is no room on the floor; let's go check it out anyway!"

As we attempted to move forward, squeezing ourselves between the crowds, pushing, and shoving became necessary.

I turned to Jim and said, "Jim, where are we going? Maybe we should stay here and wait for the mass to clear."

"No, that's the way to the bar!"

"Oh, in that case, push! And I will back you!"

And so we pushed and struggled our way through. When we finally got there, it felt like going through a wrestling match and winning it.

"Al, what will you have?"

"Oh, man! It has been longer than I thought. You really don't remember?"

"Actually, I do. I was thinking maybe you switched."

"Jim, old habits die hard!"

We sat there for a while, watching the crowd jump, then a woman appeared and squeezed herself between us. She placed her arm around Jim and gave him a kiss on his cheek.

"Al, meet Jessie! Jessie, meet Al!"

"Al, we will go get loose. I hope you don't mind."

"Of course I don't. Jim, wait! Who is she?"

"Hopefully my girlfriend! I will be right back!"

I was watching them dance and speculating that she was his type, all right. However, she was also all to herself. She danced like there was no one there besides her.

Jim constantly tried to be noticeable. Regardless of his attempts and his moves, she would not look at him or give him a moment of time on that floor. I did not like what I saw, and was glad when he returned, leaving her where she was.

"Hey, Al, how are you doing?"

"Jim, where did you find that blond?"

"Oh, her! I think she is a friend with the bodyguard! Did you like her? Nice, huh?"

"What I like is irrelevant. The question is; what are you trying to pull?"

"What do you mean?"

"If she is spoken for, why would you interfere? Especially with the bodyguard's girlfriend. Are you suicidal?"

"Al, stop worrying; you were right. Old habits do die-hard. Besides, I heard they broke up."

"You heard that? Did you confirm it? Not to mention, she is neglecting you. I saw they way she danced with you; she behaved like you weren't even there; doesn't this bother you?"

"Al, look; she is an upscale girl. It takes effort to get her attention. She did kiss me, though. She gave me a sign to make the move."

"What move? What sign? She probably did that to make her ex jealous; she is using you, Jim. Open your eyes!"

"Okay, Al. I understand where you are coming from! I do; but this is different. Trust me, and . . . Wait a minute! Where did she go? Do you see her?"

"No; she was next to that guy in the blue shirt, but now I don't see her there."

"I will go find her; wait here."

"No, Jim; let's go home. Forget about her."

"Al, please. I'll be back in a few."

"Okay, then I'm coming with you!

"No, Al. Please, just once, do as I ask, okay?"

"Alright; fine."

So, I stayed there. What else was I supposed to do? He never asked me for anything before, not like this, anyway I remembered only one occasion when Jim had sincerely asked me for a favor and I refused. My family came, and our world turned into a nightmare. So, this time, I decided to avoid any arguments and obey his request. Jim had been right in the past; who says he was wrong this time?

After he left, I did not drink much, and did not see Jim, either. After waiting two hours, it was time to go home. I thought he probably found her, got overexcited, and they moved along. How could I blame him? She was very attractive woman.

I grabbed a cab back home, and when I arrived, as anticipated, Jim was not there. Pap was asleep. It was four o'clock in the morning when Jimmy walked in. He looked exhausted and very upset.

"Hey, Jim; did you get lucky?"

"Hey, Al; what are you doing in the living room? I thought you would be asleep by now."

"My thoughts won't let me rest, and it's a good thing, too; I get to see you."

"Al, please don't turn on the light!"

"Oh! Man, where did you get that shiner?"

"Why did you turn the light on? You never do as I ask!"

"What? A few hours ago, I did that, and look at you now! Tell me what happened."

"Forget it. I am going to sleep."

"No! You are not going anywhere until you tell me. Be brief about it, I don't care."

"Okay. I went to look for Jessie, and could not find her any where in the club, so I went outside, and that is when I saw her!"

"And?"

"And, we argued, and that's it."

"No, it's not; what happened next?"

"Nothing, Al; let me go to bed."

"Not until you tell me who gave you that shiner."

"I think it was her boyfriend. Okay, are we done now?"

"You think? What you mean, you think. Your eye is all swollen; you had to see who threw the punch. It's not like someone hit you in the back, so stop playing with me and tell me!"

"Okay, it was him, alright?"

"Damn! And I thought you knew what you were doing! I guess there is a need to step away, and look from the side to comprehend the situation! Forget about her, and him. Look on the bright side; at least you did not get married."

"No, I will not forget this; that bastard will pay!"

"Jim, you have to let it go. Put yourself in his shoes. What would you do if someone were coming on to your girlfriend? Think about it. You told me long time ago that you were learning from my mistakes! So what happened to that rule? I presumed you will live by it!"

"It was not me; she came on to me. I did not do anything."

"That's where you are wrong. You played along; you are as guilty as she is. There is a word for what you did. I'm sure you are aware of it."

"Why are you taking their side? He insulted me in front of everyone. Does that mean anything to you? Well, it means my dignity, and that is all I have left!"

"Jim, people abuse, and get abused; they throw punches, and get hit. It happens all the time, and everywhere. That is the act of nature. Nobody can escape it or avoid it. We can only accept it and move on! Please, listen to me, and let it go!"

"You should be a preacher! I will think about it; that is all I can promise you now."

"Well, it's a start, and better than nothing. Go rest."

"Okay, goodnight! Or good morning! Whatever!"

Somehow, I believed that this time I had got to him, and he would forget this night as if it had never existed. That's what I would have done, anyway.

Afterward, I went to my workplace, and arrived earlier than usual. Cars and cabs were already waiting in line. It brought me joy to watch the rebirth of that station; moreover, I was pleased with myself, because that task I accomplished alone.

Although the gas pumps were someone else's, I was satisfied with my repair shop. There were three mechanics on payroll; cars were constantly coming in and my profits exceeded my expectations. That small shop had turned into a moneymaking machine, and Jim was the only missing part. I hoped that someday soon he would change his perspective and join me for a lifetime ride.

The next day, at my office, I decided to call Mother, and as soon as I picked up the phone, it rang!

"Hello!" I answered.

"Hey! Al, how are you? Long time no speak! You would not believe what I had to go through to get you number. I mean it was terrible, a nightmare!

"Who is this?"

What, you don't recognize me? That's great! I will be a rich man! It is I, Abe! Your uncle."

"Abe, oh! What do you want?"

"We miss you. I miss you; anyway I wanted to invite you to a wedding!"

"What wedding? And who is we?"

"Well, how fast do we forget? You know, we are your family whether you like it or not, and Tom is your dad. Anyway, Tom's nephew is getting married; they ask that you be at the wedding."

"Who is the nephew?"

"His name is Alex. He is a son of Tom's, or maybe he is. Oh, never mind all that; write down the address. You must attend this Saturday at eight p.m."

"Okay, Abe, give me the information, but I can't promise anything. I don't hear from any of you in years, and now you pop out of nowhere with an invitation to the wedding of someone I've never met. Is that crazy or what?"

"Maybe it is, but you must attend."

"So how did you find me, anyway?"

"By chance. Apparently, your shop provides services for some of our limos, so we got to talking and before I knew, I realized it was you! Can you believe the coincidence?"

"Man, when it comes to you, I would believe anything!"

"Take care. I will get back to you."

After all this time, without warning, he appeared. I took down the information; however, going to that wedding was not something I wanted to do.

Afterward, I called my mother. "Hi, Mom. As promised, I am calling you with a sober head."

"Thank you, Al. What are you trying to tell me, that you were drunk for the past four months?"

"No, Mom; that's not it. By the way, I hope you are joking. I just had some issues to resolve! Oh, and Jimmy is back with us!"

"Really? That's great news. I am happy for you."

"What do you mean? And what about Jim? Aren't you happy for him?"

"Look, Al. Jim and I don't get along; we never did! I just wanted for both of you to get together again. You should have seen yourself then. I could not bear looking at you the way you were!"

"What do you mean, the way I was?"

"Al, you were miserable! What mother can stand that?"

"So, you attempt for us to make up was basically for me?"

"Of course; what else?"

"And I thought all this time that you actually cared about Jim. How blind can a person be? Why am I so stupid?"

"Al, what are you talking about?"

"Nothing! Mom, the reason I called is Dad. He is miserable without his family. Please come back; we don't drink any more!"

"Al, are you sure that he is not drinking?"

"Yes, I am sure. So please, what do you say?"

"I was staying with a friend; however, now her husband is coming back from . . . well, it's a long story. Okay, I will come back next week."

"Why next week? Why not now!"

"I can't now. I promised to baby-sit the kids; she is working. I will return when her husband arrives, okay?"

"Okay. Thanks; see you soon."

"Bye, Al; be good!"

That evening I was happier then ever, I could not wait to tell Pap the good news, I also had special surprise just for Jim.

When I walked in, there were both home, Jim was watching TV, and Pap was arranging the table with dinner.

"Hey, people, how are you doing? Pap, I have great news for you!"

"Hi, Al: what is it?"

"Mom is coming back with the girls!"

"Excellent! When?"

"Next week."

"Why next week? And where is she? Leaving like that is completely inappropriate!"

"Pap, be happy for what you have! Besides, don't start any issues because any argument would backfire on you. I'm sure you know what I mean!"

"Excuse me! Anyone? Is there anybody in here? I'm just kidding, I am happy for you, Dad!" Jim said, while walking to the kitchen.

"Jim, I know how you feel about this, so I think we need to move out! Look, I brought newspapers, and have already begun to search. So get ready, because we are starting over! Aren't you excited? I am!"

"Al, hold onto your seat!"

"Why, Jim?"

"Because that bus has already left, and you are not on it!"

"I don't understand? And why I am not on that bus?"

"Well, maybe because you got overexcited at the station! Okay, Al, placing all jokes aside, you are late. I settled down already; my apartment will be complete next week! What a coincidence, huh!

"Jim, why didn't you tell me before?"

"Given that you are and will be happier here, why bother?"

"You presume that I am happy here! You should have asked me!"

"I did not presume anything! Who said that a picture is worth a thousand words? Who was that? What? You don't recall. I know it was you!"

"Your point being?"

"My point is exactly what I just said. You believe in that phrase too! When I look at you, it is obvious that you are happy here with them! It was clear when they were coming here, and is clearer now! You should have seen yourself talking about your mom coming back your eyes were sparkling with joy! Dad, tell him."

"Jimmy, I was against this ordeal from day one, but Al's mother insisted, and you know how persuasive she can be. However, I had no idea you are so against us. Al never said anything to me."

"I am not against you, Dad, or the girls. I just don't get along with Al's mother. Is that a crime?"

"Jimmy, you are holding a grudge and I understand, but life is also about forgiveness. Can't you forgive and forget?"

"No, Pap. Jim doesn't do that. Not too long ago, I said those words to him, but he neglected me and moved along."

"Al, mind your own business, and Dad, I have forgotten everything, and I thank god for amnesia by choice. I do not want to live next to her, and also thank god, for giving me a chance to move on."

"Okay. Guys, let's change the subject before it gets out of hand; knowing the way we all are, we better stop now!" I said, and we all sat down to eat.

We were all quiet through the entire dinner, and it was not because we were eating; mainly, none of us had anything to say.

After dinner, Pap went to his bedroom; Jim and I stayed by the table, looking at the leftovers, circling the plate with the fork, and feeling that something was missing.

"Jim, you know, I think talks like that have a bad influence on me."

"Yeah, I know what you mean. I can relate to that. I also have a cure for that influence!"

"Really, you do? So am I! Tell you what; you go get your medicine and I will bring mine. We'll see if our souls are still connected!"

"You got it!"

While I hustled to our bedroom, Jim rushed out the door. I could only presume he was running to his car. When we both got back, laughter ignited the room. We looked at each other and began laughing hysterically, then set down and both placed a bottle of vodka on the table.

The bottles were same size and same brand.

We talked for hours, as we used to in our previous life, on irrelevant subjects that had no meaning at all. We cherished each other's company, and that's what counted most. When the leftovers were all gone, one bottle was full, and the other half empty. We were tired and decided to call it a night.

I turned to Jim and said, "You will not believe who turned up."

"If you are aware of that fact, why don't you tell me?"

"Okay, smart ass. Abe! Remember him?"

"No shit! What brought him back to you?"

"I do not understand why, but he invited us to some nephew's wedding. He said to be there this Saturday. Will you join me?"

"Sure, why not. I have never seen a wedding before!"

"Okay; then, it's settled. We are going! Goodnight, Jim."

"You too, Al."

I was in a great mood the following morning, as well as for several mornings afterward. Saturday came and my self-esteem did not change, but Jim's, on the other hand, was not as expected.

"Jim, are you ready to go have some fun?"

"Can't assure you of fun, but I will be ready for anything soon!"

"Well, I guess it will do."

We decided to take my car. While driving to the restaurant, we were quiet and I was surprised how comfortable silence could be. When we arrived and walked in, all the guests were already indulging in food and beverages. As it turned out, the time Abe gave me was incorrect, and we missed the ceremony.

After a short tour around the restaurant, we finally found our seats. As I was about to commence dining, Abe showed up and spoiled my appetite.

"Hello, Al! You are a hard man to find!"

"I wish you would disappear!"

"What did you say? Sorry, I could not hear you; that band is very loud."

"I said I'm happy to be here!"

"Oh! Okay, me too! Excuse me, but I need to attend my table."

"Drink and die!"

"What?"

"Go get high!"

"Jim, why are you laughing?" I asked him.

"What? How you expect me to behave? I am between you two!"

"I didn't think you'd hear. Can you believe this smock?"

"You know, I believe in god, and love him, but in cases like this, I wonder what he was thinking while creating someone like Abe!"

"Jim, when Abe was created, god was not around."

"Al, do you see that bottle on the other side of this table? See if you can get it closer to us before it dry's out."

"Okay!"

As I approached the other side of our table, a man sitting next to our bottle decided to refill the glasses, and grabbed our bottle.

Thank god, I got there in time, and said, "Do you drive? A . . . well . . .?"

"You mean, white Ford?"

"Yes, that's it! Well, sorry, but someone ran into it! They told me to go find you!"

He jumped out from his seat and ran toward the exit, and I took our bottle and placed at the right spot.

Then Jim asked me, "Al, what did you say to him?"

"I don't remember. Hey, bottoms up!"

"Yeah! However, somehow I feel that your memory will revive upon his return! Did you see the size of that mountain?"

"No, I didn't! I was looking at the bottle. Besides, he can go get another from the bar."

"Yes he can, but it's not a free bar!"

"What? No way! How was I supposed to know that? Look, I did not mean to steal it!"

"I believe you, Al. Let's just hope that he will!"

"Why!"

"Look! He is coming back! And for some reason, he is not as happy as he was before!"

"Okay, pour me another; let me feel like a thief before the accusation!"

"What do you want me to do? I think both of us can take him!"

"That shot gushed in smoothly. Jim, pour me another!"

"Al, didn't your hear what I said? We can take this guy!"

"Are you crazy? We will kill this wedding. No, it shall not come to that!"

"Hey you! Wiseass! Why did you lie to me?"

"Al, I think he is talking to you! Damn, this guy is bigger than I thought."

"Yes, Jim, I know! Don't interfere!"

"Stop boiling, you may overheat! Why don't you sit down, and calm down."

"Okay, little shit! Stand up while I'm talking to you!"

"Look, giant, I will not dance with you and mess up this party; however, if you want a piece of me, then let's meet outside."

"Okay, let's go."

Then I got up, walked up close to him, and said, "While you walk there, ask yourself the most important question of your life! Are you bulletproof?"

He looked at me, and shouted, "What! Are you nuts! That's bullshit!"

"Did you really think I'd go rounds with you? Are you that stupid? Come on! Let's go, you will find out soon enough!"

I was stunned to see him turn around and walk back to his seat, then look the other way.

"Al, I do not believe my eyes. What did you whisper to him?"

"I told him I was gay! And if he kept it up, I would fall in love with him!"

"Yeah! Right! I don't believe you."

"Go, ask him."

"No way; you have to tell me. I never saw anyone get out of a fight as you did. What was it? Al, tell me!"

"Jim, it's not about what you say; it's all about how you say it!"

"What do you mean?"

"Jim, mean what you say, and make others believe that. I cannot explain the details! Pour me another shot, will you!"

"Al, I'm going to mingle with the crowd; see if there is anyone out there that likes me!"

"Go, be my guest; meanwhile, I will attempt to conclude with this bottle."

"Just make sure that bottle does not conclude with you! See you soon!"

Jim left, and so did everyone else. I was alone by the huge table with food, and a bottle of alcohol. The table was neat; looking at all the cuisines reminded me that I wanted to eat, so I tried food from every plate, repeatedly until, when I could not move anymore.

Then Jim returned. "Al, what did you do?"

"I ate! You all left me; what else was I supposed to do?"

"What a mess, I think we need to leave, Now!"

"I don't think I can walk; you will have to roll me out of here!"

"Okay, come on! You can do it."

As we slowly walked out of that place, I looked around searching for that bull. For some reason, I thought he might be dumb enough to wait for me by the exit, but we had cleared the exit and approached my car.

"Al, give me the keys."

"Why, you think I can't unlock the doors? Think again!"

"Oh, man; let me drive!"

"Why would I? Look, I promise you, I will be extremely careful, and slow! So, don't you worry, get in!"

"That is exactly what worries me; you can get pulled over for that as well, you know!"

"For what?"

"For driving too slow."

"Okay, watch and tell me how I am doing."

We drove halfway home, and I thought I was doing okay. Then, Jim shouted, "Al, let's go! Why are you stopping at the green light?"

"Just being cautious; maybe a drunk driver is now speeding through the red light. If I pass and do not look, he might run into us. Is that what you want?"

"You are dull when you drunk; it's not even funny. Okay, we looked. There is no one there! So now what?"

"I am not dull, and I did not look yet; however, wise guy, know it all, fine! Let's go!"

"Wait! Al. Stop! The light is red now! STOP!"

Afterward, all I remembered is hearing a huge blast!

When I woke up, Jim was right alongside me. I looked around, and saw we were in the center of the intersection. Jim showed signs of life. I shook him up a little, and said, "Jim, are you all right? What happened?"

"I think we got hit; look at this. He ran right into my door. Man, Al, look at your car!"

"Fuck my car! Are you okay?"

"Yes! I'm fine, I think."

"That's the car; look over there! But how did he manage to hit that post?"

"His car probably bounced off us, and then into the traffic light post."

"How could this be? I looked twice at the intersection and never saw him coming! Where the fuck did he came from?"

"Al, you went through the red light; what did you expect?"

"What? It's three o'clock in the morning. Look around you! Red light, green light, who gives a fuck! There is nobody anywhere!"

"Shit, Al, I think I did get hit. My right side is beginning to hurt!"

"Where exactly!"

"At the hip, I think."

"Okay don't move; I'm going to take you to the hospital. Hey look, the person in that car is moving. Thank god he is okay!"

"No hospitals; besides, start her up. We may be stuck here until further notice, you know!"

"Hey, it started!"

"Now! Drive away from the center, and get the hell out of here!"

"Jim, you want me to leave this accident scene?"

"Do you have a better idea? That guy was speeding, but it was your fault anyway, not to mention that you are fueled with alcohol!"

"Shit, I forgot about that."

"So, go! Al, go!"

And so, we drove away. The top speed of my car at the time was ten miles per hour, and we were both grateful for that. Luckily, there were no cops on our way, either. It took forever to get home, but we eventually did get there.

When I parked by our house, it was five in the morning. I went out and circled the vehicle while Jim was crawling his way out through the driver's side. I estimated my damage, and could not believe what I saw.

It looked fine on the driver's side, but the passenger side had caved in to the passenger's seat. Because of that, the front and rear bumpers turned toward each other. That car had turned into a "V" shape.

Jim came next to me, and said, "Well, Al, look at the bright side!"

"What bright side? Look at this car! It's dead!"

"Yeah! But we are alive! Besides, it died with a sign! Think of it as a 'Victory. 'Let's just hope there is enough life in that thing to get to your shop! Anyway, I had a great time, and I am certain I will never forget this night; goodnight and good run!"

Jim went home, and I drove to my shop. The whole time driving I was praying to God, I think he heard me, because I arrived without any problems.

By the afternoon, my car was dismantled into pieces, and around two p.m., my workers pushed a skeleton onto the street. They left it a few blocks away, so now I was relieved.

One issue bothered me, though. I felt bad for the other driver, so I called a few hospitals, tried to find out any emergency intakes due to a traffic accident, but there were none. The next day, I went to the accident location looking for clues, hoping to find something that would lead me to the man trapped in his car. Unfortunately, except for broken glass and black tire marks, there was nothing for me to find.

Eventually, I let that incident pass me, as it never happened at all. Sanitation also helped, when they towed that junk away! I watched them; how smoothly they participated in my conspiracy. They were loading the only evidence to a hit and run case.

After that incident, all and all, things were as they should be, normal. As Jim use to say, from home to work, from work to home, and nothing else. I always wondered why people call that normal. I could only assume, when an act is repeated, without a desire to alter, best too describe it, is normal! And with time, some call it accomplishment!

I, on the other hand, got very annoying with that routine life, and with myself, because I could not come up with something more interesting or exciting.

On my few attempts, I left the station for a few hours; however, on each occasion, I returned to a war zone; customers were screaming at the mechanics and at each other, fighting for their turn in line, and periodically, I could hear, some one yell, "Where the fuck is Al?" So, my accomplishment became my cage. I was in a prison of my own creation, where the only time I had to myself was close to bedtime when I was too tired to do anything else.

I had no idea that self-employment could be so unsatisfying, it was not about working hours, mainly, the hassle and problems which I had to resolve on a daily basis.

Clients and their needs, creditors and their demands, suppliers and our needs, handling state regulations and laws, employees and the payroll, the business books, myself and the monthly rent. All those matters and more were unfamiliar to me, and now, when I was acquainted with them, I did not want them anymore. Besides, I was making much more money before, with much less responsibility.

Going back to my prior doings was out of the question I needed to settle down, and the only way I knew how was by adding a few drops of joy to my daily routine.

So whenever I was bored, there was always a bottle of joy on standby in my drawer, and after a small dose, my surroundings would gain color, and I walked around the shop with a smile on my face. At first, no one at the shop could understand my sudden mood shift. I could see it in their eyes, but, seeing me angry in the mornings and then shifting into a fairy after lunch was something everyone got use to very quickly. Soon enough, my workers were all waiting for me to get in the office, and when I did, I would soon after walk out as a different man.

One morning, my best mechanic told me, "You know, boss, we would like to replace morning coffee with lunch."

"Jose, I know what you mean! So, you basically are asking me to have my coffee with alcohol, is that it?"

"No, boss; there must be something else to calm your nerves."

"I will think about it! Meanwhile go back to work, and make some real profit today. I don't get anything for oil changes and brake jobs!"

"You see, boss! That's what I mean. How can I bring in additional work when there is none?"

"You are the mechanic! Find some! If there are no problems, then create one! Do you expect to get paid by the end of the week? Where do you suppose I will get that money? So, you get the idea! Don't you?"

"Yes, I think I do."

"Good. I sure hope so!"

Soon after our conversation, the next thing I noticed were clients coming in for estimate requests on major repair work, so I approached the head mechanic again.

"Jose, is that car in need of a replacement of the rear end?"

"No, but you give him cheap price, we remove, paint, and put back!"

"What the fuck are you talking about? Why would you paint it?"

"Listen, boss, you said make more money! So, I make! Okay, tell him three hundred and fifty dollars. We remove, paint, and put back!"

Then I realized what Jose was talking about, it was a scam! But it's only a scam when people know about it, so, I went ahead with Jose's plan.

Afterward, our repair shop slowly transformed into a paint shop. We always provided the needed services, but on any given day, good parts were painted anyway.

Because no car departed with the problem it arrived with, clients were always happy, and I felt a relief, because now, billing and other expenses were easily paid, and at the end of each week, I had a profit beyond my expectations.

Soon enough, that station converted to a gold mind; so now, there was more money than I actually needed, and the next step was to acquire a partner. That would give me free time whenever I needed, and the only candidate I could think of was Jim, of course. Who else would I be able to trust the way I trusted him?

One evening at home, I decided to approach him with a lifetime proposition. "Hey, Jim; how was your day?"

"Same shit on a different day!"

"That saying belongs to plumbers, unless you're into toilets now and did not tell me!"

"No, of course not; why do you ask?"

"I have a proposition for you! Let's work together! My shop is bringing more money now than I can handle, and with you there, we would most likely double it. The best part about it, each of us would only work three days a week! Can you imagine that?"

"Al, there you go again. I thought we spoke about this, and I said NO! Case closed. Why do you bring this up again?"

"Because, back then, that place was a ghost town and now it's a gold mine!"

"No, thanks; somehow, I will manage on my own!"

"Really; and why is that? Is it because of what happened between us before? I thought you forgave me; apparently you are still mad at me."

"No, Al, I am definitely not mad at you! I just have some matters on my mind, so please, let me enjoy my drink; plus, some peace and quiet will not hurt either! So, no thank you! I am happy where I am!"

"You have not been happy since the day you came back; you are not the same, not to mention that we hardly talk! Hey, do me a favor. While you're in the kitchen, pour me some of the mix you are drinking! "

"Okay, here you go! Let's drink; please I have nothing to say. Is that a problem?"

While he handed me that glass, I saw bruises all over his face.

"No Jim, I don't have a problem. However, I think you do! Besides, no man would refuse such an opportunity, and I am not asking for any investment! So, what's wrong? Tell me; maybe I can help."

"Al, for the last time! Get me off your list and find someone else!"

"Okay then, tell me, Jim. Whom did you fight? Also, can I see the other guy?"

"No one to see. I was bitten."

"What? What happened?"

"It all started because of one woman; what a bitch she turned out to be!"

"Is that the one you introduced me to; the one in the nightclub?"

"Yes, her! You were right about her! And about the step away part.

"So, what happened?"

"I went to that club again, this time with a guy that I know. We had a few drinks, and then, when she came in, it all started."

"Go on!"

"Well, she gave me that look, you know, so I approached her; we hugged and began talking."

"That's nice. Wait; don't tell me. When you wanted some, she kicked the shit out of you, and you could not hit her back. Am I right?"

"No, you fool. We were having fun, actually, until her boyfriend came in."

"I knew it! However, what is the big deal? You were just talking, or were you?"

"Yes, we were just talking, but then that bitch jumped into his arms. I could not believe my eyes! I don't know what that bitch told him; however, it was not good. Because, right afterward he came up to me and said, 'Let's go outside; we need to talk', so I went."

"Why didn't you leave? I told you before to avoid those confrontations, only because they are useless!"

"I did not do anything. When I got out of there, some guys jumped me. I didn't have a chance to respond! So, the results you see on me, but what really pissed me off is that one of them was a cop!"

"How do you know that?"

"Nick, the guy that was with me, told me. He knows that place well."

"So where was your friend, Nick? Why didn't he help you?"

"He was there, and he said he could not interact because of his probation."

"Some friends you have, Jim. Hey, forget about this! No big deal!

"Don't mark my friends; you don't know them."

"You are right! I'm sorry! Then let me be there for you; tell me what you need."

"Al, you can't help me, and if you could, I would never accept it."

"Why? What's the big deal? I hope you are not planning revenge!"

"It doesn't concern you, so relax; and let me relax."

"You know, Jim, your attitude is beginning to irritate me. I don't know why you are pushing me away! But because of that, I am very disappointed with you. I thought we were as one; apparently, I was wrong! Let me have some of what you are drinking again."

I took my drink and went to the other room; while sipping my drink, I glanced at Jimmy as he was standing in the kitchen. A strange smirk appeared on his face. He looked at me and began smiling.

His behavior awoke a peculiar feeling deep in my soul. By that smile on his face, I could tell that something terribly wrong was about to happen.

At that time, his stubbornness did not allow me to talk to him, so I decided to put this aside for now and resolve the matter in the morning, after our dad came home, I went to my bed.

I plunged into deep sleep, when suddenly, that feeling was broken.

"Al, Al. Wake up."

"Who is this? Go away!"

"Al, it's your dad; please wake up. Wake up now!"

"What? What the hell do you what from me?"

"Jimmy . . . Jimmy is dead!"

I woke up, sat on the bed, looked at my dad, and saw he was in a tremendous panic. I thought I was dreaming, and then, those words ran through my mind, "Jimmy is dead."

"Pap, wait a minute. Tell me, what did you say?"

"Jimmy; Jimmy is dead."

"Stop saying that; are you out of your mind? He is here! Sleeping! Look!"

Then I looked at the bed next to mine, and there was nobody there. I looked at the clock; it was five in the morning and my father was standing in front of me, crying.

I was far away from reality. I did not want to believe what I heard; it could not be, not Jimmy. I just saw him, and he was smiling. Wait a minute; that smile. I remember that smile. Damn!

"Pap, where is Jimmy?"

"Outside, in his car."

I scurried outside with nothing on but my underwear. As I rushed toward his car, my pace began to slow down, and with the final steps, I approached slowly. When I approached the vehicle, my feet were shaking. I felt as if the ground beneath me were collapsing. I could hardly walk anymore, and I could hardly stand.

I have never been so scared in my life, walking the last few steps and hoping that he would not be there, and that was all a mistake, a misunderstanding that my father had dreamed.

I then turned around, looked at the house, and saw our dad standing there by the entrance, holding his head and crying. That is when veracity had pulled me down to earth. I turned back and completed my last steps toward the end of the road, where Jimmy, my soul mate, my only true friend, the only person I trusted and cherished in this life, was now lying in his car, dead.

I could not open the door nor could I look at him anymore. Slowly, I took myself into the house, sat on our couch, picked up the bottle that was on the coffee table, and proceeded to guzzle right from it.

"Al, stop drinking; we have to do something."

"To do . . . ? There is nothing to do, anymore. Call the cops if you like."

The cops were already by the car. Someone heard gunshots, and called them. I was sitting on the couch like a living corpse, and did not care about anything anymore.

One of the detectives approached me. "Are you Al?"

"Yes I am."

"Your father said to talk to you."

"Okay, can you tell me how my brother died?"

"Of course, we have concluded this case as a suicide."

"I don't believe it! He would not kill himself; somebody else shot him."

"Sir, please listen to me. There were two shots. First, he shot himself in the stomach, and then in the head."

"When did you ever see a suicide that involved two bullets? That's a bunch of bullshit!"

"I'm afraid it's not; and I have seen it before. Some suicides take more than one bullet."

"Well, I have never heard about it, and I will never believe that. Somebody killed my brother, and it's your job to find out who it is."

"Sir, this case is closed. I am sorry for your loss, but there is nothing else we can do."

Cops circled around the house for a few moments, and then took off; meanwhile, I drank that whole bottle of vodka and was clear and sober. It had no effect on me, just as if I was drinking water. So I went to the kitchen to get another. While pouring myself a shot, I saw a glass on the counter with leftover liquid and signs of white powder beside it.

Jimmy was drinking that same glass from last night. I did not want to taste it, but it became clear to me as to why he would have that mixture. He was looking to get high, so that meant he knew of the morning engagement, and probably predicted the consequences as well.

Two days later, my mother, and sister arrived.

"Oh, Al! Poor baby! How are you?'

"Hi, Mom; hey guys, good to see you!"

We all stood in the hallway hugging, afterward; the girls went to their room.

"Mom, let's go sit in the living room."

"So what happened?"

"I don't know, Mom. I really don't. One evening he was sitting here, and the next morning he was gone."

"Didn't he tell you anything? Maybe he had some issues."

"He had some problems with one girl, and that's all."

"This is very odd! Dad told me what the police concluded; do you think he was capable of such an act?"

"You know I don't agree with this. Besides, they closed the investigation before it was open; now, how is that possible?"

"I don't know, Al; however, I am worried about you!"

"No need; worry about your girls. I'm fine!"

"I can see why. When are you going to stop drinking? And what about your business? You can't neglect it like that; get yourself together. Life goes on!"

"Easier said than done! I called the shop a few times a day; they are doing fine without me."

"Dad said that today is the funeral. At least stop drinking for now!"

"I'll be fine, Mom. You shall see. Besides, for the past few days, alcohol has had no effect on me."

So came the afternoon and we all went to his funeral. It was odd to see so many unknown people arrived, people I had never seen or knew of their existence before. Through the whole memorial service, I was standing there, colder than ice, and did not drop one tear. Maybe because, deep inside, I still did not believe he was gone. However, afterward, when we came home, it was obvious that Jimmy's ordeal on the earth was now over.

Jimmy's friends followed us home, including his girlfriend, who I did not know. They were sitting with my family, talking and crying. As I watched them from the side, saturated by helplessness, I became furious.

"Al, can I talk to you?"

"Sure, Mom"

"I wanted to ask you; maybe it is time for you to leave New York; come with me to Philadelphia, I don't want you staying here."

"I don't feel like being here, either, but I won't leave dad."

"Okay, move out with him. We will get a bigger place and live together again. What do you say?"

"It sounds nice, but I thought you don't get along with him. How would we live together?"

"I have spoken to him; he said that this time it will be different, and I think he means it. Maybe the circumstances have played some part in that."

"Okay, Mom, I hope you are right."

"Also, I have noticed a house for rent, not too far from where I stay with the girls. I would like you to see it."

"Sure, I will."

"You need a fresh start! A new beginning will take your mind off this terrible occurrence."

At this junction, I put off all of my duties, and later, I announced the station for sale. When we went to Philadelphia to look at the house, my mother was right. I did reconcile with myself, and felt a little better. The house was great and so was the neighborhood. Without much consideration, I paid the deposits needed and the house was ours. My mother with sisters had stayed in their apartment, and we went back to New York to finalize my ordeals and closures.

When I reentered our house, it felt like the funeral parlor; no way could I stay there with a sober head, so every day after work, I would come home and drink; after dinner, of course.

My drinking would continue up to a certain point. I usually described that condition as "fuck with me and see what happens," so upon reaching that "I don't' give a shit" state, I would get in the car and go visit all of

Jimmy's acquaintances, including the people he worked with at the gas station.

I tried to seek out any information leading to his death, but unfortunately, I always came empty handed. I wanted find that asshole Jim had told me about, and give him a little taste of his own medicine. I cursed myself for not being involved in Jim's incident. As a result, I had no clue of who that guy was, and what happened afterward.

I only knew that Jimmy was committed to his promises. Thinking rationally, I could come up with only two possible alternatives relating to his death. First, Jim visited that club again, and that dirty cop, had received what was coming to him. Second, Jimmy opened a delivery package, and the result of that action we both knew the day we started.

In both cases, those people were connected, and I would never find any clues that could explain Jim's death; that would also explain why the cops closed the case so quickly. But I will never believe in a suicide conclusion. Somebody killed my brother, and now I have lost him forever.

He was so young, too young to leave life so soon. Also, he left nothing behind. There is nothing on the planet that states Jimmy lived; that part came to be the most upsetting, and horrified me from then on.

After all, he was a good person, always appearing to help. Rain, or shine, needed or not, he would be next to me. He was very reliable, and never said no, even when he wanted to say that the most.

Night after night, those thoughts circled my mind as I snooped around Manhattan, while intoxicated, of course, visiting that club on many occasions, and not once confronting that bitch or her boyfriend. It was as if the earth had suddenly swallowed them both, and nobody knew of their whereabouts.

I also visited the gas station where Jim used to work, and sat down with his replacement. He was acquainted with Jim, so we talked, and talked, until one of those nights, a man appeared, wearing dark dirty clothing. He looked homeless to me.

He walked into the office and said, "Good evening, gentleman! Is Jim here? "

My body commenced to shiver. I stood up, walked closer toward him, and asked, "Maybe I can help you!"

"No, I don't think so."

Then he slowly began to move backward, and I proceeded after him. When he turned around and attempted to run, I grabbed him from behind, and pinned him down to the ground.

"Tell me, how do you connect to Jim?"

"None of your business, get off me man!"

"The hell I will. I will stay here until you tell me!"

"What's it to you?"

"He was my brother!"

As I said that, he swiveled out from me, and got up on his feet.

I stood up, while holding him by the coat.

"What do you mean was?" he said.

"He is dead! Tell me how you know him!"

He stared me in the eyes with a frighten gaze. I could tell he was shocked, and scared at the same time; then he broke free, leaving his coat in my hand, and ran away.

"Hey! Wait! I just wanted to talk to you!" I shouted.

Part way down the block, he stopped. "Give me back my coat!"

"Listen, I don't want your stinking coat. Just tell me what I want to know. If you don't, I will rip it into pieces."

"You don't understand. I don't know give it back to me."

"You don't know? Then why did you run from me?"

"Okay, motherfucker, wait here. I'll be back."

The guy left, and somehow I did not believe he would ever return, so I went back into the office, to think this through.

When I walked in, I heard a scream.

"Hey! Come out; let's see what you've got!"

"Al, maybe I should call the cops. I don't like were this is leading," the gas attendant said.

"Don't worry, and don't call anyone!"

I stepped out, and there he was, standing there as promised, holding a board in his hand.

I quickly went toward him. "You really think that two by four will help you? Think again, you piece of shit!" Then I walk closer to him, calculating what my next move should be.

Then unexpectedly, he began to walk backward, raising the timber up higher. He shouted, "I will hit you with it! Don't think I wouldn't."

"I'll take it from you, and beat the living shit out of you with it!

"Okay! Okay, stop. What do you want?"

"I told you, some information, that's all! How did you know my brother? What can you tell me about him?"

"Look, I was buying some stuff from him, that's all!

"No, man, be frank with me. That's not all."

"Okay, he was not himself lately, and the last time, there was this guy screaming his guts out at Jim, and I came close. I recognized him!"

"So, who was he?"

"I can't tell you, man; all I can say s that the whole underworld knows him, and no one, and I mean no one, would fuck with him or talk about him. Besides, I would not tell you even if I knew!"

"Why not? Jim was you friend, wasn't he?"

"Yeah, but you said he was dead! And I don't have a death wish! Do you?"

"So, that may be the reason I always confront a dead end!"

"Maybe; or, maybe it's even beyond your approach. Now give me my coat back."

I gave him back his coat, got in the car, and drove away. On the way home, I realized that this task exceeded my abilities, and most likely, I would never reveal Jim's death.

I was never aware of how organized crime works. I had only seen it in the moves. It did not scare me, only the fact that I was helpless and lacking leads. That was the main reason for me to stop investigating this matter, although it was difficult let it slide and do nothing about it. It was even more painful to carry the loss I inherited for my entire life.

I came home, somehow reached my bed, and passed out. I slept for over a day, and it helped me to recoup and get back to my life routine.

Concerning my business, I accepted the first offer; some car service company decided to buy my station. Though the deal was below market value, they paid in cash and we completed our transaction in two days.

So I purchased a new car. I thought a white Trans Am would somehow cheer me up, and my family and I moved to Philadelphia. The year was 1989, and we were seeking a new beginning with hope to leave the past behind. Except for Jim's car, because that vehicle meant a lot to me, and I cherished it most.

However, hope got me nowhere, so it did not take long for my mind to fast track backward into my past and stay there. I had no work, was futureless and depressed. On any given day, I saw no bright side to my situation. Selling the repair shop was my only comfort. It brought lots and lots of money into my pockets, and I became a wealthy man.

Our new house was huge; three bedrooms, two living rooms, a big kitchen, and a greenhouse that was attached to the rear of the house, with a walkway toward the backyard, and the backyard was the size of basketball field I had one living room and a bedroom all to myself.

A few days later, that living room had transformed into a great bar, with alcohol and cocktails, all to my desire. There I was, sitting on the same couch, holding a glass of liquor, watching a big screen TV with a hundred and sixty channels. I was unemployed, with plenty of time to spare and nothing to do. Pointlessly spending my time was a new experience for me.

At first, I felt uselessness, but then I found it enjoyable, because in the mornings, we would enjoy ourselves with a fresh cup of Turkish coffee, then my dad will go to work, the girls went off to school, Mom would go back to whatever she was doing, and I would switch to a drink with a movie.

My favored blend was B52, an awesome mixture of Kahlua, Irish Cream, and Grand Marnier. After a few drinks, I would go out of the house and into the world of freeloading. Scanning the shopping mall became my preferred journey, and being acquainted with tasty women became a hobby of mine. It was the best part of it all.

My definition of an appetizing woman was not that simple. She had to be tall and slender, walk on long, slim legs, possess beautiful eyes (the color did not matter). She also had to have beautiful, soft, pure skin, And a harmoniously proportioned face, a long, thin neck, a nice figure with long, thin arms, and long, thin fingers. Everything else was meaningless, although I always preferred brunettes. I always wondered why some people said that I was very selective.

I had not dated anyone, excluding Victoria, of course, so achieving success upon encountering a woman came as a surprise to me. Although I never took them seriously, my outlook completely deviated from Victoria's perspective, and all that she represented. Now, I was attracted to enigmatic and somehow different women. They became a threat to me, and I only saw them as a sex object, nothing less and nothing more.

Evidently, I was a handsome man. When I looked at a woman, in most cases, I would get her attention. Shortly after that, I would find myself under her skirt.

Actually, it was easy. I would come up to a woman and ask her, "Excuse me, would you have change for a dollar?" on some occasions. If her response was no, then I knew she was not interested, and probably had a boyfriend. Who cares!

However, most of the time, they would respond, and say, "Maybe I do; let me see." Then she would look into her purse, and that was all I needed. While she was looking, I would begin a conversation, and if lucky, by trying to help her, I would accidentally knock the purse from her hands, either way we would be acquainted, and the rest was simple, I just went with the flow.

Only once I felt embarrassed, that was when I tried to meet a woman while driving. As it turned out, that is a bad idea, or maybe it was just bad luck. I stopped at the traffic light. It was red. On my right, there was this gorgeous blonde-haired person. I rolled down the window; her window was open and so I asked her, "Excuse me, miss."

As she looked at me, I babbled first thing that come up in my mind. "Can you please tell me how I should get to Ocean Parkway?" Only afterward did I realize I was in Philadelphia; nevertheless, I hit a one in a million answer.

"You need to be in Brooklyn. Do you know where you are? What kind of drugs are you taking?" she said, laughing.

At first, I was speechless, and then I said, "Thank you," and took off.

Boy, what are the odds? Moreover, did I feel stupid? I just wished to be so lucky in the lottery.

After that incident, encounters while driving were over for me, so I kept on using my charm at the malls; why change what works.

I was successful most times, except for one little factor. For some reason, they always wanted to continue the relationship, and sometimes, even commitment. In that situation all I could do, is run and escape, like a mouse breaking away from the sight of a cat.

Shortly after, through my mother's friends, I met a nice and good-looking girl. She was nineteen but looked like a woman to me. We began to hang out, and I met with her friends, including her best friend, whose name was Avalon.

She was so beautiful, I was attracted to her from the first time I saw her, but there was a problem; she had a boyfriend.

I wanted her so much it hurt, so one day we all went out to a nightclub. I asked her to a dance, which, by the way, was a bad idea, because I didn't know what to do on the dance floor.

Tension took over my thoughts and I was helpless around her. I could not help myself and stared at her while we walked to the dance floor. I stumbled on the way and fell, but I was okay. We got up on the dance floor. I did not pay any attention to the music. I wanted to feel her in my arms, and when I did, she felt great.

"Al, why are you not moving?" she asked.

"Oh, I thought I was," I said, and then I slowly began to move. "How is this?"

"Al, please dance to the music. Listen to the rhythm and merge with it."

"I am merging with you! Great song!"

"Al, this is not a slow dance. Let me go. Try to jump around."

"I don't feel like letting you go; most of all, I don't feel jumping around like those monkeys. I hear a slow dance, so dance with me, please!"

"I won't. We look foolish. Let me go, and I mean it."

"Are you embarrassed?"

"Yes, I am; let me go, please."

"Okay; give me your number and I will let go! I promise."

"What for?"

"I'd like to talk to you. There is something I need to ask you."

"Why don't you ask me now?"

"I can't; it's too loud in here."

"Okay, let me go. I will give you my number later, I promise. Now please let go. My boyfriend is watching us; he may get the wrong idea."

"I hope he gets diarrhea!"

"What did you say?"

"I said, he seems to be under anesthesia; is he always dull like this?"

"Yes, well sometimes." She then began to laugh.

"Okay, let's go, but I'm going to hold you to your promise."

She kept her promise, and I received her number. I was also dating her best friend, so I knew she could not be giving me a phony number. Besides, I did not give her a clue of my interest, which was strictly in her. Her best friend, on the other hand, would be very disappointed, since she liked me and thought we had a future.

The next day, I woke up at noon. I rolled down into my bar, enjoyed myself with few drinks, and that is how my days began. First thing I did afterward was I called Avalon.

"Hello, gorgeous; how did you sleep?"

"Fine, thank you for asking, and how was your night?"

"From the time you give me your number, my night turned to heaven. I thought about you all night. I could hardly sleep."

"Greg, is that you? Who is this?"

"Excuse me; I thought you were Avalon."

"I'm her mother, and who are you? Do you have a name?"

"Yes, I'm sorry. My name is Al, and may I please speak to Avalon."

"Hold on, Al." I heard in the background, "Avalon, who Al.?"

"Oh, Mother, he is just a friend. We went out a few times. I mean, he is Janet's boyfriend and we all went out together."

"I hope Greg knows about him."

"Mom, what do you think of me? Of course, he knows. I just told you, we were all together, and Greg was there too."

"Okay, here, take the phone. This Al guy is waiting."

"Hi, Al; sorry about that. My mom is very nosy."

"Hey, don't worry about it. So, what are you doing now?"

"Nothing in particular; why do you ask?"

Then I realized if she was asking me "why," my chances were growing. "Because I want to see you. I need to talk to you."

"Look, Al. We can talk on the phone. I can't go with you anywhere, and you know that. What would people think?"

"Look, I like you and I know you like me, too, so split up with that sleepy puss boyfriend of yours and let's go out. Be with me as I want to be with you."

"Are you out of your mind?"

"Maybe, but unlike you. I am frank. You don't love him, why stay with him? Leave him; otherwise, both of us will live in regret."

"Al, why would you say something like that?"

"Because it's true and I'm right about it, so let me pick you up. And go tell Mom there is no more Greg."

"Let me think about it. I will call you back."

Well, from that moment I knew she would be mine. "Avalon, don't think, because it will only create confusion in you. Act on your feelings. They don't lie. Bye for now."

I knew she would call me back, and in less than an hour, she did, then we went out again.

Avalon was different from other women I had met, and my time with her became extremely enjoyable. I really liked her, or at least, I thought so.

It is strange how the physical attraction that leads to intimate encounters somehow slowly fades away. No matter how hot I feel for someone, after sex, she seems to be just another practice toy.

The odd part about some of the woman I met is that they thought that by postponing sex, somehow my intimate urge would transform into greater respect, and I would develop a strong, deeper feeling that would eventually lead to a commitment. What a bunch of crap. The longer she made me wait, the more eager I would become for sex and because of that, sex would become the only agenda on my list and nothing else. That is why, in our encounters, I was always emotionally aroused did not think of anything but sex. Most of the time, I would not even listen to her. Of course, I never showed it.

Therefore, after we were intimate I was no longer interested in her. That was it, eagerness disappeared, and my only memory of her, was the sex we had, which on most occasions was not that good.

The worst memories were with the most beautiful women. Weird but true, because, they would lay there just like a sheet of plywood, and never participate. Maybe it was a beauty thing they inherit through life, thinking, "I'm beautiful, so you work and let me enjoy myself."

By no means did I give it much thought. It is hard to figure out women. Actually, that task is impossible, and those who think they have? Man, they are in for one hell of a ride to a self-hurt road, where the final destination is always disappointment.

Avalon was no different from the others. She made me wait so long that, afterward, she wasn't appealing to me, and I stopped calling her.

Regardless, she periodically showed up at my door. "Hey, Al, how are you?"

"Hi, Avalon, what are you doing here?"

"I came to see you; are you busy?"

"Yes, I am, actually."

"May I come in? I missed you, and you stopped calling me. Why?"

"Like I said, I was busy."

She went in. I poured myself a drink. We talked for a while, and I asked her to leave.

"Al, I don't want to go; please let me stay."

"No, you must go, and we have to stop seeing each other; do you understand?"

"But I love you."

"And I don't, so leave now."

"Do you remember when you told me about your feelings?"

"I lied; now go."

"Al, if I leave now, you shall never see me again; and I mean it."

"Well, that is my intention; now get the fuck out of here."

She left. Of course, all broke up and crying. Me? I did not possess the slightest remorse whatsoever.

The egotism took over me, and I was passing the days carelessly. My life had become meaningless and tomorrow was pointless for me.

Sitting as usual on the couch, with a cup full of alcohol, it was nine o'clock and I was dying of boredom, so I decided to go out and cruise around the city. After hours of cruising and looking, I finally ended up in a club. Judging by the women sitting there, I came to like that place, so I was determined to stay.

When I set myself down next to two lovely women, one of them asked me "Are you new to this town?"

"Yes I am; how did you know?"

"By the look on your eyes, it is obvious."

"Very impressive; I'm from New York."

"I thought so; you New Yorkers have that deep scanning gaze!"

"Do we? I have never noticed that on others!"

"That's because you are used to it; what are you drinking?"

"B52; Why? Do you have something better to offer?"

"Actually, I do. Why don't you try this?"

"What is that? No offense, but it looks like mud."

She then laughed, and placed her glass into my hand.

"Come on, bottoms up!"

Therefore, I did. While finishing it to the last drop, I could not stop staring at her legs they were in perfect shape.

"Was it good?" she asked.

"Actually, no. I did not get the flavor. Tell me, what was that?"

"Never mind! Hey, Erica, give him a taste of your golden mix!" She referred to the girl sitting next to her.

"Try this, its much softer and not so dry."

"You know, I think that is enough. I am not a big fan of mixed liquor."

"Have to try everything once, so go ahead maybe you will like it."

"Talking about trying everything once, let's try each other; maybe you will like it, too."

"Okay, but you first!"

Watching as she was crossing her legs from one side to the other, how could I resist such temptation?

Then she said, "Good boy."

I heard her repeat that twice. There was an echo in my ears, then suddenly I began to see double.

Then there were four of them. They were laughing and pointing at the bartender. Unexpectedly, my head hit the counter top and I was out cold.

I woke up and found myself lying on the bench next to the parking lot. I was dizzy and confused. I got up and tried to get back in, but the guards would not let me, so as weak as I was, I went to look for my car.

Searching for my keys, I discovered that my wallet was gone, and all my money. I could not see straight, so pushing on the key chain alarm button was the only rational thing to do. And it worked; my car responded. I was relieved when I got to it.

However, I was in bad shape, and driving was out of the question, so I decided to sleep it off.

When I opened my eyes, it was dawn, I felt better and commenced to drive. Somehow, driving back home was easy. The roads were familiar, especially the narrow road right before the sharp turn to our house. Nevertheless, without warning, I felt nauseous and was about to faint, but did not. I could not move my legs or my arms. I was numb, helplessly observing the situation as my car glided from the center of the road and into the parked cars along the side.

For half the block, I hit every car on the right, then for some reason, the car shifted smoothly to the left, and I hit every car along the way, on that side of the block.

Then when I reached that sharp turn, I tried with all of my strength to turn the steering wheel, but for some reason it did not move. I was bearing straight into the fence of a residential house, and then I fainted.

A loud noise woke me. I looked up and could not believe my eyes; a group of people surrounded the car. Some of them were cutting through the doors, and others cutting the roof off, while I was lying on both seats.

It did not take long for them to pull me out of there, and when they did, I saw my car wrapped around a huge tree. There was nothing left of it, and if that was not enough, firefighters had cut it into pieces.

All I could think at that moment was, Thank god for that tree, otherwise I would probably drive into and through the entire house.

They placed me on the grass. One man approached me, and asked, "Are you okay?"

"I think so, yes."

"What happened here? How did you end up on my lawn? Did you see the turn?"

"No I did not. I fainted and don't know why."

"Well, sit here."

Then a cop came, and stood next to me. He said, "Have you been drinking?"

"No sir. I don't drink."

"Then explain what happened."

"I fell asleep. I don't know why."

"Stand up. Let's go to that ambulance there."

"There is no need. I feel fine."

"You feel fine; however, we need to take a blood sample. You may stick to that story, but I don't buy it, so let's go."

"No, I refuse, and will not give you any samples I'm allergic to needles."

"I don't care. Look at the damage you have caused. You will go now." Suddenly, he snatched my wrist and attempted to twist it backward.

I broke free, and punched his jaw. He hit the ground, then, out of nowhere, two police officers jumped me from behind, pulled me down, and when they turned me over, I felt handcuffs on my wrists.

I ended up in jail; it was around three o'clock when my parents came for me.

They released me, and on my way out, one of the officers stopped me and asked, "Do you remember what happened and why you are here?"

"Honestly, I don't"

"Look at that officer's face, those marks on his lips. That is your doing; don't you remember?"

"No, I am sorry, but I don't remember anything."

"I don't believe you. Anyway, be grateful to your parents; they are good people, so no one will press charges. If it was not for them, you would be on your way to prison; instead you are going home."

"Thank you, officer."

"Don't thank me, thank them. Do you know what puzzles me the most? You car was smashed into a chunk of steel! Total loss is too soft of a word to describe that vehicle. However, they pulled you out of there with not a scratch. Now how do you suppose this is possible?"

While he was waggling his head, I slowly walked toward the exit, and finally into my parents' car.

The whole way back, they gave me lectures that I never heard before, and the most memorable came from my dad.

"Thank God you are okay, but that is not over for you."

"What do you mean?"

"Tomorrow, you will go and meet with every car owner whose car you damaged; you will apologize and offer a settlement to every one of them."

"Why? They all have insurance. Let them file a claim, and that's the end of it."

"No, you will offer them a payment for the damage you caused, and let them decide. You will also go to the owner of the house with the same attitude."

"Okay, I will."

The next day I did exactly that; however, nobody wanted to file a claim, so I spent thousands to repair all the vehicles and the fence that I drove into. Because of the enormous expense, that ordeal stayed with me for a very long time.

Two years went by; two years of nothing to do but drink and club. I was partying like there was no tomorrow. Through those years, the only worthy friend that come across my life path was my dog, which I named Max.

When I bought him, the documents claimed he was a white German Sheppard. In reality, Max was an exceptional gorgeous white Siberian wolf.

However, similar to me, he was young and ignorant, so one day he ran away, and after a few hours, he strolled back home, all beat up and worn out. We figured that a car had hit him; there was no other rational explanation.

As a result, Max developed a brain tumor, which shortly after, evolved into epilepsy. Watching him occasionally stumble in despair with epileptic seizures was painfully frightening. With time and medication, the seizures gradually faded, and after a while the rarely struck him again.

Max was the most exceptionally smart character I ever knew; he would always look for a way to comfort me and always be by my side.

One day, I found myself broke. I had no money and no job. At same time, pap was workless, and could not find any fitting position in Philadelphia, so he decided to go back to Brooklyn, for work search, and I had no alternative but to join him.

Pap had it easy, do to his skilled hands; once again, he got a job as storefront assembler, and I tugged along as his assistant.

Tony, the owner, was satisfied with Pap's performance, so during the day, work was quite effortless. However, at night, we slept on the floor in a shop, and there was no shower, no bar, and no TV; only a bottle of vodka and Chinese food, which we ate so often of, I thought it would gush out my ears.

Fortunately for me, that lasted only one month, because afterward, we rented a house and the whole family was on the move again, back to Brooklyn.

I was back in my old surroundings, and it felt great, except this time I had no money and no acquaintances, only a shitty job with small potential. I saw prospects in Tony's business because he performed construction work with aluminum and glass; there was a lot of money in that field. I heard that some of his clients did not pay him in a timely way, and others did not pay him at all.

However, for some reason, my eyes focused on a young woman sitting at his office. She periodically watched me while I walked past the office, and I was hiding my interest in her, looking away. Then, she began to enter our work area, pretending as she walked in to find something of hers that she had lost. I neglected her and walked away into the backyard, leaving her to resolve any matters with Pap.

We followed that routine practically on a daily basis. I could recognize her walk by the sound from her heels. One day, I decided to approach Tony with my idea, and when I heard my favorite heel touch the tile, I looked around, and there she was.

She was a beauty, slowly walking toward me, staring straight into my eyes. When she came up closer, I faced her, then passed her by and went to the office, and I took the liberty of introducing myself to Tony as a collector.

"Tony, I need to talk to you."

"Okay, what's on your mind?"

"Your business, actually; I could not help but notice that some of your clients don't pay you."

"Is that a fact? And how did you notice that?"

"Come on, everyone knows about it; especially when you have those phone calls and scream, 'Where is my balance, I want my money.' Am I right?"

"Okay, let's say that you are. Do you know somebody that can help me with this issue?"

"Yes I do. Me!"

"What? You have to be kidding me!"

"Why? Is it because I am young? Never judge a book by its cover. Give me a chance plus 20 percent, then you shall see the results."

He mulled over my proposal, walking back, forward, and around the office for a few minutes, the finally he replied, "Okay, I will try you for 10 percent, but remember, if anything goes wrong, you are out of here, and I don't know you!"

"Of course; make me a list. That's all I need"

From that day, I was self-employed again, and I hoped to earn large amounts, because the outstanding balances were quite large. In my perspective, the bigger the balance, the better was my day.

The first company I went to was Korean, and so was the owner, I walked into the office and asked to speak with the owner.

"And who should I say is asking" That was the secretary.

"His lost and found friend," I stated.

"Okay, please wait here."

When she returned, she said, "There must be a mistake. What's your name?"

I burst into his office and closed the door behind me, and saw a fat man sitting at his table, enjoying his lunch.

"Who are you?" He mumbled with his mouth full of the crap he was eating.

"Calm down, fat man. I don't want you to choke yourself!"

"What do you want?"

"See that list? You are on the top; time to pay your debt! What did you think would happen?"

"Look! I will settle this with Tony, not you; get out!"

"Tony passed this task to me, so I am not going anywhere! However, you can call for help and guess what? I will not stop you! There is no assault here, so I will see you again very soon. Only next time, I will bring a few of my friends to your house! Please, use you imagination for what might be next!"

He looked at me and reached for his checkbook. This one was easier than I anticipated. Twenty-two thousand dollars. That's what he owed Tony. My cut was twenty-two hundred, very satisfying after a long break from work.

However, the next individual was very obnoxious, and really made me work for my profit. I had to follow him around like a tail on a monkey, and so I did. I waited for him by his office, and then followed him around wherever he went. I even waited for him by his house, but what really got to him is when I went after him into a club. Then it hit me; that guy was gay.

I sat at the bar right across from him, and watched him flirt with other men; then when he appeared all to himself, I approached him.

He said, "Look I told you before. I don't have it. What else do you want from me?"

"Well, actually, I got all I needed; now I know more about you than your wife. I suppose she will be delighted to see all your photos, so goodnight! Oh, and have a great time! By the way, judging by your fellow friends, I'm sure that you will!"

I walked toward the exit thinking this guy must have a weak spot. I just needed to find it, get in there, and squeeze.

Suddenly I heard someone shout, "Hey you! Wait!"

As I turned around, he was coming my way.

"Okay, come tomorrow morning and I shall give you a check; just bring the photos!"

"Look, when you pay up, all this goes away! Don't worry about the photo; it's not in my interest to hurt you! Just pay your bill!"

And the next morning he did, just like everyone else. However, unfortunately for me, because things turned right for Tony, my enterprise ended, before it began. From then on, Tony was paid promptly, there were no open balances, no debtors, and on accession, they even paid him upfront. I could only assume that my work was respected, and word got around fast.

But, I stayed at Tony's firm anyway, and worked with Pap as a helper. Looking at this from the bright side, I obtained new skills, and eventually, learned his operation, as well as, where the jobs came from, and how to bid them.

I also learned of his niece. She was a long legged blonde, with beautiful green eyes and up scale class. Her name was Nicole. By the look of her, she was too cold to touch and too hot to handle. Therefore, I liked her from the start, and at the same time, intentionally neglected her. We had not spoken, but somehow I felt she wanted to start a conversation and waited for me to step forward. I tried to approach her, and for some reason, I could not.

One day after work, she decided to take over and approached me. "Hi, are you cold today?"

"Hello! I'm fine, why are you asking?"

"Well, I am freezing, and I forgot my coat at Tony's house. What a klutz!"

"You are living with Tony? I thought he was married."

"I'm not living with him, dummy. I am staying with his family. You see, my father is a good friend of Tony's. We all came here for a visit; they went back and I decided to stay for a while longer."

"Oh, I see. Hey, here is my coat. Take it; you can give it to me later."

"Thank you, you are very kind."

She took my jackets and I never wore it again. Back then, I was not aware that, in her vocabulary, later was defined as never.

Now, how could I ask for my jacket back if she wore it every day? Therefore, I decided if she were determined to keep it, I would get it back with her wearing it.

A few days later, Tony gave me the first collection slip, and it was all the way in New Jersey, so I came up to him, and asked, "Listen, Tony, I am not familiar with that location. Can you ask Nicole to assist me?"

"And how do you see her assisting you? She is a guest here!"

"Well, I can't read the map and drive; let me have one of the workers instead, I don't care."

"Workers? No way, they are all busy. Okay wait. I will go get her! Nicole, come here please," Tony said with a very light tone.

"Yes Tony? Oh, hi Al."

"Nicole, would you go with Al to New Jersey, help him find the way there? Also, it will be good for you, new sights, and all."

"Sure, why not! When?"

"Now; here are my car keys. Go wait in the car."

She went out of the office and I wanted to follow, but Tony grabbed me by my arm and said, "Al, here is some money. I want you to feed her, and I mean food. Don't get any ideas; she is like a daughter to me. Take good care of her."

"I understand, thanks, and don't worry, it will be fine. I meant to say, she will be fine!" I was thinking I would surely do my best to take very good care of her.

While driving on the freeway, we talked about trust. I do not know how this issue came up, but out of nowhere, it did. It happened, when Nicole told me a story, about how someone almost sexually assaulted her. She stated that it was not long ago, and now, there was no trust in her heart toward men.

At that time, I thought to myself, *almost doesn't count.*

As we were intensively discussing that situation, somewhere along the way, we got lost. The map did not help much either, so I stopped at a phone and called for directions.

Nicole stood right next to me. As I hung up, she came closer and asked me, "Do you have any extra gum?"

"Sure I do. I apologize for not offering."

I approached her intimately, unpredictably placed my lips onto hers, and gave her a passionate kiss, at the same time passing the gum from my mouth to hers.

Afterward, she just stood there looking at me, stunned, and had nothing to say. I guess she had never encountered that kind of approach. Actually, neither had I. I don't know what came over me, but I was glad it did.

"Nicole, did you get the gum?"

"Yes, I did. Yes, thank you. So now what?"

"Now we go; please get in the car." We drove away.

"Al, why did you kiss me?"

"You wanted some gum, so I gave you some. Did you like it?"

"Well yes! Actually, no. Is this how you share your gum, or other substances?"

"Only with you, but I won't do it again, I promise! I was referring to substances, of course."

"Of course" She said that with a smile, and that was the first time she smiled at me.

Our destination came into view and we were late, but better late than never. I went in and came right out, because there was nobody home.

"Nicole, we have to stay here overnight."

"Why? Let's go back, and return tomorrow."

"No, I can't. It's to far away; also, tomorrow is a busy day. I will get a motel room, and we will come back in the morning. Don't worry; we will have separate beds."

"Okay; you are the commodore of our parade, so let's stay. I take it you are a gentleman!"

"Don't I look like one?"

It was a good thing that she was unaware of my meaning, or maybe she knew and did not mind. Regardless, the importance of it all was that I found a motel, got us a room with two beds as I promised, and we walked in.

"Al, I will call Tony and tell him where we are," she said.

"Okay, good idea; meanwhile I'll take a shower"

When I came out of the shower, her clothing rested nicely on the chair, and she was in bed, evidently sleeping. I stood by her side for a few minutes and hoped to see her move, but she did not show any signs of awakening, so I quietly sneaked next to her, lay myself behind her, and fell asleep.

The next morning she woke me up and asked, "I don't remember you climbing in my bed; what are you doing here?"

"Do you know the phrase, a picture worth a thousands words?"

"Sure I do; why?"

"Let me show you." And I proceeded with kissing her neck, and then, well, we were practically naked. I was aroused and could not resist her natural temptations. At first, I thought she would oppose, but surprisingly, she went along with it.

That morning we were physically and mentally intimate, and in some strange way, we became as one. From that day on, I spent most of my free time with Nicole.

Nicole turned to be very talkative; we both enjoyed each other's company, and no matter where we went, in the end, we always ended up in a motel. Sex was our first priority, or maybe it was mine, and she just enjoyed the ride.

On some occasions, I would take Nicole to a bar, the same bar where Jim and I use to hang out. B52 had shifted to Black Label, which unaccountably glided pleasantly down my throat. For some reason, I felt calmer there; it also brought back warm memories. I liked that quiet and gloomy atmosphere.

Our interactions had progressed into routine, until one evening, Nicole became my politically incorrect salvation. "Al, why do we always come here? New York is a big wonderful place; let's go see something new."

"Like what?"

"Like theaters; there are plenty of shows on Broadway. I know, let's go to Carnegie Hall. I have never been there, and I'm dying to see it."

"I like it here; it's peaceful. However, I would not want you to die on me!"

"It's just a figure of speech. I want to go. I'm sick of this place; all you ever do here is drink. Besides, it feels like you are just looking to get laid with me; is that all you want?"

"Yes! But not all. I thought you like having sex with me?" Or do you?"

"I did not say that I didn't. I just want to explore; there is more to life than this bar and a cheap motel."

"You want to explore other places? Okay, let's go. I will show you a great place!"

So we left. She was happy about that, and had no idea where I was taking her. First, I stopped and went into a liquor store. I picked a bottle of scotch and some plastic cups.

"Why did you buy this? Didn't you get enough at the bar?" she asked.

"No, I did not; besides, it's a surprise!" My mind was set to see Jimmy's grave.

When we arrived, she asked, "Al, this is a cemetery. What are we doing here?"

"Like I said, it's a surprise. Just climb over the fence."

"No, you are drunk or crazy, or both,"

"If you won't go with me, I will leave you here. Besides, nothing bad can happen here, I just want to visit my brother."

After a short debate, she climbed over the fence, and we went up the hill, searching for Jimmy's grave. We walked around for over an hour. Finally, when I found his monument, I sat down on the ground, took out the bottle, and poured us both a shot. I placed one cup on his stone and drank mine.

After a while, and few more shots, and then a few more, and more, it had gotten to a point where I was hysterically screaming, "Jim, why did you leave me?"

She approached me and said, "That's it, Al; let's go. I can't stand being here anymore, watching you destroy yourself like that."

I did not pay any attention to her, and repeated the words. "Jim, why did you leave me? How could you?" Then I got up and walked to the tombstone, still screaming the same thing. I hugged the monument and tried to squeeze it, when suddenly it came loose and fell right on top of me. I landed on the ground covered by the stone. Somehow, I pushed myself away from it and came around.

That is when she ran in, and snatched me by the shoulder. I pinned her down to the ground, ripped her skirt off, uncrossed her legs, took out my penis, and penetrated her. At first, for few seconds, she struggled, but had no success breaking loose. Then she gave in, and waited for me to finish. We just lay there until dawn, and then walked back to the car, covered with dirt and mud.

While driving back, we were silent until we reached her home.

"How will I go in? Look at me! I am in dirt, and my clothes ragged, thanks to you! What I shall say to my father's friends?"

"I'm very sorry; I don't know what came over me. Just tell them that you were attacked, and I came to your rescue!"

That was the only dumb idea I could come up with, so she went out, slammed the car door, and rushed away.

After that morning, I didn't see or speak to her for a month, and then one day out of the blue, she called, and grumbled about my behavior toward her, which caused her misery.

I spoke back. "Look, I didn't tie you to me. Go and do whatever you want with whomever you want. Just stop nagging me!"

"Are you sure about that? Can you really be without me?"

"As I recall, you called me!"

The next evening, I was at the bar as usual, and for some reason, I thought she would show up, but Nicole did not, and she was not home when I called her. So after ten o'clock, I went to a strip bar, and that idea turned to be a treat.

I met many gorgeous babes there. I did not watch them on stage; instead, they were taking turns coming to my table on their break. Passing time there was incredible fun, and that continued on a nightly basis. In that place, I was a happy dude again, and Nicole, well, I forgot about her completely.

At work, collecting for Tom became uninterested to me, so I decided to open our own business. All dad and I needed were some tools and a small shop. That idea popped into my head mainly because of my father; he had a great deal of knowledge and his work was exceptional, so why use that for Tom's benefit?

I approached Tom with my resignation statement. "Tom, I need to tell you that I'm bored here, so I have decided to leave."

"I was expecting you say that; this line of work is not for you! So, what are you going to do?"

"I want to open my own business, just like yours, only on a smaller scale, so I won't become your competitor. However, my father will have to join me." Of course, I was lying; my plan was on a much larger scale, but he did not have to know that.

"That's a wise decision; good luck."

"Thank you, Tom."

At first, Pap and I started to work from our house. It had a nice size back yard, so we kept all the needed materials and some tools there.

My notebook became my bible; all Tom's clients were there, and it was just a matter of time before we took over.

Working with pap was a great pleasure, although he did not talk much, and was a very poor tutor, however, watching him, work on a daily basis was enough for me to understand and quickly pick up all the needed skills.

Nicole, on the other hand, had the tendency to idealize me. Maybe because she loved me. Unfortunately, for her, reality showed her that even the grave would not alter the humped one, which means, some people will never change.

One evening I was on my way out. When I opened the door, Nicole was there, sitting outside on the step waiting for me.

"Nicky, what are you doing here? Did you sit here for long?"

"Don't know; I don't have a watch."

"Why didn't you knock?"

"It doesn't matter, Al. I'm leaving."

"You are leaving me? Why?"

"I'm not leaving you; I'm going back to Russia."

"When are you leaving?"

"Tomorrow; my father insisted, so I came to say goodbye."

"Could you stay? I will help you."

"No, I can't. It's too late for that. Anyway, where have you been all this time?"

"Sorry, I was lonely, so I went to the strip bar for some company."

"You don't consider me as company anymore?"

"No, it's not that. I like being with you. I just did not want to argue, that's all. You are important to me. I hope you know that."

"I think I am. I love you, Al, and I don't want to lose you, but I have to go. There is no other way. If you need me, I will come back."

I did not go anywhere. That night, we spent together, yes, as usual in a cheap motel. Where else could I take her?

The next day, I escorted Nicole to the airport and watched her plane fly away. After she left my life, I became miserable.

The strip bar was not the same anymore, so every evening I stayed home, drinking, and watching TV. Sometimes my dad would accompany me in those delightful periods; he would sit next to me until I zonked myself out.

On occasion, I would visit the bar; my second home, that is, and sit there until midnight.

One of those nights, I was so smashed that my imagination took over, and I heard Nicole shouting for help. I heard her scream, "Al, please come home. I need you now."

I ran to my car and took off. On the way home, I ran through the green, yellow, and red traffic lights; actually, most of them were red. That is what the police officer stated when he pulled me over, one block from my home.

I stopped because cops had blocked the last intersection, and I saw them, thank god, so I pulled over. Suddenly, they surrounded my car, pointing guns in my direction. I just sat there and waited, until I heard, "Get out of the vehicle."

So I did.

"Turn around and put you hands on top of the car."

I did that, too.

One of the cops approached me, swiveled me around, and said, "So, where is the fire?"

"What fire?"

"You passed through six red lights. What was the hurry, and didn't you see us behind you?"

"I have a bad stomach problem, diarrhea was screaming out, and I did not want to shit in my pants."

"Well, I never heard that before; do you expect me to buy it?"

"Yes, please buy it; my stomach is killing me."

"Did you drink tonight?"

"No why?" By that time, other cops had left.

"You look drunk to me, not to mention the smell of alcohol coming from you."

"No, officer; I don't drink"

"Okay, come over here and walk that line."

"I can't. I'm sick; call an ambulance or let me go home."

"Where do you live?"

"Right around here; next block on the left."

"Get in. You can't drive. My partner will follow us in your vehicle."

He was right. I could not drive anymore, even if my life depended on it. I was completely wasted.

It was odd, but they took me home, parked my car, and delivered me with my car keys to my mother. When she opened the door and saw us, she looked traumatized.

"Is this your son?" the cop asked.

"Yes, what happened?"

"Apparently, he is very sick. According to him, he has diarrhea! However, we both know it's not true! So take him, and please for his own sake, don't let him go out again! I would hate to see him in jail!"

Then they left. I believed in that story so much that it did turn my stomach upside-down, and I was in severe pain.

"Al, what did you do this time?"

"Mom, nothing much. I just ran some red lights! It's no big deal."

"No big deal? Are you out of your mind? You could have killed somebody. What were you thinking?"

"Please, stop screaming. I have ears. Didn't you hear me? I'm sick!"

"You are blind drunk. When did you become so lucky? I cannot believe those cops felt sorry for you. If it was up to me, I would lock you in jail and throw away the key."

"Well, thank god it was not up to you! Or someone, like you, for that matter!"

"You know, some day this fortune of yours will run out you better get yourself together, or one day, there will be hell to pay."

"Stop cursing me; you have a terrible tongue. Most of your blathering is coming true."

"I am blathering? You are despicable when drunk. Go sleep it off!"

"Look who is talking about despicability. I will go when I choose to. Leave me alone."

She went to sleep and I continued drinking. I could not get up time the next morning, so I took that day off. There is some positive in being your own boss. Half the day I spend in the bathtub, and when I got out of there, the phone rang. It was Nicole.

"Hi, Al, how are you?"

"Much better now; why did you wait so long to call me?"

"Why, do you miss me?"

"I was worried; how are you?"

"I'm fine, but it's not the same without you. I miss you Al"

"Me, too; give me your phone number and tell me when you are coming back. I will send you a ticket. I want you back."

"Al, be a little patient. I'll be back soon! Have to go now; call me!"

Afterward, every evening, I would call Nicky. However, our conversations were very short and I was puzzled why she was so brief, until one night, when I called, her father picked up the phone.

"Hello, may I speak with Nicole?" I asked.

"Who is that? Is this Al?"

"Yes, sir, it's me!"

"Do you know what time it is now? Don't you ever wake me at this hour, you son of a bitch!" Then he hung up.

In eight days, Nicole returned to me. Those days passed by in a glint; maybe because I kept myself busy with work and all. It seemed as if only yesterday that she flew away, and today I was meeting her again.

She approached me with glowing eyes and a blissful smile on her pretty face. She was hot and blooming.

"Nicky, I'm so glad to see you." When she put her arms around me, I realized how much I had missed her.

"I missed you, too; it is good to be back."

"Come on, let's go home."

When we arrived at our house, my parents embraced her as if she was their own, and I was very glad to see that. Nicole moved into my bedroom, which was next to my folks, so at night Nicole felt uncomfortable, but never turned her back to me.

We all lived as one family for two months. During workdays, I was working with Pap and Nicole stayed home, but on the weekends, we always went out, and I thought she was happy.

That happy atmosphere lasted two months. One evening, when I entered the house, I saw Nicole on the couch in the living room. She had curled into a circle, and laid there without movement, so I rushed toward her.

"Hey! What happened? What's wrong?"

"Hi Al. Nothing. I have some cramps in my stomach. Don't worry, it's nothing."

"You don't know what it is! Let me take you to the hospital."

"No Al, no need. I'll be fine, just let me be."

"I can't see you like this, so I will let you be, after the hospital."

"Al, stop pulling me. I had an abortion. They said this pain will not last."

"What? When did you have it? And why?"

"I went there this morning."

"Why didn't you tell me?"

"Because I knew how you would react! And now I can see that I was right!"

"You killed a baby, and now you are worrying about my reaction! How normal is that? Tell me!"

"Calm down, Al, it was not a baby! I had been pregnant less than a week!"

"So why didn't you tell me?"

"Because you would ask me to carry it, and I am too young for that! It's not the right time for me now!"

"And what about me? Do I count for anything? Or maybe it wasn't mine?"

"Don't worry; it was yours!"

"Oh! Thank you! You made my day!"

"Okay, please, let me be. I'm very tired."

"Did my mom know?"

"No, I did not tell her."

Of course, she knew; my mom knows about those things from a mile away. I just needed to avoid her and any questions she might have.

After the first week, our home environment appeared to be peaceful, but then somehow it spoiled. A dispute occurred between my mother and Nicole, and I was misreading them both.

One day, when Pap and I returned home from our job site, when I entered the house, Nicky was sitting in the living room looking as if a spider had bitten her, and Mom was in the kitchen.

"Hey, Nicky, what happened? Are your parents okay?"

"Yes, they are fine! It's your mother. She does not let me do anything!"

"What do you mean?"

"I wanted to prepare you a dinner, so I took some vegetables from the fridge. She placed them back, and said, 'Buy and spoil your own!' And before that, I went into the basement to do laundry. She came down, took your clothing away, and said, 'Do your own laundry; my son needs a special approach'!"

"Mom! Can you come here, please?"

Yes, son! What is it?"

"Why you won't let her cook, or do my laundry? What is this? Have you forgotten who paid for this house, and I'm still paying half of all the expenses! So please stop dictating to her!"

"I am not dictating to her! She is lying, Al; don't you believe her!"

"Mom, why would she lie about something like that? There is nothing to gain here. I don't see the point!"

"Al, she is sitting next to you! And I'm saying that right into her face; she is a lying whore!'

"Okay, Mom; that is enough!"

Afterward, I tried to sort them out, but was ineffective, so the best resolution was to move out.

After a few weeks of a tense atmosphere, we finally found a place and moved out. The apartment was great, one bedroom, completely renovated, with wall-to-wall carpet. We had nothing except our clothing and each other; back then that is what counted most.

For the first few weeks, we slept on the floor, however, surprising as it was, regardless of our situation, I felt great, and it appeared that Nicole was happy as well.

It did not take me long to establish normal surroundings. I charged all of my credits to the limit, and obtained everything we needed. The best part of it all, it was our first joint purchases.

Nicole had upscale taste, so all our items were costly, and I ended up in a deep financial hole. Regardless, I came to be happy, but then something happened. It is true when people say that dating someone and living together are two different worlds. All this time, I had not believed that, until I felt it on my own skin.

It all began when she decided to obtain a degree, so she went to college. I always felt that I misinterpret her behavior. Somehow, something was missing, or exaggeratedly displayed, and no matter how hard I would try to understand her, I would be mystified and confused.

Nicole became a puzzle to me, with numerous missing pieces, and that began to trouble me. One day, Nicole was determined to get a driving license, so she signed up for a driving class.

"Al, I'm going to driving school. I will be back in a few hours."

"Okay, give me the address of the school."

"Why? What for?"

"Just in case."

It was six o'clock on a Saturday evening. I was surprised to know that a school operated at that time, and over the weekend.

Two hours passed, and she did not return. Then another half an hour went by, and she was still absent. I could not bear sitting home, so I went toward the school, hopping to bump into her on the way. The school was less than one block away, or I should say the address Nicole had given me. When I arrived at that location, that site occupied an old house. I looked around and there was no sign of a driving school, or any other agency. I had no choice but to confront the situation.

I knocked on the door, and an old man answered.

"Good evening, sir; sorry for the intrusion, but I'm in need of your assistance."

"Well, how can I help?"

"You see, I was given this address supposedly for a driving school, and obviously there was a mistake. Can you tell me the whereabouts of that school?"

"Sorry, young man; there is no school around here."

"How could that be? Are you sure?"

"Look, boy I have lived here for over thirty-five years, and I'm telling you, there is no school in this neighborhood, and never was. Can't you see it's all residential?"

"Sorry to bother you; goodnight"

So I went back home, and felt as if a ton of horseshit had just landed on me. I got back and still there was no sign of Nicole. I poured my self a glass of vodka, took the bottle with a bag of nuggets, set in the living room, and waited for my princess to show up.

It was eleven o'clock at night; most of the vodka was gone, and I began to worry. Suddenly, the princess walked in, all puffed out, and excited, with a huge smile on her face, shouting, "I passed, I passed," and I was pissed off.

"Yeah, so tell me, what exactly did you pass?"

"I passed the pre-exam of the written test. Aren't you happy?"

"Happy? Of course. Please tell me, where did you take that exam?"

"What do you mean? In school! Where else?"

"Okay, let me rephrase; where is the school?"

"What are you doing? I gave you the address."

"Come over here; look at the address again. Is that it?"

"Well, yes."

"What do you mean yes? I was there, there is no school in that area, and never was"

"What are you talking about? I just came from there."

"Oh really? In that case, let's go."

"Where are we going?"

"I want you to show me that school"

So she took me there all right, to that same place were I was before, pointing her finger at some old vacant building, she said, "This is it; happy?"

"What do you mean, this is it? That building is empty. Besides, it does not have the address you gave me. You see that little house. Supposedly, this is your school; but, guess what? An old man lives there instead, for over thirty-five years. So where was your exam? And what kind of exam was it? Don't lie to me, Nicole."

"I am not lying, I was here. Please stop screaming at me."

From that moment, I realized it was useless to prove her wrong. She believed in her lies so deeply that for her, the lie became the truth. We were living together now, so that incident wasn't enough cause to breakup.

However, through another four months, I learned that Nicole had a gift, a talent, with the ability to glue walls of lie together, and no one would ever recognize the seam between those walls. She was natural pathological liar.

Afterward, there were many similar and dissimilar incidents, but the fact of the matter stayed. Sometimes I thought that, for Nicole, lying was a privilege, and any honest day was a wasted day.

That is when I realized that my love toward her was unquestionable. I loved her imperfections more than perfection, therefore, I did not try to change her or show her another way, the so-called right way of life.

Instead, I commenced drinking, and turned my life into a ball of lies as well. It is true what they say, "One becomes alike with the one he committed to," and I did not like that, so eventually I though about splitting up.

One day, I came home hyperactive and ready to fight. As I entered the apartment, she approached me with a big smile, clutched onto my shoulders, and said, "Al, I have great news. I was accepted to college, and soon you will have yourself a criminal lawyer!"

"Really! You are a liar by nature, and if you feel the lack of criminal knowledge, go steal something. Why waste time in college?"

"I will not get into that with you, only because, I have great news for you!"

"Oh! Do you, I can't wait; what is it?"

"I think I'm pregnant! How do you like them apples?"

That was one of my rare moments in life when I was speechless. After sitting on the couch for a few moments, holding my head with my hands, I realized the magnitude of her statement. At the same time, a doubt raised some questions.

"You think? What do you mean by that? We are not talking about a virus here! So, its either you are pregnant or not! Nicole, you must be sure."

"Okay! I'm sure! I checked and rechecked, look at the result for yourself!"

"I don't need to look at anything! Besides, knowing your abilities, I would not be surprised if you had stuck that thing into one of the cats in our backyard! It's their season now, you know!"

"What did you say? How could you! I'm bringing you the news of a lifetime and you act like a complete asshole!"

"Okay, calm down! I did not mean that! So, you are really pregnant?"

"Yes, I am!"

"Whose is it?"

"I had enough of your comments for one day!" She went out the door and slammed it behind her so hard I thought it would tear from its hinges.

Meanwhile, I needed time to myself to think this through, so I went to the kitchen and got a liquid help thinker. After a few shots, I decided to call my mother for advice.

"Hi Mom! How are you doing?"

"Fine, Al; it's good that you called. I wanted to say that I'm glad that you both moved away! It's not always good to live with your parents, and especially when you are starting your own family."

"Funny that you mentioned the word family, because, I was just about to bring some good news to your table!"

"Is she pregnant?"

"Yes! How did you know that? Has she called you?"

"No, Al; after all that has happened, why would she be calling me!"

"So how did you know?"

"Oh, please, Al! Why do you always assume that only you can place two and two together?"

"Okay, Mom; so what do you think I should do?"

"Al, it's your life, maybe your wife-to-be, and maybe your child to care for! So, it's your decision!"

"What do you mean maybe my child? And, actually, that's why I called! Don't you think it's too soon for me to become a dad?"

"For a man, it's never too soon to become a father. So ask yourself, are you a man? Or are you still a grownup sucking on the nipple of vodka!"

"Very funny Mom; once in a blue moon I turn to you for advice and you came up with a joke!"

"I was not joking, Al! What did you expect me to say? You know by now that I don't like her, so why ask me?"

"I thought you did not get along, but had no idea that you disliked her! Besides, when I met her, you inspired me to date her, remember!"

"Yes I remember. Back then you were lonely, I thought she would take you away from your past and your lifestyle; you know, a fresh start! Now I can say I was wrong!"

"I was not lonely! I was alone!"

"You were never alone; we were always there!"

"Like I said, I was alone! And now I'm beginning to wonder why I called you!"

"Yeah, I was wondering that myself!"

"Okay Mom, goodbye!" And I hung up on her.

While pouring myself another shot, anger rose within me. How stupid it was of me to call my mother for advice; she never gave me one that would stick with me. Why did I think she could help me now? So I decided to go with the flow, and see where it would lead me.

When Nicole got home, I was some calmer and more understanding, or at least I thought I was. "Hey, honey! Glad to see you! I'm sorry!"

"I'm glad that you feel this way!"

"You know! Let's go out and celebrate! What do you say?"

"Sure! Let's go!"

So I took her to Pier Seventeen. We waited at the bar, then shortly after we got a nice table with a waterfront view. I sat down with a glass of scotch, and Nicole was upset because she was holding a glass with orange juice.

"I though you wanted to go out? Where is the excitement?"

"Why couldn't I get wine?"

"What are we supposedly celebrating? Are you pregnant? Or was it another fib?"

"Why don't you go back to when you said you were sorry!"

"Okay, look. I don't have to tell you that alcohol is bad for pregnancy!"

"I know that; however, I am only three weeks in. There is nothing developed yet. It's all in the beginning process, so a little wine won't hurt!"

"It won't hurt you! But your fucking wine might damage the process. What kind of mother will you be, if from the start you are careless?"

"Okay, Al. I don't want anything anymore!"

"Good! Finally! However, the way you are behaving, I wonder what kind of mother you will be. Have you ever thought about that?"

"No! I don't like to get ahead of myself!"

"Well, there you go! That's exactly my point. You always think about yourself! You don't know how to care for others! But I'm not worried. I'll be a great dad, for sure!"

"You know, mothers are by nature far more giving and caring than fathers. Besides, you will only be a father if I let you! So don't get too cocky with me!"

"What did you say? Do you really think I would need permission to be with my son! Well then, think again! And if you keep on talking like that, you won't have anything left to think with! I can promise you that!"

"That's your insecurity speaking. I don't mind. It's only hot air!"

"Okay, when the time comes, you shall see how hot my air really is!"

"I won't have to; if that time really comes, you will meet with my uncle. He is what you will be; in twenty years form now, times two."

"So now you threaten me with your uncle? Is that it? Why did you never introduce him before?"

"What for? You were always behaving!"

"You know what? Fuck you and your uncle! Oh better yet, why don't you get fucked by your uncle! Then again, you probably did!"

I got up and walked away, leaving her alone, and I was looking for celebration. What a crazy idea! I was cursing the whole way back home; how could I be that stupid?

While driving, I could see Jim in my rearview mirror, laughing hysterically, so I asked him, "Why am I so unlucky with women? Is it because I am selective? On the other hand, maybe it's just my luck! If I am too meticulous, then why every good-looking woman must have a crocodile soul? And if that's my luck, well, that would explain why I always get the broken or defective handcart.

"Jim, I have not told you before, but on any given day, when I visit the supermarket, or any major store that requires a shopping cart, I would always pick the faulty one. No matter how hard I would try to look them over up close, I would still pull the one with the most damage.

"How do I know that, you ask? Good question! Because afterward, I stand there with my selected cart by the cart array and watch how other people pull their cart out, and then smoothly glide it away.

"Once at Home Depot, after another skillful selection, I got so agitated that my frustration kept me standing there, so I stood like a moron for twenty minutes, and watched how other perfect carts got pulled out. I said to myself that it couldn't be; there must be more damaged carts, or at least one!

"Well guess what? There was none! I was holding on to the only bad one at that time, then the security guard interfered and asked me to move on, so I scrambled away.

"I recall only one woman in my life worthy of my attention, and unfortunately, our relationship did not last long, and I didn't say goodbye. Avalon and I will never know why. Then again, she took a very tiny part of my lifetime, and I did not get to know her that well, so I cannot grieve for the unknown. It's strange, but for some reason, upon a loss, I only recall the good side of the lost one."

I arrived home and went to bed. The next morning when I woke up, Nicole was sleeping by my side. She looked as fragile and sweet as a child did, to bad she looked that way only in her sleep.

When she woke up, I was on the living room couch watching the morning news and enjoying a cup of coffee.

She came in, and sat next to me, and said, "Good morning, Al; there is something I need to ask from you."

"What is it?"

"Last night, when you left me there by myself, I was very upset, so I called collect to my father. I did not tell him anything, and we did not speak for long!"

"Okay, so why are you telling me this?"

"Well, he is coming here! And I wanted to ask you, can he stay with us?"

"What! Are you nuts? We have only one bed. Where would he sleep? Besides, I have a strong feeling that we will not get along!"

"Al, it's only for little while. His visit will be very brief!"

"How brief?"

"No more than a week! I promise!"

"Fine; and when this pleasing event will transpire?"

"In two months."

"So, in two months, I shall meet your father! What a delightful thought! Your parents are probably thinking to immigrate here, and he is coming to snoop around! Am I right?"

"Yes, I think so."

"Well, why not? Having a baby would make your life easier!"

"Oh! Thank you, Al!"

After breakfast, I turned to the sports channels, and Nicole settled herself next to the phone. She would talk on the phone for hours, and I could never comprehend that. Any time she was home and the phone rang, I would never answer. Most of the time, the call was for her.

Around noon, when the phone was about to melt, she approached me a said, "Al, would you mind some company tonight?"

"What company you are referring to?"

"My school friends back from Russia are here; they wanted to stop by and say hi!"

"Okay, I don't mind; so who will be coming?"

"My girlfriend and her boyfriend, also, some guy, which I never met."

So the evening came, and Nicole's friends arrived. When she opened the door, they cheered and I could tell from the living room that it was the joyfulness of the reunion. They stood at the entry for a while, hugging and kissing.

I had to cut in, and say, "Hi there! I don't mean to break up this party, but please come on in, before the entire building joins you!"

"Oh! Guys, meet my friend, Al!"

She introduced us, and that bothered me. There were two guys in the hallway, why would she introduce me as her friend? However, when one of the guys handed me a bottle of vodka, somehow, my thoughts vanished and I invited them in.

Nicole was a terrible cook. I only presume that was because she had never cooked for me, so our best dinner table had to be dressed with pizza.

We sat in the living room, using a coffee table for our needs. I had nothing in common with them, so watching TV while drinking with them was the ideal resolution. Shortly after, one of the guys backed away, and stopped drinking; Nicole took this opportunity to her advantage, and began sliding down shots of vodka like water.

I did not interfere; after all, it's her body and her child, so who am I to say otherwise? She clearly told me so, just yesterday. Then again, her behavior aroused anger in me, so to keep myself under wraps; I took the role of a bartender and poured myself double shots.

They sat for hours, recalling prior stories and laughing. When the pizza was gone and when the bottle was empty, I suddenly felt very tired. "Okay, folks, thank you for coming; however, I need to turn in!"

"Thank you, Al, it was a pleasure. Would you mind if we stay a little longer? I don't know when we will meet with Nicole again!"

"Sure, why would I? Good night!"

"Good night, Al!" Nicole said with a pleasant, soft voice.

I went to bed and passed out the moment my head hit the pillow. Next morning, I woke up and went to the living room as usual; my head was pounding the whole time. When I approached the couch, I noticed strange marks at the spot where the talkative guy was sitting.

At first, they looked like fingerprints, then looking at them closely, they looked exactly like palm prints, two palms actually, narrow and thin, just like Nicole's.

I made myself a cup of coffee, sat next to those prints, and speculated. How could she leave her prints here? Those must be from sweat. I didn't remember her sweating, and she was sitting on the other side of this couch!

I could not wait for he to wake up, and when she finally did, I called her in, and said, "Nicky, honey, did you have a good time last night?"

"Why you are asking? You were there! Remember?"

"I meant afterward! When, I went to sleep!"

"Well, they did not stay for long. Andrew went out for fresh air, then shortly after, Matt left and I went to bed!"

"Oh yeah? How short was his stay before he left?"

"How should I know? I wasn't clocking him! Why do you ask?"

"Yeah! How could you clock him when you were fucking him instead?"

"What in the world makes you say that? Have you lost your mind?"

"In this case, I can only wish I had; maybe then I would not notice your hand prints! Yes, those marks on the couch. Do you see them? Do you also see the oddness about them? No? Well, let me enlighten you; both of them facing the wrong way! So that only could mean that you were on your knees, facing the couch while resting your palms on it, and sucking his dick!"

She did not say a word; instead, she ran into the kitchen, zoomed out with a sponge in her hand, and wiped her marks off.

There was no point in stopping her, so I went to the store for a bottle of calmness. Upon my return, she was gone, and for the better. While drinking to calm myself down, I mulled over the situation, attempting to come up with other possible explanations, just to prove myself wrong, but there were none.

What must a person do to place his palms on the couch backward? There were no logical or illogical explanations. That fact had me continue drinking, up to the point were I became frustrated. I wanted to strangle her, and was grateful that she left. What a raging bitch she turned out to be. I could not believe what was happening to me. I wanted to go away, but where would I go? So, I went back to sleep.

The next day, I went to my parents' house, only because our business was temporary located there. Pap and I loaded the van, and we drove to the job site.

After that incident, a few ordinary days went by. Nicole and I kept living together as if nothing had happened. She attempted to cover up her betrayal with her perfect duplicity, and I tried to hide my grief. However, we were both unsuccessful, so my approach toward her was never the same. We came to live with each other as close friends, satisfying one another the best we could; making love had passed, so we became fuck buddies.

Only then, I saw who Nicole really was! A gentle touch and a soft approach to her body, was not her thing; she liked hard treatment. Having her around was like a hole in the wall, always there and ready for penetration.

No bad mood or headaches, nor under any circumstances would she reject sex, or try to back away from it. That came to be a surprise for me, so one morning, prior to work, and after sex, I confronted her. "Nicole, can I ask you something?"

"Of course! What is it?"

"You know how we fuck anywhere and everywhere, on any give day and time?"

"Yes, So? Wait... don't tell me. You like foreplay!"

"No, it's not that! I was just wondering, why you never say no to me! I mean, through all of our time together, there must have been one episode when you didn't feel like it, and yet, we always had sex. Why?"

"That's funny you asked! That kind of question could only come from you! I'll tell you, there were many times I did not feel like fucking you, as you so gently put it! Actually, there were more occasions than I can remember! However, think and believe what you want, but the truth of the matter is that I love you, Al! Your needs are more important than mine, in my mind; that's why I never pushed you away. Besides, there is an old phrase regarding this issue. 'If you want your man to be loyal, satisfy his needs at home'I believe those words to be true."

"Did you behave like that with your prior boyfriends?"

"No, I did not love anyone besides you!"

"So, is it really love, that makes you participate unwillingly? I got the impression that sex for you is the same as visiting the bathroom! And I thought that all women needed a special approach."

"I do need that approach; ask yourself if you give it."

"Oh really? Ask yourself! Why would I give it? After the blowjob you give Matt!"

"So we are back on that road again?"

"No, you came back. I got stuck there!"

"Oh! Poor baby got stuck there all alone! You have a great imagination, but that same gift will ruin the best thing in your life! Learn to control it before it's too late!"

"Okay, that's enough. I know your technique; your best defense is a strong offense, so save it for Matt, or any other asshole tickling your waste hole!"

"Fuck you, Al!"

"We've done that already! So now, you can fuck yourself! Filthy bitch!"

"I don't want to talk to you anymore!"

"The feeling is mutual, bitch!"

She went to her college, and I went to work. I have to admit, what she said about love haunted me all day, I was ashamed for myself and felt awful for her. So on my way home, I thought of a way to make up, and actually found one, but when I entered our apartment, the scene made me postpone my attempt at peace.

Nicole lay on the couch, all twisted, and wrapped into a blanket. I came up close, slowly moved her hair form her cheek, and said, "Nicky, what's wrong? What happened?"

"Hi Al. I did not hear you come in. I don't feel good."

"Are you in pain?"

"Yes, some; but doctor said it would pass."

"Which doctor? Why did you go to see a doctor?"

"I had a miscarriage. I'm sorry, Al."

"What! When?"

"In class. I felt dizzy, wanted to go to the bathroom, got up, and fainted. I woke up in the hospital. "

"So, you were in the hospital?"

"Yes!"

"And when you woke up, they didn't ask you for my number?"

"Well, no! I woke up and left."

"Just like that, ha! They let you go without discharging you?"

"Yes; what is with the questions?" She then stood up, and looked directly into my eyes.

"Nicole! Please be straightforward with me! Tell me the truth!"

"Okay! Fine! I had an abortion! There! Happy?"

"Why would you do something like that? Why?"

"I though you would be glad! You never believed it was yours, so what's the problem? Besides, I'm the one that suffers!"

"No, baby, this is not suffering. The actual suffering is waiting for you, and you have no idea of the outcome for this sin!"

"Oh! Look who is noble! That baby was as much yours as it was mine, so stop talking about sins!"

"Listen to me very carefully. I will help you to recover, but if you won't close your suction hole, you will follow my unborn baby!"

She did not talk that night or the next day and the day after; in fact we did not see each other because I stayed at my parents' house. My mother never asked any questions, but I could tell that she knew the answers.

That week, I was drinking more than ever; thoughts of loosing a child brought up a big gun with a massive trigger, and again, I just went with the flow.

I was absent from Nicole's life for one week; through that entire week she never bothered to call me, so come Friday, I decided to go home. When I came in, there was no sign of Nicole; I assumed that she is still in college.

Come nine p.m., the ice queen walked in. "Hi Al, how was your vacation?"

"Judging by your mood; not as well, as yours!"

"I'm just happy to see you!"

"Thank you! Likewise, I think?"

"So, I assume you remember that my father is coming tomorrow!"

"Yes, of course." I had totally forgotten about him.

"His friend will pick him up at the airport, and the next day will bring him here!"

When that next day came, Nicole was glowing with happiness, and I did not care. That man had insulted me for calling him late, and now he would sleep over at my house? Where was the justice in that? So many events and occasions, proved one fact, my destiny was unjust!

He walked in we were introduced, and disliked each other from the start. However, being intelligent men, neither of us showed disapproving emotions. After all, Nicole was happy, so for him that counted the most, and I just played along.

I let them have their private moment, and I turned in sooner than usual. The next morning I woke up with sunrise, reached out toward Nicole's side, and she was not there. I was confused, and rushed to the living room to wake up her father, but when I got there, the scenery stunned me.

I saw Nicole and her daddy embracing under one blanket, on our small living room couch; they were whispering to each other. Her father raised his eyes, and was astounded to see me standing there. At once, Nicole jumped from the couch, pulling the blanket with her, simultaneously revealing her dad's nudity.

At that point, I wished for a camera, because that panorama was beyond my imagination, and if that was not enough, Nicole had a look of moral shock, and dropped the blanket.

So I stood there, observing her naked dad, struggling on my couch, while attempting to reach and grab the blanket, wearing nothing but underwear. Then I looked at Nicole, as she stood frozen at the same spot, wearing her regular, transparent lingerie; that same nightgown she always put on prior to sex. Her shock wave blazed into me, and I could not move!

Finally, when they both got organized, I turned around and went to the kitchen. I thought a cup of coffee would do me good, but somehow, without my knowledge, I was holding a full glass of vodka.

At that juncture, my mind was absent, and by the time the glass was empty, I was actually feeling remorse for Nicole.

Then she walked in, and said, "Al, are you okay?"

"That question is irrelevant at this point! Besides, do I look sick to you?"

"No, that's not what I meant. Look, I have cuddled with my dad since I was a baby; maybe it's not appropriate for some, but where I came from, it's normal."

"I can understand embracing a baby or a child, but you are a grown up woman! Lying next to your naked dad with all your gifts exposed. Besides, if that is normal, then why were both of you so stunned?"

"I knew you wouldn't understand, and I am not going to justify myself to you for no reason."

"Fine! Why don't you go back to your dad before he has himself a heart attack?"

She went back to the living room, and I felt the need for a shower. Afterward, they stayed home and I went to see my folks.

I spend that evening with my family, but slept at home. After that incident, Nicole's dad spent most of his nights at his friend's house, and on a few occasions when he stayed overnight at my place, we hardly saw each other. He showed up late, and in the mornings, I was leaving for work while they were still dreaming.

Nevertheless, that moment had frozen in time, and always staged in my mind. I could not let go of that image, so my only resolution was to find some common sense in that mystical situation. Of course, with any other man in a like situation, the answer is obvious, but with a father? It might be different! So the main key was her father.

Maybe it is possible for some people to be so close with their children; maybe, in a father's eyes, a child is always a child, even when she is a grown up. The only question was. What about decency? Most people are very strict in their beliefs. I had seen that everywhere, my mother would never pass by in my sight half-naked! Nor any parents I was acquainted with before. Cuddling naked with a grown up child is abnormal and odd. So how close two related adults must be, to think that's normal, and how sick they must be, not too realize this issue.

I turned multiple theories in my head for days, and came up with nothing, so one evening; I decided it was enough speculating. It was time to gather some facts, and I went to the library.

To my surprise, quicker than anticipated, I found a topic called "father and daughter sexual relationships." Upon reading, I found that I had been misinformed, and felt quite stupid, because there were many facts that I never knew existed. Apparently, for some people, having sex with their daughters on a regular basis was quite normal. After awhile, I got sick to my stomach and left.

On my way home, I felt satisfied, and not because I had proven myself right. My discovery proved myself sane. A few more days like that, and I would have lost my mind for sure.

As people go, we all have our preferences. Some might agree, some will not, but who am I to say otherwise, and who am I to judge what happens around me? Either I accept it, or I don't.

In this case, I knew what my next move should be; I also knew that no one else needed to know about this discovery. Besides, gossip was never my favorite subject.

When I entered my home, I was as normal as anyone could be.

"Hey Al! How was your day?"

"Great! We finally finished that job. Where is your dad?"

"You just missed him; he went out with his friend again."

"They sure spend a lot of time together."

"Well, Yes! They are childhood buddies."

"Wow! That is rare!"

"Yes it is! Anyway, my dad left this for you."

She then handed me a target practice sheet with a few holes in it. I could only assume they were bullet holes.

"Thanks! What is it?"

"Oh, I thought you knew! It's a target page! They went to the shooting range for practice. My dad though you might like his results."

"Well, it's not bad, I guess; however, it would look much better, if one of those holes was in the center circle! By the way, you don't think this is a hint?"

"How do you see that? A hint to what?"

"Well, maybe your father wanted me to see that he can shoot! You know, just in case!"

"No Al, it's not a hint. Why would he do that? Anyway, I am friends with a nice couple in college. They invited us for a visit; would you like to go?"

"Of course; when?"

"This up coming weekend. They live in a house with a large pool; it should be fun!"

"I believe it would be."

That evening, Nicole and I were sitting watching TV, as two strangers, and we were both comfortable with that; however, her father's gift was definitely a statement. Why else would he give that to me? He was a lousy shot.

He fired eight rounds into that target, and none of them meant to kill. If he only knew that I practiced to use only one bullet, and one bullet alone was all I ever needed.

The next day, I went to work, and while driving, I realized that working from my parents' house must end. Pap and I had completed a few projects, so we had enough funds in our business to expand. I picked up a few newspapers, and came home loaded with ambition to find a suitable shop.

"Al, what are you looking for in there?" Pap asked.

"I'm trying to find a loft for rent. Pap we cannot work from here any longer. Every estimate I attend, they always ask me our location, so I lie! I can't do that anymore. It's embarrassing; besides, we have the money!"

"I completely agree; good luck!"

"Thanks, Pap."

By noon, I found three ads, but only one was suitable for us. It was a spacious store, vacant, and located on 18th Avenue, between my place and the house of my parents. It was perfect for us.

We sign the lease that same day, and bargained one month for renovations. My first accomplishment at the place was hanging a large sign on the window that stated "Help Wanted." By midweek, we added two men to our team, and come Friday, we were open for business.

Saturday morning I was excited. I woke up early and went to the kitchen as usual. On my way there, passing the living room, I saw Nicole's dad sleeping on the couch, this time alone and with his t-shirt on. So, I sat down by the kitchen table and indulged in a cup of coffee.

Nicole walked in and said, "Good morning, Al, I'm glad you are up. We need to get going soon."

"It's seven thirty a.m. Where are we going? Oh, I remember; is this about that couple you were talking about?"

"Yes! Go get dressed."

"You still haven't told me why so early?"

"We will both find out when we get there."

I went for a quick shower instead. After all, I was not rushing from a burning apartment, and I did not see any need to hurry. She was probably making a big fuss for nothing. When I got out of the bathroom, Nicole was standing in front of me, giving me the look of a tiger hunting its prey.

On our way to New Jersey, I wanted to share my news of the new shop, but something was holding me back, and I could not give my news to Nicole. Besides, she was talking all the time; there was no room for me to cut in even if I wanted to.

When we arrived, a small crowd had gathered around three cars. I turned to Nicole and said, "I believe they are waiting for us."

"Yes! I recognize some of them; stop here!"

When we were all introduced, David came up to me and said, "Al, while they're chatting, let's go to my car. There is something I want to show you!"

He opened the trunk, pulled out a black box, and said with a huge smile on his face, said, "Do you like this toy? Nicole told us that you are from Israel. I just assumed that you might have an opinion."

"Well, I can only tell you that this thing is huge! Why did you buy a gun that big? You think size matters?"

"I am not sure; I thought you might know."

"No, Dave; I don't. Sorry to disappoint you! So, tell me Dave, where are we going so early?"

"Oh, I thought you knew. You see, my friends and I, we like guns, so once a month we all go to a shooting range for target practice, and you being from Israel and all, we presumed you might give us some pointers."

"That is the most ridiculous assumption I ever heard. Who told you that Israelis are experts with guns?"

"Al, I'm sorry. I did not mean to offend you. Just forget about it, and let's go have some fun! Okay?"

"I am not offended. I was a little surprised, but let's go; maybe you'll teach me how to shoot this monster of yours."

Dave invited us to ride in their car, while the other couples followed in separate cars. As Dave was driving, he received a phone call and placed on speaker. Apparently, the person on the other end of the phone had no idea we were all unwillingly listening.

He was asking Dave for the for the destination address in case they got lost, and then the voice said, "Dave, where is the Made in Israel guy?"

Dave looked at me with a smile, and replied, "He is with us!", and I added, "Safe and sound! Don't worry!"

Dave picked up the phone, and commenced laughing, and I thought that the best thing for me to do was to stay away from the practice.

I never liked guns anyway. I saw nothing heroic about them. Not much needed to pull the trigger, no wonder they called it a cold blood weapon. However, when Jim and I worked deliveries, we both purchased guns for protection, but. I never used mine, and always knew if I would ever pull it out, at that moment, all my choices would be voided, because I would have too pull the trigger.

When we got there, David was a club member, so all of us signed in and received equipment for practice, with the exception of the guns, of course. While they all took turns firing David's toy, I sat on the bench in the back with Nicole by my side.

She turned to me and said, "Al, don't you want to try?"

"I'm not interested; thank you!"

Hearing the gunshots brought back memories, recollections I had intended to forget. I did not spend any time in the army, yet practice for Israeli recruits in basic training was very popular and often mandated during high school years.

But, the most memorable of all was the Israeli military academy. At that place, my ability for quick adaptation worked against me, and my gift of fast learning developed into my worst enemy. That is when I became a top sniper, and at the same time, I was unaware that they attempted to recruit me to become a skilled killer, then, she sent me away.

"Al, hey! Al! Are you daydreaming?" Dave said.

"I guess I was; sorry."

"Come on; do me the honor. Fire a few shots, will you?"

I don't know what came over me, but I got up, walked slowly to the shooting booth, placed the earplugs, and looked at the target that appeared to be right in front of me. Then I looked at the range mark. It stated ten feet.

David's shiny toy was on the counter, with an open chamber and no magazine. 44 Magnum, what a powerful weapon. I grabbed the gun with my right hand, and with my left hand, placed one bullet into the chamber, then glided the chamber back in very slowly. I had to feel through my fingers how the bullet had entered the chamber.

At that moment, I could see myself back in time, where there was only me, my weapon which was my savior, and the target. I recalled that the farther away my target was, the safer I would be. So, I took that enemy further and further away from me, until it stopped and was very hard to see.

As I was aligning my weapon dead ahead with the target, my body froze, but my breathing was wrong, so I focused on the target's movement. It was nodding back and forward, back and forward.

Then my breathing readjusted to the target's movement, and simultaneously the air in my lungs floated in and out, in and out. I stood in that position for as long as that target sheet bounced, and then, when the target stopped moving, my lungs were empty, and my body had stopped breathing. Suddenly, the target dot enlarged and appeared in front of my eyes. I took aim at the center of a huge dot, and very slowly squeezed the trigger.

The gun fired, and then I moved aside and took the earplugs off. As I turned around, David and his friend gathered behind me.

"Thank god, Al! We though you had fallen asleep in that position! Wow! What took you so long?"

"I don't know, Dave. I guess I hesitated."

"Hesitated at what? I can hardly see the target from here! Why did you send it to the end?"

"Dave, do me the honor and bring it back here!"

As they waited for the target to return, I walked back to the bench and sat down next to Nicole. More people gathered by that booth and I could hear them cheer.

Nicole pinched me and said, "What is all the fuss about? Did you shoot someone?"

"Very funny! Why don't you go take a peek?"

Before she stood up, David ran in waving the target page, and said, "Al, you must see this! Look! Now, how this is possible?"

"I don't know; luck I guess."

"Luck or no luck, that man over there is waiting for you to sign your name in their book! He said they never saw anything like this before! So let's go!"

I knew where that might lead, and did not like it at all. "Dave, where is your gun?"

"I left it on the counter, why?"

"Load it for me, please. I want to see how good I am from a close range."

"Okay, lets' go. You will probably drill through it from a close range, but what the hell!"

I placed my earplugs, grabbed his gun, took aim at the target, and without a warning commenced blasting everywhere but the target. When I was done, there was no need to retrieve the page, because we all could see clearly that it was untouched. The crowd turned away disappointed, and no one was looking for my name anymore.

"Sorry, Dave. I told you; pure luck!"

He smiled at me, and said, "We both know what you did! Hey, take this for a memento." He handed me that bull's eye sheet and walked away.

I walked to Nicole, gave that sheet to her, and she said, "Wow! Now I understand what all the fuss was about; Way to go, Al!"

"Give this target to your father. Tell him it's a gift from me! Oh, in case he asks, you may tell him this is not a hint! It's a fact!"

On our way back, Nicole wasn't as talkative as before. In fact, she did not say a word, and I knew why. Sometimes, silence can be understood clearer than any spoken words, in this case, and without any questions, we understood each other like never before.

When we entered our apartment, Nicole's dad was already there. I could only assume that she had made him a key. Nevertheless, his presence was to my advantage, so I sat across him and said, "Hello, Bill! I need to tell you something that concerns your daughter."

"Okay, I'm all ears!"

"My financial situation has suddenly collapsed, and I cannot afford my apartment anymore, so, would you like to keep it for Nicole? Or shall I terminate the lease?"

Bill turned to Nicole and asked her, "Nicole, would you like to keep this place? I will pay your expenses, either way!"

According to Nicole, Bill was a professional photographer in Russia and loaded with money. Judging by his appearance, among other things, I could tell that he was wealthy. I also immediately recognized that he was despicably cheap.

I mean, the man tours Manhattan for the entire afternoon while dying from thirst, and won't spend one dollar for water; instead, he waits until he gets home, so he could drink for free.

"Dad, I really don't know what to do."

"Is it so hard to decide? It's your life, not mine! I will visit you from time to time, but you will be living with your choices!"

"Well, this place is already furnished!"

"Sweetie, I will move all you see here to any location of your choice!"

As I was listening, it came obvious that Bill wanted her out of this place. He also gave her all my furniture without my consent.

"Okay, Dad. In that case, I will move. Thanks!"

"Well then, it's all settled. Have a good night, and a good life!" Having said that, I packed my things, and left.

Within a week, I cosigned a lease for Nicole's new apartment, and then with our company van and workers, I moved Nicole and all of our contents to her new place. Bill never attempted to get involved in moving, and I did not expect that he would.

When she finally settled down, I kept the TV with the sound system, and delivered them to the only place that was open for me. My parents' house.

My mother was happy to see me back, and evermore for the result of my affairs. She was always against Nicole; maybe because of our different religion, or maybe she always saw what I could not see before.

And me? Well, I was furious, broken into pieces; my disappointment turned to anger that built up to a massive level, and I was about to explode! Drinking was the only solution to calm myself down.

And just like before, it actually helped. So, every other night, Pap and I would sometimes finish a bottle of vodka. Occasionally on the weekends, I would go out for more.

Shortly after, our company had grown; we had four employees and work was rolling in like never before. Although the jobs were small, they were steady.

I went back, and was spending nights with my previous escorts, alcohol and topless joyful babes accompanied me, although I was never intimate with any of them. The thought never even crossed my mind. It was all just a joyful innocent togetherness.

At first, my lifestyle didn't affect my work abilities, and I operated normally, climbing up the ladder and earning a fair living. Nevertheless, after work at home, our drinking continued, and Pap and I slowly turned into compulsive drinkers.

My mother could not take it or watch our useless existence. Because of it, suddenly and without any explanation, one day she took my kid sister and returned to Israel. They left with nothing but clothing and some cash.

In Israel, they stayed with a long-forgotten relative, and on the occasions my mother would call, she sounded much happier than I remembered her here, next to me.

Meanwhile, I was living with my Pap now, and at dinner, alcohol always accompanied us. Shortly, alcohol became the only spouse we knew.

For some reason, Nicole was around all the time, she periodically called me and we kept in touch. On occasion, we also went out.

Our intimate relations never ended, as well as our arguments. I was responsible for engaging in arguments, and mostly without cause or reason. I guess the angriness of breaking up played a big role and somewhere deep, that fire was still burning.

Since I was the one who created conflicts, I was also the one that ended them.

"Al, please don't make me cry; all I'm asking from you is to stop drinking! You are hurting me with your drunkenness"

"Fuck off! I don't want to see you again!"

"Why? Oh god, why do I deserve this kind of cruelty?"

"Why don't you find someone else?"

"Al, be careful what you wish for! It might come true!"

"I wish it would; meanwhile, fuck off!"

She was always crying and I never cared. In spite of all, a few day's later, Nicole would dial me again, and always find an excuse for getting us connected again. Sometimes, she would say that her scarf was missing, or her purse, so maybe she left it in my car and many other fairytales that she would make up on the spot.

The most catchy and effect deception consisted of her brief phone call. When I picked up the phone, she would immediately hang up, knowing that I had a caller ID and could see her name on the display. But what bothered me the most, was that somehow, she knew that I would call her back, and what's worse than that, I always did!

"Nicole, did you called me just now?"

"No, I did not; why do you ask?"

"Because, you did call me! Your name and number popped up on my caller ID."

"Oh, wait a minute. I might have! I'm so sorry that I called you. I misdialed. How stupid of me! You see, my friend's number is very similar to yours, except by two digits. So, I mistakenly misdialed! Anyway! How are you doing?"

I knew she made up that story, and I knew she did that deliberately, and I wanted to hang-up on her so badly! But I couldn't!

"Well, I'm fine; thanks, so, how is your life?"

"Okay, can't complain. My parents are now immigrating here, so it will be nice to have a family again, wouldn't you say so?"

"Of course I would! However, my mother has gone back to Israel with Valerie, so now it is me and my dad, and I don't consider us a family, if you know what I mean."

"Wow! I'm sorry to hear that; when did that happen?"

"About two months ago."

"Al, has it been that long?"

"That long for what? Please be more specific!"

"I meant us being apart."

"Oh, please; like you don't know! How many times do I have to ask you? Do not play with me!"

"Okay, I'm sorry; so, what do you do with yourself lately? Do you have a girlfriend?"

"Yes, a few! I was kidding. I'm working, and, well, that's it; just working."

"Are you still drinking?"

"Yes, I am; why?"

"Just asking. Hey, listen; I have two tickets to an opera. Would you like to come with?"

"Opera? Well, yes, sure. I would like that! I think."

Through our relationship, Nicole always attempted to show me a better way of life, but since Jim died, I shut my eyes to all my surroundings, and I couldn't have cared less.

Alcohol created my world and I liked it there. I would always find a motive to drink, and if there was none, well, then I would produce one, and soon enough, I was drinking on daily basis.

Regardless of my drinking, my activities did not change. I performed my duties at work and I was seeing Nicole periodically during the week, and practically on every weekends.

Therefore, my drinking did not affect me; furthermore, I had never showed up drunk. However, somehow, the fact of me drinking had influenced others; mostly it affected Nicole, because she did not like my appearance under the influence of alcohol.

Through four years of our so-called back and forth relationship, thanks to Nicole, I explored quite a few new upscale places. Some of them were quite exciting and relaxing, and others were educational.

I was always under the influence of alcohol at the places we visited, for some reason, and for her, one day, my drinking became unbearable. She wanted me to stop and confronted me with this issue.

"Al, I can't take it anymore; you have to stop drinking."

"I told you, I don't want to, because I like the way it makes me feel."

"You are becoming an alcoholic. This is a sickness. There is no shame in it. I have found a doctor, and he will help you."

"I am not going to any doctor."

"Oh, yes you are. Please do it for me. You don't understand the circumstances it might lead too. Please, just go see him."

Then she began to cry and I could not resist. I do not know why, but when Nicole cried, it hurt. "Okay, hedgehog, I will go."

I called her hedgehog because of her attitude; sometimes she was sweet and tried to be noble. However, intentionally upsetting Nicole always resulted in regretful consequences. Out of nowhere, those sharp bristles would come out, and with just a few words, she would grant extensive distress.

"Thank you, Al. Let me tell you about this doctor. He is a psychiatrist, achieving 90 percent success by using a combination of hypnoses with meditation, and he will help you forget about alcohol, just like he helped others."

"Fine, I will see him."

She was not kidding, because the next evening we went to see that psycho; surprisingly to me, he actually looked normal. I walked into his so-called office, a ten by eight foot room with nothing but a chair and a sofa next to small, shitty tape player.

"Hello, Al; my name is Doctor Ably, and I am pleased to meet with you."

"Thank you, Doctor Ably I heard that hypnoses has side effects that sometimes include memory loss. Is that true?"

"Well, no; why do you ask?"

"I just wanted to inform you that no matter what happens to me, I shall always remember you!"

"Don't be so paranoid; nothing bad will take place here!"

"All right, doctor; so what's next?"

"Okay, let's begin. There are some questions I need to ask you, so please be honest; it's for your own good."

"Fine, shoot."

"How long you have been drinking?"

"I don't remember. I guess long enough."

"Okay, do you remember your first drink?"

"What is this? If I knew when I started, I would surely know how long I have been drinking. Hey, is this a trick question? When are you going to put me to sleep?"

"I don't put people to sleep, and please, do not use that phrase here. I'm a doctor, not a butcher."

"I apologize, it didn't came out right."

"Okay, let's skip this part and go to my last question, and remember, your answer is most important."

"If it's so important, shouldn't it be the first on your list?"

"Never mind that; just answer me. Are you willing to stop drinking? Yes, or no?"

"No."

"So why are you here?"

"I promised Nicole; she is worried, you know."

"I spoke to Nicole, and she said that you are unaware of your problem."

"Listen, doc, I don't have a problem. I'm here because Nicole wanted me here."

"You see, denial is the first step to alcoholism. You do have a problem, and what's worse, you don't know it."

"Doc, do you have a problem?"

"No."

"Well, there you go; denial. So what is your problem, doc? Is there a Mrs. Ably?"

"You know, our session is over. Time's up."

"What about my hypnosis?"

"Maybe next time; go to the front desk and make another appointment for tomorrow."

That Ably sure gave me a headache, and somehow I felt depressed as well. What a therapy.

I came out of his box. Nicole was waiting for me, and I could see that she was anxious to know what went on in there, so I told her the truth.

"Al, how was it? What did he do?"

"This doctor is an idiot. He didn't do anything except asked me stupid questions, and then said, 'Time's up; make another appointment for tomorrow'. I going to the bar; do you want to come?"

"No thanks. I want to go home"

I drove Nicole home, went to the bar, and then drank until morning. Afterward, I went home, took a shower, and went straight to work.

When I arrived at work, Pap and the workers had already left for the job site, so I went to sleep on the couch in our back room. Every office that I build for myself contained a sofa; that was the first most important item. I considered an office without a couch as an empty space.

Sleeping on the couch, the day went by quickly, and before I knew it, it was time to go back and see that idiot again, so I went there as I promised Nicole. When I entered the office, there were no other clients. Actually, I was there by myself. Then a door to another room slowly opened, and a gentle voice said, "Hello, Al, come in."

So I did.

"Please, lie down and listen to the melody. While you are listening, try to imagine yourself somewhere pleasant. This is called meditation."

"Excuse me; before I lie down, there are two things I need to know. Who is this? And why am I standing in the dark?"

"It's Doctor Ably; please make yourself comfortable."

"Oh, then why are you whispering?"

"Would you be more comfortable if I turn the dim light on?"

"Yes, thank you."

I lay on his coach and waited for his hypnosis.

"Al, where are you?"

"Right here, on your couch."

"No, I told you to trigger your imagination. Think of a pleasant place, and meditate."

"I can't do it with a sober head; what is next on your agenda?"

"Nothing, you are not supposed to talk."

"You did not tell me that before."

"Maybe it is best if I step out. You listen to those sounds and try to relax."

When the psycho said that, for some reason he sounded disappointed.

Meanwhile, I listened and listened; the music sucked. I tried to find out how much more I had to listen to this crap, but it was too dark and I could not see the time. I turned the lights on, and was shocked that I had to sit there for another forty minutes.

Suddenly, the psycho jumped in, and he was outraged. "Why did you turn the lights on? This is absurd," he shouted.

"I wanted to look at my watch."

"You don't need to know the time when you are in here! I will inform you when the session is over. And believe me, I won't keep you in here past your time, not even for one second, so go back to the couch and meditate, damn it!"

"I didn't come here to meditate, and how can anybody relax to the shit you are playing? It is annoying, listening to it is disintegrating my brain, and you call this place a clinic? My body is itching because of it. I feel the need of strangle someone."

"Please calm down, and take it easy; actually, take a deep breath."

"Actually, give me my money back. That's all I'm going to take." I did not mean that, but that fool gave it all back to me, including yesterday's session. What a paranoid psycho.

I went home feeling somehow incomplete, or maybe because of my necessity to drink, I felt as if something was missing. Then it occurred to me; what if Nicole was right? What if I had a problem and do not know about it?

As I was mulling this thought, I decided to go back to the bar and this time drink only soda. I had to test Nicole's theory, and see if I was truly addicted to alcoholic.

I have to say, sitting in the bar and watching others was difficult. I practically tasted the scotch in my mouth, and the temptation was growing by the minute.

So there I was, sitting in my bar, the bar that I visited for years by myself or with unsuitable company. Regardless of the situation, in the end, I always came out of there intoxicated, from my head to my socks.

Surprisingly, this time was the first time in my life that I was drinking soda.

At my third request of, "scotch with soda, and hold the scotch," the bartender began to wonder, so he approached me. "Al, are you okay?"

"Yes, why do you ask?"

"Just curious."

"Why are you curious? Can't I just sit here with a glass of soda?"

"Listen, don't get excited. Usually people come to a bar for a drink, and it's not just soda. Did you ever go to the whore house just to admire the humming?"

"What? No, and I never went to those places."

"No matter; it's abnormal. You get my point?"

"So you are telling me you have never seen people coming here just to socialize, without alcohol?"

"They do socialize, while drinking." Then he began to laugh, and I felt even worse than before, so I left. I had no alternative but to go home.

I came home and turned on the TV, thinking that some stupid TV comedy would resolve my alcohol argue.

Unfortunately, Nicole called and the coin of willpower flipped on me. "Al, what happened with Doctor Ably?"

"Nothing. I just had to leave, and when I did, for no reason he got upset."

"This is not what I heard. Anyway, why did you leave? For once in your life, couldn't you cooperate?"

"Cooperate with whom? That psycho told me to lay down in the dark, then he asked me to listen to music that usually kills plants, and he left the room."

"Can you stop talking for a second? You promised me, and you broke your promise. Doctor Ably said that you were unwilling, so now he is refusing to see you again."

"First of all, don't cry. I hate it when you cry, and second, don't call him a doctor. He is a psycho who is desperately in need of therapy."

"That's it, Al. I don't want to talk to you again."

"Nicole, listen. I want to tell you something. After that psycho I went to the bar, and drank only soda, so you see, I can handle myself. Hello, hello? Nicole?"

She hung up on me; I never understood that behavior. Why would someone hang up without saying a few last words, or at least one word?

Me? I always say goodbye, or fuck you, but never have I hung up on someone with a sober head.

It was late and my dad came home from work. Apparently, he was drunk, and disappointed, probably because I slept through the whole day and then left. I tried to tell him what happened, but his condition got the best of him and he would not listen.

Due to all the events combined, a paradox had created in my mind. Shortly after, a contradiction emerged, and as a result, many questions rose. While I was seeking answers, a dilemma formed between right and wrong, and somehow, I lost my ability to think and became a hostage of my own thoughts. I was desperate for a friend, but the only friend I could get, was always, waiting for me in the fridge.

I grabbed him and gulped as much as I could. Soon, all those questions were gone, and my dilemma was replaced by the happy place that psycho talked about.

Over the next few months, Nicole periodically called me, but I neglected her. I did not feel the need to socialize with her, because it always led a break-up, and I really had become tired of our relationship.

I concentrated on our business, instead. When office work was slow, I went along with Pap and the guys. We were working on a school in New Jersey; that project was big and interesting, so I was learning new things.

Periodically, my mom called us. Due to the time variation, in her mornings, she would catch us at the office upon our return from the job site. One of those evenings, Pap and I we're exhausted, because school was soon to open, so we we're pressured for completion on a daily basis.

"Hello Al! It's me! What are you doing there so late?"

"Oh, hey, Mom! We just returned from the site, how are you? How is Valerie?"

"We are fine! Thanks. Let me speak with Dad; is he there?"

"Yes! Hold on. Dad! It's Mom. She wants to talk to you!"

I gave him the handset, and sat by the second desk across, then waited for him to finish and pass me the phone again, but while he was talking, I could see his mood change.

His voice got higher when he said, "But I am sending two thousand dollars every month! What else do you expect from me? That amount should be more than enough!"

He then listened for another minute, and passed me the handset, saying, "Here, Al. I can't talk to your mother anymore!"

When I took the handset, Pap walked out of the office. He appeared very upset. I only hoped he would not go home and leaving me hanging in the office. Sometimes we drove together, and that was one of those times.

"Hi, Mom. What happened between you and Pap?"

"Nothing much! As usual! Is he still there?"

"No, Ma, he left; very angry, I might add! Tell me, please, what did you tell him?"

"Al, what difference does it make?"

"I overheard him, and I believe you were asking for money? Weren't you?"

"Yes! I did. I have some loans here that I need to pay off, and if I don't, there will be some problems! Why did he get angry? Last time we spoke, you told me there was a lot of work, and your business is doing great!"

"Yes Mom; that's true! However, he has some needs, too! Besides, what you get from Pap is more than most Israelis earn!"

"Al, you and your Pap keep forgetting that I returned to Israel with nothing, and had to start over by myself! That means new clothing, new furniture, and I don't have to tell you about Valerie's needs!"

"I see; so how much do you need?"

"Only three thousand dollars!"

"Is that it? You don't have to bother Pap with that! Give me your bank information and I will wire that amount to you tomorrow!"

"Oh! Thank you, son! Thank you so much!"

When everything settled, Mom committed to her tasks, and Pap walked back in. I was glad to see him, and puzzled as to why he was holding a bottle of vodka in his hand, knowing that we had lots at home.

"Hi, Pap! Don't worry; I solved Mom's problem. Everything is okay!"

"I got some fried chicken! And something else to celebrate your achievement!

"Pap, let's go home and celebrate there! By the way, why did you buy another bottle when we have lots at home?"

"Because, I wanted to eat here!"

I was in a good mood that evening, and drinking was not on my list, but Pap hardly asked me for anything, so there was nothing I could do, except to join him.

"Al, I always meant to ask you but never got the chance; what happened between you and Nicole?"

"Nothing good, Pap. That's why we are apart."

"Nothing good. Ha! For how long you were together, four years or so, am I right?"

"I would say around there somewhere! But who is counting? Right!"

"Wrong! If you don't start to count while young, with years, it will get hard to catch up, and then when you'll get older, you will lose the track of it all, and ask yourself, where did my years go?"

"Come on, Pap! That's ridiculous! Only old-timers say that. I have a great memory! And now that I'm saying that out loud, there are so many things that I don't want to remember!"

"I know what you mean, and I'm sure that what I know is only a drop in the bucket! Hey! Look at the window. Is that who I think it is?"

"Shit! What is she doing here? Pap, what time it is?"

"Seven o'clock! Go open the door for her!"

"No way! That's exactly what she wants, and I won't do it!"

"Son, always remember that you are a gentleman! And always stand by your principles, regardless of the circumstances. She saw you already! So go open the door."

"Okay, I'm going! Pap stay, and finish your food!"

"No, I'm full. I will take our van home. It looks like you will need the car."

"Can you drive?"

"Al, look at the bottle. It's almost full. I hope it will stay the same while I'm gone."

"Yes Pap. Well, maybe I'll sip a little."

I walked Pap to the door, and she was still standing there. As Pap left, she walked in, and said, "What took you so long? I was freezing out there!"

"Well hello to you too! I did not see you!"

"Oh, yes you did! I saw you looking at me."

"You only saw what you wanted to see! Anyway, what fortune brought you here?"

"Fortune? So this is what you think of yourself now?"

"Not now; always! And you are a living proof of that statement!"

"Is that all I am to you?"

"Nicole! What do you want?"

"Close the door, Al. Hey, is that mirrored glass at the back? What's behind that?"

"My private office! It's where I do my thinking."

"I think it's where you do your drinking!"

As she passed me, she grabbed the bottle from the table, and kept on walking toward my private room. At the door, she stopped and said, "Come on, Al! Show me how you think in there!"

I picked up fried chicken leftovers, and two of our cups, then followed her in. As we sat down, she poured those cups full. Then she handed me one cup, and gulped the other empty.

I was astonished, and I kept the cup in my hand as she poured herself another and tossed it down her throat again, then another, and said, "Bottoms up!"

"Thirsty? Maybe you are confusing this with water. Are you okay?"

"What? Did you think that only you can drink? Oh, baby! Maybe you think you can, but you definitely lack the know-how!"

"Oh, and you do?"

"Have you ever seen me intoxicated? No! So I rest my case!"

"Wait a minute; you want to tell me that you drank while we were together, and I did not notice?"

"From time to time, yes, I did! Hey, you were the one looking for integrity; well there you go! Oh, why so glum? You see, being honest is not always healthy for others."

"I see, that means you were protecting me by lying! In that case, thank you! I feel much better now!"

"There you go again, being sarcastic. Let's forget about the past! And enjoy the moment!"

As she said that, she moved in closely, unzipped my pants, reached for my penis, and went down on me. While she performed oral sex, I sipped from my cup, and then lighted a cigarette.

I was getting a blowjob while sipping my drink, inhaling puffs, and thinking to myself, *wow*! All three pleasures at once. If I only had tried this before, we would never break up!

"Al what are you doing?"

"Nothing; why did you stop? Keep going!"

"I smell smoke! Al, why are you smoking? Would you like a magazine to read?"

"Nope! I'm fine! Thank you!"

I was better than fine, actually, but I knew the way she mentioned "magazine" at that moment a choice was raised for me. Should I get rid of the cigarette or stay with the hard-on for hours? So the cigarette had to go, however, I kept on sipping my drink quietly.

Somehow, she knew many ways to extend my pleasure. When the most intense moment arrived and I was about to burst, she would suddenly detract my climax sensation, and commence all over again. By the time she was done with me, I exploded like never before.

It took a while before I could speak, and while I lay on the couch half dead, Nicole was fondling my skull and running her fingers through my hair.

That was my first real feeling of relaxation. I was calm and my mind had emptied of all thoughts. I never knew that life was capable of such a gift. When my time comes, and if it's true that all I can take with me are my memories, then this moment I shall never forget.

"Oh, boy! Nicky, I never knew you had so much warmth in you! Why did you hide that before?"

"Al, every woman is warm by nature! A man with the right approach knows that! However, you somehow manage to bring out the worst in me!"

"I would not bring it if you did not provoke me!"

"You think you'll find yourself an angel. Think again! No women is made of honey we all have our good and bad days, and very few will be able to put up with you!"

"Are you angry because we broke up? Or because, these time our sex was one-sided? Where did you hide that amazing woman all this time?"

"Okay, pull your pants up. I want to go home!"

"If I offended you, I'm sorry! It's just, you caught me by surprise!"

"You didn't offend me, Al. What is worse, you don't understand me!"

While driving her home, Nicole periodically gazed at me, I could feel she was waiting for me to say something comforting, but sometimes my tongue is my worst enemy, and I said, "Was that a goodbye blowjob?"

"What? Do you think of me as a whore?"

"No! You never gave me that pleasure before, so I was just wondering."

"Because I wanted to!"

"Would you want that again sometime very soon?"

"It will depend on you!"

After dropping her off, I decided to go home as well. As I got into my bed, thinking about Nicole kept me awake. I could not comprehend all of her sides. How could a person have so many stages?

Nicole had a gift; being with her was like dating a team of cheerleaders all at once; maybe that's what attracted me to her, and same thing that kept us apart.

The next morning, as I promised Mom, I went to the bank and wired her the funds. When I returned to the office, Pap was still there, and only one worker stood beside him.

"Pap, what happened? You were supposed to be at the job site by now!"

"The guy did not show up, I can't go there with one man!"

"Well, then I will join you."

"No, Al, we were supposed to install large entrances today, and the three of us won't be able to handle that; it's too heavy!"

"Okay, Pap, let's load the van. We can pick up a few laborers on the way there."

I knew of location where men gathered on the street, and waited for work opportunity. They had no skills, and sometimes they hardly spoke English, so on a daily basis, they waited for simple labor work. I called them "male whores."

On our way there, Pap said "Al that is not the way!"

"Yes it is; we are almost there!"

"That's where Mexicans assemble! Make a right here, then on 13th Street, you'll see a crowd of Russians!"

"Pap, what is the difference? Why Russians?"

"Because I don't speak Spanish!"

"Okay! Good point!"

When we stopped at the corner, immediately a huge crowd of men surrounded our van. They were pushing and shoving each other, hustling for the prime spot next to the door.

When Pap opened the door and asked for two guys, three of them squeezed in, so I had to stop at the next block and let one go.

I heard about that place from other business owners in similar situations. I also heard them say; be careful while selecting, and screening was necessary. But how could we interview any of them in such a massive and unstable environment? There was nothing we could do except depart in a hurry, and hope that those two were relatively decent.

However, for some reason, when hoping for good, something bad always happens, and this time was no different from my prior experiences. Toward the end of the day, both of them approached me, and one of the actually spoke. "Hey, you! You Al? Need to say to you!"

"Speak Russian to me before you break the bones in your tongue."

After saying that, I noticed that he became hyperactive, and then his friend approached. "Are you trying to be funny?"

In Russian, I said, "Look, I did not hire you to socialize! What do you want?"

"It's three o'clock now. I told you that we needed to be back at four!"

"I did not hear you said that; anyway, we work here until four o'clock, and back in Brooklyn by five, so go back to work, and stop bothering me!"

"Look, asshole! I have another engagement at four o'clock. You will take us back now!"

As I was deciding how to get out of this mess, his friend came forward, and added, "What are you standing there for? Are you deaf?" Then he gave me a push and said, "Let's go!"

I swiveled and simultaneously extended my fist. Upon coming around and toward him, I threw the punch of my lifetime. They guy received a blow and lifted from the ground, landing few feet away from me and next to his friend.

He got up, wiping his lips, and said, "You sucker punched me, slim shit! I will cut you into pieces!"

They both came forward, and then stopped.

"Listen to me carefully because I will say this only once! Go and wait by the van! If you don't, your next appointment would be with God! I promise you that!"

As I stated that, both of them walked backward, and then toward our van. At that point, I really believed I had scared them, but then someone patted me on the shoulder. I turned around and there was Pap, holding a sledgehammer in his hand. Our worker was standing next to him with a crowbar.

"Pap what are you doing here?"

"I saw how that guy took a knife from our tool box, and then went toward you! What happened between the three of you? "

"They wanted to go back sooner! So, that guy had a knife?"

"Yes, in his sleeve! I think they were both ex-convicts!"

"Yeah! They seem that way! Too bad we did not notice before."

"Al, don't take them back to our shop. Those people don't forget, and always look for payback!"

"What is to remember? We had a misunderstanding; no big deal!"

"What do you mean no big deal? I would be surprised if all his teeth are still in place! Drop them ten blocks away!"

"Okay, Pap! You know, because of those assholes, I don't feel like working anymore. Let's pack and go!"

"Yes, let's go."

We assembled our tools, and came to the van. While loading, I noticed how those two were murmuring to each other, and periodically gazing at me.

As our eyes crossed, I knew it was not over. Pap was right about them; those two kept on burning. Our confrontation was just paused, and due to continue at any point.

As I was driving us back, those two had put themselves in a comfortable spot in the back. I repeatedly glanced at the rearview mirror and saw them chatting, which looked more like planning to me. I never walked around watching behind my back, and did not like that idea of living that way. So, when we entered the New Jersey Turnpike Highway, I pulled the van over, and yelled at them.

"Hey, you two! Why don't you stop babbling like whores? You look like two prostitutes! Do you want a piece of me? Then be men and come forward; let's finish it now!" I opened my door, held it open, and with overexcitement said, "Well, chicken shits! What are you waiting for?"

After I said that, both of them jumped out from the back of the van as if they were on springs, and I placed my foot down to the metal, taking off and leaving them both standing in the cloud of black smoke.

"Al, what did you do? You left them in the middle of nowhere!"

"Yes Pap! That was the plan! Did you like it? I can't believe those morons fell for it!"

"I think you misunderstood me. Besides, you could have done that anywhere in Brooklyn. They are illegal, and most likely they will get picked up by the cops!"

"Good! I hope they will be deported!"

We both had a long day. When we finally arrived at our shop, while entering the office with our hands full with tools, the phone rang. It was my mother, as if those two assholes were not enough.

"Hello, Al. I just wanted to thank you for the transfer! Is your dad there? Let me speak with him."

"I can't, Mom; he is busy organizing our tools and all for tomorrow."

"Well then have him call me back! It's important!"

"Mom, we had a long day. I don't think he will call you today. What is so important?"

"Tell him that I need money!"

"But I just wired you two thousand this morning! Why do you need more? And how could you spend two grand in one day?"

"I didn't spend it, Al. I gave to the collector, and he said it's not enough, after he took that money!"

"Mom, I'm tired. We will speak about all this tomorrow. Let me go now, please!"

"Al, please do something, or I and your sister will be on the street! Please do something!"

"Okay, Mom. I will call you back tomorrow; don't worry."

After work I could tell that Pap looked a little distressed, so I did not want to confront him with Mom's problems; however at dinner, and after a few shots of vodka, I said to him, "Pap, I forgot to tell you that I wired two grand to Mom this morning."

"Good, thank you, son!"

"Yeah, but apparently it was not enough; she needs more!"

"What? What do you mean more?"

"I don't know, Pap. That's what she said."

"You know, I didn't believe this will ever end. I need to go there, and the sooner the better! Pour me another, will you!"

"How can you go? You don't have any status here yet! If you go now, you may never come back!" And that's when I realized I should have kept my mouth shut.

"You are right, son! I can't leave now; you must go there and settle everything permanently!"

"What about work? I'm not done with all the estimates!"

"That's why your visit must be brief. I think one week is plenty, so tomorrow, you buy yourself a roundtrip ticket, and get on that plane as soon as you can!"

"Oh man! Israel again!"

"What do you mean again?"

"Nothing, Pap, I just don't feel like going there! There is something else I need to talk to you about."

"What is it?"

"I've been thinking that we need a secretary; that way I won't have to glue myself to the office, and can visit the job sites more often. I will find someone while I'm still here, and she will be here while I'm gone."

"Good idea; do you have anybody in mind?"

"No, but there is an employment agency; they might have someone for us."

The next morning when I called them, they referred someone young but not skilled; however, she was low pay. Besides, what skills does a person need to answer the phones? So I said yes to that.

The same afternoon, she showed up and entered the office. "Hello, I'm looking for Al!"

"Hi, you have found him! What can I do for you?"

"I'm here for a job!"

"Are you sure this is the right place?"

"Yes I am! Why do you ask?"

"Well, I did not ask for a model!"

"Thank you! It's funny that you said that. I am a model."

"So what brings you here?"

"Lack of work, and I can't sit home with nothing to do."

"I see! I'm sorry; I did not get your name."

"Sara!"

"Nice to meet you Sara. However, maybe you should reconsider we deal with construction sites!"

"I'm a fast learner, and will adapt quickly; just try me!"

At that point, I felt myself blushing, and at the same time, thinking, if she were a car, I would drop all my ordeals, just to drive her all day long. I wanted to try her in so many ways; unfortunately, none of them fit her job description.

"Excuse me, Al! So, would you give me a chance?"

"Yes! And then some!"

"Excuse me?"

"I meant some other things that you would have to do while I'm gone!"

"Oh, so who would guide me?"

"Well let's hope that you are edible . . . I meant capable, as you said! Anyway, sit here, write all the messages there, and I will be back soon!"

"What? Now!"

"Yes, now! Why wait? Besides, I have to go get tickets to Israel, so please make yourself comfortable! Also, I work with my dad; his name is Sasha."

At the travel agency, they gave me two options, a next day flight, or, the following week. Because this trip was not to my liking, I decided to expedite the task and get it over with as soon as possible.

When I purchased my ticket, I returned home, then called my mother and gave her the news. She was stunned and at the same time relieved. I still did not get why she had problems.

Many people have loans there, and some don't pay back, so what is the big deal? I never heard of someone becoming homeless due to his furniture loan.

Toward the end of the day, for no reason, I dialed our office. Maybe I wanted to here her voice again.

"Altitude; may I help you!"

She sounded sexy, and I got an erection from those few words. I could not comprehend what was happening to me, so I hung up.

I froze on the couch with the phone in my hand, shocked at the idea, that now; I could not call my own office. Sara was what some would describe as a perfect creation of God. Regardless, she is nice person, and pleasant as well. Now, I had found a weakness in me, which I never encountered before.

Nicole is very pretty as well, but I guess a woman's character plays a big role. Nicole possessed a manly soul, and Sara was like an angel. Anyway, my reaction was abnormal, so I decided to call back and reconcile myself with morality.

"Hi, Sara, how are you doing?"

"Hello, Al, considering that only one person called, I'm doing great."

"Some days are like that. Who was it? Anyone important?"

"I don't know. Her name is Nicole, and she was looking for you. When I asked her to leave a message she hung up!"

"Okay, thank you, Sara."

"I'm sorry if that was your wife. I should have known about her."

"Don't be sorry. I am not married. I will be leaving for Israel tomorrow and will see you next week!"

"Oh! Okay then; have a great trip, Al!"

"Would you like an Israeli souvenir?"

"No, thank you. I would like my boss to come back! And if you can, just call me when you land!"

"Okay, I will."

What was that? Was she coming on to me? No, she barely knew me, and it was probably my imagination creating ideas of my desire.

Afterward, I called Nicole to say goodbye. To my surprise, she took it quite the opposite as my mom.

"Hey, I have good news!"

"Is this about that new bimbo answering your phones now?"

"Why would you say that? She is very nice!"

"I bet she is! So tell me, how nice is she? Or is it too soon to ask?"

"Stop that. I thought you were too smart to be jealous."

"Okay Al, so what is the good news?"

"You will soon become Al-free! I'm flying to Israel tomorrow."

"You always have a strange way of wording things! When are you coming back?"

"In a week; do you want anything Israeli?"

"I already had me something while you were around! However, since you asked, bring me some CDs with European music; actually, it is for my father. They all are here, you know! So tell me, why are you leaving so suddenly?"

"My mom has some difficulties, but I am not quite sure what kind!"

"Oh, your mom! You know, log time ago, she told me that you are afraid of flying! Is that true?"

"Not exactly. I am not afraid of flying; I just don't like the idea that someone else is in control of my life, so you can say that I am scared of helplessness!"

"Wow! Al is finally scared! That is my greatest discovery yet!"

"Okay, very funny. You know, you make me smile when you laugh!"

"Thank you, Al! You see, you do possess the right approach when you want to! Let me go with those final words in my mind, before you mess up again! Have a great trip! And call me when you can!"

Knowing that my departure was right away, I rushed to downtown Manhattan, I killed some hours there, however, on my way back home, I got all I needed and more.

At home, I packed three huge suitcases with DVD players, VCR players, car stereos, and other electronic equipment; all top notch latest models, and all made for European use. Growing up in that country, I learned the importance of those items; it was difficult to obtain them, due to their high value.

With my suitcases jam-packed with electronics, I sat down on the couch, and said to myself, *Now, how in the world will I pass those monsters through Customs?*

The next day, my boarding on the plane was easy, and the extra weight fee came to peanuts in comparison to the real value of the contents.

My overseas flight was very smooth. I hardly sensed that I was airborne, and for some reason, after a few hours, I felt myself in the middle of nowhere.

Everything appeared to be running smoothly, so my feeling of helplessness slowly switched into total tranquility. The engine sounds had structured a harmony of relaxing tunes, suddenly; all of my worries had erased. I had no desires, no demands, and no ambition to land on the ground any time soon.

The atmosphere of the enormous aircraft, and the stress-free circumstances developed into one of those rare states that made me cherish my life.

Prior to landing, the steward handed me a declaration sheet, and that's when I became agitated. How was I supposed to declare any of my items? Or the large sum of cash, I carried in my sock. If I did, Israeli taxes would leave me penniless, and then I would be calling my Pap instead of Mom. So I didn't.

Israelis are, without exception, overconfident and arrogant by nature, so only for now, I decided to become one of them once again! After passing through customs, when my suitcases arrived, I placed them on my cart and kept my US passport in my hand, visible to all, then commenced walking toward the line and along the side of the crowd that had nothing to declare.

As I came closer, security guards were standing on both sides of the exit. I adjusted my speed to the crowd on my right, and, alongside them, slowly approached the cross line. The guard to my left stared at my passport and neglected my load. As I passed, I ignored him as if he did not exist, and walked by him, then past him and away.

After a long walk toward the exit, I was certain someone would catch up with me, so I stopped, turned around, and there was nobody there. What a relief that was. Walking through the Israeli airport had reminded me that this was my second unwilling visit. If life is all about choices, why do I always appear in undesired places?

Then I saw my mother.

She ran toward me, hugged me, and said, "Hello, Al! I'm so glad to see you!"

"Hi, Mom, so am I! How have you been?"

"Much better, now that you are here! Let's go quickly; our bus will depart soon!"

"No, Mom; no buses. I have a car rental. I just need to find where that is."

After a brief search, we were on our way to my Mom's home. Driving through Tel-Aviv with so many tiny cars and such narrow roads was annoying. I was surprised that it took us almost two hours to cover less than ten miles.

When we arrived, Mom's place was on the fifth floor, and there was no elevator.

"Mom, how do you climb those stairs every day? I could get a stroke just by looking at them!"

She smiled and hopped up those stairs like she had tiny wings on those shoes, and I tried to keep up. But how could I? My suitcases weighted a ton, so if one trip up the stairs was exhausting, I had to repeat that privilege twice.

When I walked into the apartment, I was stunned. The place was equivalent to a basketball court. I sat on the chair, and said, "Wow, Mom! This place is enormous. Why would you rent something like that? Or need so much space for that matter!"

"Yes, it's big. I know! You see, Valerie was very depressed from leaving her friends again, so I thought this place would cheer her up!"

"And where is Valerie, by the way?"

Oh! Didn't I tell you? I signed her up with the military school, so she spends most of her time at the Naval Academy!"

"Why did you do that, Mom?"

"Because, I needed to work, and I work two shifts, cleaning offices and houses, so who would take care of your sister while I'm gone?"

"I see! So tell me, what kind of problems do you have?"

"Come, I will show you!"

She took me to the living room, and said, "Look at this craftsmanship! This furniture is very rare, made in Italy, you know! Now how could I describe that to you over the phone? I also have a bedroom to match!"

"Mom, I don't understand; why did you buy all of that, and this apartment? You called your move a new beginning! Well it's not; you are living in large! And what is worse, you make others pay for all that! Back in the old days, Jim and I were making good money, and never could afford something like this; why did you do it?"

"Because, I was also depressed, I needed a drive to keep me on going!"

"Some drive you picked! At this rate, you will drive us all under!"

"I don't need a lecture from you! I will resolve this myself."

"I'm glad you said that, Mom! Because you will take this all back, and I will help you, even if I have to carry all this lumber on my back!"

"I can't take it back, I have tried; he told me those items are not returnable!"

"Who did, Mom?"

"The store owner, I spoke to him a few days ago!"

"Take me there."

"Okay, we will go tomorrow."

"No, Mom! We will go now!"

When we got out of the building, I asked, "Mom, how much do you owe him?"

"Well, somewhere around six thousand."

"That's in shekels, right? So how much that would be in dollars?"

"That's in dollars, Al."

"What? That lumber is not worth so much! Or is it, Mom?"

"Well, they added interest for late payment."

"Okay, Mom, where is the nearest bank in this shit-hole!"

"Al, don't talk like that. There is one next block; oh, it's the same block where that store is."

"Okay, let's go to the bank first."

When we got to the bank, I pulled one grand from the ATM, and another two thousand from my sock, and we were one our way to that store. As we walked there, I became hyper, and was dying to meet with the asshole that cheated my mom. I also noticed a storefront with familiar logos on the glass.

"Mom, stop; let me go in there for a moment."

When I came out, Mom said, "What did you buy in there? Your eyes are glowing!"

"I bought this! Well, quite a few of them actually! Please hold this bag while I sip a little!"

"Al, why did you buy three bottles? Hey, Al, stop. You said a sip; what's a matter with you?"

"Oh boy! That felt good! This is my drive! In case you were wondering!"

When we entered the store, I was pumped up, and walked right into the room with a door sign that said, "Private"

"Sorry, but I'm with the clients now. Please wait outside." A fat man said that, while sitting behind a desk loaded with papers.

"Don't be sorry. I will be brief, and you two leave now!"

"Wait a minute. Mr. and Mrs. Goldman, please sit down. There is some . . ."

"Hey Goldmens! Get up! That's it! Now to the door you both go!"

I escorted them out, walked back to the table, took one chair, and placed in front of the asshole, then stared at him and waited.

"What do you want?"

"Look at your screen behind you; nice system you have here! Do you really think it will protect you?"

"What the . . ."

"Keep looking, there. You see that woman?"

"Yes, so?"

"That lady, there! She is my mother! Because of the way you treated her, I had to fly in from New York, jus to see you fat ugly face! So tell me! How do you think that makes me feel?"

"Wait a minute; you got it all wrong. I . . ."

"Oh, you are saying that my mom is a liar!"

"No! No, I . . ."

"Shut up and listen, because I will say this only once! You see this?" I showed him my US Passport, and continued. "In case you get any funny ideas, this is my get out of jail card, and guess who I will be visiting on my first day out? Yes! You! Rest assure I will not be so nice on our next encounter!"

"Okay, what do you want?"

"Show me the documents on my mother's purchase!"

He rolled on his chair to the wall closet, opened a drawer and pulled out a file, then rolled back and handed over to me. He, said, "That is you mother's paperwork; it's all there."

"I see the entire collection had cost you eighteen hundred, and yet, you charged my mom more than triple! Why is that?"

"Because of the sales taxes, and my overhead is huge!"

"I'm sure! Here is two thousand, and before you comment, that is all you will ever see! With the deposit Mom gave you, this deal is profitable for you after all!"

"You don't understand. I must pay the sales taxes. They are almost 300 percent, and I don't . . ."
"Look, let me make something clear for you! Our problem will never go away! And I mean ever! In case of my absence, others will visit you! Now think! Do you really want me to go back and pass the bad news to my dad? You have no idea what would be coming your way, and then money won't help you!"

"Okay, so what shall I do?"

"What do you mean? You don't know the next step of the merchandising. Besides, I'm sure you'll find a way around taxes! People like you always do."

"Oh yes, of course! I will write you a receipt for the this money"

"No you won't! You will give me a paid in full statement! And then a release to any prior allegations toward my mom!"

"Okay, I will. Thank you!"

When I got out of his office, I noticed Mom looking at a dining room set. I came up to her and said, "Here are your documents to freedom!"

We left that store, and on our way back to the apartment, mom was reading the statements and asked me, "Al, it says here paid in full! Did you really pay him that money?"

"Mom, what difference does it make? You are home free, so be happy, and don't you buy anything else! I mean that, Mom!"

"No, I won't, but out of curiosity, how much did you pay him?"

"A few thousand, why?"

"I knew it! Thank you, Al"

"So you knew this would happen! Now I see why you bought this stuff, because you knew I would come here, and you would not have to pay as much! Actually, you paid nothing!"

"Well yes, I knew! Not the details, but I knew you would find a way!"

"A way to what? I robbed that man out of his profit! And for what? It's not like he pointed a gun to your head and made you buy this junk! You used me! And cheated him! Why Mom?"

"Because you have it in you, and I knew that you could! And that man is the one who cheats, not me."

"What do you mean by saying I have it in me? What do I have? You know, Jim said same thing!"

"Well, you place your foot on the ground, and you have the gift to hold it there! In the same spot, no matter what happens!"

"I'm not sure I follow you, but, how do you know?"

"Mother always knows"

"Mom, I swear to God! I will never bail you out like this again. Because it is wrong what you did, and what's worse is that you don't realize that."

By the time we got home, I was depressed, and glad of my sudden purchase, so the contents of the open bottled visited my stomach before dinner was on the table, and then, I reached for the second.

"Al, you must control yourself; your organs are not iron. You may cause heavy damage to you liver at this pace!"

"Oh, so now you are worrying about me? Where was that worry before, I was boarding EL/AL to get here?"

"Okay, that's enough, do you hear? At least eat, and eat well!"

"Mom, tomorrow I will revise my return flight, and leave as soon as possible. My work is done here; there is no need to waste any more time here!"

"And how about spending some quality time with your mother? Is that a waste, too?"

"No Mom and you know it! I would love to do that! However, Pap is there alone, and I know he needs me. You see, we have almost completed our projects, so, if I am absent, will have no work!"

"That's alright Al. You don't have to explain, I understand."

"By the way, those suitcases are loaded with electronics. I will call Danny tomorrow, and ask him to help me out."

"Danny, have you located Danny?"

"Nope! Not yet! But I will tomorrow!"

"Go to sleep Al; you're drunk!"

"My lips are drunk, by my mind is still sober, so I will be sipping more of this awful liquid! Man, it really tastes like gasoline, why do people drink this? You know, this question always puzzled me."

"Go to sleep Al. Your mind is not sober."

"Yes it is!"

"How would you know?"

"Because, I can still see you!" And then I could feel myself floating again!

The next day, I called my lost friend Danny. I did not think that he would be listed, but to my surprise, he was. We talked on the phone briefly because he wanted to see me the same day, and invited me over for dinner.

Denny still lived in Haifa and in the same neighborhood, only now he was married and had two sons. Dinner was at six pm, but I drove to Haifa in the morning.

Twelve year had passed by, and now I was dying to see the neighborhood where I grew up. Back then, I was fortunate, because the building we lived in contained many families with children around my age. So we were all friend, and most of them I considered my close friends. However, when my mother sent me away, I lost contact with all of them, and never heard from them again.

So now, it was my chance to reconnect, and to see how they were doing. However, before that, I went to the travel agency and switched my return ticket to the earliest on hand, which was the following day.

Driving into Haifa, and then up the road to Carmel, looking at the surroundings gave me the goose bumps. It was pleasant and sad at the same time, I felt as I was going back in time, everything was the same, except for the people I once knew. Then I drove up the hill to the most familiar narrow road, waiting for it to come to a dead end, because, that's where our building was.

Slowly driving in, I could visualize the crowd at the parking lot, where most of us, sat on the curb next to the cars. On any given day, after dinner and homework, all of us assembled at that same spot, passing time with stories and laughter.

While thinking about those great times, I could feel myself smiling. But, when I drove up to the dead end, there was nobody there, that whole place looked deserted. I stopped, got out of the car, and walked around for a few minutes, to the place where Jim and I use to sit.

Then walked to the building entrance, buzzed some familiar doorbells, but there was nobody home. Maybe I came there too early, and probably, later on, I would not like what I would see, so I left in a hurry, and drove to the sea.

I went to the beach where we all used to hang out on the weekends. Back then, that territory was deserted, and now, they had built cafeterias and restaurants along the entire shore, so I sat myself at a table for two, ordered a triple espresso, and sat there for hours and hours, recalling and visualizing how my life used to be.

Time passed, and I went to see my old lost friend. When I arrived at his house, all his family were there by the table, waiting for me.

"Man! Al, is that you? What happened to you?"

"Damn, Dan! It's been a long time! And you haven't changed a bit!"

"Thanks, man! What did you do to yourself? I mean, look at you! You are a fucking giant! They feed you with steroids in New York or what?"

"Oh, please stop it. I was always like this; it's the time frame!"

"Time frame my ass! You use to be thin! That's why we all called you a stick, not to your face of course, but that was you nickname!"

"Oh, now you are telling me?"

"Anyway, come and meet my family!"

"Okay, but first, help me bring a few suitcases in here. I will tell you about them later."

When he introduced me to his family, I was pleasantly surprised, and for some strange reason, I had a feeling within myself that was unrecognizable to me.

The food was delicious; his wife was beautiful. She had that innocent look on her face, with wide deep blue eyes and a smile to remember. As we were eating and drinking while recalling our past, Maureen was paying close attention, and mostly looking at me. Her appearance and manners matched my prime choice.

Through the entire dinner course, Dan kept on pouring me one shot of vodka after another.

"Dan, I don't remember seeing you drink before! When did you start?"

"Same day I got married! And then some when the little one was born."

"Yes, Al, and after I gave him a second child, he can't stop drinking!" Maureen added her few cents; she wanted to continue but Dan interrupted.

"Okay, enough about me! Let's here your story!"

"What do you mean?"

"You and I almost empted this bottle, and you don't seem to mind. Speaking of memories, I am also not recalling at any point in time seeing you drink! So what happened, Al? You used to be a one athletic dude!"

"It's a long story; however, I think my main cause is the lack of stimulation!"

"Oh, please, you are very young, there are so many babes in New York, I'm sure. Add to that all the opportunities; what else is needed?"

"Family, Dan! Babes don't attract me anymore. I had my share! Hey, pour me another, will you?"

"Sure! Here you go! Al, I remember you and the way you were! That was not that long ago! So what happened?"

"I can't find what drives me, and on a few good days, when I do, I don't seem to shift myself into the right gear. Pour me another one, will you?"

"Hey! You see, babe! And you think that I'm drinking!"

"Oh, shut up, Dan! Can't you see something is eating him up?"

"Okay, Al. I'm sorry!"

"Don't be. I'm fine!"

"Hey! How is Jim doing! He was always family-oriented. I bet he is married! So is he?"

"Jim is dead, Dan."

When I said that, silent covered the room. They both froze, and I felt responsible for that moment.

"Hey, guys! Wake up! Look; that's life. And it was long time ago, so let's move forward, please!"

"Al, how long ago? Tell me what happened."

"Look, Dan, my life story is like a barrel with no end! If I begin to tell it, we will be sitting here for weeks, maybe months. Instead, I propose we change the subject. Let's talk about the two of you!"

Dan let the subject go, and I was very relieved. Our meet was coming to its end, and as I was walking toward the door, Dan said, "Al, don't forget your suitcases!"

"Actually, they are for you! I need to ask a favor from you."

"Sure, what is it?"

"You see, my mom is short on funds, so I brought some systems to sell, but have no time to sell them. They are all in the suitcases. Can you take care of this matter for me, and pass the funds to my mom?"

"Yes! Of course!"

"Thanks, man! I appreciate that! Oh, by the way, before you sell it all, pick something for yourself, as a gift from me!"

"Thanks, but I won't; your mother needs all she can get."

"I insist; besides, there is more here than she really needs. Look them over! You'll see."

"Thank you, Al. I will! And I will! Don't worry."

As I drove back to my mom's place, all the roads were empty, so I got thinking about Dan, and how lucky he was, having that family around him. His sons we're amazing, and Maureen was one of a kind; very hard to find and worthy of so much, and yet, Dan hardly noticed her.

It is simple to neglect someone that comes only once in a lifetime, for most, that good luck never arrives at all. Why is it that a person realizes the true value of love and friendship only upon its loss? That is exactly what happened to me with Jim. I loved him truly but did not really show it, and now, I would give anything just to say it to him once.

And then, it hit me, Jealousy. That was it! That's what I felt when I saw Dan's family. I never encountered this feeling before. No wonder I got confused; what a lousy state of mind.

I have never envied anyone in my life, never had any reason to, until the day where darkness took over and placed me in its black region. No matter how hard I try to break free, sometimes, I feel like a squirrel in the wheel; in spite of his speed, he is always in the same spot.

Since Jim left me, my mind had become my worst enemy, and every so often, my thoughts would not let me be in peace. I couldn't stop rationalizing or analyzing my actions, and what's worse, I don't seem to come up with any clear solutions.

There is some good to every bad event. Thanks to my thoughts during driving, I arrived at Mom's building in a glint, and did not get lost. I rushed upstairs for one reason; I needed to clear my head and there was only one way known to me, so I pulled the second bottle out the bag, sat in the kitchen and poured myself a shot.

"Hi Al! Why are you sitting here in the dark?"

"Hello, Mom; did I wake you?"

"No, so how was your reunion?"

"Fine! Dan has a great family!"

"I can see it bothered you a little. Don't worry, your time will come!"

"I don't think so. Sometimes I feel like I'm going against the current! It's like, when the crowd is running downhill, I'm the first climbing up. Do you know what I mean?"

"Yes, I know what you mean, but I don't see you that way. My image is different, and quite the opposite of yours. You have achieved a lot, and also obtained losses, but that is the way of life, and no one can change that! Be grateful for what you have!"

"What are you talking about? What do I have? I have nothing! No family, no girlfriend, even my work is not steady, so what do I have?"

"Al, you must know yourself before complaining! No one could control you, or tell you what to do, since you were a little boy, that's because, you are destined to rule. That's why, with no funds at hand, you became self-employed, and if your personal life does not suit you, it's only because of what you have chosen."

"I did not choose anything. This glass is the only thing that calms me down. Without it, I would be a nervous wreck!"

"Yes! But with it, there is no one else besides you!"

"What are you saying?"

"Life is all about choices! Those who choose difficulties acquire a family; you have chosen the easy way in life, where there are fewer struggles, so you sit with this bottle. However, life was not destined to be easy! With time, that bottle will take you to the worst phase of your life, where there will be no return. That is why I left. I don't want to live to see that day, and see you suffering."

"So that's why you left? And I thought it was because of Pap."

"Why would you think that? Pap began drinking when he was in diapers! That is the way of the Russian population; everybody knows that, and I knew that when I married him. But unlike you, he knows his limits, and he never commits to anything after one drop of alcohol; moreover, he is reliable! Have you ever seen him not show up for work? Or arrive late?"

"I never gave it much thought, but no, never!"

"There you go! So, if you could control yourself, we would not be having this conversation; and what's more, you would have a family. No worthy woman would be next to a drunk! And we both know you won't ever settle for anything less! So, now I will be honest with you about Nicole. I was not against her only because of your drinking problem. When you are drunk, she is perfect for you! But when you are sober, she is not your type, and not your significant other! You see that, don't you? That's why you always break up! And she will use you because she sees that there is nothing else for her! She is very smart, you know. She can outsmart you on any day of the week! Remember that, and learn to control yourself, my son, because if you will let it, alcohol will control you!"

"Okay, and how do I learn that? Which school shall I attend?"

"You see; there you go again, being a smart ass, excuse my French! Look within yourself; it's there. What you don't see doesn't mean that it's absent."

"You know, I tried to dig within myself, and have to say, it turned to be my hardest task ever. I don't know if I will find what I'm seeking! Mom, do you know who you are? I mean the inner you, not your body!"

"Well, not quite yet! However, I know enough to always maintain my dignity, and constantly work on myself. We all make mistakes Al, and that is normal! What is abnormal is when we repeat them!"

"Okay, Mom, I got it, and hope it will help me; however, I need to turn in."

The next day I overslept, so the whole day began on high speed. I needed to buy CDs; afterwards mom and I would spend some quality time in a restaurant, and then my departure.

I did not let her escort me to the airport, so we said goodbye at home.

"Mom, I did not tell you yesterday. I left some items with Dan to sell, so he will call you soon. Please find a way to get to him and collect the profits."

"I don't understand, but okay, I will."

"Details are not important; just be there when he calls you!"

"I forgot to ask you about Max! How is he?"

"Max is fine! All grown up now, if you want details, ask Pap; he spends more time with Max than me!"

"Okay, I will; say hello to Max from me."

And so I left. On my flight back, I wasn't so lucky. There was a woman sitting next to me holding a newborn baby. There was no tranquility for me, and that baby was no ordinary baby; he never stopped crying. My flight was overbooked and I could not exchange seats, so instead of musical harmony, I developed a huge migraine.

When we landed and I walked out of the terminal, there was nobody there to meet me. I was sure that mom would call and give Pap the heads-up about me coming back sooner, but I was wrong again! Just last night she was inspiring me with her knowledge of proper behavior, and now, what it worth. I was neglected, and probably for no good reason.

I grabbed a cab and arrived home. I brought the last bottle with me, and thought to keep it as a souvenir, but disappointment had evolved into an inner volcano. As a result, it was eating me alive, so my souvenir was the only thing that kept my lava from bursting out.

When that bottle was half-empty, I called Nicole. "Hey! I'm back!"

"Hi Al. I thought you would be gone for a week! What happened?"

"Did I call at a bad time? I can call you back in three days if you like."

"No, don't be silly. I was just surprised; in a good way, of course!"

"Well, nice of you to add the 'good way' phrase!"

"So how was Israel? Who did you save?"

"I told you that I was going to see my mother."

"Yes, I know! Was your trip worthwhile? Or was it a bit disappointing?"

"What? Hold for a sec. Okay, so why would you think that?"

"Al, what did you do just now? Are you drinking?"

"Yes! I am! Why are you people always bugging me with the drinking shit! Do you know what I have noticed lately? The more you all talk about it, the higher my urges! As a matter of fact, sometimes I don't want to look at alcohol, but as soon as I hear about it from any of you, I'm dying for a shot!"

"Okay Al, you mother probably pissed you off, but I had nothing to do with that! So please stop with the booze, and call me only when you are sober!"

"I am sober! For now, anyway! So tell me what you did with yourself."

"Nothing much, same routine. Oh, and I was in the neighborhood, so I visited your office!"

"You knew I was not there! So why would you do that? Did you think I was lying to you?"

"No, Al, I called the airlines! I just wanted to see if her voice matched your taste!"

"Don't you find it odd that you always end up in the neighborhood? And why would you call the airline? You doubt me, don't you?"

"Stop with the twenty questions! Better, tell me, where did you find that sponge? You think her appearance will comfort you. She is a slut, Al. I think you were the one who told me not to judge a book by its cover, so what happened?"

"It's depends on the book!"

"What? What did you just said? So you do have the hot's for her!"

"Well, who wouldn't? But it's completely innocent; she sweet, that's all!"

"Sweet, you say! Maybe you thought that while observing her tits, which are half way exposed, by the way! I want you to fire her immediately!"

"I can't do that, she is very affordable!"

"I bet she is!"

"I did not mean it that way! We cannot afford a professional secretary, besides, she raises the office spirit, and it's bad for business when the doors are closed."

"She raises your penis! Get rid of her, Al."

"Okay! That's enough! Go fuck yourself! I'm tired of you!"

"You will regret that tomorrow!"

"I won't remember that tomorrow!"

"I will remind you! Good night!"

"It's still bright outside. And I mean it; get lost!"

"Al, don't play with me!" Then she hung up.

Nevertheless, I knew she wouldn't go anywhere! Nicole was a very persistent woman, and always got what she wanted. On similar occasions, she had come up with a new approach and used some of her friends as alliances. It worked in the past, but this time I did not talk to them.

I could not understand her purpose in the matter, bearing in mind that I was a drunk. Her family and her friends even gossiped about it. I was useless from all perspectives, so why would a woman persist toward a man like me?

Not to mention, that my statements to her "Fuck off" and "find someone else." Why she would want to be by my side? In the past, I had doubted the phrase, "Retraction is the best attraction," but now I saw that we were the perfect example.

Every so often, I speculated about her motives and could not come with any conclusions. Although I was self-employed and had a car, was it really enough to make me seem like a good catch? Of course, not, putting myself in her shoes, I would not want to date me, so what was that she was after? Why was she always connecting with me?

In attempt to discover her motives, I needed to dig deep and find whom she really was, not much known to me about her, only puzzles. Nicole had an upscale lifestyle; she was not making much money, but always looked like a million dollars. How was that possible? Her daddy was too cheap to finance her, so who was he? In addition, why would she pursue me while getting nothing in return?

But then again, it might have been simple? She had never gained anything worthwhile from me. Our relationship never satisfied her material needs, because her intentions were for much more. So she kept on played me, and upon each break-up, she was dissatisfied with herself. That is why she searched for a way to reconnect us again.

That would also explain our interactions, two months together and three mounts apart, and then all over again, a cycle of misery. It had no future for me, or for anyone else I could think of, so I decided not to see her or speak to her ever again.

I went to work, and things were back to how they used to be, boring and same on daily bases, for over six months.

Until one day, when Pap and I arrived home, I went in first, and that's when I felt something was missing. At first, I did not realize what it was, then I looked around, and began shouting. "Max! Where are you, boy?"

There was no response. Max always knew when one of us was coming home, and was at the door waiting prior to our arrival. I witnessed that on many occasions, when he was waiting for Pap. So when he was not there, I knew something bad had happened to him, and when I ran to the backyard, I saw him lying on the ground, still.

I approached him closely, and discovered that he was dead. He rested so peacefully, and I yelled, "Pap! Come here, quickly!"

When Pap rushed in, I looked at him and saw tears in his eyes. "Al, let's place him in my car; we need to find a place, and bury him."

"I can't go along with this. Please, Pap, go without me."

Therefore, he did. I watched him carry Max to his car, and my heart was pounding the whole time. There was so much distress accumulating within me, I thought that my body would explode, so I went to the fridge, pulled a bottle, and began drinking again.

When I arrived at my relaxation condition, I called Nicole. So much time had gone by, and I had no idea why I was dialing her number.

"Hello! Who is this? Speak up."

"Yes, hi, it's me again."

"Al, talk about lost and found! You are the last person I expected to hear from."

"I don't think so."

"I asked you before; don't call me when you are drunk!"

Then she hung up on me. With only the few words I said, how did she know my condition? So, I redialed.

"Al, when this is going to stop?"

"Max died"

"Oh boy! I'm so sorry to hear that, I loved that dog!

"I don't know what to do"

"Al, this is the way of life, and we all knew it would happen sooner or later! He was sick, remember?"

"Yes, but I thought he got better. You know, after I had my own closure with Jim, I thought that nothing would get to me, but I was wrong. For some reason, the sorrow rips me to pieces."

"Al, please go to sleep."

"Yes, I believe I will. There is nothing I could do anyway, goodnight."

I went to sleep, and when I woke up the next morning, I found myself in the same situation again, so I began drinking again. The next day, I was in the same state, and the day after; the entire week went by and I was still at the same spot.

I was absent from our business for three weeks; through that period, Pap could not get any new projects, and all the ongoing jobs were completed, so it resulted in work stoppage.

When I finally arrived at the office, Sara was gone and our business had turned into a disaster area. Workers were absent, and a huge pile of new projects for bid was collecting dust on my desk, along with a larger pile of unpaid bills.

My father was sitting by his desk. He looked at me and said, "Where have you been?"

"I was at home most of the time! Why?"

"How come I never saw you there?"

"You saw me on a few occasions, but didn't notice me, and let's not get into why! Where is our secretary?"

"Al, the business is dead. We have no work. I told her to go home, and most of our customers that I have spoken with were not happy with your absence, so they will not use us again!"

"Dad, I don't understand. Why is it that, if I'm out, everything comes down? You were here, weren't you? Why couldn't you handle it?"

"I was on the job sites with our men, working to complete the projects. How do you see me in the office estimating new jobs at the same time? It was your responsibility."

"Okay, Pap! So now what?"

"I don't know. Look at the stack on your desk. See if you can find some work. Let's try to put this thing back together again. I will go work at the car service for now. I cannot sit around here and wait for the unknown! Good luck!"

Without any further statements, he got up and left.

Pap and I had built this business from nothing, established equipment, vehicles, and all necessities for six field workers, and now, suddenly, all that had flushed down the toilet, and I was all alone again. What's odd is that I never saw it coming.

I struggled with our businesses for over a month, and could not come up with any resolutions. The situation now became catastrophic; bills were accumulating, and company funds were dissolving. Everything in the business was falling apart, and I could not do anything about it.

So there I was, sitting on a sinking vessel waiting for it to submerge. There were no choices or alternatives but to abandon the ship. So, I posted our business for sale, and hoped to retrieve some of the investment. Instead, I sold the equipment and for less by half than what we paid for it.

So there I was again unemployed. Losing all I had produced enormous emotions of guilt, and alcohol was the best way to conceal that guilt. Shortly after, I became tolerant to alcohol, and when my dosage increased, I still felt sober, odd, but true.

Our shop and the office turned into a useless space with nothing but my desk with one phone, and the couch, of course, but I was there anyway.

At eleven o'clock one morning, I went out to pick up some breakfast. On the way back, I got a bottle of vodka. When I returned, Pap was waiting for me in the office.

"Al, what are we celebrating today?"

"No not we, only me! And there is nothing to celebrate, except a complete freedom. Our business is officially dead, so, now I'm completely free of any obligations. How is your new job?"

"It's bearable, but that is not why I'm here. I have a proposition for you."

"Okay, what is it?"

"I spoke to your mother yesterday, and she is wiling to give me another chance, so you see, I decided to go back and we want you to come along."

"Pap! I just came back from there! What is going on with all of you?"

"We want to be a family again; that's what going on!"

"That is a tall step, Pap, and I'm not sure I could jump that high."

"Al, there is nothing for you here; please come back with me."

"Let me thing about it, okay?"

My father left and I poured myself a drink, thinking there was no way I would go back to Israel. Of course, I had nothing but bad debts here. However, nothing was waiting for me in Israel either, except my mom, of course.

I did not want to drink any further, so I took the bottle and went home. At home, an unexpected surprise was waiting for me at the door.

"Nicole, what are you doing here? Has something happened?"

"No, nothing. I was in the neighborhood and thought I'd stop by, and say hi."

"Okay, hi, and bye."

"Al, please wait. I want to talk to you"

"What do you want?"

"I missed you; actually, I need you, Al."

"Leave me be; go away."

I walked into the house and slammed the door, leaving her standing outside. Persistent as she was, she kept knocking, and I ignored her the whole time she was standing outside and shouting out my name.

After a few drinks, hearing her call became very annoying, so I decided to let her in, and enlighten her with details about the materialistic hypocrite bitch that she was. But I was too late, because when I opened the door, she was gone.

Yes, her train had departed and I dismantled the railroad, so that train could never return.

That was it; from that day, I no longer saw or even thought about Nicole. I engraved that resolution into my mind, and actually, felt good about it.

Being workless and with no ambition to find a job, it was practically impossible for me to stay on my own. It became clear to me that I had to join my father and return to Israel.

However, I could not see myself living in that country again. I had grown into a certain lifestyle. No matter how hard I would work there, Israel would not provide me with my casual life routines, and all the things I am use too.

Understanding my current situation and thinking about my new life in Israel brought me further despair, so instead of preparing, I commenced drinking.

On my second day of freedom, Pap came up to me and said, "Al, you need to get organized; and stop drinking."

"Oh yeah! What am I suppose to organize exactly? Can you be a little more specific?"

"Get your things packed, and if I were you, I would buy something useful, things you could sell there and make money."

"That's a good idea! You know, I did that on my last trip there, and still haven't got shit! What did you get?"

"Refrigerator, TVs, and few other small items. Mom said they are worth thousands of dollars there, so go do something useful."

"Okay, Pap, thanks for the input!"

I took a long shower, got myself together, and drove to Chinatown again. By the end of the day, I returned with sound and light equipment that would light up and rock the roof of a very large building.

When I walked home, Pap was there eating.

"Hey, Pap, you would not believe what I purchased."

"Of course not, so tell me."

"I got equipment for a pretty large size nightclub; I mean everything you'd need, and maybe some more! And I only spent sixteen thousand dollars!"

"Well, that's great! Now we have to get a container."

"Yes. I have been meaning to talk to you about that, the storeowner gave me a shipper's name. They are Israelis, so please call them to make arrangements!"

"No, Al. Please handle everything on your own."

"Okay, Pap! Oh, sorry, I forgot. Here is you share of the business!" I handed him ten thousand dollars.

"That's it? What did you sell?"

"Everything, except one office desk! The owner of Alma Glass bought it all; he also took our phone line, thinking there are customers there!"

"Al, this is peanuts!"

"I know, Pap, but that was my best on such short notice. I can't sell our van and my car"

"So what are you planning to do with them?"

"Nothing; we will leave them here and let the bank deal with it!"

"You know they will sell them at the action, and go after you for the difference!"

"Yes! But I'll be out of this country! And somehow, I don't see myself coming back!"

After closing all the issues with Pap, I took care of our shipping needs, as Pap requested, although, I also knew why he give me that task. He thought that it would prevent me from boozing, but as I drank, all our goods were on their way to the port. Afterwards, when I was wasted, they called from the port to inform me that our container was properly sealed, and all I could say was "Okay"

My final days in the USA were special days, so I cherished them from noon until midnight in the bar.

On the departure day, I called Nicole, and said, "Don't know why, but have to tell you, I'm leaving."

"Well hello to you too! Leaving for where?"

"I'm going back to Israel, in, or, about three hours."

"Okay, and when are you coming back?"

"That is the good news; never! Aren't you happy now?"

"I don't know how to react to this bullshit. Tell me that you are kidding. Is this your way of apologizing, and a reason to call me?"

"Don't flatter yourself! I just thought you would like to know."

"Yes, thank you, of course I wanted to know; where are you now?"

"Same place; where else would I be!"

"Please wait for me there! I would like to see you."

"Why? Do you need closure?"

"Yes, we'll call it whatever you want; just wait for me."

"Okay, but hurry, I have to go soon. My flight leaves in a few hours."

"Thanks! I'm on my way!"

I went back to my stool, and called to the bartender, "Hey Frank, let me have another!"

"So, what will you have this time? Vodka, scotch on the rocks, or tequila?"

"Scotch, hold the rocks, and make it a triple. Wait, better yet, bring the whole bottle."

"Here! Are you okay? What's wrong?"

"I'm going to live in Israel."

"So what is so bad about that?"

"Thinking about the life there irritates me."

"Al. listen, it could be worse; you are acting as if it's the end of your life."

"Frank, like I said, my whole situation is frustrating and abnormal."

"Let me tell you about an abnormal situation! A woman rushes into the doctor's office and says, 'Doc my life turned to a disaster zone.' Doc asks her, 'Why, what happened?' She then states, 'I find everything and all around me irritating, people walking, and cars driving by, birds, trees, and all surrounding sounds.' Do you find SEX irritating as well?' She thinks for a moment and says, 'Sex, what is that?' Doc looks at her, all confused, and says, 'It's hard to explain; instead, let me show you what sex is. Please undress, then lay-down on the couch, and spread your legs wide.' She complies and with great ambition, he penetrates her. While he is trying to perform his best practice, she lays there and says, 'Hey, doc, make up your mind, either you pull your thing out or keep it in! You are going in and out, in and out, in and out. Stop it! It's irritating!'"

"Was that a joke? I am not in the mood. What's your point, anyway?"

"My point being, Al, don't let the unknown irritate you. First find out what it is; you haven't done that yet, and already you are complaining. I've heard only great things about Israel; check it out with open mind and hope for the best."

"Thanks, Frank; your advice will be noted. I will try to remember your story, as well. Now let me tell you what's waiting for me there, and I will refer to that, by telling a joke! As you did"

"Okay! I'm all ears!"

"A rabbit comfortably rests on the grass on the side of a road. Suddenly a wolf drives up; he stops, rolls down his window and calls out, 'Foxy where are you! I have a present for you!' Then out of nowhere, Foxy appears and runs toward his car. When she gets to his window, she asks, 'what is it, Wolf? Tell me, what is it?' Wolf responds, 'It's a surprise! You must look in!' So Foxy sticks her head in, and while observing the interior and attempting to locate her surprise, wolf raises the window and slightly squeezes her neck against the doorframe. She says, 'Hey Wolf, what are you doing? I'm stuck here! Please slide the window down!' Wolf says, 'No honey! Your surprise is coming right up!' As Foxy struggles to break free, Wolf slowly gets out from the passenger door, then walks around the car, comes up to Fox from behind and commences to sexually assault her. Meanwhile, all this time, Rabbit observed the situation, and then thinks to himself aloud, 'Well! I cannot afford a car, but a car door, I would most definitely purchase!'"

"So you see; that is what's waiting for me in Israel!"

"Wow, Al! That was a good one! The joke, I mean."

"Yeah, I know what you meant."

When Frank walked away, I glanced at my watch and saw it was getting late. I needed to get going, so I looked through the window, and there she was, running across the street and toward the bar.

She ran neglecting everything around her and underneath her. I began to observe her closely, and saw Nicole ran toward that bar like dehydrated people run for water after spending a long time in the desert. I then realized, after all, what happen between us, and all of my wrong deeds toward her. At that moment, everything was irrelevant, apparently, I meant something to her, but I never knew what it was.

If a picture is equivalent to a thousand words, that was one of those pictures. I understood and felt her desire just by watching her run.

"Hello, Al; sorry I'm late. Get me a large drink, please!"

"It's okay. You're here; that's what counts."

"Al, thinking that you were going away makes me miss you already. When are you planning to return?"

"I told you before. I am not coming back; there is nothing for me here! I sold everything I had, and purchased electronic equipment. Maybe with little luck, I'll be able to open a nightclub there."

"Al, please stay. You can open a nightclub here!"

"No, I cannot. Here, I was good in a different field. However, apparently, not as good as, I thought I was; everything failed. I failed!"

"I love you, Al. I always did!"

"That's strange!"

"What is?"

"You have a funny way of showing it!"

"Al, I don't know what you saw, but it's true!"

"Shit, I'm late. Let's go. I can't miss this flight."

I called for a taxi, and drove Nicole home. When she got out, it was very painful to see her leave, and she did not look back.

So, I was on my way to the airport.

I arrived at the departure terminal very dizzy and intoxicated. After check in, I rushed toward the boarding area as fast as my feet could carry me, but when I got there, a man in Israeli uniform was shutting the boarding door close.

"Excuse me! I need to get on that plane!"

"Nope! You are too late, son. The plane is departing."

"No way; it's not departing. It's still here! I have to be on that flight. I'm an Israeli soldier, and have to go back today!"

"Show me your boarding pass. Do you have any idea how late you are?"

"Yes, I know, I'm sorry. Goodbyes took longer than expected. I am very sorry; please let me in."

"Let me in, you say? What do you think this is? A bus? Have you been drinking?"

"Yes, I have. It is not an easy task for me. I can't proceed with a sober head. Why are you standing here talking to me? Open that hatch!"

"Go have a seat, and I'll see what I can do."

I sat myself down and watched him talking on the phone with a frustrated look on his face. "Okay; follow me."

"Where are we going? I need to board that plane!"

"And you will; the plane is still here. However, they retracted the platform, so you will be boarding from a land stand. I have to say, you are one lucky bastard. They bought your story being a soldier and all; if you ask me, I don't believe you!"

"I did not ask you! But why would you think I'm lying?"

"Because soldiers are disciplined, and you are late and drunk!"

"Wait, how many engines does this plane have? If it's only two, I'm not flying!"

"What did you say?"

"I'm not flying on a shitty plane with two engines!"

"That is a huge aircraft 747. El/AL doesn't fly anything else."

"I want and I need to see it!"

"You will see it upon boarding."

"No, I need to see it before then, or I'm not going on!"

He stopped, gave me a nasty look, pulled me toward the window, and said, "There! Look down. Do you see that monster? Four engines! Are you happy now?"

"Oh, yes; thank you."

"Okay, now get your ass down there fast! You have made many people angry! Run!"

Running away from him, I could still hear him cursing and calling me names; however, I did not care. I got what I needed, and that was my main goal.

When I entered the aircraft, everybody was looking at me in a very mean way, so finding my seat was very unpleasant, and my longest trip ever.

I finally located Pap, and sat next to him.

"Al, where have you been? When they closed the hatch, I thought that you had decided to stay, and was very upset."

"No need to be upset Pap, I'm here! How could you see the hatch from here anyway?"

"I was waiting for you next to it, until the stewardess closed the hatch, and told me to take a seat. How did you get on board anyway? We were about to depart!"

"You know me, Pap. I have my ways!"

"Al, when are you going to stop living like a child? Grow up already! What you don't realize is, while you are having fun, others worry. Today it was I, on other occasions; you know very well who they are! You need to stop thinking about yourself, and think about others for a change. Only then will your life smile back at you!"

"Okay, Pap. Here, look at this baby!"

"What is it?"

"A gallon of vodka! I need to get in the right mood while I'm flying, and this is my ticket! Do you want some?"

"No, son, thank you. But wait until we are airborne."

"Why? I'm not flying this plane! I'll just have a few sips."

"Look, son, the stewardess is coming. Put it away for now."

"No, Pap, she is probably on her way to check the bathrooms."

"Excuse me, sir! You need to dispose of that bottle immediately! We are about to take off!"

"So take off! And let me do the same!"

"Sir, you have to . . ."

"Listen, miss! You want to tell me that, this plane cannot take off because of my bottle? Is that it?"

"No, I'm just . . ."

"So go buckle up, before you fall and hurt yourself."

"Al, why do you have to make a scene?"

"I did not; she started it! Beside, look around you. There is nobody here but us! Maybe it's because we are sitting in the back; you know what they say about aircrafts. When shit hits the fan, first the tail detaches. I guess that is why, no one else is here but us. And after all that talk, we see she went away!"

"She did not, Al. She went to call for help!"

"Yes, Pap, you are correct. She is coming back with the captain of the ship! But too late, we are already taking off."

"It's not the captain, Al."

"Excuse me, sir, did my assistant tell you to get rid of that beverage?"

"Yes, I believe she did! So don't punish her; she tried very hard. However, for a woman, she would be a more persuasive in a nice and softly manner. I hate it when women like her look for their balls, and then realize they aren't there! That is because God did not give you any! You hear that babe?"

"Okay sir! Now you are being rude. I am asking you for the last time, get . . ."

"Why don't you go away, and leave me to myself. If not, then do something and stop talking! What? You are going to throw me off the plane! Well then, go ahead! When I land, I will sue your ass!"

"You are drunk!"

"Not yet, but that's the plan, so please let me be, because only then will we all have a comfortable flight."

They both finally walked away.

"You see, Pap. They let me be"

"Yeah, and who wouldn't! I'm going to try to get some rest."

"Okay, good night."

I pulled some snacks out of my bags and continued drinking; eventually, the flight became more bearable. However, shortly after, I realized I had turned into a miserable being.

There was no aspiration for a new beginning, and no perspective toward life. I was careless about any outcome. I felt as my perception had left me, and from that point, I needed nothing but alcohol, of course.

For two months, I existed in Israel, and did not try anything; however, my parents were busy with there own life problems, and I felt lonely.

I was spending my days as well as I could, but was not impressed, and had no confidence in tomorrow. I visited most of the nightclubs, and met new people, but I never saw any opportunities of my own. There was nothing for me there, just as I predicted.

Sitting home all the time was out of the question, so mostly I spent my time by the ocean. One day, I decided to take a bus into the heart of Haifa, and walk around on those long forgotten streets. When I walked onto the bus, it was almost empty and I took a vacant seat behind a young girl. After observing the surroundings, I glanced at her, and saw her holding a notepad, and sketching a gun with deep concentration.

That gun was better than real, and looked as if it was about to fire. I tapped her with my finger and said, "Excuse me! But who you are planning to shoot?"

She turned around, smiled, and said, "Hello! You know, it's not polite to snoop around!"

"I did not snoop! Besides, the way you hold it right in the open, I could not help it but look! By the way, very impressive work; all you need now is a bullet!"

"Thank you! I am working on that."

"So tell me, why a gun? There are so many beautiful things out there! If I were a psychologist, I would give you my card and insist on therapy!"

She then began to laugh, and said, "Well then, I guess it's my lucky day! I hate brain diggers! Also I need to get off, that is my stop; nice talking to you."

The bus stopped and she stepped out. Without much thought, I jumped right after her. She must have felt me next to her, because she turned around, smiled, and said, "So you are a psychologist after all!"

"No, I am not! Look, before you get any wrong ideas, let me tell you why I am standing here."

"It is your stop as well!"

"No, please listen."

"Then walk me home and then tell me."

"Okay, when I grew up here, one morning on my way to school, I got on a bus, and it was very crowded. A few feet away from me, I noticed a very beautiful girl. Shortly after, our eyes crossed, and we both were staring at each other for a very long time. I wanted to reach out to her, but it was too crowded. So after many attempts, I made it halfway, and then the bus stopped and she got off. While I was hesitating about what to do next, the doors closed and I was driven away leaving her behind."

"Don't tell me; you are riding the same bus from years ago in an attempt to cross paths with her again!"

"No, I forgot about her the moment she disappeared."

"So what is your point?"

"Well, if I had stayed on this bus now, I would remember you forever! So that is why I'm here."

"Wow! What a line! I never heard that before! Bravo! What is your name?"

"Al. Nice too meet you!"

"The pleasure is all mine! So Al, how did you know that I speak English?"

"Because, of your drawing."

"What? That gun gave me up?"

"Of course not; it's what you wrote in English. What did you mean by it? My enemy is my friend!"

"Oh, that's a very long story! And too soon, to reveal it with you."

"Okay, I'm a patient man! Actually, whom am I kidding? I have no patience whatsoever.

"Thank you!"

"For what?"

"For walking me home."

"What is your name?"

"Gale!"

"Gale, I would like to see you again!"

She wrote on her notepad, then folded that page and gave it to me. She said, "The feeling is mutual, and now I will not have to shoot anyone! See you later, Al."

When she walked in I unfolded that page, and I was very glad to discover her number, right next to her sketch of the gun.

I called Gale that same evening and we met at the coffee shop by the shore. We spoke for a while on subjects that had no meaning, and around midnight, she invited me home.

As we walked into her apartment, I realized she had financial difficulties. She lived in a studio with no furniture, TV, or any other necessities.

As she looked at me, I asked, "Are you in a process of moving out? Or, still moving in?

"Neither! I left it all to my ex, and don't feel like reinstating myself here."

"So you like to sleep on the floor? That's great! I heard it helps with the back."

"Oh shut up, Al. If I wanted to talk, we would still be sitting at the coffee shop!"

"She extended her hand to the wall, pushed in, and a bed unfolded toward the floor. She came up to me closely, swiveled me around, and pushed me on the bed.

"You don't look like the type!" I said.

"Oh yeah, and what type is that?" She said that while unzipping my pants, and pulling them off me.

Then she removed my underwear, grabbed my penis, and said, "Did you think I was shy?" She then commenced to arouse me.

"No! I just thought you were an old-fashioned girl."

"Yes, Al, I like it the old fashioned way! Al, you are a very gifted man! I see it's true what they say!"

"What? What do they say? Hey! Be gentle with that!"

"I am! They say, big hands, big . . .well, you know! Now that phrase proves to be right."

"Gale, wait! I don't have protection."

"I do! I have piles of protection; reach with your hand below the mattress. Just don't get the wrong idea. Relax, Al; it's been a long time for me."

Somehow, I doubted that, but at that point, my morality had departed from me, and I did not try to fight it. Gale was very hungry for sex; she availed herself of my gift repeatedly, and to a point where I thought, it would detach. When I was done for the fourth time, I thought she would finally relax.

But she went down on me again, and said, "Don't get your hopes high, this is not the end! This is the beginning of the end!"

And the entire process was repeated. I was lying there with no feelings at all, periodically glancing at my watch, and when it showed four, I could not believe it was almost sunrise. She had been going at it for four hours.

When she climbed back on top and commenced to ride me, I realized that she did not see me, and it was not about me at all; she wanted to explode and at that moment, I was her only ticket.

"Okay Gale; get off!"

"No! No! I'm almost there! There it is! There! Oh! God! Yes!"

"I'm happy to see your arrival! Finally!"

"You probably think I am a slut."

"No, I think you were eager for orgasm; when was the last time you had one?"

"I don't remember."

"Nice stuffed bear! I did not notice him before."

"That's probably because he just walked in."

"What? Is this thing alive?"

"Relax, Al, he is very intelligent."

"What is he? And why he did not come to you when we walked in?"

"He is my bodyguard, a Rottweiler, and I trained him for over two years."

"Damn, he looks vicious; I need to go."

"Okay, I will call you later."

When I left, I felt like a used whore; it would make more sense if she had paid me. That night was my longest walk ever, and when I arrived home, I was heavily depressed.

I was holding a cup of coffee and wondering how this could be possible.

I was looking for company, and what company I found. I probably gave her the wrong vibe, so what was I supposed to do now? How would I face Nicole if I ever went back to her?

I was not attracted to Gale, and thought that without desire, spending time with her would ease my staying here. At first, it was plain and simple, but then what a turn-around.

So I decided to lose her number, and forget about the day I met her.

Another useless week had gone by, and during that time, I was longing for my life in New York, and Nicole, which eventually brought me back to drinking.

I do not know why, but I missed her more than ever before, and felt as if, a part of me had ripped away. I could not tolerate this feeling anymore, so I called her.

"Hi! Miss me?"

Al, is that you?"

"Yes, how are you?"

"Not so good. I miss you; when are you coming back?"

"I told you, I left for good. There is no coming back for me. Besides, I have no relatives or friends in New York, so even if I wanted to, I would not have any place to stay."

"You can always come and stay with me!"

"You probably did not think before you said that! Look, I have not settled here yet. I don't have any income, and those phone calls are expensive, so I will have to say goodbye! We'll talk again soon."

"No Al! Wait. Give me your phone number, please!"

"Okay, but only if you promise to be civilize about calling me."

"Yes! I promise!"

"Its 555-1212 and don't dial those numbers ten times a day."

"Okay Al, thank you."

I could tell she was happy to hear from me, and I was relieved listening to her voice; sometimes my character reveals strange behavior.

When she was close by, I often ignored her, and now that she was so far away, I found that I needed her the most. Could it be that, what comes easy; is not truly appreciated, or was it just my personality? And if it was, what could I do to correct it? It might be also that we got comfortable with each other, and now, it was hard to let go.

The most frustrating thought in my mind was why I didn't remember all the bad qualities in Nicole. For some reason, all that pushed me away from her was now, suddenly forgotten.

As I was thinking, the phone rang, and I thought it was mom, checking on me. "Hello, Mom, is that you?"

"Hi, Al, it's me."

"Nicole, what happened?"

"Nothing, I just wanted to hear your voice. So, tell me, what are you up too? Do you have any plans?"

"You heard my voice five minutes ago! I thought we agreed."

"Yes we did. But I am calling you; so don't worry!"

"I have no plans. I thought to open a nightclub here, so I brought with me everything I might possibly need for that task! But, Israel is not what it used to be, I am very disappointed!"

"Okay, I will let you be. Stay there until you realize where you belong, and then come back to me! Goodnight, Al!"

"Goodbye, Nicole."

We had to be thousands of miles apart, to clarify our emotions toward each other; it was pleasing to know that Nicole needed me, and I began to believe her.

She called me again, then again, begging me to come back. She stated where her mistakes, also pledged to change, and I assured her that would not drink again.

So now, I was debating with myself, trying to figure out what my next step would be. I wanted to go back badly, but at the same time, I did not want to repeat my mistakes. And if that situation was not tiring enough, suddenly an opportunity knocked on my door. At the most wrong and unexpected time ever.

Pap had a close friend in Israel, and apparently, he had spoken to him about me, and my idea. So one evening when he came home, he said, "Son, I think your dream of creating a nightclub is about to come true!"

"No way! How is that, Pap?"

"Do you remember my friend Ariel?"

"Yes, I think I do."

"Well, he owns a big loft up in Carmel, and when I told him about your idea, and all the equipment that you brought in, he got very excited and decided to go along with you! Moreover, he said that he would invest in everything else!"

"Wow, Pap! That is some news!"

"Yes, it is. I invited him for dinner, so he will be coming tomorrow."

"Thank you, Pap. I can't wait"

Now, the idea of going back created a dilemma with Pap's great news.

Nothing is ever easy or simple, so I decided to talk with my mother about it. Something about Nicole was still bothering me, and I did not know what it was.

"Mom, can I talk to you?"

"Of course, what is on your mind; you look confused."

"I am confused, Mom. I decided to go back to Nicole. I miss her badly, but there is something that's holding me back from committing, and I don't know what it is."

"I know what is holding you, son. Disappointment is holding you; you are fearful to be disappointed again. So many times, the both of you tried and nothing good came of it. It is only normal to be scared. I am sure she feels scared as well. Let me ask you, did she request you to return, or are you doing it on your intuition?"

"Well, both, but she did ask me back."

"Smart girl."

"Why do you say that?"

"Because, son, she knows it is harder to live with regret than to be disappointed."

"What do you mean? Can you be more specific?"

"Go back to her Al, and give it your best. Only then, you won't have regrets. So go. You have nothing to lose. In worst scenario, you'll come back."

"Thank you, Mom. I understand, and I will try to make it work."

When I went back to my room, Mom called me. "Al, it's for you."

"What is it, Mom?"

"The phone, Al; some lady is asking for you."

So I picked up the phone.

"Hi, Al; was that your mother?"

"Hello, Gale; yes, it was."

"So what are you doing? Would you like to ride me?"

"No, Gale. I'm still swollen from your last ride! Besides, where were you for over a week?"

"I was busy."

"So go get yourself busy again, and this time with someone else!" And I hung up on her. However, as soon as I placed the phone on the wall, it rang again.

"Al, don't hang up on me, please."

"What do you want?"

"Actually, I need your help. My dog is sick; please stop by."

"Take him to a vet. I can't come to you. I am packing and going back to New York."

"I don't believe you! I like you, Al; please come to me."

"I like you too, Gale, but I love someone else, and I am leaving. Please don't call me again."

Afterward, she did not call me, and I was on the phone with the traveling agent, ordering my return ticket to my new beginning.

I had one week to sell all I had brought in. At first, I offered all the equipment to Pap's friend and hoped he would start a nightclub on his own, but he refused and said he was too old for that idea, and there was no one else he could trust.

So, I let my dream go down the toilet, and with it all of my purchases. I sold all the equipment for less by three fourths of my purchase price, but at least someone else was excited and happy. In the end, I took over a forty thousand dollar loss.

The next week, I flew back to New York. Whoever thought I would travel like that? Going to Israel without a purpose, and then coming back full of hope, but not really knowing when my life would ever get normal.

Great people have said that men on earth should live with one purpose, divided into three objectives. First, we must build a house; second, we must plant a tree; third and final, we must produce a child. Upon achieving those three goals, a man could confidently state that his life was complete.

While evaluating that, I understood that my life sucked. I had not accomplished any of that, and whatever I had achieved was lost. But I strongly believed that as long as I lived, my options were open.

I was not drinking during my last week in Israel, nor did I drink on the plane. I was not craving one drop of anything with alcohol; maybe it was because of my high hopes, and due to my imaginary reunion, which my mind had created for me. This time my intentions were very serious, thinking about Nicole and our reunion, significantly eased my craving, I pictured Nicole running toward me, filled with joy and passion. As she came closer, I dropped my suitcases, clutching her into my arms, and squeezed her with tremendous obsession. That thought ignited my spirit and I could not wait to see her.

When we landed, I was first to exit the plane, and first to walk into the waiting area. I was very excited, as well as eager to see Nicole. Nevertheless, when I came out, she was not there. I wandered around wondering what could have happened to her, and after twenty minutes of waiting, I left the terminal and decided to wait outside.

It was not long before an unfamiliar vehicle stopped next to me, and then someone shouted my name. I looked closely, and it was Nicole with her father. She got out of the car, took a few steps, and then stopped. We stood there for a few seconds looking at each other, she came closer and elegantly laced her arms around me; it felt cold. It was nothing like I had imagined.

We got into the car and drove away; the whole time she was talking. All the words she said, they were irrelevant and had no meaning at the end. I thought she was longing for me. What an idiot. As she continued to talk, all my hopes with all my dreams of our future together faded away.

Right there and then, I knew it was wrong for me to come back. Moreover, I should never have allowed her back into my life again, but where else I could go? I wondered what Jim would say.

When we entered her apartment, what was supposedly my new home, I placed that incident behind me. What else could I do? Nicole called my mother to inform her of my arrival; she mentioned my appearance, and the way I was dressed, but nothing else.

She talked to me casually; she did not express satisfaction or joy. She was cold, and without any feelings, placed her arm around me as if I was to her only a toy.

It was impossible to describe that emotion. I experienced a simultaneous desire to laugh and to cry. Was it due to confusion or maybe it was remorse?

I had never experienced that emotion before, and could not define it. I felt lost, vulnerable, and nothing more. I stumbled upon a deceiving person in deceptive circumstances that I had to live with.

I also had to live with the fact of the promise I made to Nicole; so alcohol was no longer a part of my life. However, considering the situation, my inner urges were growing, and I was getting more miserable on every day.

We were living together, sleeping in the same bad, hardly ever making love, and when we did, it was on the same scale as throwing away trash; a thing that needed to get done, just to get over with it, and nothing more.

Not to mention Nicole's mother, who, in some way, was a burden, because she stayed with us, sleeping on the mattress on the living room floor. But I really liked that woman; in a strange way, she was unique.

It became tough for me as I struggled to find work and the daily environment, particularly at dinners, when Nicole's father would always accompanied by bottle of vodka. They would all drink, and I had to watch and fight with my cravings, at the same time, isolating myself.

It was even worse when Nicole and I visited her friends there was alcohol everywhere, and they would all drink.

There I was, surrounded by everyone and feeling lonely; it was clear, Nicole did not care about me or my feelings, or emotional state. Nevertheless, I decided to give us a last chance, as my mother said, "no regrets."

So, on our way back home, I came to Nicole with request. "Nicole, I need to ask you for a favor, but please be honest about it."

"Okay, I will. What is it?"

"Well, when we are together, can you please not drink? It is hard for me as it is, plus your aroma of alcohol is driving me crazy."

"Okay, I will chew gum."

"No, it won't help."

"Fine, then I won't kiss you; how is that?"

"I can still smell it ten feet from you, and especially when we are in bed. What is the big deal? There are non-alcoholic beverages out there, and I'll buy them for you."

"Oh, really? Why do I deserve this misery? And why do I have to sacrifice that small pleasure of mine?"

"Okay, Nicole, forget it."

Regardless of it all, life continued and I found a job with the company that had purchased all my equipment before. Actually, the owner was happy to have me, considering my past connections. He thought I would help his business grow, and I did.

However, we agreed on my terms, and with no money down, I became his partner, for the work I provided, of course. Nevertheless, that was good enough for me.

Soon enough jobs from my end were rolling in, and I was getting stable. Employees would go to the job site while I stayed in the office. Morning breakfast was accompanied by a coffee cup filled with vodka and orange juice; it reminded me of the old days when I was working with my father, except this time I was working with Paul.

It is strange how things work out. Just a few months ago, I lost my business, had to sell everything practically for nothing, and moved thousands of miles away.

Now, that same man who purchased all my equipment had offered me partnership, so all that I sold to him, was now mine, once again; only this time, I got it back for free.

One evening, as we were about to finish our dinner, Nicole's daddy approached me with a question. "Al, how is your new job?"

"It's not a new job; I am back to where I was before, only now with a partner."

"Oh, and I thought you were working for someone! So you are self-employed again?"

"That's right! As always!"

"Well, that is great, because I have a proposition for you, and since you are your own boss, you may find the time to accomplish a great idea!"

"What is it?"

"I would like for you to come with me to my store."

"Okay, let's go."

We drove to Nicole's daddy small bookstore, just a few blocks away from Nicole's apartment. His store had a rear room, with a small kitchen and a bathroom, so he was working at that store and sleeping there, as well. We all knew he could afford to live on a much larger scale, but we also knew how cheap that man was. Besides, he found his existence very suitable.

When we entered his cramped store, he said, "As you already know, I own this small book store, and I am doing okay, but I see no growth in this place! It's too small."

"So, you'd like to move to a bigger place?"

"No, Al; why move something that's working well. Instead, I would like to establish a second store, and this time on a much larger scale."

"Okay, but why me? I know nothing about books, and don't intend to learn."

"And you won't have to. I need you to build me my dream store. I'm sure you know how costly contractors are; renovating a large store to my requirements would run into a fortune! So instead of paying a stranger, I decided to offer you a partnership! What do you say?"

"I don't know what to say to that. I am not familiar with this business."

"But I am; the profits are enormous. My small store is grossing way over my needs, and I only sell Russian language books. Can you imagine what a two-story store would bring in? And at that store, the main language will be English."

"Well, if you say so, but I cannot invest any money. I'm paying bills and saving now!"

"You won't have to. I will pay for everything, and you just have to reconstruct it to my needs."

"Do you have a place in mind?"

"Of course. I located the perfect place. It used to be a furniture store."

"Okay then; let's do it!"

We shook hands, and the next day, he called me with the details and the landlord's information, for some reason, I took the ball to my side of the field.

I negotiated his lease terms, also managed to obtain two months rent free, and in those two months, that store had to be completed. After sketching out a suitable design and obtaining all the necessary materials, I grabbed one of the helpers from Paul's shop, and together we commenced to work on the store.

For six weeks, we worked ourselves to exhaustion, and instead of remodeling the two-story building, we also converted the basement into an additional level for books.

Every evening, I spent my time on the computer, searching book trades, and at the same time, I studied book demand in most fields. At the end, that place contained twelve thousand square feet of knowledge; everything was in it, for any age or curiosity, and in two languages.

At the grand opening, Nichole came in with her daddy. They stood proud and happy as a crowd of people burst in. My helper had left, and I observed their happiness.

Nicole had a job, and did not like the idea of being stuck in that store, and while her daddy searched for a salesperson, I had the pleasure of spending most of my time there.

After a week, one morning, I was at the store as usual, thinking, *what am I doing here, and when this is going to end*? A woman approached me, holding a museum album, she said, "Excuse me, how much is this art work?"

"I have no idea, but there should be a price tag on it."

"No, I don't see it."

"Well then, look at the tag on the one next to it."

"It says forty dollars!"

"I don't have a price list here, so let's assume they are the same."

"Really? Wow, too bad you have only one. Thank you."

"You are welcome."

When she left, judging from her excitement, I doubted the price I had given her, so I called daddy.

"Hi, it's me. I wanted to ask you; where is the price list?"

"I have it here. I took it yesterday to go over some numbers. Why?"

"Because some of the merchandise is still missing price tags, and because of that, I think I just gave something away."

"What did you sell?"

"The Hermitage catalog, for forty dollars."

"What? Are you sure?"

"Of course I am sure! Why?"

"That book goes for a hundred and twenty. Our cost is more than you got! How could you do that?"

And then he began to scream. At first, I placed the phone on the counter, but I could still hear that shoddy bastard yapping, so I hung up on him.

At the end of the day, he arrived with Nicole. As they entered, he looked at me as if I was his worst enemy, and as I glanced at Nicole, it was obvious that she was aware of what happened this morning.

That same evening, I went to him. As we sat down, I said, "Look, I don't want to get into what happened. I came here to tell you that I am out. Your store is completed, and doing well. Just pay me for my work and we will be on our separate ways."

"Okay, how much do you want?"

"Unlike book prices, I know exactly the cost of the work I provided there, and for some reason, I think you are aware of that cost as well, so give me half."

"I can only pay you four hundred dollars per week for your work there, so, times six, its twenty-four hundred, and here it is; it's all yours."

"I am not going to comment on that. Besides, you know exactly what you are doing now, but I will tell you a story regarding one despicable individual.

"There was an old man, he was very rich, and he became rich mostly by cheating and taking from others. One day, his time had come, and it was his last day. As he was lying on his bed, he called his son and said, 'Son, as you know, I am very, very wealthy! Here is my will and I want you to proceed accordingly!'

"As he handed him his will, the son was glowing with prosperity, but upon reading a short paragraph, he became disappointment and said,

'Father! It says here that all of your wealth shall be buried with you. Is that correct?'

"The old man smiled, and replied, 'Yes! I will take everything with me when I go! What did you think? That I would leave it all to you. So comply with my last wish, and my attorneys will insure that you do!'

"When he died, at his burial, the old man's attorney came up to his son, and said, 'Where are the funds which your father requested? You must place them in his grave now!"

"The son pulled out his checkbook, wrote the needed amount, and placed the check on his father's grave."

"Very funny, Al."

"It was not supposed to be funny. That is what usually happens to cheap bastards, because at the end, all that they have is their shame."

He did not reply. It was pointless, at that moment, I wanted to arrange for him to meet with Jim, and I wanted to proceed with that so badly I could taste it.

In my mind, killing him would bring me satisfaction, and to the entire world as well, but he was Nicole's daddy, so his disappearance would leave her in agony, and I could not bear leading her into that state, so I took the money, and left.

As I was walking back to Nicole's apartment, it became obvious to me why she needed me back so desperately. Nicole and her daddy were a team, and that store was their dream, so finally she had found a way to use me. I saved them both over twenty thousand dollars, so this time, it was safe to say, she used me well.

The next day, I went back to Paul's shop, and while at work during the day, emotionally I was doing well. However, by the end of the day, when the time came to go to Nicole, my emotions would ring a call of distress, and my mind would drag my body to the bar.

I could not go to her sober, and I did not try. She used me and didn't sacrifice her alcohol events. Well . . . neither did I, so every evening, I arrived careless and brainless, but because of that fact, I was full of joy.

Besides the way I was treated, a paradox had torn us apart. When I drank, she acted miserable, but when I was sober, she was partying without me. Soon enough, we began to lead different lives. She revealed who she always had been! Too cold to touch, and too hot to handle; I become a compulsive drinker.

One ordinary morning, as usual, I woke up and took myself to the shower. When I came out, I thought that she was asleep, but was surprised to find that she was waiting for me in the kitchen.

"Al, come here. I need to talk to you."

"What do you want?"

"I can't live like this anymore. Seeing you so often drunk is unacceptable to me. Do you remember your promise?"

"Yes, I remember! Do you remember that favor I asked from you?"

"I don't want or need to change my lifestyle! When I drink, I am normal, and you are always drunk. Do you understand the difference between the two?"

"Listen, bitch, I'm maybe a drunk, but every morning I sober up, and I'm normal again! And you! No matter what you do, once a selfish bitch, always a selfish bitch. There is no difference! Do you understand that?"

Without saying a word, she turned around and I left.

Argumentative as she was, it did not do any good to her egoism. I needed to get out of there fast, but I could not leave her without a cause. I had left her once, and guilt pursued me, so this time, I need to be wiser!

Therefore, I saw only one way out of this mess. It was clear that my drinking revolted her, so that had to be my ticket to freedom.

It was the middle of week for normal people, but, as she stated, I was abnormal, so I took a day off. When the liquor store opened, I was their first client, and I bought a gallon of vodka, my favorite size at the time.

I got a pizza on the way back, and marched home with nothing but pleasant thoughts of diffusing warmth, which shortly inspires my soul, and reminded me of the old days.

I came home, turned up the music to the point where the walls began dancing. It was loud, but who cared? I sat on the coach that I had paid for long ago, placed the pie on my coffee table, tossed a glass of hard liquor down my throat, then another, and another, until a vision appeared, a sign stating, "Welcome to Paradise."

I walked toward that sign, but could not reach it, so I kept on walking until I heard a voice.

"Follow the footprints."

"Which footprints? I don't see anything," I responded.

"Follow them and you will be . . ."

"Al, wake up; Al, what the hell did you do?"

"Nicole, what time is it?"

"Half past seven; my mother is on her way home. Get up, and clean yourself and this mess!"

She kept on babbling, but I did not hear her. I wondered about those footprints that were in the dream I'd had for so many years now. What was the meaning of it?

A few minutes later, her mother showed up, and Nicole became furious. I had never seen her like that before. She snatched at me like a crocodile, and with tremendous aggression began to rip my clothing off while screaming, "Bastard. I wish you were dead, you piece off shit. Get the hell out of my house. I don't want to see your pathetic face again; you are a nightmare to my life. Burn in hell for eternities."

Then her mother stepped in. "Nicole, stop it. What came over you? Let him go. You are bruising him; stop it now."

I just stood there. I did not retaliate, and did not feel anything while she kept on going.

"No. You piece of garbage; I will kill you myself if you won't leave. You ruined my life. I will destroy you. Son of a bitch, get the fuck out of here! You are a miserable disease to society and, to me. Get the fuck out."

She was screaming so loud, I could feel my eardrums shake.

I broke away from her, then called Paul and asked him to pick me up. Afterward, I grabbed my suitcases and walked out of there. I was breaking free of her, and knew it was the best option, actually the only option for both of us. At the same time, that incident and the way she acted spooked me badly.

I had never seen Nicole in that condition, or anyone else for that matter. Maybe I do have a gift to bring out the worst in people.

When I came downstairs, Paul was already waiting for me. "Al, what happened?"

"Nothing; can you take me to a motel?"

"Sure, let's go."

Talk about a twist of fate. Paul took me to a motel, of course. As it turned out, it was the same motel where Nicole and I spent our quality times together.

"Al, tell me how long are you planning to stay here."

"I don't know! I have no other place to go, so probably until I find a place of my own. Why do you ask?"

"Can you return to her? Or is it that bad?"

"Yes, it's very bad, and worse! But for the best, I think. We were not meant for each other."

"I understand. If you like, for the time being, you can stay with my son. Think about it, and I'll pick you up in the morning."

"Thank you, Paul; see you tomorrow."

I requested a room with special services; one of those services included an inner soul overhaul, accompanied by the alcohol to your choice. Not many people knew about those accommodations, but I always liked to snoop around, so there I was in the same motel with a pizza pie and alcohol, of course, waiting for whomever to arrive.

When she walked in, she introduced herself, but I did not remember her name. She was pretty and young. In spite of her age, spending time with an escort girl was a new experience for me.

I gave up on love but needed some company, so I didn't cared about her line of work. Besides, who am I to judge?

"So, Al, do you like to do it the old fashioned way? Or, would you prefer new style?"

"What is the difference?"

"Well, old fashioned is on the bed, and new style . . ."

"Look, I just need a companion to drink with, before I go insane."

"Okay. I hope you realize what I do, and why I'm here. So, if you don't want to pay me, I am out of here."

"No, it's not like that! Here is your money. Just stay and drink with me."

"Thank you! Hey, that's more than double!"

"Yes, I know. I'm booking you for the whole night!"

"Fine! Then you had better take it easy on that bottle, men that drink, hardly come, and I don't intend to get fruit lips!"

"What? I heard that same saying a long time ago. How old are you?"

"I can be anything you like; just say when!"

"Let me say something else to you. I am not into that! So, just drink with me, and in return, I will entertain you with jokes. How does that sound?"

"I'm all ears; go on!"

"One evening a very old woman had an urge to relive her youth before it was too late, so she visited a house of prostitution for women. Upon entry, she noticed a sign posted for all clients, stating 'chose a room.'

"So she slowly walked into one of the rooms, where a very handsome young man rested on the bed. He looked at her and said, 'Hey Granny, are you sure you are in the right place?'

"Granny gave him the hungry look, and replied with a wobbly voice 'Yes, sonny, I am sure! What is the matter? Are you not up for it?'

"The guy pointed with his finger toward the sign on the wall, and said, 'Okay then, I will read you those choices; tell me your preference! One hundred dollars for having sex on the bed. Fifty dollars for having sex standing up. And twenty-five dollars for having sex on the floor! So which one it's to your liking?'

"She listened carefully, and then slowly came up to him. With her shaking hands, she pulled out a primitive wallet that looked like a sock. Then, for a few minutes, she struggled to open the wallet, and when she finally did, she pulled out a one hundred dollar bill. She slowly and shakily handed it over to the guy.

"The guy looked at the bill, then stared at the granny and said, 'Okay, granny; its one hundred dollars, so I take that you would like to do it on the bed! I thought so!'

"'No, sonny. Not on the bed!'

"'Well! What then?'

"'I would like you to give it to me four times on the floor, please!'"

She laughed her brains out, then, trying to keep up with my drinking evidently zonked her out, and for that, I became overjoyed, because, now evading her coming on to me was not necessary.

I woke up in the morning and went outside, leaving what's-her -name behind, setting my mind toward a beautiful day and a new beginning.

Paul picked me up as promised, but instead of going to work, we went to his son's place. Andy had a two-bedroom apartment; luckily, he was looking to rent one of the bedrooms. I did not care where he lived, or how much the rent cost, or the fact that I had nothing, and needed to sleep on the floor.

None of that bothered me because now I was on my own, establishing a new life with no strings attached.

My life with a significant other had ended. I began hauling a huge bag of despair, filled with loneliness; however, it was better to be alone rather than together with her and feel lonely.

My association with Paul substantially increased our business. As we were splitting the profits, my income grew on weekly basis. When shortly after, Paul asked me to become a full partner, it came as no surprise to me.

However, it was hard to comprehend my mother's last announcement, as she stated that Pap was on his way back to New York.

According to my mom's grapevine, Pap could not find a job to match his skills in Israel. As a result, he worked nights as a security guard, and that apparently broke him. So my mother interpreted his returning to New York as a new beginning.

Back then, I did not believe her story. Furthermore, I never thought to see him here again. However, a few months went by, and one day when I came home, I saw my father on the couch. Well, that left me speechless. Go figure. After all that had happened, seeing Pap back in New York was the last thing I ever expected, not to mention so soon.

"Pap, what are you doing here, and how did you find me?"

"I called Paul yesterday, so he picked me up. Are you surprised?"

"Hell yes. Wow, Mother told me about you, but I didn't believe her. You people are something else. She said you had left because of work problems. Is that true?"

"Yes, among other things. So, what are you up to?"

"All work and nothing more! Oh, and I left Nicole. Actually, she threw me out, but I had it coming."

"I always told you; you we're not a pair. Forget about her; it is for the best. Tell me, do you think Paul needs a worker?"

"I'm his partner now, so if you want to work with us, you are welcome."

"Thanks; can I start tomorrow?"

"Of course."

The next day, Pap began working with me, or should I say for me, and once again, it was odd the way things tend to work out.

Through my entire life, I believed that events happen for a reason; however, I could not see the logic in any of my experiences. That is why I always knew I had to go with the flow and hope for the best, what else was there?

Going with the flow was also the easiest, because it did not take a genius to accept the outcome and do nothing about it. Regardless of how bad or odd my situation was, a solution to any problem always awaited me.

Where most people were struggling with difficult circumstances, I was drinking my way past them, and the scary part about that was that sometimes, it worked out just fine. Or at least I thought it did.

Pap stayed with me at my temporary apartment for only a few weeks. Spending time with him at work made me realize that he was a unique man, a master in his own world, a world of machinery and fundamental creations. He could repair and built anything, except prosperity of course. I never understood his lifestyle, and in some ways, it bothered me.

A man with his knowledge and lacking wealth, the worst part about it was that he needed and worked for money, but never in his life did he aim too become wealthy.

He lived his days to the least, and never had the ambition or desire for more. Consequently, our family suffered, especially my mother. Because of the kids, she had no choice in the matter, so she applied her best as a woman in order to fill in the gaps that our father had created. In our youth, that appeared to be more or less all right.

As a result, my mother did not have much time to herself, and missed the joy of a fulfilled woman. She looked the other way while the best years of her life passed her by, because she looked after her children.

Pap, on the other hand, had all the time in the world. For some reason, he dedicated all his time to work. As long as he met the minimum need, he did not care much, about the setting around him, or the interests of his family. In his life, there were many opportunities to change things around, and reach toward success, but for some reason he neglected them, and let them slide.

When he decided to move out, he rented himself a very small house, and called me to celebrate.

"Hey, Pap, what is this place?"

"I can only assume you don't like it."

"Honestly, no, and why would you rent a house for yourself? I'm sure there are many apartments out there, and in much better shape; also less expensive."

"Al, it is not for me. I have great news."

"Okay, shoot; don't hold me in suspense."

"I have spoken to your mother; she and Valerie decided to come back."

"Why? I though they liked it there. What happened?"

"Nothing happened; we want to be together as a family. Is that bad?"

"No, I just don't get it. Are we Gypsies now?"

"Please stop it, and at least pretend to be happy for us."

"I am happy, I guess. So you have decided to live in this dump. Rest assured my mother will not like it."

"I think this place is irrelevant; being together counts the most."

A few days later, Pap had moved out. As I found myself comfortably secured, I decided to change my lifestyle as well, and it was time to climb up a few steps. I rented my own apartment and moved out, got new possessions and things to meet my needs. My family was getting back together again, and I overflowed with emptiness.

At work, being fast at what I do best, it took me less than an hour to put the day in perspective. Workers would go to the job site, with my father of course, so I knew the project would run smoothly. Then around nine o'clock in the morning, I was free, all to myself and with nothing to do.

My enthusiasm slowly vanished, and was gradually replaced by boredom. Eventually depression slowly began to hunt me down and slowly but surely, I turned onto a road of darkness. Without self-awareness, I was on my way to a dead end, where despair and agony awaited me. And the sad thing about it all? I never saw it coming.

That day, I committed my first step toward misery road. There was no longer a need for me at work, so I went home and this time with a case of vodka. I felt lonely, so I decided to be alone for a long time.

I came home, made a few sandwiches, and embarked on drinking. The first few shots of vodka went in with no effect, but like before, when the bottle was getting closer to empty, I felt a tremendous relief.

All my dreadful emotions departed, and a new feeling inspired me to continue and drink more. When I opened the second bottle, my hands were shaking, and I had to use all my strength to pour another glass full. While consuming it, I passed out.

I woke up on a beautiful day. I lay on a hill surrounded by flowers and trees; a gentle wind stirred between the leaves and in my hair, but I could not feel it. A gorgeous bluish ocean was below, but I could not smell its aroma. Everything seemed as real as it could be, and I got up and walked downhill. While walking onto the unknown, I could not get enough of the incredible sights that surrounded me along the entire way.

I stumbled upon a small, aged house. The door was open, and so I walked in. There were a few people moving things around, apparently not disturbed by my appearance. Except for one woman seated by a wooden table and gazing directly at me. It seemed as if she knew me.

I approached her, pulled up a chair, and sat across from her. She was very attractive. I never seen such beauty before.

"Hello, Al," she said.

"How did you know my name?"

"I know you better than you know yourself, but this is not important; do you know why you are here?"

"It was not my intention to be here. I never knew of this place before. Tell me, what am I doing here?"

"You were looking for serenity; now you have found it. Aren't you glad?"

"Of course not; because nothing excites me here. For how long do you think I can endure this peace and quiet? I just got here and am already dying from boredom!"

"Al, do you know who you are?"

"Sure I do; what kind of question is that?"

"It's an honest question; searching for joy in suitable places, and escaping from complicated situations won't bring you happiness. It will bring you complete destruction, and then you will be lost in darkness forever, in a time, without end!"

"So what are you saying?"

"All that you seek can be only found within yourself. Discover yourself and you will find happiness."

"I don't believe you. I am dreaming. None of this is real. Why are you lying to me?"

"In this place, we don't lie. There is no need for that here. What is unreal to you is not necessarily absent from its existence!"

"I'm confused. Why can't I meet with Jim? Why is there always something else but him? I want to see him at least once! Please help me find him!"

"Al, you don't belong here. You must leave."

"I don't want to. I need answers."

"You can't stay here any longer; go now."

"Make me!"

And then, I woke up. I found myself on the floor by the sofa, dissatisfied with my situation, but I realized that I had escaped reality and that was just an illusion.

Actually, that voyage was unforgettably genuine, and very confusing, as well. I wanted to go back as soon as possible, and my ticket was sitting right next to me. Therefore, I gulped as much as I could, literally from the bottle, and finally I swooned again.

When I open my eyes this time, the scenery was different. Instead of blue sky, darkness surrounded me. People and subjects were beyond description. I was terrified and did not known how to get out.

Then a thought came to me; there are no feelings in here, which means that nothing can hurt me. I just stood there watching what happened was a thrilling experience for me, especially when people walked right through and past me. After a while, that scenery disappeared and I woke up.

I kept trying to get back to the initial place again, so my drinking continued for two weeks, but I was not aware of time or of the days that passed by.

Until, the phone rang, and it was my mother.

"Al, how are you doing?"

"Hi, Mom, I'm okay, what do you want?"

"Al, what happened? Why were you drinking for so long?"

"How did you know that?"

"Al! You called me a week ago; don't you remember?"

"No. Did you say a week ago? For how long have you been home?"

"Two weeks now! Stop drinking, Al. What are you doing to yourself?"

"Pouring myself another one, why?"

"Don't you think its enough?"

"No. I'm okay. I need to go. Bye, Mom."

Then I hung up. This was the first time that I intentionally hung up the phone on someone; it actually felt good. Too bad, it had to be my mom. I kept on boozing until I dropped out again.

There was no scenery for me anymore. I would get up, regardless of when, then waste myself and pass out. That continued until my body would not take that toxic waste anymore, which took another week off my life.

Unwillingly, I would stop drinking, and just sit on the living room sofa. After a few hours, my body craved more alcohol, and I would have almost a full bottle left. However, for some reason, I could not look at it anymore. The though alone repulsed me.

I was extremely thirsty. However, as soon as I gulped a glass of water, I vomited all of it right back out. It felt as if my stomach had upturned, and all my guts were about to emerge.

Afterwards every spot of my body was aching. I felt each of my organs as they were about to explode in places I never knew existed before, and the pain was unbearable.

I had no idea of such tremendous agony, like a knife swirling in me, side-to-side, periodically cutting a piece off each organ.

That suffering exhausted me completely. But, I couldn't fall asleep, no matter how hard I tried. I could not eat and I wanted to; a glass of water began to look so mouth-watering but I was scared to drink it, and because of the vomiting, I did not drink it.

I was puzzled about how I could vomit, lacking of food and water.

My stomach had turned into an empty shell, and was shrinking rapidly. On every vomiting occasion, it felt as if my guts were climbing toward my brains, and my eyeballs were about to pop out.

That condition continued for over three days, then the pain eased a little, and I could walk slowly around the apartment. Finally, on the fourth day, when the vomiting stopped, I thankfully poured myself a glass of water, followed by another and another. At that moment, I was grateful for water, I loved water more than anything in the world.

And that was my first time bingeing! I thought my sufferings were now over!

At nine o'clock in the evening, I was worn out, so I decided to get some sleep. As I was resting my head on the pillow, cold sweat broke out on body, and the attack began. It was very annoying and strangely scary, as well. My body was producing so much sweat it turned my bed into a puddle.

That was unbearable; I tossed and turned the whole night, and was very glad to see the morning light. Finally, I took a long shower and went to work.

Three terrible weeks passed by, and through that time, I hadn't seen anything except work and home. At work, because of my staff, there was nothing much for me to do, and no one waited for me at home, either, except empty cold walls and that stupid talking box with one hundred channels and nothing to watch.

Then another month went by, and I forgot about the consequences of alcohol abuse. All I remembered was that beautiful woman. I wanted to go back there so badly I could taste it, and so my cravings commenced again.

The following day at work, I was sitting at my desk playing chess on the computer, and thinking that it was time to visit a liquor store, when, out of nowhere, an old acquainted called.

"Al, how are you? Long time no speak."

"Henry, is that you?"

"Yes, man. Listen, the guys and I decided to visit the Russian sauna. Would you like to join us?"

"It's only eleven a.m., and I'm working."

"So what? I'm sure you can make time, being your own boss and all. Come on, learn to relax."

"Oh, well, maybe you right; come and get me."

When he showed up and while driving there, I remembered a few years ago, I had visited this place with Nicole, and never entered that place again.

I found the environment quite enjoyable; the sauna always had a perfect temperature, and, as a result, the steam was just right. And the food was better than excellent.

We were a team of four men, all with one similarity, and so after three hours of refreshing ourselves and ridding toxic waste out of our bodies, I actually felt healthy again. However, shortly after, a mutual quest emerged, we we're all hungry.

We decided to visit the restaurant. While ordering, Henry appeared a bit hungry, or maybe he was in the mood for flirting.

"Look, Al, that waitress is new, and quite tasty, I might add."

"Henry, let it go. We came here to relax; besides, what would your wife say if she ever finds out."

"What she doesn't know won't hurt her. I know they don't serve bagels here, nevertheless, watch me order one, and let's see what she is going to do."

"Okay, go for it! That should be interesting, meanwhile we will order for you, as well."

"Hey! Excuse me, can you help me, please," Henry softly called to her.

"Yes sir, what can I do for you?"

"I like your question! Oh, I would imagine quite a few things that you could do for me! But first, can you bring me a toasted bagel with cream cheese?"

She smiled, and replied, "Of course, coming right up!"

"And I thought you said they don't serve any bagels in here!"

"No, they don't."

"So what she is going to bring me, then?"

"Henry, I am as puzzled as you are."

Shortly after, she returned with a small plate, placed that plate in front of Henry face, and said, Enjoy; would you like anything else?"

Henry stumbled over his tongue. As she was leaving, he looked at me and said, "Can you believe this?"

"What do you mean?"

"Look at that plate! This is not a bagel; it's a roll, hard as a rock, and who the hell can eat this?"

"Well, at least now we know for sure they don't serve bagels." I could not stop laughing while saying that.

"*Bon appétit.*"

"Very funny. I'm not going to eat this shit. Where is she? Hey, miss, come over here!"

"Yes, sir, is something wrong?"

"You bet your cute ass it is; I ordered a bagel. What is this thing?"

"It's a homemade bagel, sir!"

"Is that right? In that case, tell me where the hole is."

She then leaned over right toward him, looked at him straight in the eyes, extended her arm while showing him the finger, and replied, "You have this? Use it!"

That scene shook everybody in that place, and all of us as well. People could not stop laughing, and Henry was sitting there as if he just crawled out of the sewage.

"Hey, Henry, the food is here. Come on, dig in."

"I'll be right back."

He went to the bar and returned with a bottle of vodka. While eating, I noticed that now there were four bottles on the table. Shortly after, the food vanished, and so was all the alcohol.

Suddenly the alcohol influence began to circle my body, and when it arrived at my brain, it brought tranquility into mind and felt as if I was floating. I was so relaxed I could not get up, so Henry and the guys helped me walk to the car, and when we arrived at my building, Henry asked me, "Al, are you okay? Can you walk home by yourself?"

"Yes, sure." I opened the car door and fell on the ground.

"Yes sure, my ass. Come on; let me help you." Henry said that and helped me walk into the elevator.

"Thanks Henry, I can go on my own. Just press the third floor button for me; for some reason I can't reach it."

"There you go! Call me in the morning; take care!"

Henry left. The elevator door closed, and I went up. Boy, did it feel good or what.

Suddenly, the elevator stopped, and the door opened. I realized it was time to get out. Walking through the hallway, while holding the walls from closing in on me, was a hard thing to do in my condition. Nevertheless, I sensed the walls shaking as they became weak, but finally I arrived at my door. And was I glad to see it. I tried to position my key into the cylinder lock but was unsuccessful, so I looked into the lock, and found it was not there anymore; instead, there was a hole in its place.

I stood by the door and tried to think this through, but my mind did not acknowledge me very well, so I turned the doorknob, and suddenly the door opened!

Of course, I went in, and what I saw shocked the hell out of me, because my apartment was empty. There was nothing there anymore. My first steps were into the bedroom, because behind my headboard, I always kept a bundle of cash. When I walked in, nothing was there. Apparently, my bedroom set had disappeared; even the phone was gone, and window curtains as well. This tremendous distress somehow sobered me up a little, and I could not believe what I saw.

I went to the living room and all my furniture had vanished. My mattress was placed in the corner were the TV used to be. I began to dwell on what had happened here.

I was robbed! Who would take my stuff? And where did they find the time to take everything out? Damn, it took one helper and me a full day to bring everything in here, In addition, why they would take my phones and my lock.

I went into the kitchen for a can of soda. I opened the fridge door and there was nothing there either; the fridge was completely empty.

By no means have I heard of a burglary that involved stealing food and soda. Shit, they took my bread as well. I went to the toilet and was even more surprised, there was no toilet paper; and on top of it all, my dirty laundry and towels were missing.

So I said to myself, *Fuck it. I can't think straight, and hardly can walk. Let me go back to my mattress, and I will deal with it tomorrow with a sober head. Hey, maybe it's all a dream. Yes, I have to sleep it off.*

I took all my clothes off, dropped them on the naked mattress, and bare naked, collapsed on top of them, falling into a deep sleep.

All of a sudden, I heard someone shouting, "Hey, you! Get up."

My mattress commenced to shake. I opened my eyes and looked up there was a strange woman standing next to me shouting. "I told you to get up! What are you, deaf?" she screamed.

"Who the hell are you? Get the fuck out. Oh, you are the one that robbed me; now I got you!"

So I grabbed her by the skirt and did not let go. I thanked god for my firm grip.

"Let me go. I'm going to call the cops," she screamed.

"You will call the cops? No, no, I'm going to call the cops! But first, give me back my phone, bitch, and then I will call them. Who helped you to rob me? Tell me, where are your teammates?"

"What team? You are a miserable naked drunk! Let go of me!"

"Not before you tell me of your associates. And why would you steal my toilet paper and my dirty laundry? What kind of sick bitch are you; taking all of my food? Judging by your appearance, you probably ate it all by now. Where is my stuff? Tell me or I will hurt you."

"What are you talking about? Get out of here."

"I live here, you whore!"

"No moron! I just rented this place; go to your own home, idiot!"

She then forcedly detached herself from my grip and ran out. I put my clothes on, took a closer look around, and noticed that my blinds were gone, but there were no holes in the walls. Was it possible for me to enter a different apartment? Of course it was. I got off on the wrong floor.

Then the building super came in, followed by that woman.

"Look, here is that drunk I told you about."

"Al, what are you doing here?" the super said.

"I got lost."

"Okay, go home, please."

"Who is that lady?"

"They were about to move in yesterday, but they came late and I did not let them. Although, they succeeded in bringing in the mattress beforehand. You are fortunate she didn't call the cops."

"Come to think of it, I wanted to call them myself. Thank god there was no phone."

He was laughing the whole way to my apartment, and I was relieved when my key unlocked my door. What's more, to see my place intact really lifted my spirits.

I became happy, so the was a need to celebrate, I went out and returned with a case of vodka. Shortly after, I was bingeing again, only this time I could not stop, and was out for almost a month. During that period, I didn't go anywhere and didn't see anything except darkness.

All I remember is seeing my mother standing next to me, and she appeared traumatized, just by looking at me.

The ambulance came, and admitted me to the hospital. I stayed in the emergency room for over a day, then they transferred me to the recovery room and my doctor came in.

"Hello Al; how are you feeling?"

"Much better thank you!"

"I brought something for you. Here, take a look at this." He handed me a small glass tube that contained some black liquid.

"What is it?" I asked.

"This is your blood. I wanted for you to see it with your own eyes."

"So?"

"So, seeing you breathing is a mystery to us."

"Well, doc, it is a puzzle to me as well."

"By the way, I have spoken with your mother. Tell me, how many languages you speak?"

"Three. Why do you ask?"

"Do you speak fluently in all three?"

"Yes, to some degree, I guess."

"What a shame. Why are you killing yourself?"

"Long story, doc. Actually, I don't know. Can you release me? I want to go home."

"No. I committed you here for seven additional days, and you are in no condition to walk yet, so sleep it off."

Leaving my room, he appeared a bit disappointed. Nevertheless, I was very happy because I saw my bag of clothing by the side of my bed. This meant that I could leave from hospital.

I disconnected myself from the wiring, and without further thought, I proceeded to the bathroom. About ten minutes later, the nurse appeared, but I was already dressed and ready to go.

"Sir, what are you doing?"

"I'm going home."

"You can't leave without a doctor's release."

"Okay, then, get the release, because I am leaving." I walked out of the room and stumbled into my doctor.

"Nice to see you are feeling better," the doc said.

"Doctor, please discharge me!"

"You are in no condition to leave; you need to stay."

"I feel fine, and I'm not staying here."

"Okay, Al, please extend your wrists, and hold your palms straight up."

So, I did.

"Amazing! no sign of trembling. I don't understand. Fine, I will discharge you."

"Relax, doc. What we can't understand does not necessarily signify it is absent. I don't mean to offend you, but I hope not to see you again."

"Likewise, Al. Remember this well, if you get into this condition again, the next time we meet, you will be in a body bag."

"I understand."

"Good, because situations like this don't usually happen, and if they do, there is no second time around."

"Thanks again doc, goodbye."

I could not say his statement did not frighten me, because actually it did, so for five weeks, I was clean. Beyond that, my recollections of near death episodes faded, and I began drinking again.

I was living my life by a cycle; one month of sobriety followed by one month of complete intoxication, which always concluded in enormous agony then slowly shifted to remorse and self-hate. My existence repulsed me and lowered my self-esteem; suddenly I became disgusted with myself, and shortly after, I developed a careless attitude.

On every drinking event, I took alcohol further and further, hoping to arrive to the point of no return. Life seemed pointless; my only desire was to get to the other side. I imagined that side to be better; however, I did not think of that side as death.

That I realized when I had a seizure; that experience terrified me the first time it happened. My first seizure happened at work, just when I had come out of a long hard drinking period. I was sitting by my desk looking through my notes, and then unexpectedly, my eyes focused on one particular number.

I began observe it very closely, and could not take my eyes off it. With all of my willpower, I turned my head away, but those numbers followed and stayed in my view. I then swiveled around and toward the rear wall; however, the numbers pursued and were still in front of my eyes. I tried to take my eyes off it but I could not, and suddenly, the numbers slowly began to shift. At first, they shifted to the left. Unwillingly, my head followed. Then, they shifted faster to the right, and my head followed. Suddenly, the shifting accelerated, and reluctantly my head followed, faster and faster. Next, my head began to swing side to side with incredible force, and I could not stop it.

It felt as a huge machine was twisting my head from one side to the other; simultaneously, my arms and legs were bending into abnormal positions with increased intensity. My body squeezed into a circle, and I became helplessly numb.

In some way, seizures are alike to epilepsy attacks, but according to studies, seizures are more powerful and much stronger. I guess that explains why most people die from them. It was terrifying and intimidating.

Regardless of it all, another month passed, and I got on my feet, felt great and apparently healthy.

So there I was, back to square one. Back to drinking and hoping, that this time I would blackout and never wake up. I recalled what the doc said. "If you decide to continue abusing alcohol, the next time I see you, you will be in a body bag."

I had ten similar events, and in nine out of those ten occasions, I experienced seizures. Two of those nine times, I was at my parents' house. The rest I had alone on my couch at home.

I have never gone to a detox center, and always handled alcohol withdrawal by myself. I was aware of the consequences alcohol withdrawal is the most hazardous, and without correct medicine and medical care, death is certain. However, at that time, I welcomed it.

Nevertheless, my perspective toward life changed when I had the last seizure. That time, I practically gave up, and did not fight it, or resisted in any way. The pain came all over me as never before. I felt that I stopped breathing. Strangely enough, I was not out of breath, and actually, the necessity for air was gone. Subsequently, the pain vanished and I had complete serenity; it felt awesome.

Afterward, I saw myself on the floor by the coffee table, resting there so peacefully and calmly. I tried to look closer, then I heard a voice stating, "Don't look; you're not supposed to see yourself! If you do, your soul will be lost for eternities in darkness!"

I woke up on the floor by that coffee table.

Seeing myself from a side view really shook me up, and then when I saw my face in the mirror, I was more distressed. That sight horrified me, because my face was all crumpled, and my eyes had transformed into a dark red fire balls. I became a terrifying creature.

At that moment, I realized that I would most likely not die. It was not my time and most definitely not my choice. Eventually, alcohol abuse would only turn me into a crippled creature, and I would suffer for unknown period then ultimately die like a pig in a shit hole.

So that day, I strongly decided that, no matter what happened and regardless of my life circumstances, when my time came, I wanted to go as a man and not as a filthy pig.

At that juncture, my death-wishing days were over. I understood myself to be in an extensive fight with alcohol addiction, and commenced toward a new beginning. Under the circumstances, it was simple to understand my conclusion, but the task awaiting me appeared to be enormous and unknown to me.

Regardless, I thought this was possible, and by igniting my willpower, I could surely stop drinking on my own.

Boy. Was I wrong!

Considering my frustration toward alcohol, the first three weeks passed by easily, and I actually began to feel great. Then as always, complication happened at work.

At that time, Pap and I left Paul's location, and established a place of our own. The new place was awesome, and also a top-notch location, a spacious shop, a large office, and a huge parking space. Our new business name was different; however, when we moved to our new location, all of Paul's and my mutual clients decided to stay with us.

Nevertheless, we were lacking skilled employees and, unfortunately for me, my first relapse happened sooner than expected.

It began when my father returned from the job site with workers. He was harebrained, and the workers were without sense. When they walked in, because of the ear-piercing chattering, I could not ask anyone about the event that had brought them to madness, and he kept screaming.

"I am sick and tired of the men you send to work with me. They don't have any skills at all, and I have to do everything by myself. I am not your slave."

"Pap, you have four men. I have spoken to all of them before. They say you won't let them perform any work, and you don't teach them anything; all you do, is scream all day."

"They are not worthy of teaching. Where did you find them, anyway? Did you know that one of them used to be a gynecologist in Russia? How do you expect him to perform construction work?"

"The unemployment office sends them to us; the lady highly recommended that gynecologist. She said he has skilled hands."

"Oh really? I bet he does, only not in construction. That's it. I have had enough. I do not wish to talk about it anymore."

As he continued screaming, unaware of my actions, I went to the liquor store, which was around the corner, then rushed back in a hurry with a gallon of vodka in one hand and plastic cups in the other.

Consuming the first cup was most helpful, and I felt calm. Evidently, I forgot about my task, as well as the consequences of alcohol and the way I always abuse it. So now, my Pap became a trigger. The alcohol cravings got the best of me, and drinking began again. I was back on bingeing. Those struggles continued through the entire year, and the sequence of alcohol bingeing never stopped for me.

Regardless of my periodic absences, Pap and I continued working together, but his conflicts with workers and me continued on daily basis, and as always, he was dissatisfied. The same problems inflated each day, Pap had no one to work with, and in result, he presented himself as working slave.

Watching him scream was odd, because afterward he would calm down, while the rest of us, including the workers, would stay stressed. Some called my father Dracula; they said screaming helped him to relieve his anxiety, and sucking the mood out of others actually relaxed him.

However, only at work did I see him this way; at home or on any other given day, he was quite normal and I had enjoyed being around him.

Nevertheless, at work, I could not handle the stress he created on a regular basis, so upon his return I was absent. If there was a need for me to be there, I would always come in under the influence, and that way nothing could trouble me.

Sometimes I turned the most stressful situations into a joke, and hoped things might change for the better. One day, it was snowing heavily; around five, he drove into the shop with the crew. Hearing the door slam, I knew nothing good to be expected. Therefore, it began again!

"Hello, Pap!"

"What a surprise! I did not expect to see you here; to what do I owe the pleasure?"

"I needed to finish some paper work."

"I hope it was not a price quote."

"Actually, it was!"

"Why would you price a project on with a drunken head? Couldn't you wait to sober up, and why are you drinking again?"

"That's too many whys, Pap."

"Where is the bottle? Give it to me!"

He opened the drawer, pulled out my bottle and took it with him. I got up and rushed after him.

"Al, walk away before something bad happens."

"Pap let me tell you about something bad. A drug addict and alcoholic meet on the street. The drug addict says, 'In a half hour, I will pass here again. If we meet and my shirt is unbuttoned, it will mean that I'm high, completely wasted, and out of control, so be conscious; avoid me and walk the other way.' The alcoholic looks at him and replies, 'You see that liquor store? I'm on my way there; in a half hour when I return and we meet again, I won't give a rat's ass about you or your fucking shirt!'

"So you see the point, Pap? Give me the bottle back!"

And so he did. By the time the workers left, I was completely drunk. I had no choice but to go home with him. When we arrived, my mother was dressing the table. The food smelled appetizing and I was very hungry. I went to the fridge, pulled a bottle of vodka that was there, poured myself a shot, and continued drinking while enjoying Mother's meal.

It did not take long before Pap decided to join me. When we finished the bottle and our stomachs were full, a question popped into my head. I couldn't resist. I had to ask.

"Mom, can you tell me why we moved to Philadelphia? I still don't understand that, and in the end, we came back! Why?"

"Okay, I did not think it would come to this, but so much time has gone by, I can tell you."

"So tell me, please."

"When Jimmy died, you were losing your mind; the things that you did, and people you harassed, always trying to find out the murderer."

"Yes, I remember! So what?"

"Well, one day when you and dad were out, a police officer showed up at the door. He was very persuasive when he said, 'You had better stop your son with his craziness. He will never find anything, and if you won't stop him, you will lose him as well! Moreover, your other children will enjoy hospital food for as long as they live.' So you see, Al, stopping you was not an option. The only rational thing to do was to move away, and so we did."

"You lied to me! How could you?"

"I had no other choice in the matter. Yes, I lied. I'm sorry. However, you are here and that's all I wanted."

"Oh, please. That man was pulling your leg, and you were naive enough to believe him."

"No, that is not true. He was right; that whole situation was over your head, too big for you to handle. You had no idea what you were getting yourself into, and I'm grateful the way things worked out, and always will be."

"I need to get out of here; please call a cab for me."

Recalling that my car was at the shop, I asked the cabby to take me there. From that point, I drove home. However, being frustrated, I hardly knew my whereabouts, and the most difficult task confronted with me upon arrival, because I needed to park.

Fortunately for me, there was a vacant space available right in front of my building. At first, it seemed tight, but somehow I knew I would fit. While attempting to back up into that small space, I felt a bump, and for some reason the car stopped. Going forward and accelerating in reverse did not help either; no matter what I tried, my car would not fit in.

Then a short siren sounded. When I looked around, it seemed the noise came from the police car parked across the street. Two cops were sitting in it and silently watching me. Apparently, they were gazing at me all this time; then they got out and approached me.

One of the officers stated, "Turn off the engine, and step out of the car."

"Why? What did I do?"

"You see that broken tree by the sidewalk?"

"Yes, I do see it."

"Then why you were attempting to run over it?"

"Well, it's lying there on the road! What was I supposed to do?"

"Have you been drinking?"

He popped the million-dollar question, because, for some reason, that night I turned noble, and answered, "Yes, I have!" I said that with pride, as if a reward waited for me.

"Come on; get in the car. You are coming with us, "the cop replied while placing handcuffs on me.

Instead of a quiet sleep on my bed, I spend the night in a cell.

The next day, my parents bailed me out. Afterward, the judge revoked my driving license, granted me a huge fine and two years' probation, which turned out to be my biggest reward ever. Once a month, for twenty-four months, I had to visit and sign in at the city facility. I never understood the point of me being there, but I was, and that would ruin my whole day.

Those two years were the longest, because there was nothing else for me to do. So, I dedicated myself to work. But the necessity of driving increased and I took my chances and did not think much of the consequences.

Through those two years, our business slightly expanded, and revenue had grown. My mother knew about our tiny growth, as so when I came to visit my parents, my mom approached me, and said, "Al, you must help me!"

"With what, Mom?"

"I cannot sit home anymore; can you find me something to do at your shop?"

"I don't know! What can you do?"

"Anything you will give me! I need to get out of this house!"

"Yeah, and I can understand why Sorry for being frank, but this place is a dump! Why did you rent it?"

"It was all because of this dog. When your sister brought a puppy home from the shelter, no one said a word, and I had no idea that the dog would grow into an elephant!"

"Come on! Chase is not that big! Also, he is a Rottweiler, and they do become large!"

"Now I'm aware of that fact! Anyway, the building owner saw him, and then gave us two options, move out, or get rid of the dog! Didn't I tell you about that?"

"No, I don't remember. So that's was the reason you moved into this place!"

That house was awful. I had never seen such a black hole in my entire life. Regardless of how many light bulbs were on, it was still dark in there. Moreover, it was tiny and over one hundred years old, with two bedrooms, and one bathroom in-between. I could never tell which was larger. The living room was oriented in the hallway; because of the walk by, watching TV was unbearable.

"Hey! I asked you something; remember? Don't change the subject with this house!"

"Okay, maybe you can answer the phones?"

"Al, I would do anything!"

"Funny you say that!"

"Why is it so funny to you?"

"I remember when Vicky said same phrase, and I got the wrong opinion!"

"No, you did not. Your Vicky literally would do anything and everything to get what she wanted!"

"Mom, are you looking to get paid! How much do you want?"

"It makes no difference to me!"

"Fine, I will speak to Pap about it and see what he says!"

"In that case, tell him, three hundred and fifty per week!"

"Mom, that's a lot! But, I'll see what I can do."

She didn't wait for my answer, because the next day, I saw them arrive at work together, and that was always the way of my mom.

Afterwards, my kid sister was brought into the bargain, for additional pay of course, and so we we were all working together. Well, almost working.

On any given day, I recalled Jim, and how thing would, if he would be by my side today. Looking at what Pap and I had accomplished in such a short period, I could only imagine what we could have done together with Jim.

There wasn't a day I lived that I did not think about Jim, and all those times with ardent desire. I would to give back all I had and more if Jim would rejoin us. Afterward, I understood that would never happen, and that thought was too hard to bear. Consequently, I was on same road again, toward the worst outcome.

As I was sitting at the office thinking about Jim, Mom interrupted my stream of thought, and said, "Al! Come down to earth! What are you thinking about?"

"Nothing, I think I will go home now!"

"Oh no, you're not! I know why you decided to go home. I have noticed that stage of yours and you will not commit to that again! Instead, why don't you look at this?"

She handed me a newspaper.

"What is it, Mom? Why are you handing me this newspaper?"

"Just look! There is a sailboat for sale, and I think it's fairly cheap!"

"Yeah! So?"

"Why don't you buy it; get yourself a hobby. That will take your mind off your other awful interests!"

"I am not a sailor, Mom; however, I do love the ocean!"

"There you go! And it's summer now, so spend it on the water. Remember, what you don't know, you can learn! Try it, Al; what do you have to lose?"

"Well, for starters, seven thousand dollars! That's what they are asking for it! However, the way things are going, it's not that big a deal! Okay, let me call them. Thanks, Mom!"

While dialing the number, my mood somehow raised; maybe my mother was right. Maybe I needed to get a hobby, and that was a great opportunity to obtain one!

I arranged with the seller to meet Pap and me after work. Not knowing much about boats, I thought Pap would be a big help, so by six p.m., we were at the docks, waiting for the boat owner to show up.

While waiting, Pap asked me, "Al, do you know what are you buying?"

"Yes, a sailboat!"

"I meant; what kind of a boat? Does it have a motor, or you will be using sails only?"

"First, it's not you! It's WE! And I don't know how to sail. Hey, look at the man in that boat. He is waving at us. Let's go over there. I think it's him."

When we came up closer, the boat turned out to be larger than I had anticipated. Then, that man came onto the deck and said, "Are you Al?"

"Yes! And this is my father!"

"Nice too meet with you both! So here she is! 1989 McGregor sailboat. She is one of a kind, twenty-six feet in length, and completely remodeled."

"What do you mean completely?" Pap asked.

"Well, look for yourself I extended the height of the cabin! Installed a hydraulic steering system; those boats come with what you might call a stick. Instead, there is a steering wheel now, so it turns and drives like a car, although it doesn't handle like one!" Then he laughed.

"Well, that's great! What do you say, Pap?"

"Al, wait; excuse me! What did you say your name was?"

"Simon!"

"So, Simon, are those alterations legal?"

"Of course they are! But that's not all. The best revision was with the engine; we relocated the engine beneath the stern!"

"Yeah, where is the engine?" Pap asked.

"The engine is located beneath, at the back! So now, the surface is free for any purpose. I use that space for my barbeque."

"Do you actually barbeque there?" I asked him.

"Of course I like to fish, so when I catch a few, I throw them on that grill. The rest can be only described as delicious!"

While Simon was talking and showing off, my Pap went to the stern, opened the hatch, and said.

"Simon! You have a huge cutout here!"

"Yes, of course; you see how the engine sits nicely there!"

"The engine is sitting nicely alright, but what about that cut out, and all the water around that! You don't think water will pile up, then overrun into the front, and flood this tub!"

"No way! Look, there are four pumps by the engine, just in case! And I also boarded up the compartments!"

"How did you board them?"

"With pieces of plywood; what are you so worried about!"

While they stood there arguing, I went down below, and really liked what I saw. This boat was great it had a small kitchen, a bathroom, sleeping space for five, and there was a couch at the center, with a round table next to it.

When I came out, I said. "Okay, I will take it!"

"What? Al, you can't buy this thing. It's not safe!" Pap yelled at me.

"What do you mean it's not safe? It's perfectly safe. I sail all the time; just two days ago, me and my friend were fishing on it!"

"Yeah! You were fishing alright, right here by the dock!"

"Al, I don't know why your father is so frustrated, but if you want, we will take her out to sea right now, and I'll show you what she can do!"

"No, Simon, there is no need for that! Look, why don't you stop by the office tomorrow morning? Bring all the documents so we can settle!

"Al, tell him to bring the parking slip as well!

"Oh yes, please, that too!"

Pap was very upset on our way back home, so I tried to cheer him up. "Pap, you saw some issues with that boat, and I don't disagree with you! However, for the price he is asking, I could never get something like that. You should see the inside. I mean it's like a small house!"

"Oh, yeah? Then park it at the shop, and live in it!"

"You're funny! Come on! Besides, even if you are correct, we can fix the problems, can't we?"

"Of course we can! But why buy something that is in need of work?"

"Because it's cheap Pap! I can't afford twenty grand and more! Well, maybe I can, but why would I?"

He did not answer me, but he had agreed with me. I could see that on his face, so when we were approaching the house, I said, "Pap, we have to celebrate. There is a big cause for that. Stop by that liquor store. I'm buying." And that's when I saw Pap smile.

When we entered the house, the first thing I said was, "Mom, now you can congratulate me. I am officially a sailor!"

Then, Pap had to add, "Just don't jump ahead of yourself!"

"Why not Pap?"

"Because, that tub may become a submarine!"

"Why you would say something like that?"

"Because, your son bought a toy which may sink before it sails!"

"He is kidding, Ma!"

"Al, I see that you have brought another toy with you. What is that in your hand? We spoke about this at the office."

"Ma, we need to celebrate our new ship, or she might sink like Pap said!"

After a few hours, I looked around the house, then I came up to Mom as she was washing the dishes, and said, "Mom, it may seem to you that I don't pay any attention, but so you know, it's not true. I see what is going on, and I see how you all live here! I just wanted you to know that very soon, I will buy you a great house! I promise you that in next to no time you will move out of this dumpster and live large!"

"Oh, Al, thank you! However, if you want your mother to be happy, stop drinking! That is all I am asking from you!"

"Sorry, Mom, I did not ask for my life to roll down that road, and now that I am on it, as strange as it might seem, that poison is the only drive that keeps me going! My only hope is that maybe someday, along the way, I will stumble upon a turn with a new beginning. So you see, Mom, it is easier for me to buy you a house than to quit drinking."

She did not respond, and afterward, we all went to the living room and sat up late that night. To my surprise, we did not drink as much, maybe because of the joyful atmosphere, or maybe because of my new purchase.

Regardless of why, judging from that scene, I realized that alcohol was not the enemy in my life, because there we were using it, but not abusing it. I was fine that evening. Moreover, I did not desire more. It was odd questions arose but I could not find one answer to why.

The next morning, I went to work and so did everybody else. Simon arrived as promised, and finally, that boat was all mine. I wanted to sail so badly I could smell the aroma of the ocean, and could not wait for the week to end.

However, for my daily responsibilities, the main task was a bid for the housing authority. I had placed a bid on a project a while ago, then worked on revisions for over three months, sending documents back and forth. Then suddenly, on that day, that project was awarded to us.

We received a project containing six buildings, twenty-two stories high. The scope of work was the installation of new glass face, total contract in the sum of two million six hundred eighty thousand dollars.

While reading that contract, I assume my face changed in color, because I could feel my skin burning, and then my mother has said, "Al, are you feeling okay? You turned red!"

"I am fine! Actually, overly fine! Here, read!" And I gave her the contract.

"Okay, give it here; it's a contact, Mom! A contract for a very large project; the kind I never thought I'd possess!"

"Al, be careful! Large profits bring larger problems!"

"Oh, Mom, I am used to big problems! Large profits, is all I need, and now at last, I got it!"

As nothing comes easy, especially for me, that project was one enormous headache, with so much paperwork, numerous insurances, and bonds.

When everything settled, I received the down payment. Looking at that check wiped my memories of the prior uphill struggle and sweat. I completely forgot how hard the road was that brought me here; more importantly, I lost my focus and commitment.

That project was in need of special tactics, a so-called maneuver of a shark while hunting for its prey, but I did not understand my situation, and the fact that this job had jumped me instantly from a small lake into the ocean of sharks, when I was the only small fish among them.

I was the new kid on the block, what some called the underdog, and unfortunately, for me, I did not realize how big that block really was.

So my approach toward that project was casual, and instead of being buried in paperwork, organizing my strategy and preparing for commencement date, I awaited for the week to end, and was driving to the boat on daily basis, preparing her and myself for departure.

That weekend came sooner than I expected, and so at five a.m., I was standing on my new toy with Pap. After a short checklist, which concluded in finding the key and starting the engine, I commenced backing up from the parking space.

However, it was not what I thought it would be. Apparently, unlike cars, boats don't stop on the spot, and there was no brake pedal, either, so, as we kept gliding backward, Pap said. "Al, stop!"

"I can't!" Then we slightly glided along a few larger boats parked across the bay.

"Al, get out of here fast!" I pushed the gearshift forward, and we jumped out and into the center of the bay.

"Al, pull the lever down! We are going too fast!"

"Okay, Pap! I got it now! Don't worry!"

"Damn that Simon and his tub machine!"

By the time we entered Open Ocean, I learned to handle our boat, and it wasn't that hard. As Simon said, just like a car, only with no brakes!

That boat had fish finder radar, so after few miles, when we could hardly see the shore, Pap said, "Al, park here! I see a lot of fish on the screen!"

"Pap, I hope you know this thing don't park."

"I mean to say, shut off the engine; let her drift."

Until noon we drifting away, and caught some decent fish, then around one o'clock, we both decided to sail back.

When the engine started, I wanted to see what she had, so I pushed the lever to the metal; the boat nose lifted up and practically separated from the water; as we cut through water, it felt like we were flying. When the bay appeared on the starboard, I realized that it took us half the time to return, so I said, "Pap, can you believe the speed she's got?"

"Al, don't pass the turn to the bay."

"Pap, I think something is wrong."

"What do you mean? Al, slow down! We need to turn here; where are you going?"

"I'm turning the steering, but the boat won't turn!"

"Slow down, Al! Let me open the hatch."

So, I slowed us down, and while Pap was looking at the inner stern, I asked, "Pap, do you see anything?"

"I see a lot of things; the steering linkage had detached, but that is irrelevant to all the water gushing in!"

"What water?"

"The water around us! It must have happened while you were racing. I told you that might happen!"

"Pap, can you connect the linkage back? I will take her in slowly."

While Pap attempted to reconnect my steering, I saw water gushing into the kitchen area, so I looked overboard, and saw that we were plunged lower into the water below the safety line.

"Pap, why are we so beneath the surface?"

"That is because we are sinking! Okay, I reconnected the steering; try to turn now!"

"Yes! That great, we are turning back!"

"Al, what are you doing? Align the boat!"

"I can't! It's stuck!"

At that point, water overfilled the compartment below, and I saw cushions floating. As we were circling around the bay entry, I heard a crowd cheering. Apparently, our incident was an amusement to them.

Going in circles had brought us closer to shore, and Pap yelled, "Al! Abandon this can! Jump; and swim to shore!"

"No, please fix the steering. I will take her in; we are very near!"

As Pap continued repairing the steering, water reached my knees. Pap had finally fixed the steering, and we slowly drifted toward the bay entry.

By that time we entered the bay, the only visible boat was the sail pole and cabin extension. I floated with the steering wheel in my hand, and Pap was behind me holding onto a rail that was under water.

I could only imagine the scene from the side view. The boat itself was completely under water, and we were practically gliding on water like two ducks. No wonder a crowd gathered along the side of the pier, gazing at us, clapping, and shouting "way to go!" Someone even yelled, "The *Titanic* is coming about."

"Pap! The whole boat is under water, I can only see the rail guards! Why aren't we sinking?"

"I don't know; maybe it's too shallow here, and we are dragging along the bottom."

"No, we are not dragging. Anyway, look Pap, there is our parking space!"

"Slow down, Al; you need to drift in there smoothly. Let the stream bring you in!"

"I can't see the speed control; where is it?"

"You remember the location of the lever; reach in there, grab it, and pull it down!"

And so I did. We drifted into our parking space like professional sailors, only we were standing on water.

"Pap, don't you find it strange that this engine runs under water?"

"Not anymore! Look! Simon ran the exhaust pipe out, and tightened it to the sail pole! I bet you anything he had a similar problem before!"

"That asshole! And what about the pumps? Can you check if they are working?"

"Yes, they working; however, they are circling water within the boat, so we need to pull the end houses out!"

I was soaked, and so was Pap; however, after six hours of waiting, the boat finally began to rise, and by nine p.m., she had completely surfaced.

We went home, and not said a word to each other. Come Monday, I towed the boat to our shop, and parked her along the side of our driveway, with the intention that someday, we would fix all the problems.

So, I had my fun on the water, the kind of fun that needed to be quickly forgotten, but my wisdom of going back sailing still kept strong. However, due to the workload, I needed to stay focused on the existing projects. Instead, I could not wait for the day to end, and after lunchtime, for me, work was finally over. That's when my common sense took me to the bar.

When I walked in, two women were sitting there, giggling to each other while scanning me from my head to my toes. I sat next to them, and ordered a drink.

"Let me have double scotch on the rocks."

"Hey youngster! What's your name?"

One of the giggling women said that to me, she was very appealing, and the one next to her was good looking too! Now that I sat closer to them, they looked quite striking.

"I could be whatever you want me to be!"

"Oh really! Did you hear that, Kathy?" They both chuckled, and I pulled my stool closer.

"Are you two beauties related? Looking the way you do, you must be!"

"Actually we are! Good guess!"

"So what is your task?"

"Task? What do you think? We are enjoying each other's company over a sweet drink!"

"I don't buy that; either you tell me, or I am leaving."

"Oh, aren't we demanding!"

"Yes, always."

"Okay, tough guy, how much money do you have on you?"

"Enough too cover my needs."

"I'm sure! But would it be enough to cover our needs as well?"

"It depends; what do you have in mind?"

"There is a motel nearby; we could rent a room with a nice Jacuzzi! Are you up for a deep soak?"

"With both of you?"

"Both of us will run you two grand; can you handle that?"

"Well, now that I know what you are, let's negotiate."

"We are not a bargain!"

"Hold that thought. I have only five hundred, and if you decide to accept my offer, I'll be in the car, waiting for only few moments."

Then I got out and went to my car. As I sat there, a vision of that night with Gale came to mind, and I saw myself going through the same thing, only this time I was about to double my misery, and pay for it, as well. How stupid could I get?

So when they walked out, I slammed on the gas pedal and fled away.

The next morning, I was sitting by my desk, thinking of what to do next, and how I should approach that new project, when Mom looked at me and said, "Al, do you remember what you promised me not too long ago?"

"Yes, Mom, I only made one promise to you, so how could I forget?"

"Do you intend to keep it?"

"Of course, why would you ask that?"

"I was browsing through newspapers, and stumbled onto a very odd ad."

"Is this about the house?"

"Yes, but listen to the ad. A new two-story house approximate three thousand square feet, with a total of ten thousand square feet of property."

"That must be very expensive! What is so odd about it?"

"The price Al! They are asking a hundred and thirty-five thousand dollars! I've read many listings before, but never saw anything like that."

"Well, it could not be in Brooklyn, so where is it?"

"It says here, Riverhead, Long Island; where is that, Al?"

"Let me look it up."

And when I did, that property turned out to be deep in Long Island.

"Mom, it's far; maybe that is why the price is so low. However, in that neighborhood, real-estate is much more expensive."

"I think we should check it out."

"And I think you should talk to Pap, and ask him if he would be willing to commute; that is a long drive, Mom."

When Pap returned from the job site, it did not take her long to convince him to go, and come Saturday, we were on our way there.

As we entered that location and came in closer, the property was huge, and the house was just completed. As it turned out, the owner's husband had a gambling problem, and owed a very large sum, so his wife decided to save him and was looking for a quick sale.

At the end of our meeting, I give her a deposit, and my parents purchased that house for a hundred and fifteen thousand dollars. Shortly after, they moved to Long Island permanently, and I stayed behind.

However, from that great deal, Pap got the worst end of the bargain, because now he had to commute on a daily basis, and driving three hours a day, especially after work, really pinned his spirit down, but he never give up.

Financially, things were going great for me, so I decided to give something back, and help somebody in need. That was my worst idea ever, and it all started when I got married.

I called it "the good deed" because there was no physical attraction, no mutual understanding, no emotional attachments, and of course, love was on a fairy tale scale. I simply tried to help a young man who worked for me at the time, and was staying in New York on a temporary visa.

He came for a visit with his girlfriend, and then decided to stay. His work skills were very impressive; that man had potential of becoming a top-notch installer, who my business desperately needed, and I was very satisfied to have him on our team.

One day he came up to me, disappointed, "Al, I have to inform you that soon I will have to leave."

"Why, Michael, what is wrong?"

"Nothing is wrong. My visa will expire soon; therefore I must return to my country."

"How soon?"

"In three weeks."

"Three weeks? Why didn't you tell me before? There is nothing I can do to help you stay in three weeks."

"Al, time is irrelevant; besides, if I told you before, what would you do? All this time, my attorney filed for extension, but it was always denied."

"Mike, there is no point to talk about the past now; however, I need to think about this. Tell me, do you want to go back?"

"Of course not, but what choice do I have?"

"Let me ask you, what if I married your girlfriend? It would be a fictitious marriage, of course. In one year, she will get a green card and be legal; then we would get a divorce, and you would return to your American future wife!"

"Wow, that is great; what's the catch? Why would you do that? Hey! Are you attracted to her?"

"Too many whys Mike, however, the answer is simple. I need you here full time; my business needs you. If this is the only way for you to return, then so be it."

"Okay, I am all for that idea; just let me talk to Irene and see what she says."

"Before you do that, you will have to sign a small agreement with me. It will obligate you to work here and restrict you from working elsewhere. However, if you decide to break this agreement, you will owe me twenty thousand dollars."

"You have thought of everything, haven't you? Okay, let's do it."

A few days after he signed the agreement, I met with his beloved Irene.

However, her behavior was very strange. Her beloved was on his way back, and yet she was shining with joy. The way she was looking at me, for a moment, I thought she was flirting with me. I felt that beyond doubt when she asked me, smiling, "So, Al, when are you planning to marry me?"

"The plan is to legalize you and nothing else; don't confuse yourself!"

"Yes, that is what I meant. Also, do you have a ring? You know, they said that you will have to place a ring on my finger, so, do you have one?"

"Yes I have one, and who are they? Didn't Mike tell you that no one is supposed to know about this arrangement? I mean no one!"

"I know that. I was just curious, so I asked around."

"Don't do that anymore, please!"

When she left, I thought about the ring and the fact that I did not really have one bothered me, so I decided to purchase one. Buying a wedding ring was not easy. I did not see myself wasting money on some cheap steel and later throwing it away, so instead, I decided to purchase the real deal.

What is the worst that could happen? She will wear it for a day, and then give it back to me.

Knowing that nothing happens without a reason, I took the liberty and visited Tiffany, the most upscale jewelry store in town. When I left that store with a fancy engagement ring and wedding band, I actually felt good about that purchase. Somehow, hope had lifted my mental state toward a new beginning, and I actually believed that this act would bring me closer to myself, and finding the better half within me.

Time passed fast; Michael went back to his country, and shortly after,

I found myself standing in city hall next to Irene, with her parents and my cousin Abe behind us.

That was the first time in my life I repeated pledges to a woman that I hardly knew. Then a voice said, "You may kiss the..."

I felt her lips touching mine before the word "bride" announced, that was completely unexpected, and when we arrived at my home, it got worse.

"Al, when would you like for me to move in?"

"What? Are you joking?"

"No, we are man and wife now; we need to know everything about each other. How do you expect us to pass the upcoming interview?"

"Ok, you are right; however, you don't have to live here for that. Let's just talk; ask me what you wish to know, and I will do the same."

"No, Al, it will not work. We need to be together, and I mean live together, or we will fail, and you may go to prison."

"I see where you are going with this! Did you tell Mike about this?"

"No, why would I? Besides, Mike and I were not that close. I never intended to become his wife."

"Irene, I never paid attention to the applications we filled out. How old are you again?"

"I'm twenty; so what?"

"So what? You could almost pass for my daughter. I am not going to sleep with you! That is your intention, isn't it?"

"Too late; you should have thought about that before pledging to me in front of all those people, especially my parents!"

"Yes, tell me about your parents. I thought you came here with Mike, and there was nobody else."

"You were wrong. My parents have lived here for a long time. I stayed with my grandmother, and last year I came to US as an exchange student."

"So you attend school?"

"College, too be more precise."

"Who is paying for it?"

"I am, but that's not important."

"Well, it's important to me, because I think now I know why you wanted to marry me. Listen, I am not rich, and won't be able to support your education; talk about bad choices."

"I don't need your financial support. I make more than enough to pay for it all myself."

"So what do you want from me? Try to understand. I married you so Mike could stay and work for me; that is it!"

She began to cry, then took her bag, and ran out. I was stunned from her statements and did not know what to make of this ordeal.

I did not hear from Irene for days; then weeks went by, and not even a phone call, and that was very odd. She was so determined to stay with me, and now suddenly, she disappeared with no explanation.

And then it hit me, I placed the rings on her; after the conflict at the house, she left and took them with her.

What a scam! Or was it? For the time being, I said goodbye to sixteen thousand dollars, along with my hope.

I could not sleep that night. Why when I try to do something good at the end, my deed slammed my face into shit.

Next morning, I went back to city hall. I did not know anything about Irene, and she was smart enough to obtain all the information for herself. However, I learned her whereabouts, and that's all I needed at the time.

Apparently, she was living only a few blocks away from me; and when I knocked on her door, my new mother-in-law stood there.

"Al! How nice too see you!"

"I wish I could believe that."

"Oh, it looks like someone missed the good-mood train."

"Listen, Mom! Give me back my rings before I put you aboard the Hell Train! And I mean now!"

"Okay, calm down, let me look for them. Irene will not wear them to work, so they must be in her room. Please, sit down; I'll be right back."

I was very surprised when she returned with my rings in her hand, and said, "Here there are. Take them. I smell alcohol; have you been drinking?"

"Yes, and it's not of your business. Where is your daughter anyway?"

"She is at work."

"I did not know she was working; what does she do?"

"She works as a bar-attendant in a restaurant."

"So she did not lie when she said you don't support her; which restaurant is it?"

"Russian Tea Room, in Manhattan, and yes she is on her own."

"Listen, Mom, aren't you a little suspicious?"

"Why should I be?"

"Well, how blind you must be not to see it. She is a young woman, paying for everything by herself, including college. You really think bar-attendants make that much?"

"You got what you came for; now please get out!"

And so I did

Still feeling sober and with a desire for more, I decided to visit that restaurant. I did not want to go in on my own, so I waited outside for some time, until a group of people arrived, and I rushed in along with them.

There were only two men attending the bar, and no sign of Irene. When one of them approached me, I asked, "Double scotch on the rocks, please!"

"Coming right up!"

"What is your name?"

"Mike; and you are?" Another Mike. I would soon shiver upon hearing that name.

"I'm Al; nice to meet you, Mike. Hey, listen, where is that girl that works here? Irene, I believe her name is."

"Yes, I know Irene; why do you ask?"

"Well, I feel some awkward saying this, but I'm sure you are aware of Irene's ordeals, so I will tell you. Last night, she left her earrings at my place. They were very long, and were interfering with . . . Well; you know what I mean."

He smiled and said, "So, I guess you are her client?"

"Client slash boyfriend!"

"Whatever; she is out with another client slash boyfriend, but they should be back soon."

"Wow, that's painful. She told me I was the only one during weekdays! Thanks for the input!"

That guy was very easy to buy, and now I wanted to see how Irene would react to my awareness, so I decided to stay and wait until she returned.

It took only twenty minutes and three more drinks for Irene to show up, and when she did, she looked different. She had ten layers of makeup on her face, wearing a tight red skirt and dark blue coat, had marked her as a prostitute from a mile away.

She walked, and approached me slowly, with her masquerade smile at the bartender, she said, "Hi, Mike!"

I moved closer. She turned around, and then our eyes met.

"Hello Irene, how have you been? Are you working hard, sweetie? I call this encounter 'The curtains closed in unexpectedly.' Would you agree?"

She just sat there looking at me and not saying a word. Then tears began to roll from her eyes.

I could not help myself and said, "Stop with the crocodile tear show; I'm not buying it. Better tell me; how much do you charge?"

"Why? Would you like to participate?"

"You know better than that! I'm just curious."

"One thousand dollars; Okay! Happy now?"

"Wow! Men actually pay you that much? I would like to see the schmuck who is prepared to pay so much for one night."

"You really want to see that schmuck? Then go look in the mirror, and I get much more for the night!"

"Well, that would explain how you pay the bills on your own."

"Al, what are you doing here? What do you want?"

"I want a divorce, and as soon as possible."

"Really? And if I say no?"

"Then I will sell us out; prison doesn't scare me. Actually, it might help me with my drinking problem, and I might even enjoy it. However, you will be deported and never reenter those grounds again!"

"Okay Al, you won! I'll give you the divorce; is there anything else?"

"No! Actually, yes. You knew the arrangement we had all along! So why did you refuse me, and behave the way you did?"

"I really liked you, and thought that you might like me too."

"Yeah, right; you liked me and screwed with everybody else! You are the woman of my dreams!"

"I wanted to stop working, and was on my way there, but had no idea you would find out so soon."

"Listen, honey; somewhere very deep inside, maybe you are a nice girl. However, we are completely opposite, not to mention the age difference. There were many times in my life where I neglected to face the facts, but unfortunately for me, truth always had a way of finding me."

I left that place disappointed, upset, and drunk. Driving back home was difficult, and thinking about Irene the whole time did not make me feel any better. For some reason, my eyes were piling up with tears. It became hard to see the road, and I did not feel like stopping. So many individuals living and performing unwilling acts, if life is about choice, then why do people chose to sell themselves?

We all commit wrong actions just to establish a better way of living; moreover, we chose that because it's the easier way to get there. It is unfortunate and very depressing to see how people neglect hard work, and instead are willing to sacrifice their own body, and sometimes there souls, and for what?

I always thought and believed that, a woman would give up her precious and valuable natural gifts only in exchange for passionate feeling. As romantic desires, physical attraction, and when she is seeking love. But women like Irene use their gifts to improve their lifestyle, or maybe it's true, that everybody are for sale, it's just a matter of price.

But then again, I'm an old-fashioned man; my comprehension had ceased to exist a long time ago, and now, nearly all I saw around me repulsed me.

Most of the time, I said to myself that reality was a nasty dream, and that was what triggered me toward drinking. Because then, I could wake up in a more suitable world, a world that was closer to my heart and my beliefs.

The next day, I went to work, and closed my thoughts to all that had happened. After a few months, Irene and I divorced, and my life routine went back to normal again, or how it used to be.

Because of the distant commute, and no other alternatives, Pap left the company, and shortly after, he obtained a new job that was closer to his home, and worked as a welder.

I was very happy for them, especially for my mother, because that house had a huge property, so gardening became her favorable hobby, and she had finally received her paradise.

But then again, I was completely alone, and now isolated from my family once again. I knew there was no one I could depend on, and if I should relapse or be absent from work; I would lose everything again, only this time for good. Regardless of those facts, and no matter how hard I tried to cut myself loose from alcohol, some event would always bring me back to the bottle, and with every occasion, my drinking got worse.

Another year of my existence went by and was meaningless; through that period, I saw nothing nor did I accomplish anything. In fact, I became miserable, and all my prior achievements slowly vanished.

Soon enough, a crack in the wall was created between me and my family; losing all of my friends and acquaintances came as no surprise to me either, and my business appeared to be next.

Because of my lifestyle, I was absent from work on a regular basis. As a result, one of the biggest job sites had shut down, and before long, the others followed. I was lacking cash, so all the employees took leave, and my company embarked on a rapid dive. It was just a matter of time before all of it would sink completely. At that juncture, I saw my life and all its contents crashing before my eyes once again.

How many times did I need to trip at the same spot, into the same swampy hole, before realizing there was a need to walk around that location? The main cause was obvious to me, but I could not stop on my own, so I began for a quest for assistance, and that became my first priority.

The yellow pages was a helpful source of finding the help I needed. I located substance abuse programs, although regrettably, the first few I tried turned out to be very disappointing, and I was on the brink of losing hope toward turning my life around. I thought, *this is it, I have reached the end, and there is no coming back.*

Every outpatient place I visited could offer only group therapy, but most of the clients we're mandated, so no one cared about their therapy or the addiction they had.

Actually, those people were sitting there with only one agenda, a desire for the time to pass so they could leave and continue with their lifestyle routine.

Me? Well, I felt out of balance just by being in the same room with them. Not that I had anything against them. We just had different goals. I was looking for help, and a new beginning, and they were only waiting to run out of there as soon as it was possible.

On every visit, I departed with such depression that my first thought was toward a glass of scotch, so right afterward I rushed to the bar, that same bar that I called my second home. While sitting there, having one drink after another, I could not stop thinking of the treatment I had chosen, and the therapy that sledged me even further down.

I was completely lost and helpless, so my visits to the bar never ended only with a few drinks; as a result, I was back on bingeing again.

That situation was unbearable to me. I came to force myself to drink alcohol and did not understand my reasoning anymore. Why would I drink liquid that my body strongly opposed? In addition, vomiting right after alcohol consumption and persisting to drink more, to the point where the body organs would give up resisting and accept whatever came in next.

Those proceedings continued for hours and brought tears to my eyes; that toxic drink became fatal to me, and still I was pouring that poison into my body and unwillingly letting it slide down my throat. It was the most confusing state of mind I had ever encountered.

I always believed in God! Nevertheless, I was never a religious individual. However, wretchedness and the irrational behavior of alcohol consumption had brought me to a massive cry for help. "God, why won't you help me? Please help me. I want to stop, but I can't." I cried out while consuming the entire bottle, and then I passed out.

"Look at the footprints."

"I heard that before! And I see no footprints"

"Find morality; distinguish right from wrong at every step you make! For only then the footprints become visible"

"Why am I going back on living? There is nothing there for me! I want to say here!"

"It is not for you to decide; you must complete your task."

"How will I know that I succeeded?"

"Agony will stop, fortune will reveal itself"

"Well, it did stop. I don't feel any pain!"

I woke up in a sweat; thinking about the final chapter in that dream that had inspired me to go back. There were nothing but problems waiting for me in reality, so why suffer? That thought really helped me, and my drinking continued until I passed out again.

This time, I appeared as a spirit in a normal society, working in the factory. Then, unwillingly, my shape penetrated through walls. At first, I really enjoyed that trip, until the last wall, where I passed through and stumbled in front of two young girls who appeared to be twins.

They both looked at me, and with one tone, said, "This is your last chance! Use it wisely!"

"Wait a minute! What are you two doing here? You are both just little girls! And I thought I was talking with God before!"

"We are here to guide you! High stakes placed on you! And you are neglecting your destiny! This is your last chance!"

"How old are you? And why are you talking simultaneously?"

"This is your last chance, Al"

Then my figure commenced to retreat. I was going through the same places, the same walls, only backwards passing through each wall faster and faster. Suddenly, the walls appeared from the left, and then from the right. I flew into them with enormous speed; next, a massive agony carried me back to reality.

I woke up with anguish all over my body; my hands were ripping apart, and my head was twisting side to side with massive force, that seem to continue for the longest time. When it finally stopped, I was relieved.

After that experience, I could not sleep anymore I realized that a seizure had visited me again, and this time it happened when I was sleeping.

It was very odd; seizure only arise upon alcohol withdrawal, so why did it happen to me while under the influence? That was a new discovery for me.

That dream which haunted me for years finally made some sense, so apparently, my footprints are what I leave behind when I'm gone! And through all my years, I had nothing to show for; how could I be so selfish.

I have never thought about this before, and that incident made me pause drinking. I just lay there, looking at the ceiling, and thinking. *Will this ever stop? How far do I need to go to reach the end, and how much more do I need to suffer? What else do I have to go through in order to obtain peace?*

The task to discontinue drinking was always very difficult; besides the tremendous pain, my body had no balance whatsoever. Walking became harder than a baby's first step.

However, for some reason, that time was different. As I rose from my bed, my condition surprised me because there was no body aching, my balance was normal, and in comparison to prior events, I felt good.

Recalling the years of my prior conditions and experiences, then considering the amount of alcohol I had had this time, that state of body and mind seemed abnormal to me.

So, once more, I began to scan the yellow pages with the hope to encounter a truthful help. As I was going through the pages, disappointment awakened and rose in me with every flipped page. Coming nearly to the end of one section, for some reason, my eyes halted on one particular organization that apparently I had ignored before, because previously I had highlighted everything on that page except this ad.

I could not help but wonder why, so curiosity encouraged me to try it, and without giving it second thought, I picked up the phone, and that same day I went for Intake.

The intake process was a new and interesting experience for me, although paranoia grew in me upon when they asked what I thought were stupid and pointless questions, which I thought were irrelevant to my problem. The counselor they assigned to me bothered me the most.

At my intake, my counselor, in my understanding, had no personal knowledge or experience concerning the addiction, not to mention her experience was less than a few years. In my eyes, she was unskilled and a waste of my time.

To receive proper treatment, I needed someone with experience of my situation; how else would they understand what I was going through, and how could they help me? However, regardless of whom she was or what she knew, I was desperate and decided to keep my appointment, so I went to see her anyway.

I was sitting in the waiting area in anticipation of my session when a woman walked in and called my name, I thought to myself, *that's all I need now, a sexually appealing therapist.* I really wondered what she could possibly do for me, and she probably had no plan for my treatment. For her, I was just another individual, who had bitted the dust.

When I approached her, she introduced herself and then said, "Please follow me."

So we went toward what I presumed to be her office. As we arrived, I pulled the door open and showed her in, but she refused, then shifted aside and displayed a hand motion showing me to go first.

I couldn't interpret her actions; maybe it was a professional courtesy, or maybe she didn't want me to behave in a gentleman's manner. Regardless, I went into her office, and sat down.

She asked me the same questions I had answered before. While replying to them again, I could not stop thinking, what annoying process I got myself into. Then it hit me; she was trying to come up with a suitable answer so she could have a dialog on a suitable subject, and so it was. I was right, because eventually I said what she wanted to hear, and she hit a jackpot.

Then she said, "So, why are you here?"

"I'm tired from my life routine, I need to stop drinking, and I can't achieve this task on my own."

"Need? Or want?"

"Is there a difference?"

"What do you think?"

"Okay, I want to stop drinking!"

"When did you start?"

"Long time ago."

"Whom do you live with?"

"No one!"

"I'm going to give you some homework; you will write down all of your positive qualities on one side of this page, and on the other, all your negatives."

"And this is going to help me how?"

"Same principle; for your feelings and thoughts!"

"Okay, and then what?"

"And then we shall see where it leads us."

Our session came to its end. I got up and walked out, and knew that this bullshit homework would not change anything in my life.

The following few sessions I found very difficult and I was resistant in some way, but after that, without self-awareness, I came to be talkative; and that was her method of turning me around.

Apparently, I was completely shut, and away from everything else. I existed in my own world at all times, and set myself aside from all others. With my alcohol addiction, my dilemma was most critical. I had that problem through many years and did not even know it.

My encounters with the counselor continued; we met twice a week over one month. During that time, I became to feel somehow better concerning my self-esteem and all that surrounded me. I guess I was wrong about her.

At the same time, I continued to work, only now with two helpers, and without Pap. I was performing small jobs, but that was enough to keep me in business and acquire some money flow.

When Pap left, that business was on a low level; however, it also became my most important substance, which I cherished the most. During work, I was missing Pap on a daily basis, and in difficult situations, I could hear him yell. Then I would stop and think, *what would Pap do in this matter*, and that always guided me toward a resolution I had not seen before.

But after a workday, when I returned home, cold walls closed in on me. A thought of Jim, and what my life would be like, if he was around, brought me back to escaping reality.

Through a short period, I relapsed several times, and my addiction toward alcohol was still strong, the cycle had never stopped or changed. Although my inner spirit was growing, at least I thought it was; my soul sometimes was at ease. But my addiction remained and with every relapse, at the end, my body and mind tolerated agony like never before.

The most unforgettable occasion took place prior to the alcohol withdrawal event, when I was consuming alcohol unexpectedly seizure took over; that was my last experience of miraculous pain. Regardless of it all, and just like in the past, when I woke up, the drinking continued. I was sitting in the apartment alone, without a clue of what was going on in the world, holding a glass of vodka, with a steam cloud in my eyes.

Running out of hope and strength, I could no longer admit to anything positive. Not having a choice in the matter and knowing that this was the end of the road, I decided to call that office for help. When that woman answered, hearing her voice somehow clutched faith to my stream of sadness.

"Hello, Monica! I need your help."

"What happened?"

"I am drinking again; this time I can't stop. Please help me."

"What would you like me to do?"

"Send me to a rehab! There is no way in this world I can help myself with this matter."

"Are you sure?"

"Yes, I have never been so sure about anything before."

"Okay, let me see what I can do. I will get back to you."

I was waiting all right. As soon as I hung up, the drinking continued, and my brain slowly started to boil. Strange how the human brain works; my brain, that is. It felt as I was split in two halves; someone in my head shouted "Stop gulping that acid," and right afterward someone else with more powerful influence screamed, "This is not acid; keep it up and do not let it go to waste."

It is not hard to figure out which side prevailed, so there I was, soaked with alcohol from my toes to my ears, and there was nothing I could do about it. As I sat there, I wondered about others with similar problems, I also was puzzled, as to why was I lacking fear?

Fear for all humankind is a most valuable feeling. It prevents us from hurting ourselves, and keeps us alive. Without fear, our life would be a short existence.

We don't place our hands into a fire because the mind is aware of the consequences, and fear prohibits us from that act to avoid future damage. So why, in the case of addiction, where the outcome is on a much larger scale, had my fear fallen asleep behind the wheel, and allowed me to drive into the worst harm ever?

I was consuming a liquid that had became strongly revolting to me, and despite that fact, my hands reached out and poured one shot after another. The stronger my soul resisted, the more alcohol my body consumed.

That was the first time in my life that my brain acted without my consent, and carried out a command against my will. And that unforgettable feeling finally scared me the most.

In all prior episodes, I never admitted or encountered such powerful interaction between the brain and my soul. My willpower helplessly seized by the urge of addiction. I always thought I was in control; but this state prove me wrong.

It is unreal how alcohol had manipulated my subconscious and made my body commit unwilling actions. All that was wrong and forbidden suddenly became possible and permissible. In my mind, there were no consequences for my wrong behavior; all and everything became possible, and that is why fear was always absent.

I then stepped away from my actions, and two questions rose in my mind. Why do I purchase liquor when I am aware of the outcome and revolted by it? And why can't I stop, if I desire to stop?

Deep inside, I knew how powerful my addiction really was, and still, those questions were hunting me down, unwilling behavior and forthcoming state of mind devastated me.

I could not find logical explanations to my peculiar conduct, and only then, I realized how helpless I really was. I was now at the bottom and saw no way out; therefore, bingeing began.

When the phone rang, my body was home but I was absent.

The most fulfilling sentiment of drinking is the arrival of a state of lifelessness, because then, I was within serenity and the stillness of time. It is one of the most peaceful states of mind ever, and maybe that is what makes it the most terrifying and in most cases untreatable illness.

That feeling was great, but not so comforting when I woke up not knowing or remembering my prior behavior, and experiencing a tremendous urge generated by the mind for more alcohol. However, I could not take alcohol any further. Suddenly the phone rang.

"Hello"

"Hi, it's me; how are you feeling?"

"Oh, hi Monica, not so good. Actually, I don't really know."

"Okay, there is an open bed at one of the rehabs. I can arrange for your intake this Monday."

Monday meant that I would have to struggle with this revolting situation for two more days.

"Can't you find something sooner? I don't think I can wait that long."

"No, that is the only available facility at this time; besides, you need to be selective in this matter. In some rehabs, most of the crowds are mandated. You will not benefit in those places, so listen to my advice and if you really ready for treatment, be at my office by two p.m."

"I don't think that's a good idea. I can't drive."

"Take a cab. You need to come in for paperwork, Monday morning at six a.m.; a car will arrive to pick you up. Are you listening to me?"

"Yes, I am. Okay, I'll be there."

Therefore, I got up, and on my way to the bathroom, I glanced at myself at the mirror that covered the entire hallway wall. What a scary view. I thought I would take a shower, but lack of strength prevented me from that luxury, not to mention the difficulties that confronted me as I was dressing myself. And even more so seeing the empty bottles around me. They were everywhere.

Those two days seemed endless, considering that sleep was out of the question, nights were even worse, although a strange thing happened to me during the night I fell asleep.

One of those many unforgettable journeys took me to a mysterious place where an old woman was sitting by the edge of a huge mountain. The sky was dark and full of grey clouds; the debris around her surrounding seemed to be frozen.

When I decided to approach closer, she turned her head and said, "Stop, my son! You don't want to come closer."

"Why not?"

"I know why you are here, my son."

"Yes! I'm dreaming again! Who are you?"

"Irrelevant question my son. Why won't you ask me something worthy?"

"Like what?"

"Like why are you miserable, my son; don't you want to know?"

"Well, actually, yes, I do."

"You think wretchedness is all that surrounds you; is that true?"

"Yes, of course!"

"Tell me, my son, what would make you a happy?"

"Okay" And I proceeded to tell her all my needs; the list was long but truthful.

All my hurt, with all my wishes, poured out of my mouth like water from a fountain.

I never knew of my fast talking capabilities before then.

Nevertheless, what really bothered me was that when I completed my last sentence, she turned her had to me and said, "If I grant you all your wishes, would you be happy?"

"Oh yes, of course I would."

"Well my son; you should know that life in itself is a gift; each additional grant, is presented in a mysterious way! But, upon its arrival, something else will always depart! Because, where there is a grant, there must be a seizure! Those are the rules, and without them, life would not be worth living!"

"So, you are trying to tell me that there is always a catch! Okay, that I learned the hard way! So, don't lecture me! Whatever I have to give, I will. Besides, I have nothing now! All I cherished most, I lost!"

"Then, when you wake up, all your wishes would come true! How will you feel?"

"Are you kidding me, great of course, how else?"

"You will lose your sight. You will not see your wishes! However, your joy shall come from other new senses! Would you still be happy?"

"My life is such a dilemma, and now that dilemma has consumed my dreams! Why?"

"Be happy for what you have, and very cautious about asking for more! Now go."

Then I woke up.

Monday finally came. It was five o'clock in the morning, and I was rolling around the apartment like a dying fish in the water. At last, I managed to pull myself together. Somehow, I got myself dressed and rolled out of the building. The van was already there.

I got in and the driver said to me, "I was about to leave; why are you so late?"

"Why, what time is it?"

"Six thirty. You were supposed to be here at six a.m."

"I'm sorry; I thought it was five thirty." I could barely speak.

"Okay, man, take a seat. Buckle up and stay there. In your condition, I don't want you rolling around my van."

He was right. In fact, I had no condition at all, and apparently, it took me an hour and a half just to get out of the building.

We drove for over three hours to that facility; it was painful to sit like that for so long, with the van rocking from side to side and hitting every bump on our way.

However, the place was nice, and the intake was fast and easy. Then, they gave me some pills and I went to sleep.

I liked being there for the first few days, but then something happened. Those sessions drove me nuts; one after the other with only a five-minute break, and sometimes no breaks at all. The only free time we had was at breakfast, lunch, and dinner. That was it!

I could not take this abuse anymore; it felt like in prison, so I had a strong desire to leave. I called Monica and told her.

"Listen, I can't take this torture anymore. I told them to release me and they are preparing the paperwork"

"How many mistake have you made in your life? Just think for a moment. How many? This will be your biggest ever! You're strong man; suck it up and go with the program."

I hung up and went to my room, waiting for them to finish my discharge documents. While I was there waiting, I thought to myself; *Am I really a coward? Can I handle pressure? Why run? I have to be stronger. All my life I had ran from problems, and hardly faced one. It's about time to change that.*

Then the counselor walked in, and said, "Okay, Al. You are free to go!"

"No, I decided to stay."

"Are you sure?"

"Yes, I am."

And that, is how a few days turned into twenty-eight days. I have to say that the place was tough. However, some of the group therapies were interesting, helpful, and impressive. They did help me understand and realize things that had never known existed.

I found the facility owner to be most impressive; he was forty years on the wagon. He stated the main reason for that was, due to his place, he didn't have time for anything else.

However, he was not nice to everyone, especially those with stupid questions. When a bald guy approached him and asked, "What time it is?" he replied, "Time to grow some hair!"

I think he was right; why would he need to know the time when there was no place to go?

Upon my release, I went to his office, and asked him, "My counselor advised me to find a psychologist on the outside; can you recommend anyone?"

"Of course; he is very good and somewhat expensive, but somehow I think you can afford him."

When I got out, the first thing I did was call him, and we arranged my first session.

"Hello, Mr. Lave"

"Hi, Al; how are you? How do you feel?"

"Okay; I just don't know what to do. As I told you on the phone, I have an alcohol problem, and I do not want to start bingeing again. Hey, may I ask you a question?"

"Of course; that's why we are here."

"Can you tell me how long my treatment will be?"

"Well, tell me; how long have you been drinking?"

"Fifteen years, I think."

"That is the length of your treatment!"

"WOW, are you kidding me?"

"No, I am not. Also, we will have to start from your childhood."

I was sitting there in shock. I have to come here for fifteen years. I did not know if I could handle that.

"So, Al; tell me about your childhood. What do you remember?"

"Excuse me, doc, but how old are you?"

"I'm sixty-two. Why do you ask?"

"Well, if I have to come here for fifteen years, you might not live half of that time, so then what?"

"Don't worry; we'll find you a replacement," he said, laughing.

"Okay, and then I will have to start all over again with him?"

He got up, and was laughing while waling to his desk, then he picked up a file and said, "You see that? We keep records. By the way, you are a smart guy; maybe you should treat me instead."

"I have to go to the bathroom." He commenced to laugh, and I flew out of his office, before he would finish.

While driving back to Brooklyn, I did not know where to go or what to do. My parents lived far away, and with time, somehow we all grew apart. I decided to go home and invite Monica over.

I arrived home and called her. "Hello, Monica; I'm home."

"Well, great; how was it? How do you feel?"

"I'll tell you all about it if you will come over for coffee."

"Okay; I will see you soon."

When she came over, we talked for hours, and with time, became real close friends. After a while I realized, we we're more than friends. There was some connection between us, and I recognized that feeling, because it was identical to what I felt for Jimmy.

Monica turned out to be one incredible woman; she was smart, warm hearted, and very naive at the same time. Nevertheless, our relationship never went beyond friendship.

Some say that friendship between a man and a woman only commences before or after sex. Well, in our case, they were very much wrong; there was nothing intimate between us except for our souls.

All I cared about was for her to be healthy and happy. I also wanted her to smile more often, because she had an incredible smile, one that could light a room.

We came to spend more time together, and I could only assume that she was worried about me relapsing and returning to that misery road once more.

When I returned to my shop, that place had turned to a graveyard, so Monica helped me financially to restart my business and begin to work again.

Apparently, Monica believed in me, and she was the only one I trusted; with her help, I moved to a new location, and with time, hard time that is, I turned that place into an operational business once again.

The task was getting back on my feet, I wanted to be financially stable again; moreover, I wanted to see the world through sober eyes, so work kept me occupied and away from bad urges.

Due to new location and phone lines, all our previous connections were lost, and instead of my Pap, I had an ex-sailor as a helper. This time around, starting over wasn't as simple as it used to be.

Because of that, I struggled to get work, and then, upon getting small jobs, due to a lack of workers, I struggled to complete each project. Then, when the project was finally done, no one paid me on time, so in the end, I struggled financially.

For two years, I borrowed funds from one source to cover another, but, at the same time, my work provided me up scale reputation, and one day, somehow things turned around.

Gradually new estimates were piling up, then unnoticeably, I had two teams, which were constantly working, and after a while, I got some free time again. That's when I experienced, that patience result in reward.

One morning, I was browsing through internet sites and came across a very attractive ad. "House for sale, with a beautiful lake view, for ten thousand." That ad magnetized me, so after a phone call I jumped into my car and rushed there.

It turned out to be in, Pennsylvania. The area was magnificent however, when I arrived at that beautiful house, things were quite different.

"Hello! Al, I presume."

"Yes, and you must be Beth!"

"That's right; nice to meet with you. Let me show you the house."

As we walked toward the lake, I began to wonder where that house might be. The entire space was loaded with tiny structures, one squeezed next to the other with hardly any walking space between them.

"Okay, that is it!" she said, pointing toward an old wreck which looked like it was about to fall apart at any moment.

"Is that it? Are you kidding me? My bathroom is bigger than this wreck!"

"What did you expect for that kind of money?"

"Beth, you should have told me on the phone that this is a five yard toilet! Do you know how long it took me to get here? I mean, come on! What kind of business are you running here? This is nothing like what I saw on the internet, and I would never have come here for this junk!"

"Okay, Al, tell me what are you seeking."

"Well, first, I want to be isolated. A lake is good but not a necessity. The structure is not important. I just need a large space so I could build there!"

"I have just the place for you; there is nothing there now and the community has no building regulations, so you can build whatever you like."

"Show me!"

That had really inspired me; especially, her phrase "whatever you like" rang a bell in my head all the way there.

When we entered the community, everything seemed the same as at the prior location, although the houses were larger. However, I followed her as she climbed toward the top of the mountain, where there was nothing but forest on a huge, isolated summit.

We reached the peak of the mountain, and she stopped. "This is it!" she said, smiling.

"Yes, Beth. That is it!"

I was standing at the top of the summit; there were no houses around me, the lake beneath me; there was nothing but me, the sky, and the forest, at the top of nowhere, surrounded with so many trees, it was hard to count.

"Hey, Al, come back to earth!"

"Sorry, Beth; okay, I'll take it."

"This location is unique, and also much more expensive."

"How much is it?"

"The asking price is ninety-six thousand; however, there is a room to negotiate."

"Quite a mark-up from what you showed me before."

"What did you expect? There is almost an acre and a half here; besides, look around you! You wanted to be isolated; it can't get any better than that. You get what you pay for."

"Yes, that phrase is well known to me. Okay, let's go to your office. I will give you my offer, and please make it happen!"

As I was sitting in her office, she came out and said, "Your offer was accepted! Congratulations."

"Thank you, Beth!"

I purchased that property for about ten thousand less than its asking price, and I was short by half for the total amount needed.

So I came home, and asked Monica to stop by. "I have some great news!"

"I can tell; your eyes are on fire! What is it?"

"I bought land, and I want to build a house there, but not just any house; it will be one of a kind!"

"That's great!"

"Well, yes and no! I don't have the entire amount, and you know I don't believe in banks, so I need your help."

"Okay, how much do you need?"

"Forty thousand dollars."

"Wow, that's quite a number!"

"Not really; the way my business is going, I will pay you back in three months!"

"Are you sure about that?"

"Positive!"

"Okay, but I don't have all of it, so I will borrow some from my father and my friends. But Al, be sure you pay it back!"

The following week, I give Monica all my funds and she mailed them a full payment, then shortly after, that property was mine.

I was there on the day the excavation company commenced working; watching them cutting the trees down was very painful for me. That day, I pledged to plant a new tree for every tree they removed, which turned to be over fifty.

Afterward, every evening, I sketched my dream house, and when my sketches were complete, I called an old acquaintance of mine and asked him to visit my shop.

The next day, he showed up.

"Hello Nicholas; long time no see!"

"Hey, Al; what brings me here?"

"I need your help. I purchased a property in Pennsylvania, and I want to build a house there, so I made some sketches and I need you to turn them into architectural drawings."

"Al, I am not an architect, and I do not know the building codes, especially in Pennsylvania."

"I know that. I can't afford an architect; just make the drawings without codes and specifications, then I will find a local architect and pay him for final submittals."

"Okay, give me the sketches. I will call you in two weeks."

Nick was sixty-five years old, and a very talented engineer. His major experience and knowledge was in structural steel, which I needed the most because I had no idea of the structural steel process. I had only seen it upon completion, so I hoped he would join my team when construction began.

However, at that point, I decided not to tell him about my plans. This was all new to me, and quite a big challenge, so I needed to approach this one phase at the time.

The following week, I took Monica to the dreamland; of course, she was aware and involved in my plan from the day of the purchase, however, as it turned out, knowing and seeing somehow rested on different sides of the scale.

"So, what do you think? Do you see the marks there?"

"Wow, this property is enormous. Yes, I see them; what are they?"

"Those are the points of where the house will be."

"That is some distance! Are you sure about that range? It seems overly big!"

"Yes, I'm sure, and it's not that big, only a hundred feet long and forty feet wide, or maybe forty-five."

"Well, standing at one end, I hardly can see the sticks on the other side. Actually, I don't see them! How is it not big? It's huge!"

"It just seems big because of the open space; trust me, when a structure is raised here, you will not think that."

As she walked around with her eyes glowing, I knew I had made the right choice; however, I had no idea what waited for me later on.

Nick did not call me; instead, he showed up at my work unexpectedly. He placed a roll of drawings on my desk and said, "Here they are! Al, I have to say, you don't know what you getting yourself into!"

"Why you would say that?"

"Well, first of all, that structural steel is enormous! And if that is not enough, you are looking to place it on a cliff! For that, you will need massive concrete support. However, what puzzled me and my assistant, is that most of the building is glass! Why?"

"Nick, you know why; this is what I do. That way I will be able to perform most of the work on my own! I am not rich, Nick. I can't afford to hire contractors, and besides, I think it will look great!"

"Oh yeah, it will look great! Nevertheless, I still think it's crazy to built something like this at that location; you may have problems from the local building department. I don't think they would approve this structure there! Pick a flat space! I saw there are many there; why would you choose the cliff?"

"Because only then, would it stand for what it's really worth! And we'll see about that building department. I believe in a phrase, "Where there is a will, there must be a way!"

"I Hope you are right Al, good luck!"

"Thanks Nick. Wait. I will need your help upon approval. I want you there building the structural steel. I will pay you, of course. There is no one else I trust, and you know I have no knowledge in steel work."

"Okay, Al. First get the approval, and then we'll talk about building it."

Nick left in a hurry, and did not discuss any terms with me; he also seemed a little disappointed. I guess he assumed that my dream would collapse and nothing would come of this.

Regardless, I was very enthusiastic about that project, Nick's willingness to participate, had inspired me even more, so now there were no doubts but to proceed further, and so I did.

After a few weeks of constant search, I finally located an architect who was willing to take my idea further and apply for a permit. When we met, at first, he was leaning toward a complete drawing remake. However, after a thorough explanation and ten thousand dollars, I managed to persuade him otherwise, and he proceeded with my initial idea.

Two weeks later, he called me, and said, "Al, I got your drawings and engineering calculations back from the township."

"And?"

"And they were all approved! Just mail a permit fee, and you are ready to go!"

"Oh boy! That is great news! How much is the permit?"

"Two thousand dollars!"

"Thank you, Charlie; it's on the way to you!"

"My pleasure! Listen, I have to say that in all my years here, I had never seen anything like your project, and I think they approved your structure because they don't believe you will build it! I saw it in their faces, and wanted you to know they are looking for you to fail."

"Well, I will give them something to look at! No doubt about that!"

"Al, would you need me for construction?"

"No offense, Charlie, but I cannot afford you. Take care; and thanks again."

When he gave me that news, a huge load of pressure came off me, and doubts raised as well. When so many people have misgivings, it could mean only one thing: big problems were waiting ahead for me.

I had never believed or recognized outsiders' opinions, but I was also familiar with the law of the many. When someone says you look pale, ignore him, but when you hear that from many, it's time to visit a doctor!

I had to talk to someone, and there was no one available but Mom, so I called her.

"Hi, Mom; it's been a long time. Sorry; I was very busy."

"Hi, son Busy is good, but not busy drinking I hope!"

"Mom, I bought a property in Pennsylvania."

"That's great! What are you going to do there?"

"I am planning to build a house. I had some issues in the beginning, however, now everything is approved, and I can finally start construction."

"Congratulations! I'm very happy for you; if you recall, when you were a kid, you always said to me that you would build your first house. So, you see, dreams do come true!"

"Yes, Mom, but why are there always so many difficulties along the way? Sometimes, I see people find a coin on the street and pick it up with no trouble. I never try that because I know I would trip and break my head before I reached it. Why am I so unlucky?"

"You're not unlucky, Al! Don't say that. Do to your high standards, you have chosen a difficult life path, and now you are complaining."

"I don't have high standards, Mom. Why would you say that?"

"Oh yes you do, and the sad thing about it is that you don't even know it! Try to analyze your way of living. You were never satisfied with a paycheck and always wanted to be your own boss. Well, that's difficult! Nothing ordinary ever attracted you! You were always attracted to the opposite, and that brought you even more problems. Then, when all the problems combined, you made the worst choice ever! You decided to run and hide behind the bottle; that is when your most horrible nightmares began! So don't complain; be grateful for what you have!"

"I think I heard that before! Okay Mom, and thanks. I have to go."

"Before I forget, why don't you buy a camera and keep a life log of your progress."

"Okay, Mom, that's a good idea I will!"

Damn, I was feeling low. I thought she might help bring me back in the mood; instead, she lowered me into a barrel of shit. Now I really felt awful, I had not spoken to her in months, and now had no will to speak to her for another four months.

Buying a camera was the only helpful advice from her, and thank god all the submittals were now behind me, and I could start with construction,

The following week, I met with Nick and we agreed on our terms, then he organized and assembled a team of welders and I rented a trailer nearby. Then we all went to Pennsylvania to start work.

I ordered all the necessary steel and materials to arrive at the site, and on Monday morning, when Nick and his men were preparing the equipment, two trailers came in loaded with steel beams.

That day, Nick and his men began fabricating my future home; meanwhile, the excavation and mason companies were working on the foundation.

I watched all of them for one day, and then had to return to my tasks in New York. My men and our projects were in need for me, so I was in New York during the working days, then going to Pennsylvania on the weekends.

I played the role of a yoyo for two months, which came to be very trying. However, the main positive outcome was that I forgot about my addiction. I steamed forward and never looked back.

One Saturday morning when I arrived at the site, the foundation was completed and half of the steel structure fabricated.

When I drove up the hill, Nick was already there. He looked at me with a smile on his face, and said, "Hello, Al! What is that lift doing here?"

"You mean that forklift by the pile of steel?"

"Yes! That's the one!"

"I rented it, and left you a note in the trailer. Didn't you get it?"

"Nope! We wanted to use that lift for moving the beams around, but I did not find the keys."

"The keys are in the glove compartment; too bad you did not call me and ask. Anyway, now it should be easier with that machine."

"Yes, of course, but we managed without it. The men rolled the beam on pipes! They are used to it now, so you can give the lift back."

"No, Nicholas; I will need it for installation!"

"Al, you will have to get a crane for that! Those steel columns are heavy!"

"I cannot afford the luxury of a crane. Because, they rent cranes only with an operator, for fifteen hundred dollars per day! So, for a few weeks' rental, the amount is significant! I don't have that kind of money to spend!"

"Well, I assumed you knew about this expense, and were ready for it!"

"Yes, I knew about it, and now I am ready for it with the forklift."

"Al, this lift cannot handle it. It's meant to move heavy items around, but not lifting them up in the air for assembly!"

"Nick, it has a sixty-foot reach! And I will use it for assembly; you shall see!"

"Do you have any experience on this lift?"

"Nope! But I'm a quick learner!"

"Al, you are going to kill somebody with this thing!

"Stop worrying, Nick; it will be okay!"

But he did not stop worrying, and after two weeks, my projects in New York were completed. My men and I went to Pennsylvania to begin the assembly.

Due to my lack of experience, my first approach toward the lift operation was very calm, but after a short while, managing that lift came to be a simple task. So, I raised the first column up in the air, and then drove with it to its location, then slowly lowered the column onto its anchors, then my men came and secured with bolts.

"Nick! Did you see that? Like I said, it's not a big deal!"

"Okay, just make sure all of them slide in that way! Because, with the second floor will not be that simple."

And so, men and I proceeded to install the rest of the beams; the next three units went in more or less the same way, and everybody felt comfortable about it. In addition, a few mason men had returned, and began to remove some of their planks, which they had left behind.

As we got to the center of the house, we were all working at a good pace; then each column was more than double in length of the others, so bringing that huge piece took longer than usual. I began to raise it slowly, then it reached its height, and the chains broke and that monster slowly commenced to tilt away.

At first, my men froze, then I yelled, "Run!" and they broke away faster than rabbits, then the mason team ran as well. Every one of them ran in a different direction, while the column for some reason was still slowly tilting down.

All this time, I was sitting in the lift, secured by a heavy cage, observing the situation, and did not attempt to move. I felt a desire for laughter, which needed badly to burst out of me, but I held it in and did not laugh.

Then finally, that column fell down with a tremendous noise and crushed the ground.

Nick with his men ran into the site, and yelled, "That was exactly what I was talking about! Thank God it came down clear!"

"Relax, Nick; they all had plenty of time to move away. That column was practically standing on it own! Anyway, did you see how they ran?" Then I commenced laughing.

"Oh, now you think it's funny? I don't see anything funny about that."

"I know; it's seeing them run the way they did; it was hilarious! Too bad you missed it!"

"Look! Those mason men are leaving."

"Let them go; they were probably scared shitless. They will come back."

Then one of the mason men came to me and said, "Look, Al, with all due respect, we cannot stay here! However, we will return in a month. I hope by then you will be out of here. Yes?"

"Yes, George! I don't blame you; go be safe!"

"So, Al, now will you call for a crane?"

"No, Nick! Now I know exactly what to do! And this will not happen again, I promise!"

"You are a crazy guy!"

"Yes, everybody around here thinks that about me! And now, those mason men will spread this story around, and it will stand for a fact! So be it!"

We did not leave. After a short break, I assembled all of them, and we continued as nothing happened. We repaired the column, and then raised it back up again. Only this time, I affixed so many chains around it, that now it could only flip along with the lift.

We assembled the structural steel in one week, and in the end, there was now a first stage of a house.

It took Nick and my team, two months to raise the entire steel structure, then, they all left for home, and I was a little depressed. However, the memories stayed with me, because I asked one person to record most of our construction.

Looking at that structure somehow raised my spirit, and I wanted Pap to see it badly, so after a few months, one weekend, I brought my parents for a visit. When we arrived, they were both amazed, and my Pap was very impressed with what he saw.

As we walked around the house, he said, "Al, I thought you told me that only the structure was complete."

"Yes, Pap, but that was over a month ago! So now, the concrete floors are completed, and the roof, as well."

"Yes, I see that; very impressive! I don't mean to get your spirit down, but I have to ask you, do you really know what kind of task you took upon yourself?"

"Yes, of course!"

"Well, son, by the way you answered, I don't think you understand the magnitude of this idea!"

"Can you please explain?"

"No, only time will tell!"

Then we all set out by the trailer, and enjoyed nature's silence along with other amazing gifts.

"Look, Al; is that a deer?"

"Yes, Mom, they always walk this way."

"Unbelievable! I had never seen a deer up close."

"We are in the forest, Mom; many creatures come here. Once a swan landed here, and then came closer, so I gave him some bread. They are treated well here you know, so they are not scared by people"

"Why would a swan come here?"

"Free food Mom, what else? They live at the lake below."

"Al, I have to say, paradise finally found its way to you. This place is beyond description! I am really happy for you!"

"Thanks, Mom."

After dinner, we sat out until midnight, then stayed overnight, and the next morning I took them back to New York, and from there, they drove back home.

The exterior construction held me back for another year; through that time, I mostly worked on the house, and could not commit to my business. As a result, the house was completed, but on the exterior only, and my business in New York sustained tremendous work loss.

Only afterward, I realized that my appetite was bigger than my stomach could handle. Nick was right; I had no idea what I was getting in to, and my Pap was right as well.

I stood proud when I looked at this magnificent building, as its blue glass reflected the sunlight onto the surroundings, turning the entire area a bluish color, but I also felt lost upon realizing the magnitude of interior work awaiting me.

I had exhausted my funds, and had no running projects at that time, so to survive, I had to forget about my dream house and concentrate on getting my business back on track once again.

However, when it rains, it pours; finding work was harder than ever, and my problems accumulated along the way. So without self-awareness, I found myself home with a bottle again, so instead of a searching for solution, my problems only grew.

My drinking cycle had changed, and so had the amount of alcohol. I consumed a smaller amount, for a much shorter period; however, at the end, self-hate never departed from me, and the same questions of why stayed with me on a daily basis.

I could not understand my thoughts and my behavior. I felt like a two individuals who where completely the opposite of each other.

Monica and I visited our house on every free occasion; however, one time, it was quiet different because my forgotten cousin Abe called my cell.

Actually, it was his wife. “Hello, Al!”

“Hi, who is this?”

“Its Jane, I'm sorry to bother you, but something awful has happened.”

“Hi, Jane, we haven't spoken in a long time, and frankly, after all what your husband said to me, I thought we would never speak again?”

“It was not my intention to call you; I just had to.”

“Why? What happened?”

“Your father is in the hospital, Al. He is dying. Doctors said there is nothing they can do; you are the oldest son. His wife and my husband begged me to notify you!"

"I thank you; please ask Abe to give me a call. I need to speak with him."

"He is right here; hold on. I'll put him on the phone."

"Hey, Al, how are you? How is your business?"

"Tom is dying and you ask how I'm doing? Better tell me what's wrong with him."

"Doctors said everything; and this is it. He has not much time left. You have to visit him before it's too late"

"He never wanted to know my whereabouts nor my wellbeing while he was okay. I'm sure he dose not care of my presence."

"Al, maybe you are right. So tell me, how is your business? How many men do you have working for you now?"

I always thought that, this cousin had mantle issues, but I had no idea of how far his mind had drifted away.

"Abe, are you drunk? What is the matter with you? We don't talk for ages, then out of nowhere, you inform me of such terrible news and ask me questions about my work, or moreover, my accomplishments. Is that important to you now?"

"No, however, you must come immediately!"

"I am far away now, and I will try, but no promises."

When I hung up the phone, I walked to Monica and said, "My natural father is dying; what do you think I should do?"

"Well, I think you should be there."

"Monica, he never wanted to be next to me; why would I rush there now?"

"Because, he is your father!"

"I never told anyone this before. When my most cherished dog died, that day, I was first to arrive at home. I found him lying in the backyard, and when I realized he was dead, I got myself drunk, and I think, only due to my condition, I called Tom. Do you know what he told me? 'Don't worry I will buy you another one'! So many years have gone by, and we have never spoken. Max was the only creature loyal to me; he understood me. I could see it in his eyes. Most people, including my parents, thought I trained him, but the truth of the matter is; I did not."

"Al, please; calm down."

"You know, when Max first met Nicole, I observed a very odd thing. It happened when I introduced Nicole to my parents; so, when we walked into the house, Max was sitting in the hallway. He was always aware of my arrival, and always jumped at me at the entrance. However, this time he was sitting still and watching me closely. I shall never forget that moment."

"So why do you think he was behaving like that?"

"He tried to protect me; he was watching Nicole while figuring out if she was a danger to me. As we went to the living room and sat on the couch, he jumped between us and did not let Nicole move. Only when I approached Nicole and hugged her, did he lower his head and walk away. That is who Max was, and Tom said, 'I'll buy you another one,' not realizing that some things are irreplaceable."

"Okay, Al; regardless, we all make mistakes. I'm sure he meant well. I think you need to see him before its too late."

"No, I don't! And I won't. That man never wanted me around; he always avoided me. Our last encounter was not that long ago. One day I met with him at the car wash, and practically begged him to follow me to my shop, and when he finally agreed, we sat there for less than five minutes. He looked around and said, 'Al, you have to get married; you are way past due. Do it now, before it's too late' He then got up and left. He did not want my presence, and I didn't need his advice, so I am not going. Besides, they probably found me after all those years just for one reason."

"What reason, Al?"

"Money! What else? No one on that side cares about me. Why do you think Abe was asking me about my work at a time like this? He wanted to know of my wealth. Materialistically speaking, how much I could contribute toward the funeral; that was his main agenda and nothing else."

"So, as I understand it, you will not go?"

"You understand right. I am not going to be there. I don't care about them!"

Thinking about all I just said made me feel worse. I did not mean that. However, in those few moments of conversation with Abe, I got frustrated and disappointed due to the way things had turned out. Of course, I wanted to be there, but no one on that side of the family ever liked me or wanted my presence at any events, and felt that from day one.

So, I did not go. Those same thoughts periodically haunted me, and it was hard in the beginning, but with time and me dedicating myself to work, I forgot about Tom and any troubles.

After that day, I kept running periodically with a few men to

Pennsylvania. We began to work on the basement, trying to convert it into a one-bedroom apartment, but because I was lacking funds, many issues were overdue, and I could not complete them.

No one believed that I could built something like that at the summit of the mountain; nevertheless, it was done, and whenever I went there, that building reminded me that some impossible tasks are sometimes possible.

During my work at the house, and simultaneously at the business, I did not need any other complications, but my life could not exist without unexpected major issues and problems.

Another two years passed, and those were the better years of my life because I accomplished most of my major goals.

Although the house was only completed on the exterior, and there was nothing inside except a huge empty space. Still, it was the greatest feeling I ever encountered.

Shortly after, new bids for projects were rolling in, so I was planning to continue working on my building.

But, in 2009, recession came through my doors late, and suddenly there were no jobs for me. I lost all the bids and had no new leads. I was aware of the situation; however, it never affected me before, when everyone else was complaining for lack of work, I was getting new contracts with deposits.

But that day, all work had turned around, and at the same time, due to the lack of fund, our running project had canceled. I could pursue them legally for breach of contract, and probably would have won. However, pressing on someone who had already suffered a loss, did not feel right. I guess I did changed in some way; in my early life, I would not care about someone else's problems, and would have kept on squeezing everything out of them until there was nothing left to squeeze.

But today, I think and approach life in a different way. After so many losses, it had become clear to me that money is meaningless; it's only a necessity that unfortunately no one can live without.

So there I was, sitting alone in my shop again, with no work, no workers, and thanks to my enormous idea, now I had no funds.

When I thought how it could not get any worse, my mom called. "Al, we have a big problem!"

"What happened, Mom?"

"For the past two months, your dad has been visiting doctors like there is no tomorrow, and I only discovered that recently when bills arrived in the mail. You should see those bills! Thousands of dollars, for test!"

"So, what's wrong with that? He is sixty-eight, working as a welder, and always around black smoke. Do you know how bad that is? Let him check himself!"

"He did, and that's when the problems began, the results are bad. He has lung cancer. I'm sorry, Al."

"Please stop, Mom! Those doctors made a mistake; it can't be."

"No, Al, they didn't. As I told you, several tests were made, and then confirmed by others, as well."

"So what did they say?"

"He has less than one year."

"That's bullshit. I don't believe that. Have him take additional tests."

"We can't, Al. He triple checked, and it's very expensive. Here is your father; he wants to talk too you"

"Al, son; how are you?"

"Okay, Pa. What's wrong with you? Mom has told me the terrible news, and you sound different. What's going on?"

"Nothing; everything is fine. I wanted to talk to you about my car. It did not pass inspection here; apparently, my car needs some repair, but we can't afford that. Do you think you could help me?

"Of course, Pap; bring the car here, and I will do the rest"

We decided to meet at the repair shop. When he showed up, he looked a little bit different, maybe because I had not seen him for a while, or maybe because I had not paid attention to his appearance before. Overall, he seemed fine, and I was very relieved by seeing him that way.

Looking at him, I realized that I loved him very much; however, for some reason, I did not tell him that. Instead, I said, "Hey, Pap! Good to see you again!"

"Hello son. Seeing you are more important than this inspection; why don't you visit us anymore?"

"Sorry Pap. I was working on my house all this time. The house in enclosed now, so I would like to take you there. I want you to see it, and tell me your opinion!"

"Of course! Mom showed me the photos you mailed; they look great. I would like to see it very much!"

"Pap, give me the car keys. I need to drive it in."

I got into the car, thinking, and realized that a very long time had passed by since I last visited them.

"Pap, your car passed; they are placing the inspection sticker now. Where would you like to go now? Maybe you would like to stop by my shop?"

"Thank you son, I would like to go visit your kid sister now, and from there, I will go home."

"Okay, Pap; go on! I will see you soon; I promise."

It brought me joy to see him doing okay. The doctors didn't know what they were talking about, and he was fine, the way he acted.

When he left, I went back to my worthless workplace, but there was nothing for me to do, so the next day I decided to go visit my house and stay there for two days.

When I arrived, my mother called. "Al, your father was hospitalized."

"Mom, I just saw him a few days ago. He was fine! What happened?"

"Al, his doctor was wrong. His latest tests came back, and he doesn't have much time left. You must come now before for it's too late."

"Mom, what are you talking about? To late for what? I don't believe them; do not listen to them. Besides, I am in Pennsylvania. I cannot come now. Please let me speak with him."

"I wish I could; he is unconscious."

"Mom, what happened? How did he end up in the hospital?"

"I was in the kitchen; I thought he was asleep. Then when I turned around, he was standing next to me. He said he was thirsty, and then collapsed on the floor. I was scared and called for help. Al, they said he is dying; just yesterday, we went to your sister's graduation. I don't understand how that could be."

"Mom, why did no one tell me about her graduation?" Once again, she showed that her interest in me was only financial."

"That's not true, Al. She is your sister and she loves you."

"So you say. She doesn't love me; she loves only herself. All I remember is when she needed money, so I called her to pick up two thousand dollars. She had drafted herself up in front of my door before I could hang up the phone."

"Al, stop that! Instead, why don't you remember where you were wrong? Anyway, I don't want to talk about it now."

"Well I do, and I won't stop! It was always like that; my baby sister turned into a selfish, materialistic bitch. When she needed a car, whom did she turn to for financial help? And I was stupid enough to give her that help. I will never repeat that mistake again! And it's most definitely not about the money! Around a year ago, she came with her boyfriend, her husband now, and they placed an envelope in front of me. I could only presume that she was attempting to pay me back. But when I looked in her eyes, it was obvious that paying me back was not her intention; they came in with enormous hope that I would not take it. It was so obvious, and so I didn't!"

"Al, she was in need, and there was no one else but you."

"Yes, but she could have presented that need differently! Don't you understand? I wanted her to appreciate me as a brother! And not as a financial agent! If I was a shitty brother because of my lifestyle, then so be it! Then don't talk to me. I would understand her behavior toward me! But she was always selective, and only approached me upon a need; now that is low! So I don't care about her! Now, our feelings are mutual! Okay, enough about them; tell me what's going on with Pap."

"He is in bad shape Al. You need to come and see him before its too late."

"Okay, Mom. I'll call you later."

After all that she said, I still did not believe it. I had just seen him recently, and he appeared to be perfectly fine. I had to admit, it shook me, so the next day, I left all my responsibilities behind and went to see Pap.

It was a long drive back to New York, and at five o'clock in the morning, the roads were empty of cars, and there was nothing for me to do but think. I though of what it would be like living without my pap. It is strange how that had never bothered me before. I hadn't seen him that often lately, but now, it was very important for me to be around him. Apparently, I was too busy to be around those I love, I had been satisfied knowing that he was fine, and nothing else mattered; as long as he was living the life to the best he knew how, and I could always choose to visit whenever I felt like it, nothing else really mattered.

However, I had one enormous loss in my life, and forgot about the main rule in the nature; all things tend to repeat themselves at one point in time or the other.

Thinking about the consequences, I suddenly saw myself driving onto the belt parkway. Somehow, the steering wheel turned and I exited on Ocean Parkway Avenue. I guess my subconscious was not ready to see my Pap in his condition, so instead my concealed will took over and drove me home.

Of course, on the way, that same will made me stop at the liquor store. When I walked into my apartment, I was holding a bottle of poison again.

My first steps were toward the kitchen. I got myself a glass and filled it with alcohol. That was my last act of the day; like on many other occasions, I ended up on the couch with a glass in my hand, leftovers on the table, and no one to talk too.

Monica did not know what happen; she thought I was still at the house, so I decided to call her.

"Hey, how are you doing?"

"Al, you came back! Why so soon?"

"My mother called me. Pap is very sick; they diagnosed lung cancer. I was on my way to see him, but could not make it. I don't know what to do"

"Did he get a second opinion?"

"Yes he did, and according to Mom, more than one. She asked me to be there, but I cannot go, and can't explain why. Besides, I just saw him couple days ago; he was fine!"

"Okay then. Don't go. Get yourself together first; however, judging by the way you talk, I think you are doing the opposite. Am I right?"

"Meaning what?"

"Meaning, you are getting drunk!"

"Yes; that comforts me. Nobody loves me as she does. Nobody wants me like she does."

"Stop it, Al. What is the matter with you? Why are you singing? And who is *she* anyway?"

"Vodka! Who else?"

"Okay, Al. Stop drinking and get some rest; you will feel better afterward."

"Okay, goodbye."

I kept on drinking anyway. There was a strange urge for something to accompany my misery, so I played a *Titanic* DVD. That way, the alcohol consumption came to be supportive.

While watching the move, I glanced at the bottle and I noticed that it would soon be empty. Before the remains could vaporize, I poured another full glass.

The *Titanic* had commenced to sink, and I was sitting at the edge of the couch, waiting to see what would happen next. I had seen this movie so many times I lost the count, but this time, I was watching it, as I had never seen this movie before.

Then my cell rang. "Al, I though you were coming. Where are you?"

"I'm home, Mom. I could not make it; sorry."

"It's okay. I understand; what are you doing?"

"Nothing much; how is Pap? Is there any news?"

"He is awake now, and doing much better. The doctor said they will keep him for observation and tomorrow I will take him home."

"That's great news. You see, I told you there is nothing wrong with him."

"No, Al; don't get your hopes high. He is sick. The cancer is spreading. Get yourself together. Stop drinking and come here. I will call you later; try to get some rest."

I finished the bottle to its last drop, and passed out on the same couch.

"Hey bro! Long time no see!"

"Jim, is that you?"

"I guess so! You have certainly changed, and why are you destroying yourself like that? Why suffer? Make it quick, like I did, and get it over with once and for all!"

"You mean to tell me you did that to yourself? I don't believe that! You are not my brother; you are not him."

"I am whatever you want me to be. Believe what you want, but not all is meant to be exposed, no matter how much you seek it."

"I don't seek anything anymore. I gave up a long time ago. My pap is dying."

"He is not your father; he is mine, and he is not dying. He is leaving you to be with me; the time has come! Al, remember! What cannot be changed shall be accepted!"

"I have to say, you look great. What is that noise?"

"Goodbye, Al; you shall never see me again!"

I woke up; the phone was ringing off the walls.

"Hello."

"Al, did I wake you?"

"How can it matter now? I am awake, aren't I? What's wrong? We just spoke!"

"We spoke in the morning. Its three p.m. now. Anyway, this morning the doctor told me to go home, so I did, and now the hospital called me. Al, they said that your dad has died!"

"What! How can this be? You told me he was doing better!"

"Yes, I know. That's what they told me, and I saw him awake. Al, I don't know what to do; please come quickly."

"Mom, calm down. I want to call the hospital. Give me their number, and I will call you back soon."

I dialed the number she give me, but for some reason Monica picked up the phone.

"Monica is that you? What are you doing there?"

"Al, I am at work. Where else would I be? What's wrong? Why are you shouting?"

"Pap died, and I don't know what to do. Something is wrong with me; please come over now."

"I can't, Al; please calm down. Call the hospital and find out what happened."

"Okay, I will call them now."

And just as I hung up, my caller ID showed Mom again.

"Mom, I was about to call the hospital. I will get back to you."

"No need, Al, I'm here; they made a mistake! Pap is fine! Well, what I mean is, he is alive! And they are discharging him!"

"How can someone make that kind of mistake? Wait a minute; you said they are discharging him? But before, you stated that he died! Are you sure you did not misunderstand them before?"

"What do you mean?"

"I mean that they called you before and said that he is discharged, and you thought that he was deceased! Am I right?"

"Well, I don't know! Look, you must come now."

"What do you mean you don't know? I almost had a heart attack because of you."

"Okay Al, maybe I misheard them; but please come."

"Okay, I am on my way."

When I arrived, I ran past everything, my mom included, into my father's room. I traumatized upon the entry; my legs were crumbling beneath me. I wanted to speak but I couldn't, for few moments I stood by his bed, completely numb.

A completely different man was lying on that bed. My hands began to shiver. I recalled hard situations in my life before, but nothing like this ever. I was never at this stage.

Finally, I sat down by his side, took his hands into mine, and could not comprehend how that large strong hand had turned into a small, fragile carrier of skin and bones. His face and all of his body had turned into a skeleton, and there were no muscles anywhere.

"Pap, what happened to you? I just saw you a little while ago; you were fine. What did you do to yourself?"

He opened his weary eyes, and looked right at me. It felt as if he gave his last energy to answer me.

"Sonny, Hi! I am so very happy to see you! Thank you son!"

"Pap, please don't give in. You are strong! Remember!"

"I can't, son; there is too much pain. I can't bear it anymore."

Then, my Mom as always, had to add her few cents at the wrong time. "Don't be scared, Sasha! Accept it, ask for forgiveness from everybody, especially from God, and keep asking. I forgive you, Sasha. I want you to know that!"

I was out of breath, and could not think straight. Was this really the end? Would I never see him again? Something inside me was accumulating, and there was so much of it; but I didn't know what it was. I felt like a balloon that was about to explode. "Pap, please be strong. Don't worry; this is just a transition to a new beginning. I can't explain it, but I know that it's not the end."

He reopened his eyes, and said, "Quicker already! " Then he passed out.

"Mom, I can't take this anymore. I must go outside."

"Okay, Al, go. I understand"

As I walked outside, tears burst out of me and I could not stop crying. Not too long ago, I had seen him, and he was doing fine. What happened? Why did it happen so fast? And why is it always happening to me? I could not stay there any longer, and could not endure his present condition, so I left. While driving, tears fell from my eyes the whole way home.

I came home broken in pieces, and then my mother called me.

"Al, your father did not respond to anything, so I had to call the ambulance He is in the hospital now. The doctor said . . ."

"Mom, what did he say?"

"He is dying, Al; this is it."

"Mom, how could this be? You told me before that the doctor said he had more time."

I threw the phone into the wall, and ran to my car, unaware of my behavior. I drove to the liquor store and bought the biggest bottle they had.

I always hated those stores because, for some people, they were selling poison and profiting from that act. However, this time, I was glad that place was there and open. I did not care for anything else anymore; at the same time, my youngest sister was nine months' pregnant, and was about to give birth.

In my previous life, she was the baby I loved the most, and now she was about to become a mother. Years flew by so fast, and life goes on. With time, only a few people changed for the better, and some for worse. It was unfortunate and very painful to realize, that a sweet little baby had grown up and managed to develop only the worst in her. She did not comprehend that. I guess for some, ignorance is bliss. Too bad, it had to be my sister.

Sitting on my couch at home and drinking, I could not stop thinking about my father's last words. He had said to me, "Quicker already." Why he would say something like that? Why did he want to die? Maybe he said that because of the pain he endured.

As I was thinking about Pap's unwillingness to fight for his life, I realized that actually there was nothing meaningful in my life to hold on to, either. I had no family, no children; only a structure that I had created, which needed my attention for completion, and I cannot complete it, no matter how much I wanted to. And if I did have a way to finish it, who would enjoy it after I was gone? Was that enough for me to keep on struggling with life?

What would be the result if I ended it? Right then, I understood that my life was meaningless, and that became even more depressing. I had no idea of what to do next.

Then my mother called again.

"Al, I am so sorry; your father is dead!"

I could not respond to that news. I fell onto the floor and stayed there; my whole body felt like a bag of steel that I could not move. I could not feel my legs or my arms. I tried to get up but I could not. Lying on the floor, I repeatedly said, "Pap, why did you leave me so soon?"

When I pulled myself back together again, I called Mom. "Mom, when is the funeral?"

"Tomorrow morning."

"Okay, Mom. I will see you then."

It was five o'clock in the evening, I wanted too get wasted, but there was no way I would miss Pap's burial, so I called Monica and told her what happened. Shortly after, she came in.

She walked in, hugged me, and said, "I'm so sorry, Al. I know how much you loved him."

"Thank you; I still cannot believe that he is gone. I wanted him to live so badly! There is so much that I wanted to show him. I thought when he would see my construction and, he would be proud of me, maybe give me some pointers for my mistakes."

"Al, he was always proud of you. I could see it in his eyes!"

"You know, he was a great man! He never placed himself first, and always went to the end of the line. He was like that on all matters; even at dinner, he would wait until everybody's plates were full, and only then place food on his plate, and always select the worst looking meat from the table, leaving the good ones for his family."

"Yes, I noticed that when I visited."

"Pap dedicated his entire life to someone else's needs; he was not rich, and did not give much, but for me, his attention and presence was always more than I ever needed. My sisters, however, were never satisfied with him."

"Al, when is the funeral?"

"Tomorrow morning."

"I want to come with you."

"I don't think it's a good idea. I will go alone."

"No, Al. I am going with you, and don't argue with the elderly!"

"Oh, please! Looking at us from a side, I am double your age in every way; but, you can come if you want."

So the next morning we were on our way to see Mom. My mom never liked Monica. She had a wrong impression about us, and assumed that we were dating. However, when we arrived, Mom was the opposite of what she used to be, and to my surprise, the gathering was very warm.

At the funeral, and when they placed his casket into the ground, I was burning on the inside. Then the Rabbi came to me and said, "Are you his son, Al?"

"Yes I am."

"Please take a shovel and participate in the burial."

"Why?"

"Because, according too Jewish tradition, children must bury their parents."

"I don't care about you stupid traditions! I will not, and cannot bury my pap."

"What do you mean, you don't care? You are Jewish, aren't you?"

"I am a human who respects, loves, and believes in God! That's all I can tell you." Then I walked away, stood by my car, and watched them from a distance.

I watched my two sisters, and was surprise by the scenery. They were working those shovels overtime. They threw soil on my pap's casket so intensely and rapidly it looked as if they were competing for a prize.

I always knew that they both loved him, and the shovels were probably an exercise of emotional stress, but for strangers, it must have appeared as if they were burying their worst enemy.

When the ceremony was completed, Mom came up to me and said, "Al, Rabbi is leaving, and no one as has paid him yet; can you take care of this?"

"Here is one hundred dollars. That's all I have."

"Thank you. Also, they are hungry. Would you like to go get some food?"

"No Mom; no food! I'm going home!"

When we arrived home, Monica left and I climbed back up on the couch, thinking that life moved so fast! I had a father, and now, in the blink of the eye, I didn't have him anymore.

I kept on drinking and drinking and drinking, until my stomach could not take it anymore; my body refused it, but I kept on pushing it in.

With every shot, I was vomiting my guts out right after, but that did not stop me, I proceeded and went beyond the ordinary drinking and to the unknown.

At that time, I did not think of the consequences, and didn't care about the abyss that appeared in front of my eyes, and waited for me like a black hole with nothing except gray smoke shaped like a smile.

There was nothing for me here; the only truthful person in my family was Pap, and now he was gone. Everyone else in my family had a need of my existence, only for their own satisfaction. I always felt that, but Pap was just there for me, on any given day of my life, just like Jimmy.

While the drinking continued, I realized that I was not wanted; no one really needed me for who I was, and I was just a figure who was able to help others in any situation; that thought repulsed me completely.

I could not finish that huge bottle; instead, the contents finished me, and I woke up in the hospital. When I looked around, Monica was standing by my bed.

She did not say much, but was glad to see me awake. I spent over one week there, and when they discharged me, I left the hospital half the man I used to be.

Apparently, this time my drinking had evolved into pancreatic problems, and as a result, I lost twenty-six pounds in seven days. When I came home and looked at the mirror, the reflection reminded me of Pap, and the way he appeared the last time I saw him.

After a long shower, I went to my balcony. I sat there thinking, *how much does one person need to suffer? When this will end? No matter what I do, and regardless of how hard I work to better myself, at the end, I find myself in much worse crisis than ever before. And as I struggle to climb out of there, soon enough I am back to where I was before, only now, my strength and my body are not what they used to be.*

I remembered the day Nicole sat down next to me and asked me, "Why do I feel so miserable? Is it because of my sins in the past? Or maybe I am paying now with my misery, to acquire happiness in the future!"

She said that a very long time ago, and only now did I understand the meaning of her words. We are paying for everything, one way or the other; not too long ago I heard a rumor that she was happy, and a newborn child had lighted her life.

Back then, I was joyful hearing that news, and now I just think, *When will my bills would be paid; how much more do I owe?*

I also recalled what Mother told me about the way of life I had chosen. Back then, I was angry and neglected her, but now I understood her point of view.

Maybe she was right. Maybe, through all this time, it was I, who ignited the agony in my life, and into my body. I was my worst enemy, and because of that, people next to me suffered as well. So many problems with so many loses, and so much pain, for so many years, only because of my wrong preferences, and wrong choices.

Wasting so many years with twisted preferences and abnormal choices, had brought myself numerous problems and huge losses. I experienced so much pain, and for what?

Most likely, it's true what they say, choices we make define whom we are, but I never understood that before, and that is the main reason why my life turn upside down. As a result, not reconciling with myself, I never attempted to recognize who I was, or who I wanted to be. My appetite was larger than my stomach; each need became my first priority. Satisfaction was vital, and I did not give thought to the consequences or penalties waiting for me from a distance.

It is only now I understand that, penalties had always waited for me, nothing goes

Unpunished, and the worst sentence ever, is when it comes from a higher power,

From somewhere or something that cannot be seen, or touched.

Today, I would give back anything and everything for one chance to reverse time, and sit once again next to Jimmy and Pap. However, nothing could ever bring them back, so I have to go on living my life with sorrows, and regrets, and that is the worst sentence ever.

If I only knew then what I know now, I would never have attempted to stand or blend in where I did not belong. I would never have aimed for an elevated lifestyle, just because it appeared to look better from my point of view.

Maybe that is why any living creature, by nature, somehow always knows his place on this world. Never would a deer approach a tiger, a dolphin would not swim next to a shark, and a wolf, well, no matter how well he to be treated, he will always keep his eyes toward the forest, its just a matter of time before he will vanish into the wild life.

Human society always divided into cultures, religions, and regions. The rich do not mix with the poor, and on some rare occasion when it happens, in most cases it never lasts.

That is exactly what occurred in my life, nothing had ever lasted with me. All of my doings and all my relationships always came to a short term. In addition, the higher I climbed, the further below I fell, and with each time, my fall was harder and more painful.

Looking back at my life, I see a man with ambitions and great potential, but for some reason, he always carried a bag of bricks on his shoulders, while walked in the wrong direction. My moral and immoral thoughts were always on a wrong path; there was nobody to point or guide me onto the right one. On occasion, when someone attempted to show me the right way of life, I always neglected to see it, because my way looked better at all times.

In the past, I took life with everything in it for granted, creating many mistakes, and instead of finding a way to cope with difficulties, I always selected the simple solution, with an urge to escape from it all.

There is no escape from reality, like escaping by abusing alcohol or drugs, and those who had found that way, walked through it, and liked it; had never cared for anything else afterwards.

I was one of the many who found that route, and stayed there with my eyes shut toward all surroundings. I enjoyed my stay, and did not see how lust for my goals, turned my life into dust.

However, as every beginning always concludes with the end, I was fortunate to depart from alcohol, before it concluded with me. What is more, walking that path brought sense into me, because without my nightmares, I would never have come to appreciate simple facts, and life.

In the past, when I attempted to change, by creating an idea for a good deed, shortly after, that idea backfired on me, because each good deed I created mostly for my own benefit.

Back then, I did not know the basic rules, rules that always existed, and will never vanish. Upon giving, never ask or expect anything in return, and be grateful for that wonderful and rare feeling, which interpreted as love. If both sides are willing to sacrifice, patience will result in reward.

However, I never had patience, so instead of that great feeling, I experienced losses. There is no amount of money or high material status that can replace the sorrow and pain of the loss of a loved one.

Understanding my wrongdoings was not enough there was a need to remember the verdict that appeared after every escape, because every action is due for reaction, and I did not have a substantial reason to face the consequences. Unfortunately, there are many who still do not care for anything else; they are unaware of the consequences, so they only exist to welcome the end.

Twenty-two years passed by in a glint, and now I always feel there is not enough time for me, no matter what I do, there is always a feeling that I could achieve more.

While chasing after wealth, I neglected to see life's gifts and its wanders. Powerful and great creations were always around me, when observing them; it makes me appreciate life evermore.

There is no need to escape from reality, and life is not overrated. Life is a short-term gift and not to be wasted.

I neglected to see where I was and all that nature had offered me, so now I must enjoy them more often. The aroma of the ocean and the sound of waves, embraced by clouds surfing through an enormous sky, all surrounded with sunshine. Observing closely, I realize how tiny we really are.

Relishing the blue sky on a hammock on the balcony of my current apartment, now I shall only think about today and tomorrow. Life is too short, and any given day could be the last day, so my main agenda has became to explore each day to its fullest. However, it is difficult to fulfill each day, but then again, why should it be easy.

Long ago, someone once told me: Never postpone for tomorrow what you can accomplish today. Most likely, I will never succeed with this task, but challenging my efforts is comforting.

Desires are normal by nature; they are also our drives, need to deal with them carefully, and with great concern. We depend on our desires, for they are our drives, and help us cope with the complexities of living. Without needs, we lose our willpower, and shortly after, we lose our hope.

However, when our desires overflow our aptitude, difficulties arise, and afterward, we struggle with anxiety, on occasion lust turns to dust.

Desires need no struggle or isolation from our thoughts; we need to learn to control them, or substitute them with moral cause. If we will not control them, they will certainly control us.

As we go through our life path, some of us change, and most of us don't, and those that paused and missed their train, at times, fate would grant them with a second chance to get on board again.

I know I was, so the biggest question I face now is, what do I do with it?

THE END